KU-460-600

Skilled Immigration Today

Skilled Immigration Today

Prospects, Problems, and Policies

Edited by

JAGDISH BHAGWATI

and

GORDON HANSON

UNIVERSITY OF WOLVERHAMPTON
LEARNING & INFORMATION
SERVICES

2470022	CLASS
	001
CONTROL NO.	331.
0195382439	62
DATE	SITE
-2 OCT 2009	Q
	SK1

OXFORD
UNIVERSITY PRESS

2009

OXFORD
UNIVERSITY PRESS

Oxford University Press, Inc., publishes works that further
Oxford University's objective of excellence
in research, scholarship, and education.

Oxford   New York
Auckland   Cape Town   Dar es Salaam   Hong Kong   Karachi
Kuala Lumpur   Madrid   Melbourne   Mexico City   Nairobi
New Delhi   Shanghai   Taipei   Toronto

With offices in
Argentina   Austria   Brazil   Chile   Czech Republic   France   Greece
Guatemala   Hungary   Italy   Japan   Poland   Portugal   Singapore
South Korea   Switzerland   Thailand   Turkey   Ukraine   Vietnam

Copyright © 2009 by Oxford University Press, Inc.

Published by Oxford University Press, Inc.
198 Madison Avenue, New York, New York 10016

www.oup.com

Oxford is a registered trademark of Oxford University Press

All rights reserved. No part of this publication may be reproduced,
stored in a retrieval system, or transmitted, in any form or by any means,
electronic, mechanical, photocopying, recording, or otherwise,
without the prior permission of Oxford University Press.

Library of Congress Cataloging-in-Publication Data
Skilled immigration today : prospects, problems, and policies / edited by Jagdish Bhagwati and
Gordon Hanson.
p.   cm.
Includes bibliographical references and index.
ISBN 978-0-19-538243-3
1. Alien labor.   2. Skilled labor—Supply and demand.   3. Emigration and immigration—Economic
aspects.   4. Emigration and immigration—Government policy.   5. Labor mobility.   I. Hanson,
Gordon H. (Gordon Howard).   II. Bhagwati, Jagdish N., 1934–   III. Hanson, Gordon.
HD6300.S55 2009
331.6′2—dc22   2008030364

1 3 5 7 9 8 6 4 2

Printed in the United States of America
on acid-free paper

Preface

This volume has grown out of a conference that was organized at the Council on Foreign Relations and at Columbia University, with financial support from both the Russell Sage Foundation and Columbia University's Program on International Migration: Economics, Ethics, and Law, which one of the editors, Jagdish Bhagwati, directs at the Columbia Law School.

The topic of skilled immigration, as noted in the introduction, has become an important part of the immigration debate today, reflecting the steady move by many countries, especially the rich countries of immigration, to bias their *legal* immigration systems in favor of skilled migrants. The other important issue today, of course, concerns the *illegal* immigrant inflows that overwhelmingly involve unskilled migrants.

While the questions about skilled immigration and its effects on sending countries (many of them poor) were raised and discussed with considerable sophistication in the 1950s and 1960s, the issue retreated from both public attention and economists' interest. It has now been revived, and it seemed necessary to revisit the phenomenon, the problem, and possible policy responses. The conference was a result of this perception.

Almost all of the main researchers in the area became involved, with a productive mix of theorists and policymakers, of current researchers and those who were pioneers in the earlier debates of the 1950s and 1960s. The resulting volume, while inevitably not exhaustive, nonetheless brings several insights to bear on the policy framework that will emerge as policymakers focus increasingly on skilled immigration and its consequences.

Our thanks are due to a number of excellent research associates at the Council on Foreign Relations who have overseen two years of revisions undertaken by the authors in light of the editors' and the referees' comments. Tanya Finnell helped organize the conference; Melanie Gervacio and Seth Flaxman provided excellent support afterward. We also received splendid suggestions from Francisco Rivera-Batiz, Mihir Desai, and Caglar Ozden; and many others at the conference, including Joseph Chamie,

Avinash Dixit, Arvind Panagariya, Andrew Samet, and David Weinstein, gave us helpful comments.

Suzanne Nichols at the Russell Sage Foundation and Terry Vaughn and Catherine Rae at Oxford University Press helped with expeditious handling of the manuscript.

Contents

II   Effects on Source Countries

Overview

African Template: The Return of the Brain Drain

Indian Template: Taxation

Contributors

Jagdish Bhagwati is University Professor of Economics and Law at Columbia University and senior fellow in international economics at the Council on Foreign Relations. He has uniquely combined scientific contributions to the postwar theory of commercial policy, strengthening greatly the case for free trade, with several best-selling books and op-ed essays in leading newspapers and magazines on current trade-policy issues. He has been economic policy adviser to the director general of the General Agreement on Tariffs and Trade (1991 to 1993) and special adviser to the United Nations on globalization. He has been the honoree at six festschrifts. He has received several honorary degrees and awards, among them the Freedom Prize (Switzerland), the Bernhard Harms Prize (Germany), and the Thomas Schelling Award (Kennedy School, Harvard). His honors also include the highest civilian awards from the governments of India (Padma Vibhushan) and Japan (Order of the Rising Sun, gold and silver).

Micah Bump is research associate at the Institute for the Study of International Migration at Georgetown University and associate editor of the journal *International Migration*. He holds an M.A. in Latin American studies with a certificate in refugees and humanitarian emergencies from the Graduate School of Foreign Service at Georgetown and is currently pursuing his J.D. at Georgetown Law Center.

Frédéric Docquier is professor of economics at the Catholic University of Louvain (Belgium), research associate at the National Fund for Economic Research (Belgium), and consultant for the World Bank Development Research Group (United States). He holds a Ph.D. in economics from the University of Aix-Marseille II (France). His research interests are in international migration and development economics, growth theories, and computable general-equilibrium models. He has edited three books and

ix

published in many journals, including the *Journal of Economic Theory*, the *Economic Journal*, and the *Journal of Development Economics*.

William Easterly is professor of economics at New York University, joint with Africa House, and codirector of NYU's Development Research Institute. He is also research associate of the National Bureau of Economic Research, as well as nonresident fellow of the Center for Global Development in Washington, D.C., and nonresident fellow at the Brookings Institution. Easterly received his Ph.D. in economics from the Massachusetts Institute of Technology. He is the author of *The White Man's Burden: How the West's Efforts to Aid the Rest Have Done So Much Ill and So Little Good*, *The Elusive Quest for Growth: Economists' Adventures and Misadventures in the Tropics*, four other coedited books, and 59 articles in refereed economics journals. He is associate editor of the *Quarterly Journal of Economics, American Economic Journals: Macroeconomics*, the *Journal of Economic Growth*, and the *Journal of Development Economics*.

Sherry A. Glied is professor and chair of the Department of Health Policy and Management of Columbia University's Mailman School of Public Health. She is the author of numerous articles and two books, *Chronic Condition: Why Health Reform Fails* and, with Richard Frank, *Better but Not Well: Mental Health Policy in the US since 1950*. She is a member of the Institute of Medicine, a member of the board of AcademyHealth, a member of the National Academy of Social Insurance, and a research associate of the National Bureau of Economic Research.

Gordon Hanson is director of the Center on Pacific Economies and professor of economics at the University of California, San Diego, as well as coeditor of the *Journal of Development Economics*, research associate at the National Bureau of Economic Research, and member of the Council on Foreign Relations. He has published extensively on the international migration of high-skilled labor, the causes and consequences of Mexican migration to the United States, and global outsourcing.

Guillermina Jasso, who received her Ph.D. from Johns Hopkins University, is Silver Professor and professor of sociology at New York University. Her research interests are basic sociobehavioral theory (including distributive justice, status, and inequality), international migration, mathematical methods for theoretical analysis, and factorial survey methods for empirical analysis—topics on which she has published numerous scholarly articles. She served as special assistant to the commissioner of the Immigration and Naturalization Service and as director of research for the Select Commission on Immigration and Refugee Policy, and she is currently a principal investigator of the New Immigrant Survey. Jasso was a fellow at the Center for Advanced Study in the Behavioral Sciences, is a research fellow at the Institute for the Study of Labor (Bonn), and is an elected member or fellow of the Johns Hopkins Society of Scholars, the Sociological Research Association, and the American Association for the Advancement of Science.

Lynn A. Karoly is a senior economist with the RAND Corporation whose research has focused on labor-market behavior, human-capital investments, child and family well-being, and social-welfare policy. She is a coauthor of *The 21st Century at Work: Forces Shaping the Future Workforce and Workplace in the United States.* Her other recent research focuses on self-employment and retirement patterns among older workers and the economic returns to early-childhood investments. Karoly received her Ph.D. in economics from Yale University.

B. Lindsay Lowell is director of policy studies for the Institute for the Study of International Migration at Georgetown University. He was previously director of research for the congressionally appointed Commission on Immigration Reform. He completed his Ph.D. in demography at Brown University and has published more than 150 papers on immigration policy, the labor force, economic development, and the global mobility of the highly skilled.

Susan Martin, the Donald G. Herzberg Associate Professor of International Migration, serves as executive director of the Institute for the Study of International Migration in the Edmund A. Walsh School of Foreign Service at Georgetown University. Her most recent book is *Managing Migration: The Promise of Cooperation.* Martin received her B.A. from Rutgers University and her M.A. and Ph.D. from the University of Pennsylvania.

John McHale is associate professor of economics and Toller Family Research Fellow at the Queen's School of Business (Ontario). He has published numerous articles on migration in refereed journals and edited volumes and has coauthored (with Devesh Kapur) *Give Us Your Best and Brightest: The Global Hunt for Talent and Its Impact on the Developing World.* He has also served as consultant to the World Bank on migration and development projects.

Yaw Nyarko is professor of economics at New York University (NYU), with research interests in growth and human capital theory and game theory. He is director of Africa House and codirector of the Development Research Institute, both at NYU, and is also former vice provost of New York University. The associate editor of the *Journal of Economic Theory,*

Nyarko received a B.A. in economics and mathematics from the University of Ghana and an M.A. and a Ph.D. in economics from Cornell University.

Constantijn W. A. Panis is labor economist and senior manager in the economic and statistical consulting group of Deloitte Financial Advisory Services. His work straddles public-policy analysis, quantitative business consulting, and litigation support. Panis has served as an expert witness in a variety of cases, concerning areas such as health care, employment, and general business litigation. Before joining Deloitte, Panis performed economic research for many years at the RAND Corporation, directing federally funded research on labor, demographics, health care, and econometric forecasting. His academic research also includes work in pensions, financial-choice behavior, health-care utilization, and the benefits of marriage. He is a frequent speaker at professional meetings and has published extensively in leading journals in health care, labor economics, and demographics. His book *The 21st Century at Work: Forces Shaping the Future Workforce and Workplace in the United States* is cited widely by policymakers and journalists. Panis holds a Ph.D. in economics from the University of Southern California.

Hillel Rapoport is professor of economics at Bar-Ilan University and EQUIPPE, University of Lille, and is also affiliated with the Center for Research and Analysis of Migration, University College, London. He serves or has served as consultant on migration issues for the World Bank, the Inter-American Development Bank, the G-20, and the UN World Institute for Development Economics Research. His research focuses on the growth and developmental impact of migration on source countries. He has done theoretical and empirical work on the brain drain, remittances, the effect of migration on inequality and educational attainments at origin, ethnic discrimination in a context of migration, and the links between migration and FDI. His other research interests include the economics of ethnic and religious minorities and economic history.

Mark R. Rosenzweig is Frank Altschul Professor of International Economics and director of the Economic Growth Center at Yale University. He is one of the principal investigators for the New Immigrant Survey. Rosenzweig earned his B.A., M.A., and Ph.D. from Columbia University. He was a junior faculty member at Yale, 1973 to 1979, before becoming director of research for the Select Commission on Immigration and Refugee Policy in Washington, D.C., 1979 to 1980. Before returning to Yale, he taught at the University of Minnesota, where he was codirector of the Economic Development Center; the University of Pennsylvania, where he chaired the economics department; and Harvard University, where he held the Mohamed Kamal Professorship in Public Policy at the Kennedy School and was director of the Center for International Development. Currently editor of the *Journal of Development Economics*, Rosenzweig has served on the editorial boards of such publications as the *World Bank Economic Review*, the *Review of Economics and Statistics*, and the *Journal of Economic Literature*.

Debojyoti Sarkar is vice president at Analysis Group, an economic, financial, and business-strategy consulting firm. He has developed innovative economic and econometric models to analyze a variety of complex issues related to securities and financial instruments, antitrust, labor and employment, economic damages, contract disputes, and general business litigation. He has also delivered expert testimony in trials. Debojyoti received his B.Sc. from Presidency College (India), his M.A. from Delhi School of Economics (India), and his Ph.D. from Columbia University.

Kenneth Scheve is professor of political science at Yale University. He also serves as codirector of the Leitner Program in International and Comparative Political Economy and director of graduate studies in the Department of Political Science. His research focuses on the mass politics of globalization, the determinants of income inequality and welfare-state development, and the electoral behavior of voters and elites in ethnically heterogeneous societies and the consequences of this behavior for economic policymaking and democratic performance. He has recently been fellow-in-residence at the Center for Advanced Studies in the Behavioral Sciences and has been a visiting scholar at the Bank of England and the London School of Economics.

Matthew J. Slaughter is associate dean of the M.B.A. program and professor of international economics at the Tuck School of Business at Dartmouth. He is also research associate at the National Bureau of Economic Research, senior fellow at the Council on Foreign Relations, academic adviser to the McKinsey Global Institute and the Private Equity Council; and a member of the academic advisory board of the International Tax Policy Forum.

David E. Wildasin is the endowed professor of public finance and professor of economics at the Martin School of Public Policy and Administration of the University of Kentucky, having previously held positions at Indiana University, Vanderbilt University, and numerous academic and research institutions in the United States and abroad. His research focuses on public economics with an emphasis on fiscal policy in urban, regional, and international contexts. He holds a Ph.D. in economics from the University of Iowa.

John Douglas Wilson is professor of economics at Michigan State University and was previously chair of economics at Indiana University.

He currently is editor-in-chief of *International Tax and Public Finance*. He has also served as coeditor of the *Journal of International Economics* and was a member of the board of editors of the *American Economic Review*. He holds an A.B. in economics and applied math from Brown University and a Ph.D. in economics from the Massachusetts Institute of Technology.

L. Alan Winters is professor of economics at the University of Sussex, research fellow of the Centre for Economic Policy Research (London), and fellow at the Institute for the Study of Labor (Bonn). From 2004 to 2007, he was director of the Development Research Group of the World Bank. He has been editor of the *World Bank Economic Review* and associate editor of the *Economic Journal* and is about to become editor of the *World Trade Review*. He has published more than 200 articles and 30 books, mostly on international trade and migration.

Skilled Immigration Today

1

Overview of Issues

JAGDISH BHAGWATI

It is widely believed that skilled immigrants create fewer assimilation problems and are more desirable in modern knowledge-based economies than unskilled immigrants. Whereas unskilled workers migrating on a permanent basis into major countries of immigration (unlike the temporary importation of workers legally under the *gastarbeiter* programs of postwar Europe or the Bracero program of the United States for agricultural workers) are typically entering illegally or have entered legally and stayed on illegally, the entry of skilled workers has been through legal mechanisms. Equally, international migration of skilled workers from developing to developed countries is increasingly a feature of the legal immigration systems of many developed countries.

The resulting focus on skilled migration raises a host of questions, for both "receiving" and "sending" countries, many of which are addressed in this volume.

Developed Countries Shift Legal Immigration toward Skilled Immigrants

The shift toward skilled immigrants in the legal immigration systems is by now a well-documented phenomenon. As Lynn Karoly and Constantijn Panis argue in chapter 2, a forecast of the developments in the supply of and demand for skilled labor in the United States suggests that robust demand for skilled labor will continue to outstrip its supply.

So, we can expect that the shift in immigration systems toward skilled immigrants will continue. Perhaps the most reluctant country to make this shift has been the United States, which has traditionally relied on family-unification and refugee admissions for the bulk of its legal immigrants. This does not mean that the skill composition will not rise over time, even among the familial categories. When the family-preference categories allow entry of brides married abroad to holders of green cards for permanent

3

residence or naturalized citizens, economic incentives operate to raise skill levels. This is because when a young man, for instance, goes home to choose from among several potential brides (all unknown to him) who respond to matrimonial advertisements and line up to marry him, he will pay attention to which bride will add to his family income, leading to his preferring a better-educated, more highly skilled mate. But the bulk of the skill upgrading of legal immigrants comes simply from a shift of immigration quotas in favor of what the U.S. system calls professional, technical, and kindred (PTK) immigrants under the so-called third-preference quotas. In addition, the United States has temporary skilled immigrants who come under a relatively small H-1B visa program. In both cases, prior approval by the Labor Department is necessary so that the skilled immigrants are sponsored by employers and certified as essential (and hence noncompetitive) for the employers in question.

Other countries, chiefly Australia and Canada, have what is known as a point system. This is more of a supply-determined system, in which skilled immigrants qualify to come in, whereas the U.S. system is based on labor certification and employer sponsorship and is demand-determined. During the last year of the failed immigration reform in the U.S. Congress in 2008, an attempt was made to change the U.S. system in the direction of Australia's and Canada's point system. The failure of the reform meant also the failure of the proposed skilled-immigration change.

Chapter 5, by Susan Martin, B. Lindsay Lowell, and Micah Bump, systematically describes and analyzes how Labor Department–certified immigration of the skilled is handled in the United States, differently from the point system of Australia and Canada.[1] This work is nicely complemented by the careful analysis of selection criteria and the insightful empirical examination of the effects of these criteria on the actual skill composition of immigrants in a comparative analysis of the U.S. and Australian systems in chapter 6 by Guillermina Jasso and Mark Rosenzweig.

At the same time, chapter 7, by Sherry Glied and Debojyoti Sarkar, offers an important analysis of how professional societies, in their case the American Medical Association, can effectively condition and restrict inflows, virtually acting as gatekeepers. When Sarkar was my student at Columbia, I asked him to investigate a hypothesis I had come up with, that the entry examinations for foreign medical graduates might be made more or less restrictive depending on the state of medical earnings in the United States, tightening when earnings were under pressure and relaxing when conditions improved. At my suggestion, he worked with my colleague,

---

1. These authors also have a useful discussion of the different ways in which "skills" are defined in the legislation, making international comparisons tricky.

Glied, who is a far better econometrician than I am, and the result is intriguingly in conformity with what I had hypothesized. This chapter is important insofar as it shows that when skilled immigrants are involved, professional societies find it possible not merely to lobby for restrictions but also, in some cases, to apply prior restraint by manipulating professional qualification procedures. It has a counterpart in the recent studies of outsourcing X-rays to be read by radiologists in Bangalore rather than in Boston. It turns out that the radiologists in foreign countries who do this must be board-certified, so that despite the huge scare about most radiology being outsourced, this has not happened; no radiologists in the United States have lost their jobs, and their average income remains exceptionally high.

It is also interesting to ask whether the public attitudes toward skilled and unskilled migration are different and whether individuals are less opposed to immigration when the ratio of skilled to unskilled migrants is high. The argument is that the average citizen will feel less threatened by skilled immigrants, for assimilation reasons and because the skilled immigrants are not perceived as a drain on the fiscal situation. Gordon Hanson, Kenneth Scheve, and Matthew Slaughter examine this issue in chapter 8 for the United States, using the data for different states, and find that the skilled-to-unskilled composition of immigrant inflows does matter in shaping public attitudes toward immigration policy.

The fiscal consequences of skilled immigration and perceptions thereof are relevant to public attitudes about immigration. In chapter 4, David Wildasin offers a sophisticated analysis of this issue in the wider setting of interactions among fertility, migration. and fiscal policies, drawing together the empirical and theoretical findings from several studies, relating especially to western Europe. Wildasin emphasizes the fiscal implications of age-imbalanced demographic structures in advanced economies, the impacts of these imbalances on age-sensitive expenditure and revenue systems, and the prospects for fiscal adjustment along demographic, tax, and expenditure policy margins in a global economy characterized by increased competition for mobile capital and labor.

These analyses are set against the historical backdrop of early postwar European experience with skilled immigration by L. Alan Winters in chapter 3. With its officers decimated as much as the foot soldiers, Europe was characterized by inflows of skilled people, not just the unskilled *gastarbeiters*.

Developing Countries: Two Templates

At one time, in the 1960s, there was massive concern in the media and among policymakers in many countries, including India, about the costs of the "brain drain." Today, that is no longer the dominant narrative. We have moved on in our understanding of the phenomenon of out-migration of the skilled from the developing countries. As it happens, the emigration, permanent or temporary, of the skilled from the developing countries today fits two alternative templates.

The "Brain Drain" Template

On the one hand, some countries in Africa regard the outflow of their skilled nationals (whether through stay-on after education abroad or through physical out-migration) as a threat, recalling the refrain in India and elsewhere in the 1960s about the problems raised by the brain drain. On the other hand, some countries today, such as India again, which is now a rapidly rising world economic power after wide-ranging economic reforms, regard emigration of their skilled nationals as an opportunity.

As it happens, if the present-day participants in the debate, such as the former physician (but not social scientist) Lincoln Chen at Harvard and, tangentially (as part of his technocratic exhortations for more aid regardless of absorptive capacity in Africa),[2] the activist Jeffrey Sachs at Columbia, were to familiarize themselves with the massive discussion of these issues in the 1960s and 1970s, by Harry Johnson, me, and other international economists, they would know, for instance, that even when countries "need" skilled manpower, the ability to absorb it is quite another matter, and one would therefore have a very different and nuanced view of the skills shortage in the African countries that worry about the brain drain.

The older literature recognized, after the early alarms, that salary structures and incentive mechanisms often do not reward the skilled. Also, professionals often out-migrate because social legislations such as divorce and family laws are rooted in old cultures and conflict with the needs of the modern classes. Again, bureaucracies interfere with the free functioning of these classes. In India, academics such as myself had to get permission from Ministry of Finance bureaucrats to attend scientific conferences abroad. I recall being asked why I was invited to a particular conference, to which I reacted icily: "Well, because I am smarter than you." Of course,

---

2. Sachs seems to be unmindful of the enormous literature in the 1960s and 1970s on the various ways in which foreign aid may be unproductive or counterproductive. At the time, there were serious econometric studies of concerns that foreign aid, even when given so as to supplement domestic savings, may actually substitute for them, leading to "dependence," some even going so far as to describe it as part of the malicious design of neocolonialists. Again, as today, the question was extensively discussed of whether food aid would harm domestic agriculture and set development back.

I knew the top bureaucrat in the ministry, so there was no risk attached to my retort. There are also the extreme versions, in which, as was the case with Soviet Jews, many were denied the visa to go abroad, especially to Israel, ostensibly because their skills were deemed essential, whereas they were simultaneously displaced from their work as soon as they applied for exit visas.

This dissonance between need and effective demand led some of us to recognize at the time that the concept of a brain drain had to be handled with care and that the policy responses had to be sophisticated and informed, or else they could easily be unproductive, even counterproductive. Thus, it was quite fashionable for many then, as it is for many now, to ask for a restraint on such outflows of the skilled from the developing countries. This restraint was considered seriously by social scientists and policymakers in the developing countries (e.g., a famous economist in India wrote that no one younger than forty should be allowed to emigrate). The rich countries of destination such as the United States were also shamed into enacting return visa arrangements, such as exchange-visitor visas, which required that skilled nationals visiting or working under them were to return for two years before they could reapply for entry. Today, the literature on the African brain drain eerily asks for similar restrictions, urging Canada, the United Kingdom, and the United States not to let in doctors, nurses, and other professionals from Africa.

But these proposals do not merely ignore the difference between need and demand. They also ignore the fact that today, as the right to emigrate has become an important human right, it is ever more difficult to put obstacles in the path of those who wish to emigrate from a society.

So, the discussion of even African problems with skilled labor cannot be cast, as many do, in a simpleminded lament and a restrictionist format that the original brain drain literature often gravitated toward at the outset. Besides, as William Easterly and Yaw Nyarko emphasize in chapter 11 (as the 1970s literature did), personal incentives are stacked in favor of emigration in many of the African countries that have outflows of skilled labor. From a policy perspective, the relevant questions then change. If people will not return from study abroad to work at home or will leave soon after they return, how do their countries of origin still get some value from them? Can they make short forays back home, such as Ghanaian professors spending the summer at educational camps for local professors in Legon or even at Columbia? In short, we have to work with promiscuity, since marriage is impossible. A variety of ways to harness the goodwill of émigré nationals to reduce the handicap on skills would be useful.

Again, a lot of money must be spent educating Africans. True, for the foreseeable future, they will settle abroad because of inadequate governance and growth at home; and policies to get them to assist on a "promiscuity" basis, as outlined above (and in other ways that I will mention), will help the African countries to get some value from them. Eventually, however, you can be sure that they will provide the augmented stock of nationals abroad who will return home maybe 15 to 20 years from now, once their home countries in Africa have taken off into sustained growth.

But in the meantime, Africa is going to need skills for virtually every developmental problem of consequence. For example, doctors, nurses, and extension workers are needed, even in a well-endowed and efficient country such as Botswana, if diseases such as AIDS, malaria, yellow fever, and others are to be treated and also contained. But think also of trade, which (despite the occasional skeptical statements of a handful of economists) is widely seen now to be an important aid to growth. But if exports are to increase, say, in agriculture, these nations have to be prepared to cope with the inevitable invocation of sanitary and phytosanitary (SPS) standards to keep exports out. SPS standards may be cited to exclude imports for legitimate safety reasons, but every trade expert knows that as tariffs and subsidies decline, the temptation to use SPS standards simply for protectionist purposes will be great and has already been indulged. Such illegitimate use of SPS standards can be challenged via the World Trade Organization's Dispute Settlement Mechanism. But how will African countries be able to find skilled experts in pesticides, bacteria, and microbiology to plead their cases? Wherever we turn, we will find skills shortage as a critical impediment to development.

I have suggested that using the demographic aging of rich-country populations, we could fund a "Gray Peace Corps," which could take, at wages that include a hefty "tropical premium," large numbers of skilled professionals of all types to the African nations during the years when we are training large numbers of their nationals who will mostly become the diaspora abroad. Members of this diaspora can be mobilized to make contributions (in the "promiscuity" mode discussed above) and will eventually find their way, somehow, to their home countries after their takeoff. The Gray Peace Corps, carefully designed and managed, can fill the vacuum until the "reverse migration" of the diaspora begins, as it will, down the road, as economic and social reforms take root and development takeoff occurs. I am told that specific programs to take retired business executives to skills-short countries are in place in Europe and the United States. But the program I suggest would be far more extensive and would also require systematic planning across very many different types of professionals and diverse countries.

The "Migration as an Opportunity" Template

In regard to the template in which policymakers in countries such as India today see exportation of their skilled professionals as an opportunity rather than a threat, the diaspora model is overwhelmingly the relevant one. Remittances, now a huge number for many countries with migrants abroad, are often cited as important, but they are largely from migrants who come from poor families. For skilled migrants, while remittances can be identified in some data, they are far less important. This is because, by and large, skilled migrants come from better-off families, and the typical pattern is not to send money home since the need to do so is much smaller.

But what seems to be happening increasingly is that when the diaspora is cultivated by the home countries through offers of dual citizenship and other rights, many want to use their wealth and income to finance primary education and medical hospitals, to fund nongovernmental organizations, and to build research institutions and much else. The skilled generally tend to send "social remittances"; the unskilled send "family remittances."

Nonetheless, along with the improved rights (e.g., dual nationality and voting rights) for the diaspora, I have recommended that the obligations of the diaspora also be increased in the form of a tax on citizens settling abroad.[3] Originally, in 1973, I proposed this idea as a "brain-drain tax," now popularly known as the Bhagwati tax, much like the Tobin tax, which relates to capital flows instead. There were several rationales proposed. First was that, since immigration in a world of restricted entry enabled one to earn "rents" (i.e., get the premium associated with restricted entry), this provided a source of revenue that could be tapped, without serious allocative inefficiencies, to be spent in turn on social use of one kind or another. This aspect has appealed to many, even to this day, who are looking for proposals that would raise revenues for provision of public goods, for example, at the international level. But, as with all such proposals—such as proceeds from mining manganese nodules underneath the high seas, the Tobin tax, or the global-environmental carbon tax levied by an international authority—the political salience is limited, for several reasons. Why should India agree to have its nationals abroad taxed only to see the proceeds go into a global fund? Who would run the fund? And so on.

I quickly shifted to other rationales. An appealing one came from the prevalent view that out-migration of the skilled would have adverse impacts on those left behind (TLBs). Therefore, those who migrated could be justly asked to compensate the TLBs. Indeed, if one decomposed

3. There is a huge literature on this proposal by now. For the early discussion, see, in particular, J. Bhagwati and Martin Partington, eds., *Taxing the Brain Drain: A Proposal* (Amsterdam: North Holland, 1976); J. Bhagwati, ed., *The Brain Drain and Taxation: Theory and Empirical Analysis* (Amsterdam: North Holland, 1976); and J. Bhagwati and John Wilson, eds., *Income Taxation and International Mobility* (Cambridge, MA: MIT Press, 1989).

(as Koichi Hamada and I did in some of our work) in simple models the "world" gains from migration, these gains would accrue to migrants and to the population in the receiving countries, whereas the TLBs would lose. But then the Bhagwati tax proposal in that format raised heckles from human-rights activists who wrongly thought of a parallel with exit taxes and from economists who argued that there was no such adverse effect on TLBs because often the migrants had not been effectively utilized, anyway.

Then again, another rationale was that the migrants ought to repay their educational costs to the countries from which they came. But this did not hold water in many cases, because many migrants were stay-ons, who had been educated in universities in the countries to which they were migrating. If their education was paid for by the countries to which they had migrated, as was often the case with the United States, why should they pay taxes to India? (Today, that objection seems far less cogent, as several highly skilled migrants, whether temporary or permanent, come with exceptional education from leading educational institutions in key exporting countries such as India and South Korea, with that expensive education fully financed by the governments.)

The rationale that finally became dominant was a different one: that citizens settling and working abroad, as long as they were citizens, could be legitimately taxed as members of the community making up the nation-state. That is, it was an attribute of citizenship that one owed a tax obligation. Many objected that if one lived abroad, one derived no benefits, so why should one pay? But that implies that taxation should be benefits-related. By contrast, in a modern progressive state, taxation is delinked from benefits, and the rich pay more to provide for the poor and to offer a progressive share of the burden of public goods.

I discovered accidentally that this was, in fact, what the United States was doing, taxing by citizenship, not by residence (as the Europeans did). The U.S. practice was the one that finally fit my thinking neatly, and so the Bhagwati tax took the final form of extension of income-tax jurisdiction to nationals abroad. Many in the developing countries liked the proposal, as long as they mistakenly thought that I was advocating a tax to be paid by the United States to India, for example. When they discovered that I was asking that the Indians in the United States be taxed (until change of citizenship) by the United States for India, their enthusiasm shrank greatly.

While the Bhagwati tax became a hot issue, including in the United Nations, in the 1970s, I felt that it had little chance of being adopted and turned to other aspects of immigration research. But now that the incomes of skilled migrants have reached exceptionally high levels, and even a small surcharge levied on U.S. income of Indian citizens in the United States would raise sums of money that could add significantly to the Indian budget, for example, the issue has come back into economic research and public debate. One of the major participants in this revival is John McHale, who has written an excellent analysis of the Bhagwati tax in chapter 12.

Equally, the analytical issues raised by public-finance theorists who have looked at the issue of optimal income taxation when people can move out of a tax jurisdiction have addressed a great number of analytically interesting questions of tax design. There is a huge literature on the subject now, to which John Wilson has made important contributions. He provides an overview of the latest thinking among public-finance theorists in chapter 10.

Frédéric Docquier and Hillel Rapoport, in chapter 9, examine the Bhagwati tax and other issues concerning the impact of out-migration of the skilled in alternative frameworks that supplement the Wilson analysis. They also provide an excellent survey of 40 years of research on skilled out-migration. They have up-to-date comparative data on the brain drain, as well as case-study evidence that generally supports the view that outflows of skilled labor are in practice beneficial, rather than harmful, to the source developing countries.

I

Underlying Trends and Policy Changes in Receiving Countries

Labor Markets and Demographics

2

Supply of and Demand for Skilled Labor in the United States

LYNN A. KAROLY AND
CONSTANTIJN W. A. PANIS

We aim in this chapter to identify the forces that are expected to shape the supply of and demand for skilled labor in the next several decades in the United States. By supply, we mean the population that is willing and available to work and the skills they bring to the labor market. By demand, we mean the number of jobs employers seek to fill and the skill requirements of those jobs. Following the neoclassical economic tradition, compensation in the form of wages and benefits is assumed to adjust to balance labor supply and demand, although other factors such as immigration may serve to meet excess demand for skilled labor. In much of the chapter, we discuss skilled labor as if it refers to a well-defined, homogeneous group of workers. Naturally, this characterization is overly simplistic. Skilled workers may be young or old, male or female, white or nonwhite, native-born or immigrant, and so on. Our primary metric of skill follows much of the recent literature in focusing on educational attainment of the workforce. However, we also consider other measures of skills relevant for the labor market.

Following our analysis of the future of the workforce and the workplace in the United States (Karoly and Panis, 2004), we focus in particular on three factors that we expect will affect both supply of and demand for skill: demographics, technological change, and globalization. Demographic shifts caused by changes in the size and composition of the population, combined with patterns of educational attainment and labor-force participation, will affect the supply of skilled workers. For example, population aging and more racial or ethnic diversity affect the composition of the U.S. workforce, including its skill composition. Demographic trends will

We thank Robert E. B. Lucas, Michael Piore, and Joseph Chamie for their helpful comments. The opinions expressed in this chapter are those of the authors and not necessarily those of the RAND Corporation or Deloitte Financial Advisory Services LLP.

also affect the demand for skilled labor caused by differential consumption patterns across different demographic groups (e.g., younger versus older households) and the outsourcing of home production with increased female labor supply. Immigration patterns play an important role as well, and immigration policy offers a lever to address projected excess demand for skilled labor.

The future pace and direction of technological change will also influence the demand for skilled labor in the years ahead. The consensus among economists is that technological progress in the past several decades has been skill-biased, raising the demand for more highly educated workers. We assess the likely future course for technological progress in such areas as information technology, biotechnology, and nanotechnology and how the path may be expected to affect skill demand. Finally, the extent of integration between the U.S. economy and the rest of the world in terms of trade, capital flows, labor mobility, and knowledge transfers will also influence the U.S. labor market. Globalization—essentially a form of international specialization—changes the mix of labor demanded and makes a supply of skilled labor from overseas available for work in American production processes. By understanding how globalization in recent decades has shaped the supply of and demand for skilled labor, we will gain insight into the expected future effects.

If the recent past is any indication, these underlying forces shaping labor supply and demand can be expected to influence the structure of wages in the United States. Notably, as seen in figure 2.1, the wage differential (measured as the real median hourly wage) between lower-educated and higher-educated workers has been increasing since 1979. (All wages are indexed to equal 100 in 1979.) Between 1973 and 1979, real wages fell somewhat for more highly educated workers, so that, for example, the college wage premium relative to high school graduates fell. After 1979, wages grew more rapidly as the level of education rose. In fact, workers with a high school diploma or less actually experienced real-wage declines until the mid-1990s. During this period, the wage premium for a college graduate relative to a high school graduate increased from 40 percent in 1979 to a peak of 76 percent as of 2001. Real wages for the least educated workers recovered to some extent with the business-cycle expansion in the 1990s, although, as of 2003, real wages for dropouts remained 16 percent below the 1979 level. In the last two years covered by these data, the college wage premium stopped growing and remained flat. More recent data through 2004 indicate that this pattern has continued, leading some economists to suggest that the era of rising wage differentials by education levels may be over (Uchitelle, 2005). In the analysis that follows, we seek to understand the extent to which these patterns in the wage structure have been influenced in the past by demographics, technology, or globalization. This provides the basis for understanding the likely future implications of these forces.

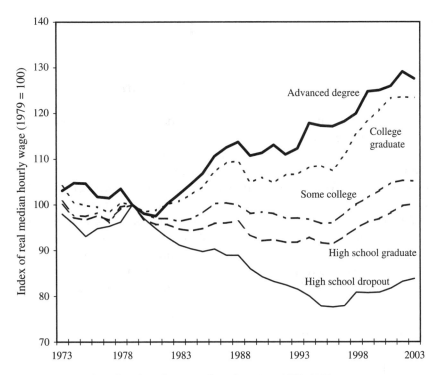

Figure 2.1 Real median hourly wages by education, 1973–2003.
Source: Authors' calculations based on Mishel, Bernstein, and Allegretto (2005), table 2.17,
online at www.epi.org/content.cfm/datazone_dznational (accessed June 9, 2005).

Our analysis draws on relevant literature and existing data to document recent trends and assess future projections (e.g., population trends and occupational and industry projections). We do not seek to provide a full general-equilibrium model of supply and demand forces—a complex undertaking beyond the scope of this chapter—nor do we endeavor to estimate precise supply and demand quantities. Rather, our approach is to provide an informed basis for understanding the likely future course that supply and demand for skilled labor will take in the decades ahead.

Forces Shaping the Supply of Skilled Labor

Several factors will affect the future supply of skilled workers. As noted above, the mix of skills may vary across subgroups of the population. Thus, we begin by discussing the broad demographic shifts on the horizon. We then place the spotlight on educational differentials across these subpopulations and show that the average number of years of schooling is not expected to rise as fast as it did in the past few decades. We also consider workplace skills (rather than education) from an international perspective.

Shifts in Demographics and Labor-Force Participation

Among the most influential demographic developments of the second half of the 20th century were elevated childbearing rates during the baby boom and increased participation of women in the labor force. The baby-boom generation, born between 1946 and 1964, started entering the labor force in the mid-1960s and is currently beginning to retire. Concurrently, women increased their participation in the labor force from 40 percent in 1966 to 60 percent in 2000 (Bureau of Labor Statistics, 2005). Together, these two trends generated a temporary burst of labor-force growth, as seen in figure 2.2. After growing by 1.1 percent annually during the 1950s, the labor force expanded by 1.7 percent per year in the 1960s and 2.6 percent annually in the 1970s. Since then, growth has slowed to 0.9 percent

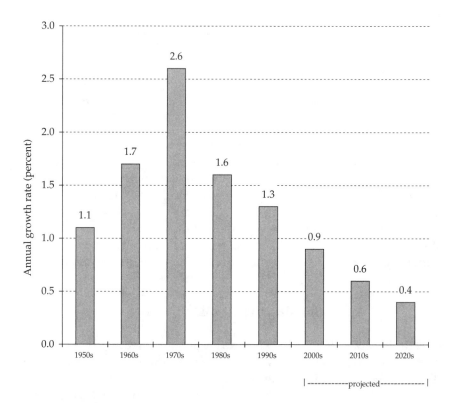

Figure 2.2 Annual growth rate of the labor force, 1950–2030.
Source: Toossi 2006, chart 1.

annually in the 2000s. The impending retirement of the large baby-boom cohort and the stabilization of female labor-force participation since the mid-1990s are projected to result in yet slower labor-force growth, to 0.6 percent per year in the 2010s and 0.4 percent per year in the 2020s (Toossi, 2006).

Underlying the slowdown in the growth of the future labor force is the aging of the population, caused by lower fertility and longer life spans. The top panel of figure 2.3 shows the distribution of the population by age and sex in 1960 (U.S. Bureau of the Census, 2002). It is pyramid-shaped, indicating that there were far more young children than older people. The bottom panel shows the projected distribution in 2020, when the population

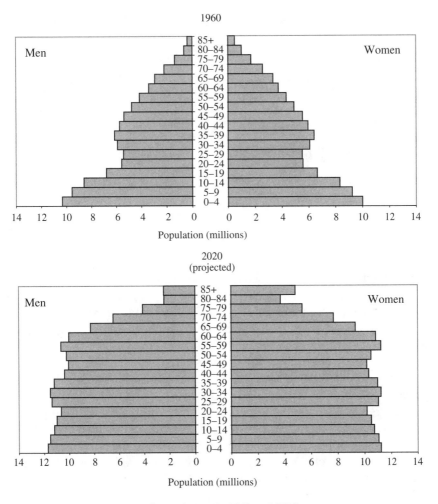

Figure 2.3 Age structure of population in 1960 and 2020.
Source: U.S. Bureau of the Census (2002).

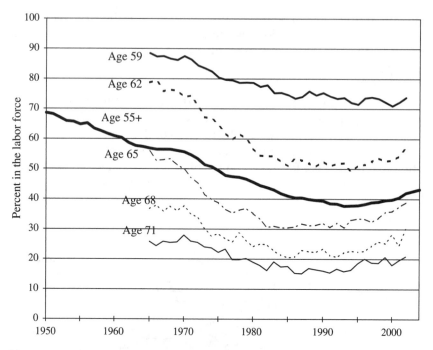

Figure 2.4 Labor force participation among men age 55 and above and at selected single years of age, 1950–2004.
Source: Age 55-plus series based on Bureau of Labor Statistics (2005), series LNU01324231; single years of age series based on unpublished tabulations of the 1965–2002 CPS provided by the BLS.

pyramid will be better described as pillar-shaped up until age 65. After age 65, the force of mortality turns the pillar into a pyramid. As a consequence of the underlying population shifts, even with no change in labor-force participation rates by age, the future workforce will be more balanced in its age structure.

As the baby-boom generation nears retirement, however, labor-force participation rates at older ages appear to be changing, as seen in figure 2.4. Through much of the second half of the 20th century, older men had been steadily reducing their participation in the workforce. For example, the labor-force participation rate of men age 55 and older declined from 69 percent in 1950 to 61 percent in 1960, 46 percent in 1980, and 38 percent in 1993. After decades of retiring younger, mature men have increased their participation during the past decade (Costa, 1998; Quinn, 1999). Since the low of 38 percent 1993, the labor-force participation rate for men 55 and older has increased to 43 percent as of 2004 (Bureau of Labor Statistics, 2005). As seen in figure 2.4, this reversal of the downward trend in labor-force participation rates is not evident for 59-year-old men, but it is prominent for the other older ages shown (ages 62, 65, 68, and 71).[1]

The recent upswing in labor-force participation among mature men may be a result of several factors (Karoly and Panis, 2004). First, traditional defined-benefit pensions, typically with strong incentives for early retirement, are being replaced with 401(k) and other defined-contribution pensions. Second, the normal retirement age of Social Security is moving from 65 to 67, thus lowering monthly benefits at any particular retirement age. Third, health-insurance costs have risen sharply, and many companies are restricting health insurance for retirees. Fourth, workers today enjoy longer life spans and are capable of working to higher ages than previous generations. All of these factors are likely to persist, so we expect that the recent reversal of retirement trends is not a temporary phenomenon. The trend toward delayed retirement will reinforce the underlying demographic shifts toward an older workforce.

Given earlier retirement among men during the latter half of the 20th century, one reason the labor force grew as rapidly as it did was the entrance of large numbers of women into the workforce. A century ago, only 20 out of 100 women participated in the workforce. The rate grew steadily to 38 percent in 1960, accelerated to 60 percent in 1997, and leveled off to 59 percent in 2004 (U.S. Bureau of the Census, 2004). The increased participation took place across the board. Many working women are married; in fact, married women increased their participation the most, from 41 percent in 1970 to 62 percent in 2003 (Goldin, 1990; U.S. Bureau of the Census, 2004). Many also have children; participation among married women with children up to age 17 was 69 percent in 2003, and more recently, participation rates have increased among unmarried mothers as well. A similar pattern holds for women age 55 and older, whose labor-force participation rose from 17 percent in 1948 to 23 percent in 1993 and 31 percent in 2004. While women's participation in the labor market rose, increasingly early labor-force withdrawal meant that men reduced theirs from 86 percent in 1950 to 73 percent in 2004 (Bureau of Labor Statistics, 2005). As a result, the fraction of the labor force that is female rose from 30 percent in 1950 to 47 percent in 2000.

The workforce is becoming more balanced not just in gender but also in race and ethnicity. As shown in figure 2.5, non-Hispanic whites made up 82 percent of the workforce in 1980. By 2000, their share was down to 72 percent, and it is projected to decline further to 63 percent in 2020 and 51 percent in 2050 (Toossi, 2002, 2006). By contrast, Hispanics account for a growing fraction of the workforce, from less than 6 percent in 1980 to 12 percent in 2000 and 17 percent in 2020. The fraction of non-Hispanic blacks in the workforce is rising slowly, from 10 percent in 1980 to 11 percent in 2000 and 2020.

---

1. To avoid cluttering the graph, we show only every third year of age. Participation rates among those ages 55 to 61 remained essentially flat over the 1990s.

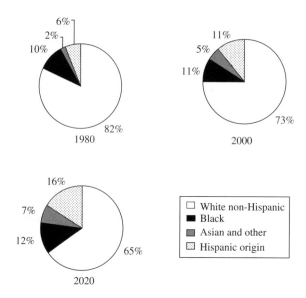

Figure 2.5 Racial/ethnic composition of labor force, 1980, 2000, and 2020.
Source: Toossi (2002), table 5; Toossi (2006), table 4.

Proportionately, the remaining group (Asians, American Indians, Alaska natives, native Hawaiians, other Pacific Islanders, and those of multiple racial origin) is growing the fastest, but their numbers are still relatively small.

The growing share of ethnic and racial minorities in the workforce reflects, in part, the influx of immigrants in recent decades. Notably, in 2000, 11.1 percent of the U.S. population was born outside the United States, up from 7.9 percent in 1990 (U.S. Bureau of the Census, 2003b). While the numbers fluctuate, the annual flow of immigrants is substantial. In 2003, 706,000 immigrants were admitted legally, down from 1,064,000 in 2002 and also below the 1990–2003 average of 962,000 immigrants per year. In 2003, 70 percent of immigrants were admitted to reunite with family members and 18 percent through the diversity lottery, as refugees, or otherwise (U.S. Department of Homeland Security, 2004). Only 12 percent (82,000 immigrants) were admitted on the basis of employment. While the number of undocumented aliens is difficult to establish, they further add to these flows. Approximately 7 million undocumented aliens were thought to reside in the United States in 2000. A little more than half of them originated from Mexico. The population of undocumented aliens is estimated to grow at about 350,000 per year (Immigration and Naturalization Service, 2003).

Migration flows can substantially alter the growth rate and the composition of the future workforce. The number of people legally immigrating into the United States each year is about 900,000. There is about one emigrant for every four immigrants, and the illegal immigrant population increases by roughly 350,000 annually, so net migration is about 1.0 million. In 2001, the natural increase of the U.S. population—the difference between 4.0 million births and 2.4 million deaths—was about 1.6 million (National Center for Health Statistics, 2002). Net migration thus boosted U.S. population growth by about 60 percent. The effect on workforce growth is even larger, because immigrants are more likely to be of working age than the general population (71 percent of immigrants were ages 20 to 64 in 2001, compared with 59 percent of the population).

Educational Attainment and Skills

The overall growth of the labor force is likely to stagnate, and we can expect more older workers, more women, more minorities, and a continued large share of immigrants. The implications of these trends for the supply of skilled workers are determined by the present and future educational attainment of these groups.

PATTERNS OF EDUCATIONAL ATTAINMENT. Overall educational attainment among the U.S. population increased rapidly throughout the 20th century. Figure 2.6 shows the trends in the educational attainment of the population ages 25 to 34 since 1940. In 1940, only about 4 in 10 persons in this age range (cohorts born as early as 1905) completed high school. By 1980, more than 8 in 10 persons (cohorts born as early as 1945) reached this level of educational attainment or higher. During this 40-year period, the proportion completing a college degree or more rose from 6 percent to 24 percent. These large cohort differences imply that there was a steep age gradient in educational attainment. Consequently, those workers retiring in the latter half of the 20th century after a 40-year career were replaced with considerably better-educated labor-force entrants and larger absolute cohorts as a result of the baby boom. After 1980, however, that age gradient had flattened considerably, although educational attainment measured at ages 25 to 34 began to rise again after the early 1990s (see figure 2.6). One consequence of the slowdown in the trend toward higher educational attainment is that the difference in educational attainment between cohorts entering and retiring from the labor force is becoming smaller. Thus, it would appear unlikely that the United States will realize future growth rates in the educational level of the workforce comparable with those experienced in the past.

The changes in educational attainment in the recent past and those we can expect in the future depend on the schooling patterns of various demographic groups in the population and changes in the composition of the population among those groups. Table 2.1 shows the fraction of the population age 25 to 29 who completed college for men and women in

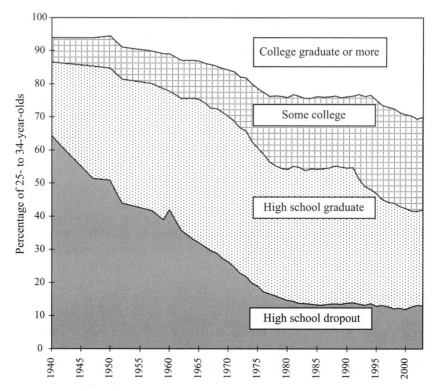

Figure 2.6 Educational attainment of 25–34-year-olds, 1940–2003. Data available for selected years between 1940 and 1964.
Source: U.S. Bureau of the Census, Educational Attainment, historical tables, table A-1, online at www.census.gov/population/www/socdemo/educ-attn.html.

three racial or ethnic groups: non-Hispanic whites, non-Hispanic blacks, and Hispanics. College completion rates are generally higher for females than for males (except among blacks), and they vary considerably by race or ethnic group. Overall, non-Hispanic whites are more than three times as likely to graduate from college than Hispanics, and they are nearly twice as likely to do so as blacks.

The low level of educational attainment of Hispanics reflects, in large part, current immigrant patterns. Many recent immigrants are very well educated, but most come to the United States with relatively little formal schooling. This has made educational progress among Hispanics, in particular, look low. The fraction of Hispanics who completed high school increased only 15 percentage points during the last 20 years, compared with a gain of 30 percentage points among blacks (Day and Bauman, 2000). However, the number of lower-educated Hispanic immigrants here today is much higher than it was 20 years ago. A cohort analysis excluding

Table 2.1   Percentage of College Graduates among Persons Ages 25
to 29 by Sex and Race/Ethnicity, 2003

Race/ethnicity	Male	Female	Total
Non-Hispanic white	31.4	37.1	34.2
Non-Hispanic black	17.7	17.4	17.5
Hispanic	8.4	12.0	10.0
Total	26.0	30.9	28.4

Source: U.S. Bureau of the Census, Educational Attainment, historical tables, table
A-2, online at www.census.gov/population/www/socdemo/educ-attn.html.

immigrants showed that educational progress among Hispanics has been
nearly identical to that among blacks (Bean and Tienda, 1987). Smith (2003)
applied an analogous analysis to the schooling and wages of three generations of Hispanic immigrants. He concluded that the apparent slow progress among Hispanics stemmed from immigration. Indeed, schooling
and wages of the children and grandchildren of immigrants grew faster
than those of native non-Hispanic whites, so that their economic statuses
converged (see also Smith, 2001).

While many immigrants enter the United States as adults with low
levels of schooling, immigration policies do allow for selective immigration of high-skilled workers. For skilled workers, the most relevant temporary visas are the H-1B and L-1 visas. H-1B visas apply to well-educated
or skilled "specialty occupation workers." L-1 visas are for intracompany
transferees (for aliens transferring from a foreign location to a U.S. location
of their employer). H-1B petitions are approved for up to three years, with a
possible extension of up to another three years; L-1 petitions are for a maximum of seven years. These visa holders are generally highly educated.
In fiscal year 2001, 98 percent had bachelor's degrees, and 42 percent had
master's degrees or higher. Their labor-force participation is, by the terms
of their visas, 100 percent.

IMPLICATIONS FOR EDUCATIONAL ATTAINMENT OF THE FUTURE WORKFORCE.
To the extent that recent differences in educational attainment persist, the
rising share of women in the labor force should favor higher educational
attainment, while the rising share of Hispanics in the labor force will work
in the opposite direction. Depending on how immigration policies are implemented, immigrants may be a source of both skilled and unskilled labor.

The implications of population shifts and educational-attainment patterns for the skills of the future workforce have been the focus of several
studies. Day and Bauman (2000) reconsider earlier findings of a stagnation

in educational attainment for the future workforce. Prior analyses were typically based on cross-sectional data and the assumption that educational attainment stops after a certain age. However, this understates college-graduation rates for younger cohorts because they have had fewer years to complete their degrees. For example, according to the 1998 Current Population Survey, the fraction of white men who completed college was stagnant at 30 percent for the 1953–1957, 1958–1962, 1963–1967, and 1968–1972 birth cohorts (see table 2.2). When measured during the same age range for every cohort, college-graduation rates rose from 26.3 percent among white men born in 1953–1957 (determined in 1983) to 30.4 percent among white men born in 1968–1972 (determined in 1998). College-graduation rates among young white women, as of ages 26 to 30, now surpass those among their male counterparts. White female college-graduation rates rose very strongly, from 22.7 percent in 1983 among women born in 1953–1957 to 34.2 percent in 1998 among women born in 1968–1973, again when measured as of ages 26 to 30 for each cohort. Here, even cross-sectional data show an upward trend, but they again understate actual attainment growth. It is therefore important to measure successive cohorts' educational attainment at the same age—one must use multiple years of data.

Based on characteristics across cohorts and educational attainment rates by sex, race or ethnicity, age, and nativity status, Day and Bauman (2000) project that educational attainment will continue to increase among the very youngest birth cohorts. Overall, in the next 25 years, they project that the proportion of the population age 25 and older who will have completed high school will rise 4 to 7 percentage points above the current 83 percent. The probability of finishing college will rise 4 to 5 percentage points above the current 24 percent. The largest gains will be realized by

Table 2.2   Percentage of College Graduates by Sex and Birth Cohort, in 1998 and at Ages 26–30

	% College graduates			
	White men		White women	
Birth cohort	In 1998	At ages 26–30	In 1998	At ages 26–30
1953–1957	30.4	26.3	28.8	22.7
1958–1962	29.5	25.7	28.3	24.5
1963–1967	30.4	27.2	32.6	27.1
1968–1972	30.4	30.4	34.2	34.2

Note: "White" includes both Hispanic and non-Hispanic white.
Source: Day and Bauman (2000), table 1.

women, particularly non-Hispanic white and Asian women. Non-Hispanic white men are also projected to reach higher levels of educational attainment. Minority men should robustly increase high-school-graduation rates, but their gains in college-graduation rates are subject to more uncertainty.

Ellwood (2001) paints a somewhat less optimistic picture in projections of educational levels for the future labor force (he also projects future labor-force participation rates, unlike Day and Bauman). He points to educational stagnation in the 1970s and 1980s. While younger cohorts may have greater college-graduation rates, it will take a very long time for the large baby-boom cohort educated in the 1970s and 1980s to leave the labor force. Under his preferred assumptions, he suggests that college-graduation rates for the labor force are likely to remain little changed from their current level. Even under the assumption of high growth rates in college enrollment, there will be only modest gains in the college-graduation rate. Between 1980 and 2000, the share of college graduates in the labor force grew from 22 to 30 percent; Ellwood projects that share to rise to 32 to 35 percent by 2020, at best.

While the projected changes differ to some extent between the Day and Bauman and Ellwood studies (in part because of a focus on population projections for the former study and labor-force projections for the latter), to the extent that educational levels are projected to increase in the future at all, the rate of increase in the next several decades will be slower than what was experienced in the past several decades.

LOOKING BEYOND EDUCATIONAL ATTAINMENT TO MEASURES OF SKILL. Thus far, we have focused on the supply of skilled workers as if educational attainment were the primary determinant of skill. However, an educational credential does not necessarily confer the needed skills that will be valued in the future workplace. For example, technological change and shifts in the nature of work are expected to place a premium in the future on such skills as abstract reasoning, problem solving, communication, and collaboration. Yet several sources of internationally comparable data indicate that the level of skills acquired by U.S. students and workers is outmatched by their counterparts in other developed countries.

Consider first data from the Organisation for Economic Co-operation and Development (OECD) Programme for International Student Assessment (PISA). PISA compares the performance of U.S. 15-year-olds on mathematics, reading, and other assessments with persons of the same age in other high-income countries (OECD, 2004, 2007). PISA, implemented for the second time in 2003 and the third time in 2006, administered internationally comparable standardized tests of reading, mathematical literacy, and scientific literacy in 41 countries. Tables 2.3 and 2.4 show how the United States ranks in comparison with other developed economies on the

Table 2.3   Student Performance on PISA 2003, Reading Scale

Country	Mean score	Level 1 or below (%)	Ratio 90th percentile to 10th percentile
Finland	543	5.7	1.47
Korea	534	6.8	1.48
Canada	528	9.6	1.55
Australia	525	11.8	1.63
New Zealand	522	14.5	1.71
Ireland	515	11.0	1.55
Sweden	514	13.3	1.62
Netherlands	513	11.5	1.55
Hong Kong	510	12.0	1.53
Belgium (Flanders)	507	17.8	1.79
Norway	500	18.2	1.72
Switzerland	499	16.7	1.65
Japan	498	19.0	1.76
Poland	497	16.8	1.65
France	496	17.5	1.67
United States	495	19.4	1.72
Denmark	492	16.5	1.60
Iceland	492	18.5	1.69
Germany	491	22.3	1.83
Austria	491	20.7	1.74
Czech Republic	489	19.4	1.68

Note: Countries are ranked by mean score.

Source: Organisation for Economic Co-operation and Development (2004), tables 6.1 and 6.2.

reading and mathematical-literacy scores.[2] We show mean scores (which are used to rank the countries from highest to lowest score), as well as the fraction scoring in the lower tail of the distribution. The ratio of the scores at the 90th and 10th percentiles provides a measure of score dispersion.

On the reading score, the United States ranks 15th out of the 29 countries shown and has one of the highest fractions in the lower tail of the score distribution measured as the fraction proficient at reading level 1 or lower (out of a possible five levels). Proficiency at reading level 1 indicates that a student

---

2. Because of a printing error in 2006 test booklets, reading performance in the United States could not be estimated. We therefore discuss reading scores from 2003 and mathematics scores from 2006.

Table 2.4   Student Performance on PISA 2006, Mathematical Scale

Country	Mean score	Level 1 or below (%)	Ratio 90th percentile to 10th percentile
Finland	548	6.0	1.47
Korea	547	8.9	1.56
Netherlands	531	11.5	1.56
Switzerland	530	13.5	1.62
Canada	527	10.8	1.53
Japan	523	13.0	1.58
New Zealand	522	14.0	1.61
Belgium	520	17.3	1.71
Australia	520	13.0	1.56
Denmark	513	13.6	1.54
Czech Republic	510	19.2	1.71
Iceland	506	16.8	1.58
Austria	505	20.0	1.69
Germany	504	19.9	1.69
Sweden	502	18.3	1.60
Ireland	501	16.4	1.53
France	496	22.3	1.67
United Kingdom	495	19.8	1.61
Poland	495	19.8	1.59
Slovak Republic	492	20.9	1.65
Luxembourg	490	22.8	1.65
Norway	490	22.2	1.63
Spain	480	24.7	1.62
United States	**474**	**28.1**	**1.65**
Portugal	466	30.7	1.67
Italy	462	32.8	1.71
Turkey	424	52.1	1.74
Mexico	406	56.5	1.72

Note: Countries are ranked by mean score.

Source: Organisation for Economic Co-operation and Development (2007), tables 6.2a and 6.2c.

is capable of only the least complex reading tasks measured in PISA, which is designed to assess "reading for learning" (reading literacy as a tool for acquiring knowledge and skills) rather than just reading fluency. Those scoring below level 1 are not able to perform routinely at even this most basic level.

Table 2.5   Performance of Adults Ages 16 to 65 on the IALS 1994–1998, Prose Score

Country	Mean score	Level 1 (%)	Ratio 90th percentile to 10th percentile
Sweden	301.3	7.5	1.51
Finland	288.6	10.4	1.54
Norway	288.5	8.5	1.44
Netherlands	282.7	10.5	1.48
Canada	278.8	16.6	1.78
Germany	275.9	14.4	1.51
New Zealand	275.2	18.4	N/A
Denmark	275.0	9.6	1.39
Australia	274.2	17.0	1.69
United States	273.7	20.7	1.90
Belgium	271.8	18.4	1.68
United Kingdom	266.7	21.8	1.75
Ireland	265.7	22.6	1.71

Note: Countries are ranked by mean score. N/A = not available.
Source: Organisation for Economic Co-operation and Development (2000), tables 2.1, 2.2, and 4.13.

In the United States, 6.5 percent score below level 1, while 12.9 percent score at level 1, approximately in the middle of the OECD ranking. The dispersion in reading scores in the United States is higher than in most other OECD countries. In the mathematical-literacy scores shown in table 2.4, the United States ranks below average on mean scores and fraction scoring at level 1 or below and has a wider dispersion than most other OECD countries.

When the United States is compared with other developed countries on the workplace-literacy skills of adults, a similar pattern emerges. The OECD International Adult Literacy Survey assesses the distribution of adult literacy skills in three domains relevant for functioning in white-collar jobs: prose literacy (the ability to process narrative text), document literacy (the ability to process forms, charts, tables, schedules, and maps), and quantitative literacy (the ability to perform practical arithmetic operations) (OECD, 2000). Table 2.5 shows how the United States ranks among 13 of the 20 other countries on the prose score, measured for persons ages 16 to 65.[3] Once again, the United States falls below the middle of the distribution among the countries studied. The fraction scoring below level 1 is an indication of those with very poor literacy skills (e.g., they may be unable to determine

3. The seven countries excluded from table 2.5 (Chile, Czech Republic, Hungary, Poland, Portugal, Slovenia, and Switzerland) all scored below the United States.

the correct amount of medicine to give to a child based on information printed on the package). For the U.S. population of adults, that fraction is 20.7 percent. Slightly higher fractions score at this same low level for document literacy (23.7 percent) and quantitative literacy (21.0 percent). Among the countries shown in table 2.5, the United States also has the largest gap between the 10th and 90th percentiles in the prose-literacy score.

Technological advances will also require a workforce with training in the sciences and engineering in order to undertake the basic research necessary for scientific and technological innovations, to develop applications from the advancements, and to bring new products to market. Considering the educational trends discussed above for recent cohorts, it is relevant, then, to consider fields of study for U.S. graduates, especially given the growing importance of women among holders of bachelor's degrees. As of 2001, 28 percent of bachelor's degrees awarded to women were in the sciences and engineering, compared with 37 percent for men (National Science Foundation, 2004b). However, the share of degrees in these fields awarded to men has been gradually declining over time, having stood at 46 percent in 1966. In contrast, the share of degrees in these fields has been steadily rising for women. Moreover, in absolute terms, the number of bachelor's degrees in the sciences and engineering awarded to men each year has changed little since the mid-1970s. Perhaps strikingly, even though women earn bachelor's degrees in these fields at a lower rate than their male counterparts, the larger absolute number of women graduates means that the absolute annual number of female graduates in these fields now surpasses the number of male graduates.[4] The combined effect is a slight decline in the share of all bachelor's degrees awarded in the sciences and engineering, from 36 percent in the late 1960s to 32 percent as of 2001.

Forces Shaping the Demand for Skilled Labor

We now turn to the forces that will affect the future demand for skilled labor. We focus first on demographics and the role that population shifts play in altering the demand for goods and services. We then turn to technological changes and the expected effects that advances in information technology and other fields will have on the demand for skilled labor. We also consider the importance of economic globalization for shifts in the demand for skilled workers.

4. In 2001, there were 202,583 female graduates with bachelor's degrees in the sciences and engineering, compared with 197,623 male graduates. The absolute number of female graduates in these fields first surpassed the number of male graduates in 2000 (National Science Foundation, 2004b).

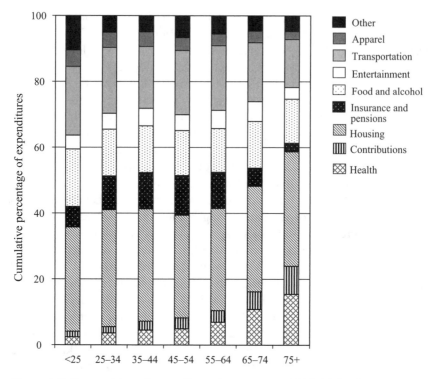

Figure 2.7 Composition of expenditures by age group, 2003. "Other" category includes personal-care products and services, reading, education, tobacco products and smoking supplies, and miscellaneous.
Source: Bureau of Labor Statics, Consumer Expenditure Survey, 2003, table 47, online at www.bls.gov/cex/2003/share/age.pdf.

Shifts in Demographics and Consumption Patterns

The demographic shifts discussed above also have implications for the demand for skilled labor in the coming years. To the extent that demographics affect the underlying demand for goods and services, changes in the composition of the population will alter the mix of jobs employers will need to fill in order to meet that underlying demand. For example, older persons have very different consumption patterns compared with younger persons. Figure 2.7 shows the share of consumption in 2003 in various categories of goods and services disaggregated by age group of the household head. It is evident that older households spend a larger share on health care, contributions, and, to some extent, housing, while spending relatively less on insurance and pensions, entertainment, transportation, apparel, and the residual "other" category.

Consider health care in particular, where outlays range from 2.4 percent of spending for those in households with a head younger than 25 to 10.8 percent and 15.4 percent for those whose heads are 65 to 74 and 75 and older, respectively. This difference in spending shares actually understates the gap, since it does not reflect social expenditures for health care through Medicaid and Medicare, which are dominated by spending on those older than 65. As the older population continues to grow in absolute numbers and as a share of the population, demand for health-care goods and services will expand in step. This will affect the demand for workers in goods-producing industries, such as pharmaceuticals and medical devices, and also those in the service sector that provide health care, such as doctors' offices, hospitals, and long-term-care facilities. Concern about the rising costs of health care and the growing share of gross domestic product devoted to health spending may lead to efforts to stem this growth, but such efforts are unlikely to alter the basic trend toward greater consumption of health-care goods and services.

Another key demographic shift discussed above is the increase in labor-force participation among women, especially those with young children. As women have entered the labor market in greater numbers, the demand has increased for goods and services formerly produced in the home, such as prepared meals, cleaning services, gardening, and other personal-care services. Likewise, the demand for child care, whether in the home or in another facility, has risen. The latest trends show, for example, that the share of four-year-olds in prekindergarten programs has doubled in the last three decades, from 28 percent in 1970 to 67 percent in 2002. The share of three-year-olds in such programs has tripled in the same time period, from 13 to 42 percent.[5]

Occupational projections prepared by the Bureau of Labor Statistics (BLS) illustrate the implications of these demographic changes in terms of the expected shifts in the occupational mix (Hecker, 2004). Figure 2.8 shows the top 20 detailed (four-digit) occupations with the fastest projected employment growth between 2002 and 2012, while figure 2.9 shows the top 20 detailed occupations with the largest projected absolute growth over the same period.[6] Reflecting an aging population, 10 of the 20 occupations projected to grow the fastest are in the health-care field or personal-care services.[7] Notably, these fast-growing occupations—medical and physician

5. See U.S. Bureau of the Census (2004), table 237, and www.census.gov/population/www/socdemo/school.html.

6. Overall, all occupations are projected to grow 14.8 percent between 2002 and 2012. The 20 fastest-growing occupations in figure 2.8 exceed the average growth rate by a factor of 2.5 to 4.

7. The growth in these occupations also reflects a wealthier population willing to devote more resources to health care and technological advances in the health-care field that allow for more aggressive treatment (Hecker, 2004).

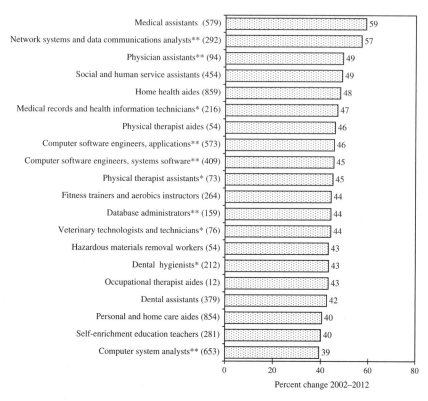

Figure 2.8 BLS projected top 20 four-digit occupations with fastest employment growth, 2002–2012. Number in parentheses next to bar label is absolute employment level (in thousands) projected for 2012. Education or training level required by most workers to become fully qualified is (*) associate degree, (**) bachelor's degree, or (***) doctoral degree. Those with no asterisk may require a postsecondary vocational award or varying levels of work experience or on-the-job training. *Source: Hecker (2004), table 3.*

assistants, physical therapist aides and assistants, dental hygienists and assistants, occupational therapist aides, medical records technicians, and home health and personal and home-care aides—all support higher-paid professionals, such as physicians, dentists, and therapists, or substitute for institutional care (e.g., hospitals or nursing homes). This reflects, in part, the push for cost savings in the provision of health care. Two of these fast-growing occupations are also projected to add large absolute numbers of jobs: home health aides with 279,000 and personal and home-care aides with 246,000. Other large gains are expected for registered nurses (623,000) and nursing aides (343,000). As a group, health-care practitioners and technical occupations and health-care support occupations (two categories that include the detailed occupations mentioned above) are slated to increase

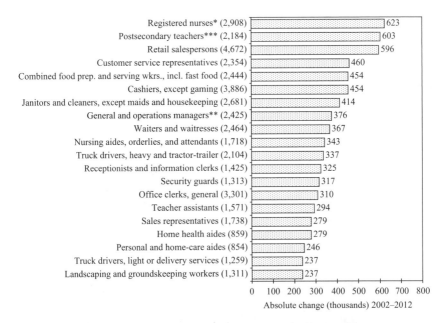

Figure 2.9 BLS projected top 20 four-digit occupations with largest employment growth, 2002–2012. Number in parentheses next to bar label is absolute employment level (in thousands) projected for 2012. Education or training level required by most workers to become fully qualified is (*) associate degree, (**) bachelor's degree, or (***) doctoral degree. Those with no asterisk may require a postsecondary vocational award or varying levels of work experience or on-the-job training. *Source: Hecker (2004), table 4.*

over the decade by 26 percent and 35 percent, respectively, while employment will grow 15 percent overall.

Another category that dominates the fastest-growing occupations shown in figure 2.8 is occupations related to the information technology (IT) field. Computer network and system analysts, computer software engineers, and database administrators are all projected to grow rapidly. As a whole, computer specialist occupations and computer and information system managers, two aggregate occupational groups, are each expected to grow 36 percent over the decade. These gains reflect the growing importance of IT for most industries, as discussed below. Among the occupations with large expected absolute gains are those that are growing, in part, as a result of higher female labor-force participation and the substitution of purchased services for home production. These include food-service workers as well as landscaping and groundskeeping workers and teacher assistants. Preschool teachers just miss the top 20 fastest-growing occupations, with a 36-percent projected growth.

The occupations with the fastest projected growth rates and absolute growth represent a mix of skill requirements. BLS categorizes detailed occupations by the education and training needed by most workers to be qualified. Among the 20 fastest-growing occupations shown in figure 2.8, 4 are classified as requiring an associate degree, and another 6 are in the bachelor's degree category. The other 10 require vocational or on-the-job training or work experience. Postsecondary education is required for the IT-related jobs, along with the more highly skilled health-care support occupations. On-the-job training is sufficient for most workers in the fast-growing health-care support occupations, although a few require an associate or bachelor's degree. Adding the next 10 fastest-growing occupations (ranks 21 to 30) brings in 9 of 10 other occupations that all require postsecondary education. At the same time, only 3 of the 20 occupations shown in figure 2.9 with the largest absolute growth require postsecondary education. Six of the next 10 occupations with the largest absolute growth do require a bachelor's degree or higher, however. Overall, the fastest-growing occupational group—professional and related occupations—includes mainly occupations that require postsecondary education. At the same time, none of the top 30 occupations with the largest projected declines is classified in a postsecondary-education category. Thus, the largest losses are expected in fields that require short- to long-term on-the-job training.

Technological Change

The BLS occupational projections signal the importance of technological change, notably in occupations directly related to the IT field. However, technological advancements more generally have had, and can be expected to have, even wider-ranging effects on the demand for skilled labor throughout the economy. Indeed, the last several decades marked a transition in the United States from a production-based economy to an information-based economy. The transformation is evident in the rapid pace of innovation in IT, as well as emerging fields such as biotechnology and nanotechnology. These technological advances are manifested in the rising demand for more educated labor, changes in business organization, and the wage structure.

The last few decades have been marked by a rapid pace of technological change. Consider the speed of developments in the adoption of computers. The Bureau of Economic Analysis first recorded stocks of computer equipment and peripherals in the nonresidential sector in 1963, around the time that mainframes came online. As of 1980, nine years after the invention of the microprocessor, these stocks were less than 1 percent of the level they would attain by the turn of the century, and even by 1990, the stock was still less than 10 percent of the level reached in 2001 (Karoly and Panis, 2004). During the 1990s, advances in semiconductor and other technologies vastly expanded computing, storage, data transmission, and networking capacities, all while prices per unit fell dramatically. Software advances improved user interfaces and allowed widespread adoption of computers throughout the economy. As of 2001, 54 percent of the workforce reported using a computer on the job, more than double the rate estimated as of 1994 (Freeman, 2002; Hipple and Kosanovich, 2003). And the influences of the computer revolution extend beyond computing and telecommunications equipment. Microprocessors and other semiconductors have been incorporated into a wide array of products, from machine tools to consumer electronics. Estimates indicate that 50 to 70 percent of worldwide semiconductor sales in the late 1990s were for products other than computers (Congressional Budget Office, 2002).

However, there are differences in the extent of IT investment in different sectors of the economy (Karoly and Panis, 2004). Investment in IT has been the highest in absolute terms in transportation, communications, and utilities, as might be expected. Other sectors with large investments include financial services, wholesale and retail trade, and services. Use of computers in the workplace also varies in predictable ways. Notably, computer use rises sharply with education levels, from 16.2 percent among workers without a high school diploma to 81.9 percent among those with a college degree (Hipple and Kosanovich, 2003). Likewise, use of a PC on the job is much more common for managerial and professional workers (almost 80 percent) compared with operators, fabricators, and laborers (less than 20 percent).

All indications are that the pace of technological change will continue, in terms of developments in the IT field and in other areas as well. Current estimates indicate that advancements in integrated circuits will proceed on a similar trajectory for another decade or so before physical limitations of silicon technology become binding (Congressional Budget Office, 2002). In practical terms, these advances will allow greater processing speed, higher storage capacity, and wider applications than what is currently available (e.g., robotics and artificial intelligence) (Anderson et al., 2000). These advances will be accompanied by and will complement developments in other fields such as biotechnology and nanotechnology. In the biomedical sciences, advances on the horizon include new approaches to the diagnosis and treatment of disease, including sophisticated medical devices and specialized pharmaceuticals (Garr, 2001; Wortman, 2001; Goho, 2003). Other evolutionary and revolutionary technologies are anticipated from future developments in the field of nanotechnology (National Science Foundation, 2001; National Nanotechnology Initiative, 2005).[8] The

---

8. Nanotechnology refers to the ability to measure, manipulate, and organize matter at the atomic scale and bridges the fields of biology, chemistry, physics, engineering, and computer science.

National Science Foundation (2001) projects that investments in the field of nanotechnology will exceed $1 trillion annually in the United States by 2015, with implications in the 21st century as significant as the combined effects of antibiotics, the integrated circuit, and synthetic polymers were in the 20th century.

While many of the more dramatic contributions of nanotechnology may be farther off in the future, the combined effects of even near-term advances in IT, biotechnology, and the emerging field of nanotechnology will be increased demand for a skilled workforce able to generate scientific discoveries, translate them into commercial applications, and bring the resulting products to the marketplace. More generally, technological change has been identified as an important source of rising demand for skilled workers throughout the economy, where worker skill is typically defined by educational level. While new technologies in theory may be either a relative complement or a relative substitute for skilled labor, the consensus among most economists is that the technological advances for most of the 20th century have favored more highly skilled workers (Goldin and Katz, 1998; Bresnahan, Brynjolfsson, and Hitt, 2000; Acemoglu, 2002; Autor, Levy, and Murnane, 2003).

To illustrate the shifts in demand over time, Autor, Levy, and Murnane (2003) analyze the skill content of jobs during the last four decades using data on the distribution of occupations from the Census Bureau and the Current Population Survey combined with the Dictionary of Occupational Titles. Figure 2.10 shows these trends in terms of five skill categories, all plotted as the mean task input in each year as a percentile of the base-year (1960) distribution. The figure illustrates that in the last 40 years, there has been a steady shift in occupations toward those requiring nonroutine cognitive analytic (problem-solving) and interactive (communication) skills, especially during the 1980s and 1990s as computers came into widespread use. These represent the set of skills that require flexibility, creativity, problem solving, and complex communication and are therefore not easily programmable for computers to perform. In contrast, just as demand was rising for nonroutine skills, the occupational mix shifted away from jobs that require routine manual or cognitive skills, precisely those types of clear, repetitive tasks that can be translated into computer code. There has also been a steady shift away from occupations requiring manual skills.

Autor, Levy, and Murnane (2003) investigate the drivers of these economy-wide trends by industry, occupation, and education groups. Their analysis indicates that industries that adopted computers most rapidly during the 1970s, 1980s, and 1990s increased their usage of nonroutine analytic and interactive skills more rapidly than other industries, at the same time as they had the largest decline in routine task input. Moreover,

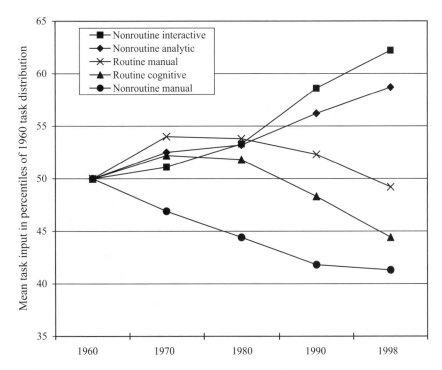

Figure 2.10 Economy-wide measure of occupational task input, 1960–1998. Data for 1960 and 1970 are from the Census Bureau; data for 1980, 1990, and 1998 are from the Current Population Survey.
Source: Autor, Levy, and Murnane (2003), table II.

these shifts toward nonroutine skills in industries with rapid computerization occurred within educational groups, indicating task shifts away from routine skills at all educational levels. Shifts toward nonroutine skills also occurred to a greater extent within occupations that had the largest increases in computer use. They concluded that technological change is a key underlying factor that shifted demand in favor of more educated workers in recent decades. A related study by Autor, Katz, and Krueger (1998) concluded that the relative demand for skilled labor (college equivalents) grew more rapidly between 1970 and 1995 compared with the 1940-to-1970 period, with the greatest degree of skill upgrading taking place in those industries with intensive computer investment.

Complementary evidence on the relationship between technology and the demand for skilled labor comes from firm-level analyses. For example, Bresnahan, Brynjolfsson, and Hitt (2000) studied a sample of 400 large U.S. firms and found that the demand for human capital and workforce skills was higher for firms with larger investments in IT and higher IT intensity. These authors, through case studies and firm-level data analysis, found evidence that IT investments are associated with complementary changes in the organization of firms (Bresnahan, Brynjolfsson, and Hitt, 2000, 2002; Brynjolfsson and Hitt, 2000). IT adoption, for example, is associated with better measurement and communication within the firm and associated changes in management and organizational structures, such as increased outsourcing of noncore business functions. These complementary workplace practices, along with the automation and substitution traditionally associated with IT adoption, provide a more complete explanation for the rising demand for more educated workers.

The shifting demand for labor associated with changes in technology is evident in the BLS occupational projections discussed above. High-growth occupations include many associated with the IT field. At the same time, 13 of 30 occupations with the largest declines are in office and administrative support and include occupations such as word processors and typists; secretaries outside the legal, medical, and executive domains; telephone operators; data-entry keyers; order clerks; and brokerage clerks (Hecker, 2004). Demand for these occupations will fall with the expansion of electronic commerce, as well as advances in computing, optical-scanning, and voice-recognition technologies. Automation will also affect production-related occupations such as electrical and electronic equipment assemblers, team assemblers, and chemical plant and system operators. Electronic publishing will reduce the demand for prepress technicians and workers, and the Internet will displace travel agents. As noted earlier, none of these occupations that will experience large declines in the decade ahead requires postsecondary education as a significant source of training.

Technological change and the associated increase in the demand for skilled labor have been identified as significant factors in the increase in wage inequality in recent decades, summarized earlier in figure 2.1. The rise in the college-education wage premium occurred during the 1980s and 1990s at the same time as the relative supply of college-educated labor was increasing. This suggests that the demand for skill was rising even faster. Skill-biased technological change is a leading demand-side explanation. Indeed, a review of the extensive literature on this topic by Acemoglu (2002) concluded that "an acceleration of [skill-biased technical change] during the past few decades appears to be the main cause of the increase in [wage] inequality" (p. 9).

The evidence that technological change played a role comes from studies of the changes over time in the college-education wage premium that account for changes in relative supplies of educated workers and attribute the unexplained residual wage change to technological change (see, e.g., Bound and Johnson, 1992; Katz and Murphy, 1992; Murphy and Welch, 1992). Other studies offer more direct evidence of a relationship among various measures of the wage structure and technological change (Mincer, 1991;

Allen, 2001). While there is a consensus that technological change played a role in growing wage inequality, studies vary in the share of the growth of inequality attributable to this factor.

Technological change, however, may not explain all aspects of the changing wage structure in recent decades, such as the rise in wage inequality within education groups and the slowdown in the growth of wage inequality in the 1990s (Card and DiNardo, 2002a, 2002b). Rather, a broader set of supply- and demand-side factors likely played a role. We discuss below the role of globalization. Other factors that have been linked to the rise in wage inequality include a slowdown in the growth rate of the college-educated labor force, rising immigration, declining unionization, a falling minimum wage, and economic deregulation (Card and DiNardo, 2002a, 2002b; DiNardo, Fortin, and Lemieux, 1996; Freeman, 1996; Fortin and Lemieux, 1997; Topel, 1997; Katz and Murphy, 2002).

Globalization

The growing importance of global economic integration in recent decades is another key trend that has implications for the demand for skilled labor in the U.S. economy. Globalization is evident in the relative size of exports and imports as a share of the U.S. economy, in the magnitude of international capital flows, in the mobility of labor across national boundaries, and in the relative ease of knowledge and technology transfers across countries. Consider the value of exports and imports as a share of GDP. During the 1960s, the share was about 10 percent of economic activity. In the following decades, the share of trade in the economy began to rise, reaching about 25 percent of GDP by the millennium (Karoly and Panis, 2004). During this period, the composition of trade shifted toward a greater share in services, thereby subjecting a wider range of industries to competition from international trade. For example, the share of service exports (e.g., travel and transportation, telecommunication services, education, financial and business services, technical services, and royalties and license fees) increased from 18 percent of exports in 1980 to 30 percent by 2002.

A key feature of contemporary trade patterns is "vertical trade," the phenomenon of finished products composed of inputs produced and assembled in stages in different countries (Krugman, 1995; Feenstra, 1998; Hummels, Ishii, and Yi, 2001). Carving up the production process allows more labor-intensive stages of production to take place in low-wage countries, while more capital-, knowledge-, or technology-intensive stages are located in higher-wage settings. Such "disintegration of production" is enabled, in part, by the IT advances discussed above, combined with falling costs for communication and transportation.

The technology changes have also facilitated the growth in outsourcing of higher-skill service-sector jobs to lower-wage settings (Karoly and Panis, 2004; Mann, 2005). IT-enabled services such as business-processing services, computer programming, and call-center operations are increasingly outsourced to countries such as Hungary, India, Ireland, the Philippines, and others, where educated workers perform tasks at lower wages compared with their U.S. counterparts. Work outsourced overseas also extends to such other fields as preparing architectural blueprints, analyzing financial data, and reading CAT scans. The work products in these information-based occupations can be easily transmitted over high-speed data lines and monitored over electronic networks.

The media attention centered on white-collar outsourcing has raised concerns that the growth in high-skilled workers overseas in countries with lower wages will reduce the demand for high-skilled workers in the United States, through either layoffs or a slowdown in the creation of new jobs. Yet government statistics provide only crude data to assess the importance of offshoring for the U.S. economy (General Accounting Office, 2004). What limited evidence is available suggests that the impact of such outsourcing has thus far been small. For example, recent statistics indicate that offshoring plays only a minor role among the reasons for layoffs. In a study of companies with at least 50 layoffs in the first quarter of 2004, the BLS estimates that 4,633 workers lost their jobs because of relocation of production overseas (Bureau of Labor Statistics, 2004). This represents 1.9 percent of mass layoffs, or 2.5 percent among job separations for reasons other than seasonal or vacation events. These numbers exclude smaller-scale layoffs, but Brainard and Litan (2004), based on forecasts of IT consulting firm Forrester, conclude that offshoring-related layoffs will represent less than 2 percent of involuntary job separations between 2004 and 2015. U.S. import data, especially imports of services that most closely measure relocation of skilled work, provide another metric to quantify offshoring. Schultze (2004) found that the number of jobs affected by offshoring has increased over time but is very small compared with the number of jobs affected by recent domestic productivity increases. In all, offshoring appears to play a minor role in affecting the demand for skilled labor in the United States, but it remains an area to monitor.

Equally limited data are available to examine the opposite phenomenon: the outsourcing of jobs to the United States by companies located in other countries. One recent anecdote is suggestive of how global markets take advantage of high-skilled labor in the United States. China's largest computer maker, the Lenovo Group, purchased IBM's personal computer business in 2005. The Chinese company moved its headquarters to the United States and appointed a senior IBM executive to manage it. More generally, foreign direct investment in the United States by foreign multinationals is estimated to be an important source of job creation, as well as a source of technology transfer (Karoly and Panis, 2004).

With the growing importance of trade in the U.S. economy, economists have examined the effect of trade on the demand for labor of varying levels of skill and the resulting consequences for the U.S. wage structure. The expectation that changes in the wage structure are linked to trade derives from the Heckscher-Ohlin-Samuelson two-factor two-good model of trade. The theorem predicts that trade between two countries will result in the equalization of factor prices, such as the wages of lower- and higher-skilled workers (Bhagwati and Dehejia, 1994; Helpman, 1999). Until the recent phenomenon of outsourcing higher-skilled white-collar jobs, globalization was generally expected to have the greatest effect on lower-skilled U.S. workers, given the abundance of low-wage counterparts overseas.

Although trade theorists debate the validity of the model and its various extensions, in terms of the prediction of factor price equalization, economists have looked for empirical evidence of a link between trade and the wage structure. While there are several approaches to quantifying the effect of trade on wages and while there are some differences across studies, most find at most a modest effect of trade on wages (see, e.g., Freeman, 1995; Richardson, 1995).[9] These studies suggest that 10 to 20 percent of the relative decline in wages of low-skilled workers could be attributable to trade. Generally, trade is thought to be a smaller factor in changing the wage structure than others such as technology.

Conclusions and Implications

Our review of the forces affecting the supply of and demand for skilled labor points to several key conclusions.

- The labor force will grow considerably more slowly in coming decades compared with the recent past. The labor-force composition will change in favor of subgroups that currently have higher rates of educational attainment (e.g., women), as well as those with lower rates of educational attainment (e.g., minorities). The delayed retirement of older workers will keep older cohorts with lower educational levels in the labor force longer.

- We can expect some additional upgrading of the educational attainment of the U.S. workforce in the future, but the changes

9. For discussions of the strengths and weaknesses of alternative approaches to quantifying the effect of trade on wages, see Burtless (1995), Freeman (1995), Collins (1998), Krugman (2000), and Leamer (2000).

will be more modest compared with the gains experienced in the 1960s and 1970s. While years of schooling of workers may continue to rise, there is some question about the quality of the education they obtain. International comparisons of U.S. students and adults place the United States well below many other developed countries in terms of measures of skills. The U.S. skill distribution is also more dispersed, with relatively more low-skilled and high-skilled individuals. Moreover, the fraction of degree recipients in the sciences and engineering is stagnant at best, with whatever absolute growth there is driven by female graduates.

- Demographic shifts, technological change, and globalization also have implications for the demand for skilled labor. Occupational projections by the BLS reflecting these influences indicate that the fastest-growing occupational group—professionals and related occupations—mostly require a bachelor's degree or higher. At the same time, the largest losses are expected in occupations where skills are largely acquired through on-the-job training. Countering these changes are demographic shifts (e.g., population aging and higher prevalence of dual-earner couples) that are increasing the demand for workers with less education in health care and various personal services.

- Changes in technology in the last several decades have been identified as an important source of rising demand for skilled workers in a wide range of industries and occupations. New technologies favor nonroutine skills such as flexibility, creativity, problem solving, and complex communication. Computers and other new technologies complement workers with these skills. In contrast, information technologies tend to substitute for routine skills that can be translated into programmable steps for computers to execute. Complementary changes in workplace practices further increase the demand for workers with high skill levels. All indications are that such technological advances in the future will continue to place a premium on higher-skilled workers.

- Until recently, globalization was viewed as reducing the demand for lower-skilled workers in the United States, who increasingly competed with low-wage counterparts overseas. The advent of outsourcing higher-skilled IT-enabled white-collar jobs has raised concerns that trade will also reduce the demand for higher-skilled workers in sectors now subject to greater competition from workers overseas. However, the limited data available suggest that the magnitude of white-collar outsourcing is too small as a share of overall labor-force activity to have had a large effect to date.

- Technological change has been estimated to have increased the demand for higher-skilled workers at a pace that exceeded the increasing supply. This, in turn, resulted in widening wage differentials by education groups. Other factors that have been identified as affecting the wage structure include a slowdown in the growth of college graduation, increased trade, the influx of immigrants, declining unionization rates, a falling minimum wage, and economic deregulation.

These conclusions follow from an extrapolation of trends in demographics, technology, and globalization of the past few decades. Naturally, major disruptions of historical patterns could change some of the conclusions. For example, the supply of skilled workers in the United States could be boosted by targeted public policies or an adverse economic shock inducing students to remain in school longer. By contrast, the supply of skilled workers from overseas could be reduced by tighter immigration standards or rapid economic progress in India or China, improving prospects for high-skilled workers in those countries. Similarly, demand for skilled workers in the United States may decline if rapid technological developments result in large-scale offshoring of high-skilled labor. All of these developments have occurred in recent history, left their traces, and may occur again. However, if they were to occur again with unprecedented vigor, our conclusions may need to be adjusted. Assuming no major breaks with historical trends, we now draw out several implications of our findings.

If future labor-force growth matches the projections presented earlier, the U.S. economy will likely face tight labor markets during periods of rapid economic growth and potential shortages in key occupations, most likely highly skilled ones (Lofgren, Nyce, and Schieber, 2003). One potential outcome is an increase in wages in light of such shortages. To the extent that shortages affect higher-skilled work, this would further raise the wage premium associated with higher levels of education. High wages may, in turn, increase labor supply or, alternatively, induce employers to substitute other inputs, including possible foreign sources of labor through offshoring. Employers may also recruit workers more aggressively, with more attractive benefits, or from nontraditional labor pools, including specialized immigrant workers. There may also be a supply-side response in the face of future shortages of skilled workers, albeit with a lag. In particular, it may be the case that prospective students will respond to the increased wage gap between lower-educated and higher-educated workers. Indeed, there is some evidence of a supply response in the pattern of educational attainment shown earlier in figure 2.6.

Thus, against the backdrop of a slowdown in workforce growth, one possible outcome is that employers will advocate for increased immigration through greater numbers of employment-based visas such as the H-1B and L-1 visas discussed above. Indeed, the 1990s, with its tight labor market, was a period when the number of highly skilled temporary foreign workers admitted increased substantially. In fiscal year 2001, 331,000 temporary work-based (H-1B) visas were approved for specialty occupations, 58 percent for computer-related jobs (U.S. Department of Homeland Security, 2005).[10] Nearly 60,000 other visas (L-1) admitted intracompany transferees (Migration News, 2003). A rough estimate, assuming an average stay of two years per H-1B approval and four years per L-1 visa issuance, is that the stock of H-1B and L-1 beneficiaries is about 800,000. Ultimately, the future outlook for immigration flows—both high- and low-skilled—is uncertain, in part because their size and composition are subject to congressional policy.

Immigrants who come to the United States for advanced education have also been a source of high-skilled labor in the past. For example, top students from universities and engineering schools in China, India, Korea, and Taiwan receive their doctorates in the sciences and engineering from U.S. universities, and many remain after they complete their degrees. Recent estimates suggest that as many as 70 percent of foreign-born U.S. Ph.D. recipients remain in the United States rather than returning to their country of origin (Bhagwati, 2003). In high-tech areas such as California's Silicon Valley, immigrants make up a substantial portion of the scientific and engineering workforce, as well as corporate leaders (Saxenian, 1999). Overall, estimates from the 2000 U.S. Census indicate that 22 percent of all college-educated workers in the sciences and engineering were foreign-born (National Science Foundation, 2004a). Among engineers with doctorates, the share of foreign-born was 51 percent, and it was 45 percent for individuals with doctorates in the life, physical, mathematical, and computer sciences. Yet more restrictive immigration policies in the wake of events on September 11, 2001, coupled with increased competition from universities in other countries have led to a decrease, at least in the short term, in the number of foreign students studying for advanced degrees in the United States (Dillon, 2004). If this recent experience continues, the United States may find it increasingly difficult to attract highly skilled immigrants or to retain those who are educated at U.S. colleges and universities, thereby limiting the supply of scientists and engineers in the U.S. labor market (National Science Foundation, 2004a).

In light of the prospect of near-zero growth in the workforce, employers are likely to step up recruitment among subpopulations that are currently underrepresented. We already discussed older workers, women, and immigrants. Another potential source of workers is persons with

---

10. The following year, the number fell to 198,000 as a consequence of the retrenchments in the IT industry.

disabilities. Not surprisingly, labor-force participation among persons with disabilities is lower than among those without. In 2002, workforce participation among the disabled versus the nondisabled ages 16 to 64 was 29 and 82 percent, respectively (U.S. Bureau of the Census, 2003a).[11] This difference translates into roughly 12 million persons with disabilities who are left out of the workforce. The trend in workforce participation among the disabled is slightly downward, by 3 percentage points between 1995 and 2002. However, several technological and institutional developments are under way that may reverse this pattern (Karoly and Panis, 2004). Medical technology is undergoing rapid change, so that some disabilities may be cured, prevented, or rendered more manageable in the future; progress in IT may help persons with disabilities perform tasks that they currently cannot, either by helping directly with the task or by enabling remote work from home; and the Ticket to Work program of the Social Security Administration aims to induce more disability-insurance recipients to return to work. Countering these developments, however, is the prospect that the prevalence of disability may be on the rise as a result of general population aging and the increasing prevalence of such precursors to disability as diabetes, asthma, and obesity (Lakdawalla et al., 2003).

The growing importance of skill in the U.S. economy, both for new labor-force entrants and for current workers, highlights the need for an education and training system that can prepare workers to enter the labor market and offer opportunities for skill upgrading throughout an individual's working life. At the primary and secondary level, a focus on improving educational outcomes in mathematics and the sciences is critical, given the expected pace of technological change and the extent of global competition (National Commission on Mathematics and Science Teaching for the 21st Century, 2000). There is also a need to develop opportunities for lifelong learning through formal and informal training programs, whether offered by employers or public or private educational institutions. One challenge is that opportunities for employer-provided training typically increase with education levels, so that lower-educated workers do not have the same opportunity for upgrading their skills as their higher-educated counterparts (Ahlstrand, Bassi, and McMurrer, 2003). At the same time, the Internet and other communication technologies have great potential for improving worker skills through technology-mediated learning that is available anytime, anywhere (Karoly and Panis, 2004). If lower-skilled workers, in particular, can take advantage of such technology-driven learning opportunities, it may allow for skill upgrading of the current workforce in response to the anticipated growth in demand.

---

11. Other sources suggest different rates, depending on the strictness of the definition of disability.

References

Acemoglu, Daron. 2002. "Technical Change, Inequality, and the Labor Market." *Journal of Economic Literature* 40, no. 1 (March): 7–72.

Ahlstrand, Amanda L., Laurie J. Bassi, and Daniel P. McMurrer. 2003. *Workplace Education for Low-Wage Workers.* Kalamazoo, MI: W. E. Upjohn Institute for Employment Research.

Allen, Steven G. 2001. "Technology and the Wage Structure." *Journal of Labor Economics* 19, no. 2: 440–83.

Anderson, Robert H., Philip S. Anton, Steven C. Bankes, Tora Kay Bikson, Jonathan Caulkins, Peter Denning, James A. Dewar, Richard O. Hundley, and C. Richard Neu. 2000. *The Global Course of the Information Revolution: Technological Trends, Proceedings of an International Conference.* Santa Monica, CA: RAND.

Autor, David H., Lawrence F. Katz, and Alan B. Krueger. 1998. "Computing Inequality: Have Computers Changed the Labor Market?" *Quarterly Journal of Economics* 113 (November): 1169–1213.

Autor, David H., Frank Levy, and Richard Murnane. 2003. "The Skill Content of Recent Technological Change: An Empirical Exploration." *Quarterly Journal of Economics* 118, no. 4: 1279–1333.

Bean, Frank D., and Marta Tienda. 1987. *The Hispanic Population of the United States.* New York: Russell Sage Foundation.

Bhagwati, Jagdish. 2003. "Borders Beyond Control." *Foreign Affairs* 82, no. 1 (January-February): 98–104.

Bhagwati, Jagdish, and Vivek H. Dehejia. 1994. "Freer Trade and Wages of the Unskilled: Is Marx Striking Again?" In Jagdish Bhagwati and Marvin H. Kosters, eds., *Trade and Wages: Leveling Wages Down?* Washington, DC: American Enterprise Institute, pp. 36–75.

Bound, John, and George Johnson. 1992. "Changes in the Structure of Wages during the 1980s: An Evaluation of Alternative Explanations." *American Economic Review* 82, no. 3 (June): 371–92.

Brainard, Lael, and Robert E. Litan. 2004. "Offshoring Service Jobs: Bane or Boon and What to Do?" Brookings Institution Policy Brief No. 132. www.brookings.edu/comm/policybriefs/pb132.htm.

Bresnahan, Timothy F., Erik Brynjolfsson, and Lorin M. Hitt. 2000. "Information Technology and Recent Changes in Work Organization Increase the Demand for Skilled Labor." In Margaret M. Blair and Thomas A. Kochan, eds., *The New Relationship: Human Capital in the American Corporation.* Washington, DC: Brookings Institution, pp. 145–84.

———. 2002. "Information Technology, Workplace Organization, and the Demand for Skilled Labor: Firm-Level Evidence." *Quarterly Journal of Economics* 117, no. 1 (February): 339–76.

Brynjolfsson, Erik, and Lorin M. Hitt. 2000. "Beyond Computation: Information Technology, Organizational Transformation and Business Performance." *Journal of Economic Perspectives* 14, no. 4 (Fall): 23–48.

Bureau of Labor Statistics. 2004. "Extended Mass Layoffs, Associated with Domestic and Overseas Relocations, First Quarter 2004." Bureau of Labor Statistics News Release, USDL 04–1038, June 10.

Bureau of Labor Statistics. 2005. *Series Report*. Washington, DC. Series LNU01324231 and LNU01324232 for labor-force participation among men and women age 55+; LNU01300001 and LNU01300002 for labor-force participation among men and women age 16+. http://data.bls.gov/cgi-bin/srgate.

Burtless, Gary. 1995. "International Trade and the Rise in Earnings Inequality." *Journal of Economic Literature* 33, no. 2 (June): 800–16.

Card, David, and John E. DiNardo. 2002a. "Skill Biased Technological Change and Rising Wage Inequality: Some Problems and Puzzles." *Journal of Labor Economics* 20, no. 4: 733–83.

———. 2002b. "Technology and U.S. Wage Inequality: A Brief Look." *Federal Reserve Bank of Atlanta Economic Review* 87, no. 3: 45–62.

Collins, Susan M. 1998. "Economic Integration and the American Worker." In Susan M. Collins, ed., *Imports, Exports and the American Worker*. Washington, DC: Brookings Institution Press, pp. 3–45.

Congressional Budget Office. 2002. *The Role of Computer Technology in the Growth of Productivity*. Washington, DC: Congressional Budget Office.

Costa, Dora L. 1998. *The Evolution of Retirement: An American Economic History, 1880–1990*. Chicago: University of Chicago Press.

Day, Jennifer Cheeseman, and Kurt J. Bauman. 2000. "Have We Reached the Top? Educational Attainment Projections of the U.S. Population." Working Paper Series, No. 43. Washington, DC: U.S. Bureau of the Census.

Dillon, Sam. 2004. "Foreign Enrollment Declines at Universities, Survey Says." *New York Times*, November 10, p. A17.

DiNardo, John E., Nicole Fortin, and Thomas Lemieux. 1996. "Labor Market Institutions and the Distribution of Wages, 1973–1992: A Semi-Parametric Approach." *Econometrica* 64 (September): 1001–44.

Ellwood, David. 2001. "The Sputtering Labor Force of the 21st Century: Can Social Policy Help?" Working Paper No. 8321. Cambridge, MA: National Bureau of Economic Research, June.

Feenstra, Robert C. 1998. "Integration of Trade and Disintegration of Production in the Global Economy." *Journal of Economic Perspectives* 12, no. 4 (Autumn): 31–50.

Fortin, Nicole M., and Thomas Lemieux. 1997. "Institutional Changes and Rising Wage Inequality: Is There a Linkage?" *Journal of Economic Perspectives* 11, no. 2: 75–96.

Freeman, Richard B. 1995. "Are Your Wages Set in Beijing?" *Journal of Economic Perspectives* 9, no. 3 (Summer): 57–80.

———. 1996. "Labor Market Institutions and Earnings Inequality." *New England Economic Review* (May–June): 157–68.

———. 2002. "The Labour Market in the New Information Economy." *Oxford Review of Economic Policy* 18, no. 3: 288–305.

Garr, Doug. 2001. "The Human Body Shop." *Technology Review*, April, pp. 73–79.

General Accounting Office. 2004. *International Trade: Current Government Data Provide Limited Insight into Offshoring of Services.* Washington, DC: General Accounting Office, September.

Goho, Alexandra M. 2003. "10 Emerging Technologies That Will Change the World: Injectible Tissue Engineering." *Technology Review,* February, p. 38.

Goldin, Claudia. 1990. *Understanding the Gender Gap: An Economic History of American Women.* New York: Oxford University Press.

Goldin, Claudia, and Lawrence F. Katz. 1998. "The Origins of Technology-Skill Complementarity." *Quarterly Journal of Economics* 113, no. 3: 693–732.

Hecker, Daniel E. 2004. "Occupational Employment Projections to 2012." *Monthly Labor Review* 127, no. 2 (February): 80–105.

Helpman, Elhanan. 1999. "The Structure of Foreign Trade." *Journal of Economic Perspectives* 13, no. 2: 121–44.

Hipple, Steven, and Karen Kosanovich. 2003. "Compute and Internet Use at Work in 2001." *Monthly Labor Review* (February): 26–35.

Hummels, David, Jun Ishii, and Kei-Mu Yi. 2001. "The Nature and Growth of Vertical Specialization in World Trade." *Journal of International Economics* 54, no. 1 (June): 75–96.

Immigration and Naturalization Service, Office of Policy and Planning. 2003. *Estimates of the Unauthorized Immigrant Population Residing in the United States: 1990 to 2000.* Washington, DC. http://uscis.gov/graphics/shared/aboutus/statistics/Ill_Report_1211.pdf.

Karoly, Lynn A., and Constantijn W. A. Panis. 2004.*The 21st Century at Work: Forces Shaping the Future Workforce and Workplace in the United States.* Santa Monica, CA: RAND.

Katz, Lawrence F., and Kevin M. Murphy. 1992. "Changes in Relative Wages, 1963–1987: Supply and Demand Factors." *Quarterly Journal of Economics* 197 (February): 35–78.

Krugman, Paul. 1995. "Growing World Trade: Causes and Consequences." *Brookings Papers on Economic Activity* no. 1: 327–62.

———. 2000. "Technology, Trade and Factor Prices." *Journal of International Economics* 50: 51–71.

Lakdawalla, Darius, Dana Goldman, Jayanta Bhattacharya, Michael Hurd, Geoffrey Joyce, and Constantijn Panis. 2003. "Forecasting the Nursing Home Population." *Medical Care* 41, no. 1 (January): 8–20.

Leamer, Edward E. 2000. "What Is the Use of Factor Contents?" *Journal of International Economics* 50: 17–49.

Lofgren, Eric P., Steven A. Nyce, and Sylvester J. Schieber. 2003. "Designing Total Reward Programs for Tight Labor Markets." In Olivia S. Mitchell, David S. Blitzstein, Michael Gordon, and Judith F. Mazo, eds., *Benefits for the Workplace of the Future.* Philadelphia: University of Pennsylvania Press, pp. 151–77.

Mann, Catherine L. 2005. "Offshore Outsourcing and the Globalization of U.S. Services: Why Now, How Important, and What Policy Implications." In C. Fred Bergsten and the Institute for International Economics, *The United States and the World Economy: Foreign Economic Policy for the Next Decade.* Washington, DC: Institute for International Economics, pp. 281–311.

Migration News. 2003. "Labor, H-1B, L-1, H-2B, Unions." *Migration News* 10, no. 3 (July). http://migration.ucdavis.edu/MN/more.php?id=82_0_2_0.

Mincer, Jacob. 1991. "Human Capital, Technology, and the Wage Structure: What Do Time Series Show?" Working Paper No. 3581. Cambridge, MA: National Bureau of Economic Research, January.

Mishel, Lawrence, Jared Bernstein, and Sylvia Allegretto. 2005. *The State of Working America 2004/2005.* Ithaca, NY: Cornell University Press.

Murphy, Kevin F., and Finis Welch. 1992. "The Structure of Wages." *Quarterly Journal of Economics* 107 (February): 285–326.

National Center for Health Statistics. 2002. "Births, Marriages, Divorces, and Deaths: Provisional Data for November 2001." *National Vital Statistics Reports* 50, no. 13. Hyattsville, MD: National Center for Health Statistics, Centers for Disease Control, September 11. www.cdc.gov/nchs/data/nvsr/nvsr50/nvsr50_13.pdf.

National Commission on Mathematics and Science Teaching for the 21st Century. 2000. *Before It's Too Late: A Report to the Nation.* Washington, DC: U.S. Department of Education, September.

National Nanotechnology Initiative. 2005. *The National Nanotechnology Initiative at Five Years: Assessment and Recommendations of the National Nanotechnology Advisory Panel.* Washington, DC: Government Printing Office, May. www.nano. gov/FINAL_PCAST_NANO_REPORT.pdf

National Science Foundation. 2001. *Societal Implications of Nanoscience and Nanotechnology.* Washington, DC: National Science Foundation, March.

———. 2004a. *Science and Engineering Indicators, 2004.* Washington, DC.

———. 2004b. *Women, Minorities, and Persons with Disabilities in Science and Engineering.* Washington, DC, May. Figure C-1. www.nsf.gov/statistics/wmpd/figc-1.htm.

OECD (Organisation for Economic Co-operation and Development). 2000. *Literacy in the Information Age: Final Report of the International Adult Literacy Survey.* Paris: OECD.

———. 2004. *Learning for Tomorrow's World: First Results from PISA 2003.* Paris: OECD.

———. 2007. *PISA 2006: Science Competencies for Tomorrow's World, Volume 1, Analysis.* Paris: OECD.

Quinn, Joseph F. 1999. "Retirement Patterns and Bridge Jobs in the 1990s." Employee Benefits Research Institute Issue Brief No. 206, February. www.ebri.org/ibex/ib206.htm.

Richardson, J. David. 1995. "Income Inequality and Trade: How to Think, What to Conclude." *Journal of Economic Perspectives* 9, no. 3 (Summer): 33–55.

Saxenian, AnnaLee. 1999. *Silicon Valley's New Immigrant Entrepreneurs.* San Francisco: Public Policy Institute of California.

Schultze, Charles L. 2004. "Offshoring, Import Competition, and the Jobless Recovery." Brookings Institution Policy Brief No. 136. www.brookings.edu/comm/policybriefs/pb136.htm.

Smith, James P. 2001. "Race and Ethnicity in the Labor Market: Trends over the Short and Long Term." In Neil J. Smelser, William Julius Wilson, and Faith Mitchell, eds., *America Becoming: Racial Trends and Their Consequences,* Vol. II. Washington, DC: National Academy of Sciences, pp. 52–97.

———. 2003. "Assimilation across Latino Generations." *American Economic Review* 93, no. 2 (May): 315–19.

Toossi, Mitra. 2002. "A Century of Change: The U.S. Labor Force, 1950–2050." *Monthly Labor Review* (May): 15–28.

———. 2006. "A New Look at Long-Term Labor Force Projections to 2050." *Monthly Labor Review.* (November): 19–39.

Topel, Robert H. 1997. "Factor Proportions and Relative Wages: The Supply-Side Determinants of Wage Inequality." *Journal of Economic Perspectives* 11, no. 2: 55–74.

Uchitelle, Louis. 2005. "College Degree Still Pays, but It's Leveling Off." *New York Times,* January 13, p. C1.

U.S. Bureau of the Census. 2002. *International Data Base Population Pyramids.* Washington, DC. www.census.gov/ipc/www/idbpyr.html.

———. 2003a. *Disability Data from March Current Population Survey.* Washington, DC: U.S. Bureau of the Census. www.census.gov/hhes/www/disable/cps/cps202. html.

———. 2003b. *The Foreign-Born Population: 2000.* Washington, DC. www.census.gov/ prod/2003pubs/c2kbr-34.pdf.

———. 2004. *Statistical Abstract of the United States.* Washington, DC. www.census. gov/prod/www/statistical-abstract-04.html.

U.S. Department of Homeland Security. 2004. *2003 Yearbook of Immigration Statistics.* Washington, DC: U.S. Government Printing Office. http://uscis.gov/graphics/ shared/aboutus/statistics/2003Yearbook.pdf.

Wortman, Marc. 2001. "Medicine Gets Personal." *Technology Review,* January-February.

3

Skilled-Labor Mobility
in Postwar Europe

L. ALAN WINTERS

This chapter compiles some evidence on skilled-labor mobility for European countries (both among themselves and with the rest of the world) since World War II. It does not identify new primary data sources but rather puts together estimates from a variety of (English-language) sources to illustrate the broad trends and magnitudes involved. It also investigates the analytical and policy literature of the time in order to explore contemporary explanations for skills movements and the prevailing views of their consequences. Since recent data and analyses are relatively more available to colleagues, most of my attention has been devoted to the earlier part of the postwar period. The evidence and discussion are incomplete (not least because of my linguistic shortcomings), but I believe that the overall tenor of my conclusions is not misleading.

Those conclusions are:

- Broadly speaking, western Europe has evolved from a position of the net export of skills to one of net import, largely as a result of increasing relative incomes in Europe.

- There have always been gross flows in both directions, but during the 1970s and 1980s, these were probably relatively light.

- Eastern Europe has had a U-shaped trajectory over the postwar period, with strong emigration in the earlier and later parts of the period but considerable repression of the flow in the middle.

I am grateful to a referee, participants of the conference, and Patrick Honohan for comments on an earlier version of this chapter; to Vlad Manole for excellent research assistance; and to Audrey Kitson-Walters for logistical help. I absolve them of all responsibility for its remaining problems. The findings, interpretations, and conclusions expressed are entirely those of the author and do not necessarily reflect the views of the Board of Executive Directors of the World Bank or the governments they represent.

- The analysis of the early period—not attributable to economists, by the way—has a rather modern feeling about it. For example, it notes, inter alia, the reliance of rich-country medicine on immigrant providers, concerns about the fiscal costs of the brain drain, recognition of the externalities associated with the loss of very talented individuals, and the prevalence of screening in skilled migration.[1]

The Postwar Legacy

Migration was the inevitable consequence of the disruptions in Europe preceding, during, and following World War II. The first two fall outside my appointed period, but anecdotally, we know of the many scientists and artists—mainly Jews—who had to leave Germany in the 1930s and those who moved in the opposite direction from the occupied territories during the war. And these movements mattered: "In 1933 (the year of Hitler's formal rise to power), Jewish scientists were fired en masse. (Half of Germany's theoretical physicists lost their jobs.) Hitler cared little about the consequences. 'If science cannot do without Jews,' he told the physicist Max Planck, 'then we will have to do without science for a few years.' But for Hitler's misjudgment, the Nazis would almost certainly have beaten America in the race to develop nuclear weapons" (Cornwell, 2003).

In 1945–1946, some of the earlier movements reversed and, over the next few years, were supplemented by the movements induced by the division of Europe agreed on in Yalta. Attention has tended to focus on the mass migrations of the time, with about 9 million people displaced internationally by the war (Isaac, 1949, 1954). An early account by Kulischer (1948) suggests that some 5.0 million Germans were repatriated from the liberated territories, including about 2.5 million from Poland and 0.5 million from Czechoslovakia. Because of the Germans' higher average skill levels overall and the greater ability of the more skilled and the wealthier to move, Kulischer argues that these flows were significantly biased toward the highly skilled, despite the willingness of the Czechs to exempt "indispensable workers" from repatriation. There were also reflows of Czechs and Poles back to their home countries, but these were probably smaller, and we also know, anecdotally, of Russian, U.S. and U.K. policies to recruit very highly skilled Germans into their domestic science establishments.

It is difficult to judge the net effects of these movements on skills availability in Europe, but they certainly illustrate the phenomenon of skilled

---

1. Screening is a critical dimension of the brain drain, both via the disproportionate cost of losing very highly talented individuals and because its existence tends to undermine the "beneficial brain drain" argument of Mountford (1997) or Stark, Helmenstein, and Prskawetz (1997). See Commander, Kangasniemi, and Winters (2004).

MOBILITY IN POSTWAR EUROPE

mobility right from the start of the postwar period. Kulischer notes the allies' fears that the "overpopulation" of Germany, with its reduced territory and increased population as ethnic Germans returned, could spark future tensions. He also notes, however, their recognition (in an unspecified UN document) that their own problem was likely to be the reverse; the problem "most serious from the point of view of economic development is the shortage in Europe today of people with managerial training, of technicians, of foremen and skilled industrial workers." Both France and Britain sought workers overseas, although only halfheartedly and while simultaneously tolerating or even encouraging the emigration of nationals to their overseas dependencies or former empires. Isaac (1949) shows that official projections of shortages of skilled workers (a much broader category than managers and technicians) were high in the late 1940s but that actual movements were much smaller.

Part of the legacy of Yalta was a large flow of workers from eastern to western Europe over nearly the whole of the postwar period—8 million from 1944 to 1949, 2 million from 1950 to 1989, plus 3.7 million from East to West Germany from 1949 to 1961 (Roche, 1993). These flows were heavily biased toward the skilled, and Roche reminds us that the Berlin Wall was built mainly to stanch the flood of skills from east to west. The repressions in Hungary (1956) and Czechoslovakia (1968) generated outflows of about 200,000 each, while chronic anti-Semitism encouraged Jewish emigration throughout the period, especially from Poland. This was also heavily skills-biased.[2] Roche estimates outflows from Poland:

1959–1979	795,000
1980–1989	600,000

Of which:

1980–1987	academics	76,000
	technicians	36,000
	engineers	11,000

Roche reports that Poles consciously sought higher education to facilitate their westward migration (a "beneficial brain drain," perhaps).[3] She observes that of 690,000 Polish visitors to the west in 1987, 130,000

2. In 1991, as restrictions relaxed, an estimated 90,000 Jewish scientists left the CIS countries (Roche, 1993).

3. Several Polish friends rebut this view, arguing instead that there were strong internal traditions of education and that Polish qualifications did not open many western doors.

had degrees, and she implies that a significant share of these stayed on, although the number is not known.

Britain, 1946–1954: Nearly Balanced Labor Markets

A detailed study of U.K. migration in the late 1940s (Isaac, 1954) illustrates the two-way nature of the flows and also the relative importance of skills in the net flows. This has to be inferred from occupational data, because no qualification or education data were collected. Table 3.1 gives the occupational composition of U.K. emigrants from Isaac's sample (which refers to 46,000 emigrants during 1946 to 1949) with about 17 percent of the sample in the professions, technical, and managerial class. Table 3.2 reports the share of particular occupations in the flow of emigrants relative to their shares in the U.K. population (multiplied by 100), a sort of revealed

propensity measure: $100 * \left(e_i / \sum_j e_j \right) / \left(t_i / \sum_j t_j \right)$ where e_i is emigrants in

occupational class i, and t_i is total U.K. employment in that class (in June 1948). The greater propensity to emigrate among the more highly skilled segments is plainly evident (although the number for nurses may be distorted by definitional problems). Isaac suggests that many skilled emigrants were only moving temporarily to the empire ("on loan"), but there is no real evidence for this.

Table 3.3 examines U.K. immigration with labor permits—where employers have helped to initiate the inflow. It shows a huge dominance of domestic service (institutional and private) and also material inflows of

Table 3.1 Distribution by Socioeconomic Group of British Emigrants in Gainful Occupations, by Sex, 1946–1949: Sample Survey Results (in Percentages)

Group	Both sexes	Male	Female
I. Professions	17.2	20.5	8.5
II. Semiprofessions	10.4	5.3	23.6
III. Proprietors et al.	16.2	20.3	5.5
IV. Clerical workers	16.5	9.3	35.5
V. Skilled workers	26.5	32.4	10.8
VI. Semiskilled workers	7.5	4.7	14.6
VII. Unskilled workers	5.8	7.5	1.4
Total	100.0	100.0	100.0

Source: Isaac (1954).

Table 3.2 Index of Losses for Various Occupational Groups through Emigration from Britain, 1946–1949: Sample Survey Results

	Men	Women
1. Unskilled manual workers not in agriculture	46	18
2. Agricultural workers, skilled and unskilled	80	54
3. Clerks, typists, bookkeepers	116	190
4. Salespeople, shop assistants	73	36
5. Nurses	212[a]	415
6. Personal services	164	89
7. Domestic services	36[a]	58
8. Skilled and semiskilled, not in 3, 6, and 7[b]	65	52
9. Professions, proprietors, managers, officials[b]	298	190

[a] Based on samples too small to be reliable.
[b] The emigrants classed as semiprofessionals are allocated equally between these two groups.
Source: Isaac (1954).

Table 3.3 U.K. Labor Permits by Industry/Occupation, 1947–1951

	1947–1950 (%)[a]	1951 (%)
Domestic service (private)	63.11	50.37
Domestic service (institutions)	4.24	5.62
Entertainers	10.16	10.31
Industry/commerce	14.25	23.11
Hotels/restaurants	2.06	2.85
Teachers	2.86	2.65
Nurses	2.60	4.67
Other	0.70	0.42

[a] Total: 125,723.
Source: Derived from Isaac (1954), table 87.

nurses and teachers. The United Kingdom also operated an official recruitment program, which mainly supplied labor to traditional industries (agriculture, coal mining, textiles, and clothing) but which by September 1950 had recruited 2,182 female nurses (about 6.5 percent of the females entering under this scheme).

Unfortunately, Isaac does not give a country/occupation breakdown of the data, but it seems likely that there were strong imbalances at that level, with, for example, skilled workers lost to the United States being replaced by those from the British commonwealth.

Overall, Isaac records a small net outflow from Britain (1.22 million emigrants versus 1.08 million immigrants). The tables also suggest a slight outflow of skills, especially given the evidence he refers to that many immigrants downgraded their occupational status on arrival either permanently or at least while they retrained. Much migration was reported as being expected to be temporary. There is no evidence on how often this turned out to be the case, but the relatively free movement of labor within the commonwealth and the imperial tradition at that time probably did do much to keep it so. Overall, Isaac concludes that excepting a few selected sectors where further recruitment would be desirable, the United Kingdom did not face any significant labor shortages in 1950. However, the tension between some shortages and small net emigration clearly had the potential to create problems.

1955–1970: Brain Drain

Over the next decade or so, there was a growing concern in Britain—and elsewhere—about the losses of very highly skilled and highly trained scientific labor, especially to the United States and Canada. The term "brain drain" was first coined, according to the *Oxford English Dictionary*, by Peter Fairley in London's *Evening Standard* on January 7, 1963. He was reporting on the work of a committee established the previous year by the Royal Society to consider the outflow of scientists and engineers from the United Kingdom to the United States.[4] The report was debated vigorously in Parliament in February 1963 (House of Lords, 1963; published as Royal Society, 1963). A follow-up survey of a rather different kind is reported by Wilson (1966). Similar concerns had been expressed in Germany, India, and Pakistan (see *Minerva* 1, Autumn 1962). British officialdom continued to fret about the brain drain for several years, partly stimulated, no doubt, by the election of a socialist government in October 1964 with a strong devotion to "the white heat of technology" and manpower planning as the keys to British economic revival. In 1967, the government published an official paper on the subject: Committee on Manpower Resources for Science and Technology (1967).

The Royal Society study considered only Ph.D. scientists—a much narrower group than the professional occupation groups used in the official surveys above—but they implied the existence of a wider concern.[5] They

4. The Royal Society is the apex of the British scientific community; it offers comment and advice on scientific policy but is not formally a governmental body.

5. "Science" included 15 disciplines in physical and biological sciences, engineering, and mathematics.

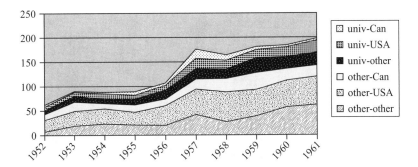

Figure 3.1 Emigration of Ph.D. scientists.
Source: Based on Royal Society (1963).

sought to identify the entire British population of Ph.D. awardees from 1952 to 1962 via surveys of more than 500 university science departments and, while not entirely successful, were close enough for their data to be quite reliable. These data do, indeed, reveal significant outflows of scientists relative to the flows of new Ph.D.s and the U.K. stock.

Figure 3.1 shows the permanent migration of Ph.D.s from university staffs and elsewhere, distinguishing North American and other destinations. The increasing trend is evident. Although that may partly reflect less complete data in early years (because the survey was conducted only in 1962 and required recall answers for earlier years), the committee argues that it is not seriously misleading. By the late 1950s, the outflow represented about 15 percent of the flow of new Ph.D.s and about 1 percent per year of the complement of university posts in science. Table 3.4 reports the same basic data but with emigrants cross-classified by year of Ph.D. and year of departure. This table shows that in the earlier years, fewer than one-half of emigrants left in the year of their Ph.D.s, but the flow continued to be significant for many years afterward (the upper right triangle of the matrix). By the later 1950s, the table shows more than one-half of recorded departures occurring immediately and leaves unanswered whether subsequent delayed departures will increase the total sufficiently to reduce the proportion to "normal."

The Royal Society also reports significant flows of an ostensibly temporary nature, as scientists moved to take up postdoctoral fellowships and other temporary appointments abroad. From 1957 to 1961, 1,053 Ph.D. scientists were recorded as leaving the United Kingdom to take up fellowships and so on (733 to the United States). By late 1962, 545 of these were known to have returned, 143 were known not to be expecting to return, and the outcome for 365 was unknown (many of these were still on their fellowships). The 143 are included in the permanent-emigrants data, but

Table 3.4 Permanent Emigrants: Year of Emigration by Year in Which Ph.D. Was Awarded

Year of degree[a]	Year of emigration													Ph.D.s awarded[c]	% emigration[d]
	1952	1953	1954	1955	1956	1957	1958	1959	1960	1961	1962[b]	Not known	Total		
1952	41	19	5	5	3	8	8	5	2	2	4	8	110	723	15.7
1953	0	49	10	9	6	7	7	6	4	2	1	7	108	770	14.5
1954	1	3	45	8	6	8	5	6	9	1	1	8	101	772	13.5
1955	0	0	1	45	10	10	6	6	4	5	5	11	103	794	13.4
1956	1	3	3	2	49	22	11	6	3	6	9	4	119	796	15.4
1957	0	1	1	2	4	71	17	14	6	9	4	4	133	823	16.7
1958	0	0	0	1	1	4	75	13	12	5	9	4	124	900	14.2
1959	0	0	1	1	2	1	3	77	13	20	13	2	132	942	14.5
1960	0	1	2	0	0	2	4	6	97	23	10	6	149	991	15.5
1961	0	1	1	2	1	0	0	2	9	94	18	1	130	1026	13.1
1962[b]	1	0	1	0	2	0	0	4	1	1	49	0	59		
Unknown	12	5	8	7	10	21	15	18	17	19	15	145	292		
Total	56	81	77	82	94	154	151	163	177	187	138	200	1560[e]		

[a] Year in which Ph.D. was awarded.
[b] Approximately January–June.
[c] Underestimated by about 14% because of incomplete returns.
[d] Corrected for (1) underestimate of number of degrees awarded and (2) number of emigrants whose year of degree is unknown.
[e] Including university staff members who received a Ph.D. between 1952 and 1962.
Source: Based on Royal Society (1963).

the likelihood is that there would be greater losses than just these. For temporary movers from 1957 to 1959, permanent-loss rates were slightly below 30 percent, and in addition, many temporary emigrants were said to have returned to the United Kingdom only briefly before undertaking permanent migration. As I have observed elsewhere (Ulph and Winters, 1994), the U.S. education and fellowship system provides ample opportunity for screening and sorting young scientists. Combining permanent and temporary emigration, the Royal Society estimates gross losses equivalent to about 19 percent of the flow of new science Ph.D.s in 1961.

The Royal Society report was largely descriptive, merely presenting data, but press discussion (see *Minerva*, 1963, pp. 342–57) and Wilson (1966) took up the causes of emigration. The salary premium of 100 percent or more in the United States was one factor, and the much better facilities and provisions for scientific research were another. The expansion of U.S. scientific effort resulting from the Russians having been the first into space, coupled with stagnation and social unrest in Britain as it struggled to define its postwar destiny, widened the gaps during the 1960s and presumably lay behind the increased numbers as the decade progressed.

Committee on Manpower Resources for Science and Technology (1967), the official report, includes a broader range of qualifications than the Royal Society but suggests that total emigration (permanent and temporary) accelerated during the mid-1960s to be about one-third of the output of engineers, technologists, and scientists by 1966. That report also records inflows of (in its broader definition) scientists. It shows net losses of about zero in 1961, increasing by 1966 to losses equivalent to 19 percent of 1963's newly qualified engineers and technologists and 9 percent of new scientists. It also argues that inflows and outflows are not comparable in quality: outflows are typically positively selected (see below), whereas inflows are substantially from new commonwealth countries and frequently "lack the training and experience" that are lost to emigration. This "ladder" effect is something that much more recent data also reveal (Docquier and Marfouk, 2005). Its net effect is to denude the lowest level and augment the highest, even if each individual in the chain moves only a little. Dedijer (1964) also notes it.

The issue of quality is among the most important and yet empirically intractable dimensions of the brain drain. The Royal Society highlights this aspect informally, noting that "several" university heads of departments ranked their emigrants as among their best staff members. More formally, they report:

- Civil Service and Atomic Energy Commission recruiters said that of British graduates interviewed in North America, 70 percent were worthy of appointments in the United Kingdom compared with fewer than 50 percent of interviewees in Britain.

- Of its own fellows, 20 (3.5 percent of the total) were in the United States by 1962, including 9 who had left between 1957 and 1962.

- Of the British university staff emigrants, 20 percent held very senior academic posts in the United States in 1962.

- Comparing the Royal Society's data with the U.S. National Science Foundation's data, which cover all scientists, suggests that U.S. scientist recruitment was shifting strongly toward those with Ph.D.s, a further source of selection bias given that U.K. output of science Ph.D.s was increasing only modestly (see table 3.4).

Wilson (1966), who received survey replies from 517 British physical and mathematical scientists in North America (out of a total of about 925 questionnaires distributed), also suggests strong positive selection bias in terms of (1) the (elite) universities from which emigrants received their degrees, (2) their performance in their first degrees relative to U.K. averages, and arguably, (3) even in the reported reasons for migrating ("being able to get to the office at 7:00 a.m. without being criticized," "welcoming change," and "despising hierarchy"). Even more interesting, Wilson hints at negative selection among returnees to Britain in terms of salaries and job quality. Although his analysis is not powerful—for example, Wilson acknowledges that it does not correct for age—this is an interesting early harbinger for the critical mechanism in the Stark, Helmenstein, and Prskawetz (1997) model of the "beneficial brain drain."

In terms of normative analysis, the scientists of the Royal Society committee made two observations. First, Britain was plainly incurring significant fiscal cost in training scientists who subsequently left (with the regressive transfer entailed in "leaving for America" identified as the principal objection). Second, and far more important, they said, was the loss of talent—lifetime leadership and creative contributions—that the emigration of top scientists entailed.

Britain was not the only country to worry about the brain drain. There were also concerns in Germany, India, and Pakistan (*Minerva* 1, 1962). For the flow to the United States, National Science Foundation data offer some direct evidence. Britain is the largest single source of scientists and engineers, especially recalling that many reached the United States via Canada and so were recorded as last resident there, but it is not the only one. For example, from 1962 to 1964, out of a total immigration of scientists and engineers of 15,286, Europe provided 8,102, of which the largest flows were from Britain (3,175, or 20.8 percent), Germany (1,219, or 8.0 percent), Poland (339, or 2.2 percent), and Switzerland (325, or 2.1 percent) (Mills, 1966).[6]

---

6. Canada is recorded as providing 1,749, or 11.4 percent.

British scientists were less likely, however, to take U.S. citizenship (Mills, 1966, table 4), which perhaps suggests a greater permanence among other immigrants.

Immigration of Scientists

The other important dimension of "other countries" is the inflow of scientists to Britain. In the late 1950s and early 1960s, the net flow from other countries was positive, but by 1963, it had become negative, as it had for North America (Committee on Manpower Resources for Science and Technology, 1967). But within the "other," developing countries were almost certainly net suppliers of skills. *Nature* (December 3, 1966, p. 965) observes the dependence of U.K. hospitals on flows of commonwealth doctors, while contributions to the *Minerva* 1962 symposium from India and Pakistan explicitly note their losses and the adverse effects that these had on local scientific communities.

Dedijer (1964) observes the flows from developing countries to the United States and Europe and notes that many were essentially unrecognized by home countries because they occurred at pre-degree levels from countries with little indigenous scientific training capacity and frequently resulted in permanent migration. In the latter cases, there is, in a sense, no net loss of scientists in the developing country, for more would have been created by the process of migration, but, as Dedijer notes, the loss of talent and the loss of pressure to develop science facilities may have been costly.[7] Dedijer notes the tendency of scientists to move from poor to rich countries, from stagnant to growing and from small to large. The last is an interesting reflection of the "economic geography" dimensions of skilled migration that are touched upon in Commander, Kangasniemi, and Winters (2004).

The Analytical Response

The Royal Society's and related deliberations caused a great deal of comment among policymakers and the science community. They also provided a fruitful and rather modern-looking discussion of the issues surrounding the brain drain. They apparently did little, however, to promote formal

---

7. Moreover, training in the United States is not necessarily subsidized by the United States. The costs of higher education could still remain with either official or private sectors in the developing country.

analysis among European social scientists, particularly economists.[8] In addition to Dedijer, mention should also be made of Brinley Thomas (1961, 1966), who offered an informal analysis of the brain drain focusing on data, fiscal costs, and the costs to lower-skilled workers of losing complementary human capital. As Dedijer did, Thomas also highlighted the plight of developing countries, citing externalities and economies of agglomeration as reasons for concern and, at least implicitly, noting that demand from Europe was a problem as well as that from the United States. More serious responses were found in the Canadian science policy journal *Minerva* and were paralleled by the U.S. National Science Foundation's collection of statistics on immigrant scientists and a symposium by the American Academy of Political and Social Science (*Annals* 367, September 1967).

The earliest significant analytical contribution from the economics profession was a major program led by Herbert Grubel and A. D. Scott (1966a, 1966b, 1966c, and others), which focused on the United States, compiling data, estimating the education costs of migrants and the returns to skills and providing an analytical model. Unfortunately, the latter was not very convincing; being based on perfectly functioning and competitive labor markets, it argued that there could only be gains from letting people who wished to move actually do so. The problem was not that this conclusion was wrong but that by reaching it more or less by assumption, Grubel and Scott provided no means of addressing the real, but analytically intractable, concerns expressed by policymakers and scientists. Thomas (1966) was an early critic of their approach.

A much more fruitful approach, but, again, not from Europe, was Bhagwati and Hamada's (1974) general equilibrium framework. This focused on labor markets and tackled the welfare implications of skilled emigration for those who were left behind and, ultimately, for the sending country. Two sets of distortions were introduced, the first relating to setting wages, which are set by negotiation, not by markets, and in which negotiators are influenced by wage levels in other countries and/or other skills-classes, and the second relating to the financing of education. The model, which was subsequently widely employed, made fairly stark predictions about losses to those left behind both via reduced employment opportunities or productivity and via fiscal losses resulting from education subsidies. In this way, it addressed and validated the policy concerns of the day.

Hamada and Bhagwati (1975) extended the model by introducing a number of refinements to labor markets in the sending countries. For example, if emigration induced a ladder effect in which remaining skilled

---

8. The evidence for this can be found by skimming the excellent and comprehensive bibliography by Dedijer and Svenningson (1967), on which I have relied heavily.

workers were now better matched to skilled jobs and thus not unemployed, emigration could indeed be beneficial. On the other hand, to the extent that the external labor market is more efficient at screening workers, the result would be the loss of the most efficient workers to the sending country.

This early literature was also notable for making explicit policy recommendations about taxing migration. Bhagwati and Hamada (1974) proposed a tax on emigrants, with that tax levied by the receiving (developed country) party and transmitted in one form or another to the sending (developing) country. In terms of the impact on the incomes of those who did not emigrate, two channels could be identified: a direct revenue effect, which would depend on the elasticity of emigration with respect to taxation, and a set of indirect effects via employment and expected and actual wages. To the extent that the elasticity of emigration with respect to the tax was less than unity, the income of those left behind would improve. However, other work in this area (e.g., McCulloch and Yellen, 1975) was more ambiguous. Not only could total labor earnings fall under plausible assumptions, but a tax would likely raise the relative wage of nonmigrating skilled workers at the expense of unskilled workers and possibly affect the relative size of modern and traditional sectors.

U.S. Census and INS Data, 1950–1980

The United States provides two other sources of data for our theme. First are the decadal censuses, which, via their detailed 1-percent survey instrument provided information on the education and origins of those immigrants who remained in the United States until census day. Figure 3.2 provides evidence on immigrants with first degrees or higher (high-skilled) resident in the United States in 1980 who had entered after the age of 22.[9] It shows that in 1980, there were roughly 150,000 high-skilled migrants from Europe who had entered the United States at an age older than 22 before 1950 and about 95,000 who had entered in the next decade. The fact that despite having had far longer in which to leave the United States (or die), there were more immigrants from the earlier waves shows pretty conclusively that the earlier waves were significantly larger, that skilled immigration from Europe declined during this period, at least until the 1970s. The geographical breakdown is also informative: the numbers from northern Europe (Great Britain, Ireland, Scandinavia) and southern Europe (Italy,

9. I focus on individuals migrating after their 22nd birthdays because that corresponds to our normal view of brain drain. An interesting question that we are not considering further is what happened to people who migrated as children and acquired their education in the United States. Could the loss of their talent be an issue?

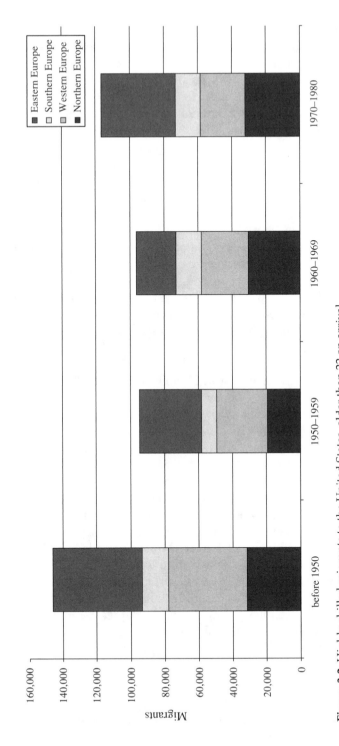

Figure 3.2 Highly skilled migrants to the United States, older than 22 on arrival.
Source: Based on U.S. Census (1980).

Vatican City, Greece, Spain, Portugal, Andorra, Gibraltar, Malta) are fairly constant, while those from western Europe (the EEC minus Italy, plus Austria, Switzerland, Liechtenstein, and Monaco), and eastern Europe (the Soviet bloc in Europe, including the Soviet Union) fall strongly, except for a turn-up for eastern Europe in the 1970s.

The second source is the U.S. Immigration and Naturalization Service (INS), which provides data on migrant inflows, with a break in 1980–1981, which I use here as the natural cutoff point for this section. The definition of skills is rather wider than previously: professional and semiprofessional workers plus proprietors, managers, and officials (after 1973, proprietors are excluded). Also, there are significant shortcomings in the occupational data. INS (1971) states that most immigrants do not report occupation, and those who have already been in the United States on a temporary basis (a large share) refer to their U.S. temporary occupation rather than their home-country one. Figure 3.3 gives a breakdown for four sample years and shows clearly the declining totals from Europe, while figure 3.4 presents annual data on the five major western European sources. The latter shows that the trend declined from Germany from the mid-1950s, but, as suggested above, the flows from the United Kingdom increased until the later 1960s. The precipitate drop in 1968 reflects the coming into force of the 1968 Immigration Act, which broadened the geographical spread of U.S. immigration and imposed overall limits on immigration from the Western Hemisphere. There were no country-specific quotas on European sources, however, until 1977 (Jasso, Rosenzweig, and Smith, 1998).

The patterns in figures 3.3 and 3.4 presumably reflect both the supply of immigrants and the demand (filtered through U.S. immigration policy). However, the discussion in Jasso, Rosenzweig, and Smith (1998) implies that there is little likelihood of skilled workers from individual European countries being constrained, and figure 3.5, which shows Europe's strongly declining share, also suggests that supply is likely to be the dominant factor. This is especially so given the evidence from the census that northern and western European migrants appear to have relatively higher incomes among skilled workers than either U.S. locals or immigrants from the rest of the world; that is, they are probably more able.

The INS data in figure 3.4 are detailed enough to allow some minor hypothesis testing about the determinants of highly skilled migration.[10] Following Clark, Hatton, and Williamson (2002) and Hatton (2003), outflows of workers from Europe to the United States are likely to be related to relative salary levels (corrected for purchasing power) and to the relative quality of facilities and complementary factors for highly skilled activities. The former may be loosely thought of as a function of average incomes and income

10. I do not include eastern Europe in this exercise because its flows are so strongly political in nature (and the requisite data are missing).

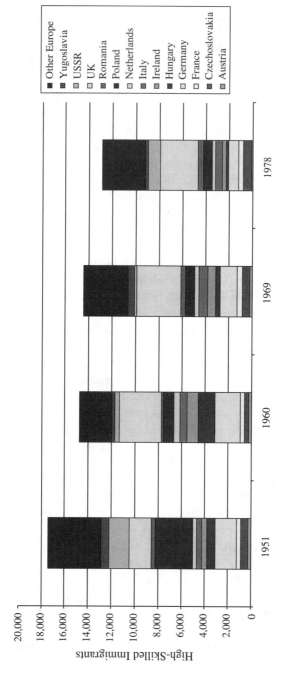

Figure 3.3 Highly skilled immigration from Europe to the United States.
Source: INS (various years).

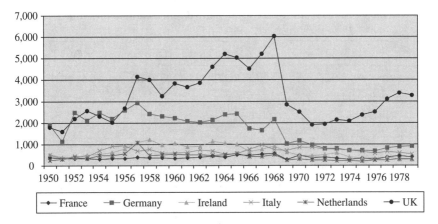

Figure 3.4 Skilled immigrants from western Europe (number).
Source: INS (various years).

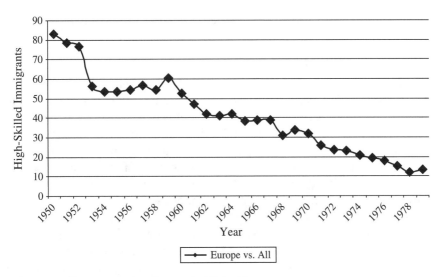

Figure 3.5 European migration to the United States.
Source: INS (various years).

distribution and, since the latter changes only very slowly, only the average for year-to-year changes.[11] Similarly, facilities and support for highly skilled workers are likely to be related to general affluence levels plus slowly evolving conventions about expenditure on research and/or tertiary education.

---

11. U.K. income inequality fell from 1970 to 1977 and rose rapidly thereafter, but for most countries, the statement is true. See Hatton (2003).

Table 3.5   Explaining European Skilled Emigration to the United States, 1950–1979

	(1)	(2)	(3)
ln (GNI pc)$_{-1}$	−0.53 (0.17)	−0.33 (0.28)	−0.61 (0.30)
ln (stock)	—	0.70 (0.60)	—
ln (stock)$_{-1}$	—	—	−0.22 (0.66)
France	—	—	—
Germany	1.18 (0.09)	0.10 (0.93)	1.53 (1.03)
Ireland	0.06 (0.14)	−0.24 (0.29)	0.16 (0.31)
Italy	0.23 (0.14)	−0.11 (0.31)	0.35 (0.33)
United Kingdom	2.00 (0.06)	0.74 (1.05)	2.41 (1.17)
R^2	0.91	0.91	0.91

Note: Robust standard errors in parentheses. See text for detailed explanation of column heads.

For the major western European source countries, therefore, I have regressed the flow of skilled workers to the United States on their gross national income per capita (GNI pc), country-fixed effects to capture the supposed influence of income distribution and local variations in the provision of other facilities for highly skilled workers as well as language and other links with the United States, and year effects capture the roles of the U.S. GNI pc and income distribution as well as of U.S. immigration policy toward western Europe. (Given a starting date of 1950, I cannot use PPP data for incomes, but given that all of the sample countries are in western Europe, this is not likely to induce much bias.)[12] The regression is logarithmic in form.

Column 1 of table 3.5 reports the regression coefficients from this simple exercise. It suggests a significant negative elasticity of migration with respect to GNI pc (lagged once to reduce the chance of any simultaneity) and positive country effects (relative to France) for Germany and the United Kingdom. The results are very similar if GNI pc is either unlagged or lagged by two years.

12. One might also worry whether the use of current exchange rates induces irrelevant variation into the income data. However, the mean "dollar-European" exchange rate is captured by time dummies, so only intra-European fluctuations affect the regression. These probably do belong in the equation as reflections of the relative fortunes of direct-source countries.

I also consider a crude measure of the initial stock of skilled migrants as a means of identifying network effects. From the 1950 U.S. census, we establish the starting stock of skilled immigrants (using four or more years of college as the threshold, the closest we can get to the INS definition) who had entered the United States after the age of 22 for each country. This is then rolled forward by cumulating the INS inflow data, assuming 10 percent wastage for two years, 5 percent over the next three, and 2 percent a year thereafter. The results are given in columns 2 and 3 of table 3.5. In the former, where year t's inflow is related to the stock at the start of t, the stock receives an insignificantly positive coefficient and absorbs more or less all of the explanatory power of the other variables. In column 3, however, where I lag the stock to reduce any spurious correlation induced by the positive autocorrelation in the immigration data, it hardly affects the equation at all. This does not seem implausible. For a variety of reasons, stock effects seem much less likely to be relevant for the highly skilled from western Europe than for the average migrant: The highly skilled have international professional networks, highly skilled jobs are more likely to be advertised or recruited internationally, the risks are probably lower for skilled than for average immigrants, and Europe is fairly well networked to the United States anyway.

Figure 3.6 plots the fixed-year effects derived from the equation in column 1 of table 3.5. No scale is shown, because these are, of course, merely relative. However, they shed an interesting light on the flow of skilled migrants from 1950 to 1979. Apart from the step change in 1969, once we allow for income, the trend is almost uniformly positive, albeit at a declining rate. That is, other things being equal, there is an increasing propensity for skilled Europeans to emigrate to the United States, but this is outweighed by the negative effect of the narrowing income gap. (Table 3.6 repeats the estimate for the whole of the period 1950–2001, excluding 1980–1981

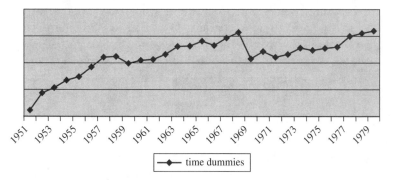

Figure 3.6 Western European migration: Time effects.
Source: Year effects from column 1 in table 3.5.

Table 3.6   Explaining European Skilled Emigration to the United States, 1951–2001

	1951–2001		
	(1)	(2)	(3)
ln (GNI pc)$_{-1}$	−1.04 (0.13)	−0.96 (0.21)	−1.16 (0.19)
ln (stock)	—	0.32 (0.50)	—
ln (stock)$_{-1}$	—	—	−0.35 (0.43)
France	—	—	—
Germany	0.90 (0.06)	0.42 (0.75)	1.43 (0.65)
Ireland	−0.33 (0.12)	−0.48 (0.23)	−0.19 (0.23)
Italy	−0.33 (0.95)	−0.49 (0.26)	−0.16 (0.23)
United Kingdom	1.77 (0.06)	1.20 (0.89)	2.39 (0.77)
R^2	0.87	0.87	0.87

Note: See text (re. table 3.5) for detailed explanation of column heads.

because of missing data. The basic results are unchanged, despite the considerably greater policy activism in U.S. immigration in the later period. Similarly, the fixed-year effects tell much of the same story as figure 3.6, although the propensity to migrate appears to dip during 1997 to 1999.)

Inflows into Western Europe

Data on the inflows of skilled workers into Europe present far greater challenges than those on outflows. European censuses are less detailed than those of the United States, and migration-flow statistics are rarely reported. The evidence at hand suggests a gradual trend toward greater proportions of skilled workers within the set of immigrants, but, of course, the workforces of both origin and destination countries are becoming increasingly skilled anyway. To some extent, this "skilling up" would be expected.

France

The best evidence probably comes from France. Figure 3.7 reports census data on people with university degrees, the closest we can get to "highly skilled." They are broken down into native and foreign-born—again, the finest disaggregation available. Similar data do not appear to be available after 1990.

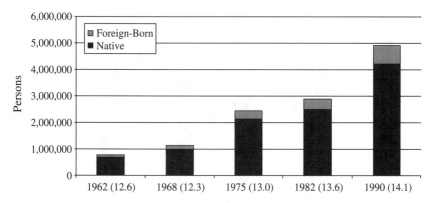

Figure 3.7 Persons completing university in France.
Source: Censuses of France.

The striking feature of the figure is the more than sixfold increase in people holding degrees. The increase in the number of foreign-born degree holders is slightly faster, with the result that their share of the total increases from 12.6 percent in 1962 to 14.1 percent in 1990. The corresponding shares for foreign-born low-skilled migrants are 5.2 percent and 9.3 percent, however, which suggests a decline in the average skills of migrants. Conversely, OECD (1982) details a gradual increase in skills within the foreign workforce during the 1970s based on Eurostat Labour Force Surveys. The share of "skilled workers" plus "supervisory staff" increases from 21.9 percent in 1971 through 31.8 percent and 36.5 percent in 1973 and 1976 to 40.0 percent in 1979.

United Kingdom

The United Kingdom has one reasonably detailed source of migration-flow data, the International Passenger Survey (IPS), an annual survey of international passengers at major British air and seaports.[13] It administers a brief survey for 0.2 percent of passengers, asking for country of residence, place and purpose of trip, occupation (by very crudely defined groups), and (intended or actual) length of stay. The sample is drawn continuously through the year and numbers about half a million a year in all. It is much smaller for migrants, of course, and the sampling frame is dependent on

13. I am grateful to Tim Hatton for making these data available to me. They are explored in Hatton (2003) and explained in more detail in Office of National Statistics (2002).

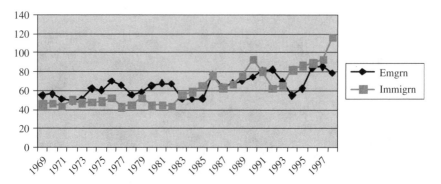

Figure 3.8 U.K. migration, professional and managerial.
Source: U.K. International Passenger Surveys.

stopping every *n*th traveler and on their cooperation. Thus, overall, the data are subject to significant error. Having said that, however, they span three decades on a roughly comparable basis.

Figure 3.8 reports absolute numbers of migrants to and from the United Kingdom in the professional and managerial category. From 1969 to 1983, there is a small but regular net emigration. Thereafter, both emigration from and immigration to the United Kingdom assume a positive trend, running in parallel for a decade and with the latter usually slightly dominating the former after that. In other words, the United Kingdom moves from a situation of net emigration of skills to one of net immigration. Corresponding to this, the share of professional and managerial in total immigration flows increased somewhat from 20.2 percent for emigration and 22.3 percent for immigration in 1969 to 1974 to 35.6 percent and 33.7 percent in 1994 to 1998.

One interesting feature of the IPS data is that they separate British from foreign residents. Figure 3.9 shows emigration by British residents and immigration by nonresidents, which I call expatriation flows, while figure 3.10 shows immigration by British residents and emigration by foreign residents, or returns.[14] From these, the trends of emigration are rather similar for British and non-British workers, but those of immigration differ. While the upturn for foreign immigrants starts in about 1983 and, apart from 1990 and 1991, only really takes off in about 1994, that for British returnees occurs from 1981 to 1986, with (noisy) constancy

---

14. Residency is defined by "place of usual residence" and requires residence for a year or more. Thus, these returns refer only to long-term migrants.

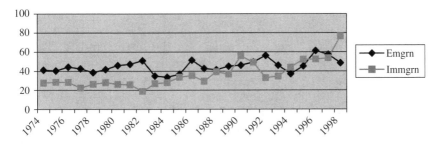

Figure 3.9 U.K. migration, professional and managerial: Expatriation flows.
Source: U.K. International Passenger Surveys.

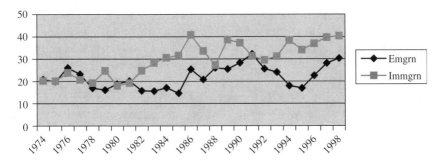

Figure 3.10 U.K. migration, professional and managerial: Returns.
Source: U.K. International Passenger Surveys.

thereafter. Possibly, the latter reflects the rather sharp political changes of the early 1980s or political developments elsewhere in the world. (Unfortunately, skilled data are not available by country of departure.) The temporary peak for foreign immigrants in the early 1990s appears from the total migration data to originate in the EU, not eastern Europe as I would have anticipated, unless, of course, eastern Europeans misrepresented their provenance. (The IPS does not ask for verification of any of the answers it receives.)

One of the phenomena that the returnees data illustrate is the importance of "brain circulation" for skilled workers. Although we do not know whether returnees are returning "home," the large numbers strongly suggest a good deal of geographical churning.

Salt (1992) presents other U.K. data based on work permits (necessary for non-EU citizens) and the labor-force survey. Both reinforce the high share of professionals within total immigration and, to some extent, its growth during the 1980s.

Other Western Europe

Salt (1992) also offers some trends data for the Netherlands and (West) Germany, as well as for the United Kingdom. For the Netherlands, immigration of scientists, specialists, artists, managers, and higher executives increased from 27,000 to 40,000 between 1983 and 1989, while other immigration was virtually static. For Germany, the employment of graduates from abroad increased by about 25 percent (for both EC nationals and other foreigners) between 1977 and 1989, while employment of foreigners overall fell by about 11 percent.

Salt argues that the dominance and growth of high skills within the international labor markets are associated with the increasing internationalization of business. Partly, it is a phenomenon of firms' internal labor markets, but in addition, multinational corporations (MNCs) recruit internationally and also employ business-services suppliers from around the world.

We lack comparable data on skills migration across European countries and time, but OECD (1997) offers a snapshot for 1995 based on the Eurostat Labour Force Survey. Figure 3.11 reports the shares of the "highly skilled" workforce originating abroad (ages 25 to 54 with completed tertiary education, ISCED 05 and above). It shows higher shares for smaller economies, which probably is just another reflection of their greater openness. Beyond that, there is a hint that shares are related to levels of technical sophistication of output and exports, but that does not tell us about causation. The very large figure for Luxembourg, for example, may either derive from or cause its importance in international banking and finance.

In fact, the data in figure 3.11 are surprisingly low. For example, the figure gives about 4 percent for France, whereas the French census for 1990

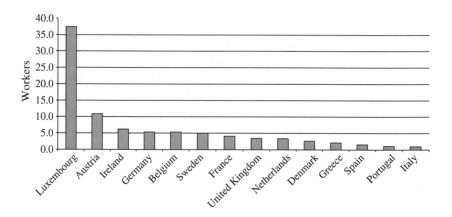

Figure 3.11 Foreigners in highly skilled labor force (%), OECD, 1995.
Source: Organisation for Economic Co-operation and Development.

suggests that foreigners accounted for 13.9 percent of the French labor force with the same definition of skill. UN Population Division (2002) suggests that the shares of the population who were foreign-born were 10.4 percent, 6.6 percent, and 6.6 percent in France, Germany, and the United Kingdom in 1990 and were 10.0 percent, 8.9 percent, and 6.9 percent in 2000.[15]

Eastern Europe

As noted above, outflows of scientists from eastern European countries were very significant in the immediate postwar period. Data are hard to find on the 1970s and 1980s, although evidence on Polish emigration in this period was cited above. Most of the discussion suggests that flows were fairly small, with Russia as a magnet and Israel and the United States attracting a constant flow and occasional spurts of immigrants from the region. Even after the liberalizations of the early 1990s, data are scarce. Much contemporary commentary refers to major outflows—from countries such as Albania—but equally, by the mid-1990s, skills were returning from the west to the more liberal of the eastern European countries. Mansoor and Quillan (2007) report a mixed picture across countries.

Docquier and Marfouk (2005) offer a moderately reliable source of data on stocks of migrants holding degrees, and their updated estimates by age of migration (World Bank, 2008) allow us to estimate migrants moving after they have received their first degrees. The latter reports the proportions of countries' total numbers of skilled (tertiary-educated) workers who are resident in OECD countries and who arrived in those countries after the age of 21. For the five countries with data, they suggest little increase in such stocks between 1990 and 2000, with Albania, Hungary, and Poland showing declines and Bulgaria and Romania (slightly larger) showing increases. Other countries do not report 1990 figures, but for 2000, the estimates for eastern Europe traditionally defined range from 21 percent for Bosnia-Herzegovina down to 6 percent for Bulgaria, while those for the countries of the former Soviet Union excluding the Baltic states are 3 percent or less. Many of these emigrants are in western Europe, but the New World is more important as a destination in stock terms. However, it is possible that Europe dominates in current flows, especially for those countries that have already joined the European Union.

Eastern Europe seems almost bound to see future emigration of skilled workers during its period of convergence to western Europe's income levels, but the evidence equally suggests that significant rates of returns are

15. For Germany, foreign citizens, not foreign-born, are counted.

also likely. Thus, while the region has been a source of considerable skills for the OECD in the last five decades, the long-run net outflow seems likely to be more moderate.

Conclusion

As I warned in the introduction, the data presented here are partial and error-prone. However, they probably contain sufficient information to suggest tentatively that the following:

- Western Europe has evolved from a position of net export of skills to one of net import, largely as a result of increasing relative incomes in Europe.
- There have always been gross flows in both directions, but during the 1970s and 1980s, these were probably relatively light; the ceteris paribus trend is toward greater gross outflows.
- Eastern Europe has had a U-shaped trajectory during the postwar period, with strong emigration in the earlier and later parts of the period but considerable repression of the flow in the middle.
- The analysis of the early period has a rather modern feeling about it, or, perhaps more accurately, the current discussion has a sense of déjà vu. For example, the discussion of four decades ago notes, among other things, the reliance of rich-country medicine on immigrant providers, concerns about the fiscal costs of the brain drain, recognition of the externalities associated with the loss of very talented individuals, and the prevalence of screening in skilled migration.

Among the remaining challenges are to confirm and substantiate the data and our view of European skilled migration; to extend the analysis to confirm that it is substantially a result of income differences superimposed on a growing degree of globalization; and, perhaps most important, to try to analyze the consequences of the migratory flows. That Europe is less innovative than the United States is not particularly controversial, but whether that can be laid at the door of emigration is very unclear indeed.

References

Bhagwati, J., and K. Hamada. 1974. "The Brain Drain, International Integration of Markets for Professionals and Unemployment: A Theoretical Analysis." *Journal of Development Economics* 1, no. 1 (June): 19–42.

Clark, X., T. Hatton, and J. Williamson. 2002. "Where Do U.S. Immigrants Come From, and Why?" NBER Working Paper 8998.

Commander, S., M. Kangasniemi, and L. A. Winters. 2004. "The Brain Drain: Curse or Boon? A Survey of the Literature." In R. E. Baldwin and L. A. Winters, eds., *Challenges to Globalization: Analyzing the Economics.* Chicago: University of Chicago Press.

Committee on Manpower Resources for Science and Technology. 1967. *The Brain Drain.* Report of the Working Group on Migration. Committee on Manpower Resources for Science and Technology.

Cornwell, J. 2003. *Hitler's Scientists: Science, War, and the Devil's Pact.* London: Penguin.

Dedijer, S. 1964. "Migration of Scientists: A World-Wide Phenomenon and Problem." *Nature* 201: 964–67.

Dedijer, S., and L. Svenningson. 1967. *A Bibliography on Migration of Scientists, Engineers, Doctors and Students.* Lund, Sweden: Research Policy Program.

Docquier, Frédéric, and Abdeslam Marfouk. 2005. "International Migration by Educational Attainment." In C. Ozden and M. Schiff, eds., *International Migration, Remittances and the Brain Gain.* New York: Palgrave Macmillan, chapter 5.

Grubul, H., and A. P. Scott. 1966a. "The Immigration of Scientists and Engineers to the United States, 1949–61." *Journal of Political Economy* 74, no. 4 (August): 368–78.

———. 1966b. "The International Flow of Human Capital." *American Economic Review* 56, no. 1/2 (March): 268–74.

———. 1966c. "The International Flow of Human Capital: Reply." *American Economic Review* 58, no. 3, part 1 (June): 545–48.

Hamada, K., and J. N. Bhagwati. 1975. "Domestic Distortions, Imperfect Information and the Brain Drain." *Journal of Development Economics* 2, no. 3 (September): 265–79.

Hatton, T. 2003. "Explaining Trends in UK Immigration," CEPR Discussion Paper Series, No. 4019.

House of Lords. 1963. Hansard, February 27, cols. 86–182.

INS (various years). *Statistical Yearbook of the Immigration and Naturalization Service.* Washington, DC: INS.

Isaac, Julius. 1949. "European Migration Potential and Prospects." *Population Studies* 2, no. 4 (March): 379–412.

———. 1954. "British Postwar Migration." NIESR Occasional Paper XVII, Cambridge: Cambridge University Press.

Jasso, G., M. Rosenzweig, and J. P. Smith. 1998. "The Changing Skill of New Immigrants to the United States: Recent Trends and Their Determinants." NBER Working Paper 6764.

Kulischer, Eugene M. 1948. *Europe on the Move.* New York: Columbia University Press.

Mansoor, Ali, and Bruce Quillan. 2007. *Migration and Remittances: Eastern Europe and the Former Soviet Union.* Washington, DC: World Bank.

McCulloch, R., and J. L. Yellen. 1975. "Consequences of a Tax on the Brain Drain for Unemployment and Income Inequality in Less Developed Countries." *Journal of Development Economics* 2, no. 3 (September): 249–64.

Mills, T. J. 1966. "Scientific Personnel and the Professions." *Annals of the American Academy of Political and Social Science* 367 (September 1966): 23–44.

Mountford, A. 1997. "Can a Brain Drain Be Good for Growth in the Source Economy?" *Journal of Development Economics* 53, no. 2 (August): 287–303.

Office of National Statistics. 2002. *International Migration, 2002.* London: HMSO. Also on www.statistics.gov.uk/statbase/Product.asp?vlnk=507&More=N.

OECD (Organisation for Economic Co-operation and Development). 1982. *Continuous Reporting System on Migration (SOPEMI).* Paris: OECD.

———. 1997. *International Migration Statistics for OECD Countries.* Paris: OECD.

Roche, Barbara. 1993. "The New Geography of European Migrations." In R. King, ed., *The New Geography of European Migrations.* London and New York: Belhaven Press.

Royal Society. 1963. *Emigration of Scientists from the United Kingdom.* London: Royal Society.

Salt, John. 1992. "Migration Processes among the Highly Skilled in Europe." *International Migration Review* 26, no. 2, Special Issue: The New Europe and International Migration (Summer): 484–505.

Stark, O., C. Helmenstein, and A. Prskawetz. 1997. "A Brain Gain with a Brain Drain." *Economics Letters* 55, no. 3 (July): 227–34.

Thomas, Brinley. 1961. "Trends in the International Migration of Skilled Manpower." *Migration* (Geneva) 1, no. 3 (July-September): 5–21.

———. 1966. "From the Other Side: A European View." *Annals of the American Academy of Political and Social Science* 367 (September): 63–72.

Ulph, D. T., and L. A. Winters. 1994. "Strategic Manpower Policy and International Trade." In P. R. Krugman and M. A. M. Smith, eds., *Empirical Models of Strategic Trade Policy.* Chicago: University of Chicago Press, pp. 157–94.

UN Population Division. 2002. *World Population Prospects: The 2002 Revision.* New York. (Medium projections.)

Wilson, James A. 1966. "The Emigration of British Scientists." *Minerva* 5, no. 1: 20–29.

World Bank. 2008. Measuring International Skilled Migration. http://econ.world bank.org/WBSITE/EXTERNAL/EXTDEC/EXTRESEARCH/0,,contentMDK:2 1085139~pagePK:64214825~piPK:64214943~theSitePK:469382,00.html, accessed April 29, 2008.

4

Public Finance in an Era of Global Demographic Change
Fertility Busts, Migration Booms, and Public Policy

DAVID E. WILDASIN

The rich countries of the world, especially those of western Europe, are in the midst of a truly remarkable demographic experience. Fertility rates are now far below the replacement rate, and the populations of these countries are therefore aging rapidly. At the same time, the rich countries have been receiving substantial flows of migrants from elsewhere in Europe, North Africa, and the third world generally, partially offsetting low native fertility rates. For the foreseeable future, western European countries will confront a policy trade-off between population aging and migration. This trade-off—which involves not only "migration policy" narrowly construed but a whole range of other fiscal and structural policies such as EU enlargement—has far-reaching consequences, since immigration affects all aspects of economic and social life.

The following discussion draws together empirical and theoretical findings from several branches of inquiry in order to identify some of the important interactions among fertility, migration, and fiscal policies. The basic theme here is that demographic change, past and prospective, carries major implications for the fiscal systems of the advanced economies, especially those of western Europe. Differing levels of economic development create strong and persistent incentives for both skilled and unskilled workers to migrate from relatively young third-world countries to relatively old rich countries. Both skilled and unskilled workers affect the highly redistributive fiscal systems of advanced economies, the first as net contributors, the second as net beneficiaries. Global competition for labor and demographic changes create incentives for the adjustment of fiscal policies, especially in advanced economies, where the public sector plays a major role in the redistribution of income. In particular, skilled workers generally offer a fiscal premium for the nations in which they reside. Competition for these workers affects the allocation of skilled labor throughout the world, with implications for earnings and income levels and distribution, output, and other important economic outcomes.

It is impossible to foresee with any precision how these powerful forces will interact. As the demographic developments of the past several decades show, our ability to predict fertility and migration behavior is quite limited, and, of course, economic forecasting is a notoriously inexact science. To these uncertainties one must add the difficulties of predicting policy changes through political processes, which are sometimes democratic, sometimes not so, sometimes peaceful, sometimes violent. With these qualifications in mind, there is still at least a basis for a presumption that competitive pressures will work to limit the extent of redistribution in rich countries, including not only intergenerational redistribution but also other forms of explicit and implicit redistribution. At the same time, global integration of factor markets should promote more productive utilization of the world's productive resources, including human capital. Factor-market integration can also strengthen incentives for human capital investment, in both rich and poor countries.

The Demographic and Economic Setting

Fertility Rates and Age Structures

Some of the basic demographic facts facing the countries of western Europe are by now relatively familiar. In particular, these countries are experiencing a true fertility bust. The total fertility rate—the number of children borne by a woman in her lifetime—is a standard demographic measure for which data are available for many countries and many years. The benchmark fertility rate is 2, the number of children each woman must have, on average, if a population is to replenish itself over time. As shown in table 4.1, fertility rates in EU countries are now at remarkably low levels, ranging from a low of 1.15 in the Czech Republic to a high of 1.97 in Ireland; for the EU-15 countries as a whole, the fertility rate is 1.53, far below the replacement rate. Figure 4.1, which focuses on western European countries that belong to the Organisation for Economic Co-operation and Development (OECD), shows that today's low fertility rates are hardly a new phenomenon. Whereas the simple unweighted average fertility rate was 2.7 in 1960 for the countries shown in figure 4.1, this average had fallen below 2.0 by 1976, below 1.7 by 1984, and below 1.6 for most of the period from 1994 to 2003 (data drawn from World Bank, 2007). The consequence of low and falling fertility rates, combined with rising life expectancies, is an aging population. Figure 4.2 illustrates the basic trend. For western European countries, the old-age dependency ratio (population older than

Table 4.1   Current and Projected Fertility Rates, EU

	2004	2010	2020	2030	2040	2050
Austria	1.40	1.42	1.44	1.45	1.45	1.45
Belgium	1.62	1.66	1.69	1.70	1.70	1.70
Denmark	1.76	1.78	1.79	1.79	1.80	1.80
Finland	1.76	1.78	1.79	1.80	1.80	1.80
France	1.89	1.87	1.86	1.85	1.85	1.85
Germany	1.35	1.41	1.44	1.45	1.45	1.45
Greece	1.29	1.41	1.49	1.50	1.50	1.50
Ireland	1.97	1.89	1.81	1.80	1.80	1.80
Italy	1.31	1.38	1.40	1.40	1.40	1.40
Luxembourg	1.65	1.73	1.78	1.79	1.80	1.80
Netherlands	1.75	1.76	1.75	1.75	1.75	1.75
Portugal	1.45	1.52	1.59	1.60	1.60	1.60
Spain	1.30	1.36	1.40	1.40	1.40	1.40
Sweden	1.74	1.84	1.85	1.85	1.85	1.85
United Kingdom	1.72	1.74	1.75	1.75	1.75	1.75
Cyprus	1.47	1.43	1.49	1.50	1.50	1.50
Czech Republic	1.15	1.24	1.44	1.50	1.50	1.50
Estonia	1.39	1.45	1.54	1.60	1.60	1.60
Hungary	1.30	1.33	1.51	1.59	1.60	1.60
Latvia	1.30	1.42	1.53	1.59	1.60	1.60
Lithuania	1.29	1.30	1.41	1.55	1.60	1.60
Malta	1.66	1.49	1.54	1.60	1.60	1.60
Poland	1.21	1.19	1.42	1.58	1.60	1.60
Slovakia	1.19	1.18	1.33	1.52	1.59	1.60
Slovenia	1.18	1.27	1.46	1.50	1.50	1.50
EU15	1.60	1.64	1.66	1.66	1.66	1.66
EU25	1.48	1.51	1.58	1.62	1.62	1.62

Source: European Commission (2005), table 2.

65 as a percentage of total population) has risen from 10 to more than 15 percent (a simple unweighted average) since 1960. This "graying" of the population has been gradual and well documented.

Predicting the future is harder than documenting the past. In some respects, however, demographic extrapolations are easier than economic

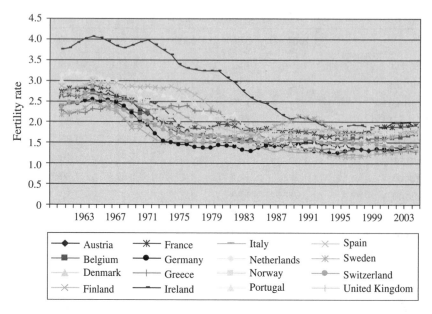

Figure 4.1 Fertility rates, western Europe, 1960–2005.

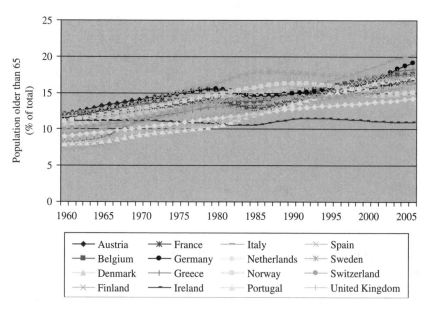

Figure 4.2 Old-age dependency ratio, western European countries, 1960–2006.

forecasting because of the inertia of demographic change. For example, all of those who will be 50 years old or older in 2050 are already born. Fertility rates in the future can certainly change, but typical projections, such as those shown for the EU in figure 4.1, postulate continued low fertility in Europe and in most OECD countries elsewhere in the world. Barring major wars or epidemics and abstracting from migration, which is discussed further below, the evolution of the old-age dependency ratio for the next several decades will increase for decades to come—for instance, as shown in table 4.2 for EU countries, from current levels of about 25 percent to about 50 percent by 2050.[1] This basic pattern is found throughout Europe, including the newer EU member states in the east as well as those in the west.

These demographic data carry obvious implications for the public-pension and health systems of developed countries. As shown in Dang, Antolin, and Oxley, (2001), the aging of populations in OECD countries is expected to put fiscal systems in these countries under increasing stress. For instance, spending on old-age pensions currently amounts to about 7.4 percent of GDP for OECD countries, and this proportion is projected to rise to about 10.8 percent by 2050 under midrange demographic and economic assumptions. For France and Germany, current spending is much higher, at about 12 percent of GDP, and is projected to rise to about 16 percent of GDP by 2050. For other countries, such as the United Kingdom and the United States, this category of spending is much lower (about 4.3 percent of GDP) and is projected to rise relatively little (about one percentage point for the United States) or even to fall (about 0.7 percentage point for the United Kingdom). As a whole, however, the low fertility rates of the western European countries mean that old-age-related spending (including not only pensions but also health-care and other spending) will rise substantially over time, in the absence of significant demographic or economic change.

International Migration

A full appreciation of the demographic situation facing western Europe cannot omit migration, which, in turn, depends critically on demographic and economic conditions in this region relative to the rest of the world.

First, although fertility rates worldwide have been declining for some time, they remain quite high in regions such as the Middle East, Africa, and southern Asia. As shown in figure 4.3, fertility rates in these regions

---

1. The low-fertility/rising old-age-dependency pattern is far less pronounced in the United States than in other OECD countries, a reflection, in part, of several decades of high rates of immigration.

Table 4.2   Current and Projected Old-Age-Dependency Ratio, EU-27, 2005–2050

	2005	2010	2020	2030	2040	2050
Austria	23.5	26.3	30.3	40.8	50.4	53.2
Belgium	26.3	26.4	32.2	41.3	47.2	48.1
Denmark	22.7	24.8	31.2	37.1	42.1	40
Finland	23.8	25.4	37	45	46.1	46.7
France	24.9	25.9	33.2	40.7	46.9	47.9
Germany	27.8	31	35.1	46	54.6	55.8
Greece	26.8	28	32.5	39.1	49.8	58.8
Ireland	16.4	17.5	22.5	28.3	35.9	45.3
Italy	29.3	31.3	36.6	45.2	59.8	66
Luxembourg	21.3	21.6	24.7	31.5	36.7	36.1
Netherlands	20.8	22.2	29	36.7	41.6	38.6
Portugal	25.2	26.5	31.5	39	48.9	58.1
Spain	24.4	25.4	30	38.9	54.3	67.5
Sweden	26.5	28	34.4	38.5	41.5	40.9
United Kingdom	24.3	25.1	30.3	37.4	43.8	45.3
Bulgaria	24.8	25.6	33	40.4	48.8	60.9
Cyprus	17.3	19.1	25.5	32.9	36.1	43.2
Czech Republic	19.8	21.9	31.8	37.1	43.8	54.8
Estonia	24.3	24.7	28.7	33.4	36.6	43.1
Hungary	22.7	24.3	31.2	35.1	40.3	48.3
Latvia	24.1	25.2	28	33.4	37.4	44.1
Lithuania	22.3	23.4	26	33.4	39.3	44.9
Malta	19.3	20.4	30	36	35.9	40.6
Poland	18.7	18.8	27.1	35.7	39.7	51
Romania	21.1	21.2	25.1	29.6	39.6	51.1
Slovakia	16.3	16.9	23.5	31.7	38.1	50.6
Slovenia	21.8	23.6	30.8	40.4	47.7	55.6
EU-15	24.3	25.7	31.4	39.0	46.6	49.9
EU-27	22.8	24.1	30.0	37.2	43.8	49.5

Source: EUPHIX (2008).

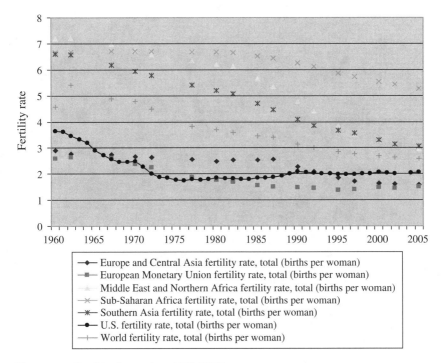

Figure 4.3 Fertility, by region, 1960–2005.

range from 2.8 (sub-Saharan Africa) to 3.3 (Middle East/North Africa), well above the replacement-rate benchmark of 2 (see UN, 2004, for additional analysis). Thanks to their high fertility rates (and shorter life expectancies), countries in these regions have much younger and more rapidly growing populations than the nations of Europe, western or eastern.

Furthermore, the populations in these other regions are relatively poor. As illustrated in figure 4.4, the countries of western Europe (identified in World Bank data as the countries of the European Monetary Union) have real per-capita incomes far higher than the nearby regions of eastern Europe, central Asia, the Middle East, and northern Africa, not to mention the somewhat more distant regions of sub-Saharan Africa and southern Asia. In 2006, the EMU countries had a per-capita GDP of $21,704 (in 2000 dollars). Of the other regions shown in figure 4.4, Europe and central Asia (a classification that includes eastern Europe and the countries of the former Soviet Union) has the highest current per-capita GDP, at $2,689 in 2006. While per-capita GDP in the Middle East and northern Africa in 2006 was $1,839, in southern Asia, it was $605, and in sub-Saharan Africa, it was $583. As figure 4.4 shows, the trends of the past half-century provide no basis for any expectation that the gap in per-capita incomes will close to

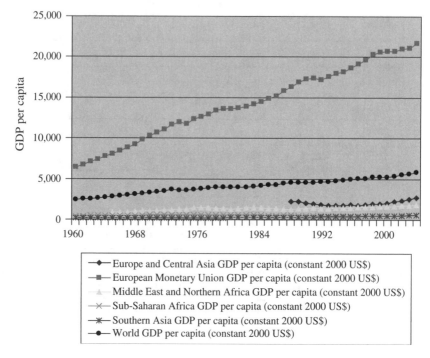

Figure 4.4 GDP per capita, by region, 1960–2006.

less than a factor of 5 in the next several decades. Income differentials of this magnitude swamp measurement errors.

Strong current and future demographic potential and economic incentives for people to migrate to western Europe from eastern Europe and from many poor regions of the world are apparent from the data just described. The effect of these incentives, even in the face of somewhat restrictive migration policies, is easily seen.

To begin with, table 4.3 displays inflows and outflows of population, expressed as a percentage of total population, as well as net and gross flows, for western European countries. These countries generally exhibit positive net migration since 1988, though, of course, with some variation.[2]

2. The migration data in this and the following tables reflect *legal* migration. By its nature, illegal migration is difficult to document. The U.S. Office of Immigration Statistics (2003) estimates that there were 3.5 million illegal immigrants in the United States in 1990, a number that grew to 7 million by 2000, representing an average annual inflow of about 0.35 million. These figures may be compared with a flow of 4.5 million *legal* immigrants during the decade from 1971 to 1980, 7.3 million from 1981 to 1990, and 9.1 million from 1991 to 2000, suggesting that illegal immigrants make up about 20 to 30 percent of the total annual U.S. immigrant flow in recent decades. More

Table 4.3 International Migration Rates, Selected OECD Countries, Selected Years, 1988–2005

		1988	1990	1992	1994	1996	1998	2000	2001	2002	2003	2004	2005
Austria													
	Inflow						0.73%	0.81%	0.92%	1.15%	1.20%	1.33%	1.23%
	Outflow						0.55%	0.55%	0.63%	0.48%	0.57%	0.59%	0.57%
	Net						0.18%	0.27%	0.29%	0.67%	0.63%	0.74%	0.65%
	Gross/net						7.28	5.11	5.3	2.4	2.8	2.6	2.8
	Gross						1.29%	1.36%	1.55%	1.63%	1.77%	1.92%	1.80%
Belgium													
	Inflow	0.39%	0.51%	0.55%	0.55%	0.51%	0.50%	0.67%	0.64%	0.68%	0.66%	0.69%	0.74%
	Outflow	0.33%	0.27%	0.28%	0.34%	0.32%	0.36%	0.35%	0.31%	0.30%	0.33%	0.36%	0.37%
	Net	0.06%	0.24%	0.27%	0.22%	0.19%	0.14%	0.32%	0.34%	0.38%	0.34%	0.33%	0.37%
	Gross/net	11.9	3.3	3.1	4.1	4.3	6.0	3.2	2.8	2.6	2.9	3.2	3.0
	Gross	0.71%	0.78%	0.83%	0.89%	0.83%	0.85%	1.02%	0.95%	0.98%	0.99%	1.06%	1.11%
Denmark													
	Inflow	0.27%	0.29%	0.33%	0.25%	0.24%	0.23%	0.43%	0.47%	0.41%	0.35%	0.35%	
	Outflow	0.10%	0.09%	0.09%	0.10%	0.11%	0.15%	0.16%	0.17%	0.16%	0.16%	0.17%	

continued

Table 4.3 *(continued)*

	1988	1990	1992	1994	1996	1998	2000	2001	2002	2003	2004	2005
(Denmark)												
Net	0.17%	0.20%	0.23%	0.15%	0.13%	0.09%	0.27%	0.30%	0.25%	0.19%	0.17%	
Gross/net	2.2	1.9	1.8	2.3	2.8	4.3	2.1	2.1	2.3	2.7	3.0	
Gross	0.37%	0.38%	0.42%	0.34%	0.36%	0.38%	0.58%	0.64%	0.57%	0.51%	0.52%	
Finland												
Inflow		0.13%	0.21%	0.15%	0.15%	0.16%	0.18%	0.21%	0.19%	0.18%	0.22%	0.24%
Outflow		0.02%	0.03%	0.03%	0.06%	0.03%	0.08%	0.04%	0.05%	0.04%	0.08%	0.05%
Net		0.11%	0.18%	0.12%	0.09%	0.13%	0.10%	0.17%	0.14%	0.14%	0.14%	0.19%
Gross/net		1.3	1.3	1.5	2.3	1.5	2.6	1.5	1.8	1.6	2.2	1.5
Gross		0.15%	0.24%	0.18%	0.21%	0.19%	0.26%	0.25%	0.25%	0.22%	0.30%	0.29%
Germany												
Inflow	0.83%	1.06%	1.50%	0.95%	0.86%	0.74%	0.79%	0.83%	0.80%	0.73%	0.73%	0.70%
Outflow	0.46%	0.59%	0.76%	0.76%	0.68%	0.78%	0.68%	0.60%	0.61%	0.60%	0.66%	0.59%
Net	0.37%	0.47%	0.74%	0.19%	0.18%	-0.04%	0.11%	0.23%	0.19%	0.12%	0.07%	0.12%
Gross/net	3.5	3.5	3.1	9.2	8.5	-37.1	14.0	6.3	7.6	10.7	20.8	11.1
Gross	1.29%	1.65%	2.26%	1.71%	1.55%	1.52%	1.47%	1.44%	1.41%	1.33%	1.39%	1.29%

Luxembourg	Inflow	2.19%	2.44%	2.50%	2.28%	2.21%	2.49%	2.47%	2.49%	2.44%	2.56%	2.76%	2.97%
	Outflow	1.41%	1.44%	1.43%	1.31%	1.35%	1.57%	1.62%	1.71%	1.84%	2.09%	2.40%	2.37%
	Net	0.77%	1.00%	1.07%	0.97%	0.87%	0.91%	0.85%	0.79%	0.60%	0.47%	0.35%	0.59%
	Gross/net	4.7	3.9	3.7	3.7	4.1	4.4	4.8	5.3	7.1	10.0	14.6	9.0
	Gross	3.60%	3.88%	3.94%	3.59%	3.56%	4.06%	4.09%	4.20%	4.28%	4.64%	5.16%	5.34%
Netherlands	Inflow	0.39%	0.54%	0.55%	0.44%	0.50%	0.52%	0.58%	0.59%	0.54%	0.45%	0.40%	0.39%
	Outflow	0.14%	0.14%	0.15%	0.15%	0.14%	0.14%	0.13%	0.13%	0.13%	0.13%	0.14%	0.15%
	Net	0.25%	0.41%	0.40%	0.30%	0.35%	0.38%	0.44%	0.46%	0.41%	0.32%	0.26%	0.24%
	Gross/net	2.2	1.7	1.8	2.0	1.8	1.7	1.6	1.6	1.6	1.8	2.1	2.2
	Gross	0.54%	0.68%	0.70%	0.59%	0.64%	0.66%	0.71%	0.72%	0.67%	0.59%	0.54%	0.54%
Norway	Inflow	0.55%	0.37%	0.40%	0.41%	0.39%	0.60%	0.62%	0.56%	0.68%	0.59%	0.61%	0.68%
	Outflow	0.22%	0.23%	0.19%	0.22%	0.23%	0.27%	0.33%	0.34%	0.27%	0.31%	0.20%	0.27%
	Net	0.33%	0.14%	0.21%	0.19%	0.16%	0.33%	0.29%	0.23%	0.41%	0.27%	0.41%	0.41%

continued

Table 4.3 (continued)

		1988	1990	1992	1994	1996	1998	2000	2001	2002	2003	2004	2005
(Norway)	Gross/net	2.3	4.3	2.8	3.3	3.8	2.6	3.3	4.0	2.3	3.3	2.0	2.3
	Gross	0.77%	0.60%	0.59%	0.63%	0.62%	0.87%	0.95%	0.90%	0.95%	0.90%	0.80%	0.95%
Sweden	Inflow	0.53%	0.62%	0.46%	0.85%	0.33%	0.40%	0.38%	0.49%	0.53%	0.54%	0.53%	0.57%
	Outflow	0.14%	0.19%	0.15%	0.18%	0.16%	0.16%	0.14%	0.14%	0.16%	0.17%	0.18%	0.18%
	Net	0.39%	0.43%	0.30%	0.67%	0.17%	0.24%	0.24%	0.35%	0.37%	0.37%	0.35%	0.39%
	Gross/net	1.7	1.9	2.0	1.5	3.0	2.3	2.1	1.8	1.9	1.9	2.0	1.9
	Gross	0.67%	0.81%	0.61%	1.03%	0.49%	0.56%	0.52%	0.64%	0.69%	0.70%	0.71%	0.74%
Switzerland	Inflow	1.13%	1.48%	1.60%	1.29%	1.03%	1.04%	1.20%	1.36%	1.33%	1.23%	1.30%	1.27%
	Outflow	0.83%	0.87%	1.15%	0.90%	0.94%	0.82%	0.77%	0.72%	0.68%	0.63%	0.65%	0.67%
	Net	0.30%	0.61%	0.45%	0.39%	0.09%	0.22%	0.44%	0.64%	0.65%	0.60%	0.65%	0.60%
	Gross/net	6.5	3.9	6.1	5.7	21.5	8.4	4.5	3.3	3.1	3.1	3.0	3.2
	Gross	1.97%	2.35%	2.75%	2.19%	1.97%	1.85%	1.97%	2.08%	2.00%	1.87%	1.95%	1.94%

Note: Data shown only for years in which both inflows and outflows are available.

Source: Inflows and outflows, OECD (1999a), table A.1.1 (for 1988–1990 data); OECD (2003), tables A.1.1, A.1.2 (for 1991–2000 data); OECD (2005), tables A.1.1, A.1.2 (for 2001–2002 data); OECD (2007), tables A.1.1, A.1.2 (for 2003–2005 data). Population, U.S. Bureau of the Census, International Data Base.

(The implications of high *gross* migration rates are discussed later.) The cumulative effects of net immigration *flows* are shown in tables 4.4 and 4.5, which present two measures of the *stock* of "immigrants," corresponding to two different measures that are typically used in population records. Table 4.4 shows that the stock of "foreign-born" individuals in several western European OECD countries (Austria, Ireland, the Netherlands, Sweden) amounts to more than 10 percent of the total population, close to (or exceeding) the U.S. figure of 12.9 percent. Table 4.5 shows stocks of "foreign" population for a number of (mainly western European) countries. The key difference between foreign and foreign-born is that an immigrant who acquires citizenship, though still foreign-born, is no longer counted as foreign. Foreign populations are generally smaller than foreign-born populations, especially in countries with high rates of naturalization, as is apparent from a comparison of those countries for which both measures are available. For instance, there are more than twice as many foreign-born as foreign persons in both Sweden and the Netherlands.

Immigrants account for a significant share of the populations of western European countries today. A sense of what the future may hold can be obtained by comparing migration flows in recent years with the other sources of demographic change: fertility and mortality. As shown in figure 4.5 (see OECD, 2003, chart I.10), the combination of sustained positive net migration and low fertility means that for the EU as a whole and for a number of individual countries, the rate of net migration has exceeded the rate of natural increase since the mid-1980s.[3] Immigrants are younger than native populations, and their fertility rates reflect those of their native countries until they become assimilated into their new countries of residence.[4] For both of these reasons, the demographic, economic, and fiscal impacts of immigration are certain to become more prominent in the near future. The foreign-born population, and their immediate offspring, will make up a growing fraction of the western European population for several decades. As a matter of demographic inertia, this would be true even if immigration flows were assumed (say, as the result of unrealistically

recently, the Department of Homeland Security has estimated that the population of "unauthorized" immigrants was approximately 8.5 million in 2000 and that this figure had risen to 11.6 million by 2006 (see Hoefer, Rytina, and Campbell, 2007). Similar figures might be presumed for western Europe, in which case the figures shown in tables 4.3, 4.4, and 4.5 significantly underestimate the net immigration flows and stocks.

3. Figure 4.5 illustrates clearly that while net migration rates fluctuate over time for individual countries, the overall net migration rate for the EU is relatively stable, showing the importance of local short-run variations in labor demand as well local migration and other policies.

4. See, e.g., Bauer, Lofstrom, and Zimmermann (2000) for a review of the literature on the assimilation of immigrants.

Table 4.4 Stocks of Foreign-Born Population, Selected OECD Countries (as Percentage of Total)

	1990	1992	1994	1996	1998	2000	2001	2002	2003	2004	2005
Austria					11.2	10.5	11.1	10.8	11.4	13.0	13.5
Canada				17.4	17.8	18.1	18.4	18.6	18.7	18.9	19.1
Denmark		4.0	4.3	5.1	5.4	5.8	6.0	6.2	6.3	6.3	6.5
Finland				2.1	2.4	2.6	2.7	2.8	2.9	3.2	3.4
France											8.1
Hungary				2.8	2.8	2.9	3.0	3.0	3.0	3.2	3.3
Greece							10.3				
Ireland				6.9	7.8	8.7	9.3	10.0	10.5	11.0	11.0
Luxembourg				31.5	32.2	33.2	32.8	32.9	33.0	33.1	33.4
Netherlands	8.1		9.0	9.2	9.6	10.1	10.4	10.6	10.7	10.6	10.6
Norway			5.4	5.6	6.1	6.8	6.9	7.3	7.6	7.8	8.2
Sweden		9.6	10.5	10.7	11.0	11.3	11.5	11.8	12.0	12.2	12.4
United States	7.9		8.2	10.3	10.8	11.0	11.3	12.3	12.6	12.8	12.9

Source: OECD (1999a), table A.1.5 (1990 data); OECD (2003), table A.1.4 (1991–1992 data); OECD (2005), table A.1.4 (1993–1995 data); OECD (2007) table A.1.4 (1996–2005 data).

Table 4.5 Stocks of Foreign Population, Selected OECD Countries (as Percentage of Total)

	1988	1989	1990	1991	1992	1993	1994	1995	1996	1997	1998	1999	2000	2001	2002	2003	2004	2005
Austria	4.5	5.1	5.9	6.8	7.9	8.6	8.9	8.5	8.6	8.6	8.6	8.7	8.8	8.9	9.2	9.4	9.5	9.7
Belgium	8.8	8.9	9.1	9.2	9.0	9.1	9.1	9.0	9.0	8.9	8.7	8.8	8.4	8.2	8.2	8.3	8.4	8.6
Czech Republic					0.4	0.8	1.0	1.5	1.9	2.0	2.1	2.2	1.9	2.0	2.3	2.4	2.5	2.7
Denmark	2.8	2.9	3.1	3.3	3.5	3.6	3.8	4.2	4.7	4.7	4.8	4.9	4.8	5.0	4.9	5.0	4.9	5.0
Finland	0.4	0.4	0.5	0.8	0.9	1.1	1.2	1.3	1.4	1.6	1.6	1.7	1.8	1.8	1.9	2.0	2.1	2.2
France			6.3									5.6						
Germany	7.3	7.7	8.4	7.3	8.0	8.5	8.6	8.8	8.9	9.0	8.9	8.9	8.9	8.9	8.9	8.9	8.9	8.8
Hungary							1.3	1.4	1.4	1.4	1.4	1.5	1.1	1.1	1.1	1.3	1.4	1.5
Ireland	2.4	2.3	2.3	2.5	2.7	2.7	2.7	2.7	3.2	3.1	3.0	3.1	3.3	4.0	4.8	5.6	5.5	6.3
Italy	1.1	0.9	1.4	1.5	1.6	1.7	1.6	1.7	2.0	2.1	2.1	2.2	2.4	2.5	2.6	3.9	4.2	4.6
Luxembourg	27.4	27.9	29.4	30.2	31.0	31.8	32.6	33.4	34.1	34.9	35.6	36.0	37.3	37.5	38.1	38.6	39.0	39.6
Netherlands	4.2	4.3	4.6	4.8	5.0	5.1	5.0	4.7	4.4	4.3	4.2	4.1	4.2	4.3	4.3	4.3	4.3	4.2
Norway	3.2	3.3	3.4	3.5	3.6	3.8	3.8	3.7	3.7	3.6	3.6	3.7	4.0	4.1	4.1	4.3	4.6	4.8
Portugal	1.0	1.0	1.1	1.2	1.3	1.3	1.6	1.7	1.7	1.8	1.8	1.9	2.1	3.5	4.1	4.3	4.5	4.1
Spain	0.9	0.6	0.7	0.9	1.0	1.1	1.2	1.3	1.4	1.6	1.8	2.0	2.2	2.7	3.1	3.9	4.6	6.2
Sweden	5.0	5.3	5.6	5.7	5.7	5.8	6.1	5.2	6.0	5.9	5.6	5.5	5.4	5.3	5.3	5.3	5.3	5.3
Switzerland	15.2	15.6	16.3	17.1	17.6	18.1	18.6	18.9	18.9	19.0	19.0	19.2	19.3	19.7	19.9	20.0	20.2	20.3
United Kingdom	3.2	3.2	3.2	3.1	3.5	3.5	3.6	3.4	3.4	3.6	3.8	3.8	4.0	4.4	4.5	4.7	4.9	5.2

Source: OECD (1999), table A.1.6 (1988–1990 data); OECD (2003), table A.1.5 (1991–1992 data); OECD (2005), table A.1.5 (1993–1995 data); OECD (2007), table A.1.5 (1996–2005 data).

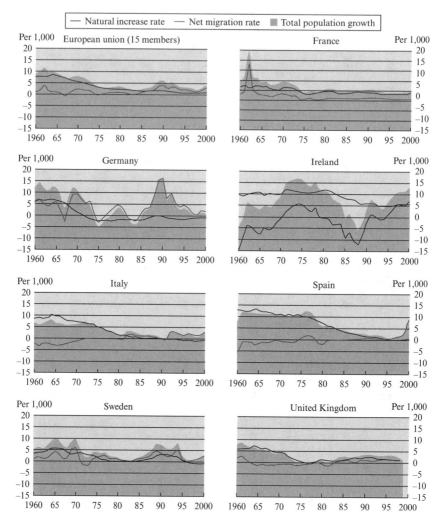

Figure 4.5 Components of total population growth in selected OECD countries and in the European Union, 1960–2000.

draconian policy restrictions) to drop instantly to zero. As we have seen, however, the fundamental incentives for immigrants to come to western Europe from the younger and poorer regions of the world are large and highly persistent. Variations in local economic conditions and policies may deflect future immigration flows from one country to another, but the share of immigrants and their immediate offspring will certainly rise for many decades to come.

Age-Related Spending: Migration to the Rescue?

If the populations of western Europe are age-imbalanced because of sustained low fertility, and if the populations of poor countries are relatively young because of continued comparatively high fertility, and if large income differentials create powerful incentives for the latter to migrate toward the former, can international migration restore a more age-balanced demographic structure in western Europe, providing the active labor force needed to finance social benefits for the elderly? In short, will migration provide a solution to the age-related issues facing the fiscal systems of western Europe?[5]

It is impossible to forecast migration flows and their impacts without forecasting migration policies, and part of the task of the discussion here is precisely to assess the incentives for rich and aging countries to adjust their migration policies. Nevertheless, it is instructive to consider hypothetical extrapolations of migration trends to see how they could possibly affect the populations of destination countries. An analysis by the UN (2000) provides best-guess projections for migration and demographic structure and examines what migration flows would permit the attainments of various demographic targets.

The midrange projections of this study find that western European countries will experience continued net immigration for the next half-century. Under these projections, immigration will mitigate but not fundamentally alter the basic demographic trends implied by low fertility. The European Union is projected to absorb approximately 16 million immigrants by 2050, but the "support ratio," that is, the number of people ages 15 to 64 divided by the number of people older than 65, would still fall from its 1995 value of 4.30 to 1.97 by 2050. Although this "medium-variant" projection is higher than the projected 1.89 under the assumption of zero net migration, it also indicates that continued immigration, at rates similar to those experienced in recent decades, will not dramatically affect the age structure of the population (UN, 2000, tables IV.4, IV.5).

Indeed, to maintain the 1995 support ratio of 4.3, the EU countries would need to absorb about 12 million immigrants *annually*, in contrast to annual flows throughout the 1990s of at most 1.3 million. Sustained over the next 50 years, this tenfold-higher immigration rate would result in about 700 million net immigrants; by 2050, about 75 percent of the total EU population would either be immigrants or the descendants of post-1995 immigrants, in contrast to the medium-variant projection of 6.2 percent (UN, 2000, tables IV.4, IV.7). One can use these two cases—a constant

---

5. Storesletten (2000) examines the impact of immigration on the U.S. Social Security system.

support ratio compared with one that falls by somewhat more than half in 2050—to gauge the migration implications of various intermediate cases. In the absence of extremely high immigration rates, sustained over many decades, low fertility rates and long life expectancies imply that the countries of western Europe will face age-imbalance demographic structures, and their fiscal consequences, for the foreseeable future.

Fiscal Impacts of Migration

Immigrants affect a country's fiscal system in many different ways, starting from the moment of arrival and continuing throughout the life cycle (or as long as the immigrant remains in the country).[6] This section focuses on the impact of immigration on public-pension systems, an important issue for advanced economies in view of their current demographic, economic, and fiscal circumstances as described above. Before turning to a detailed discussion of public pensions, however, it is useful to consider the fiscal implications of migration in a somewhat broader context.

To begin with, note that immigrants, like all of a country's residents, contribute to public-sector revenues and impose public-service burdens in a multitude of ways, direct and indirect. These effects depend on the immigrant's age, sex, health, consumption patterns, education level, earnings, savings behavior, legal status, and other socioeconomic characteristics. Most of these characteristics change over time and vary from one person to another, and the fiscal impacts of immigration are as diverse and complex as immigrants and fiscal systems. Accurate and comprehensive assessments are difficult, and generalizations, though possible, can easily be misleading or inappropriate for the analysis of important types of policy questions. This becomes increasingly apparent as one reviews systematically the revenue-side and expenditure-side interactions of migrants with a country's fiscal system.

Consider the revenue side first. In western European countries, social insurance contributions, personal income and payroll taxes, and value-added taxes are major sources of tax revenues. Legal immigrants (or their employers) pay taxes on earnings, through either payroll taxes or personal income taxes, in amounts that depend positively on the immigrant's

---

6. Emigrants also affect fiscal systems. Many of the remarks that follow are equally applicable, in reverse, for emigrants, and both are important. Obviously, the fiscal effects of migration, in either direction, are especially critical in countries where fiscal systems are large, that is, in practice, in rich countries. By conventional measures, redistributive fiscal policies in poor countries are quite limited, and the fiscal impacts of migration are accordingly much smaller.

earnings. Both legal and illegal immigrants pay value-added taxes, in amounts that depend on consumption preferences as well as income. These sources of revenues will be relatively small for low-income immigrants but larger for those with higher incomes—which, in turn, means (on average) for those with better education, better health, in the peak earnings part of the life cycle, and with greater amounts of accumulated nonhuman wealth. Note that all or most of these attributes are potentially observable and can be (and in practice are) used as explicit or implicit screens for determining "desired" types of immigrants. Moreover, changes in tax policy—the mix of different taxes, their rates, and their administration and enforcement— change the tax treatment of immigrants relative to natives and of different types of immigrants, offering important opportunities for differential fiscal treatment of immigrants.

Immigrants also generate revenues through nontax sources. Prices or fees are or could be used to defray the costs of public services such as health, education, transportation, and housing. As a matter of policy choice, these revenue instruments can be used more or less intensively, and, in some cases, they are or can be used differentially for immigrants. For instance, fares for public transportation are commonly collected from all users, independently of citizenship status and, for that matter, usually independently of legal status. As in the case of tax policy, however, there are many ways in which the structure of transportation pricing differentiates implicitly, if not explicitly, between native residents and different types of immigrants. As one illustration, special discounts or subscriptions are sometimes made available for the elderly, students, or other demographic or economic subgroups, a price structure that differentially affects immigrants. Similarly, access to hospitals and clinics may be differentially priced for those who participate in national health systems, effectively discriminating among users based on citizenship or legal status. In the United States, at least, it is common for explicit tuition charges at public colleges and universities to distinguish between in-state and out-of-state students, with noncitizens included in the latter category, and financial aid programs, utilized by students attending both private and public institutions, can and do discriminate based on the characteristics of students (and their families). Although prices for access to higher education in western Europe are normally much lower than in the United States, this is a policy choice, and the option exists to alter the policy, including in ways that would require foreign students to bear a larger share of the costs of education provided to them.

On the expenditure side, immigrants will, of necessity, benefit from nonexclusive public goods and services, even though these may be congestible, that is, even if immigrants impose *added costs* of service provision and, in this way, affect the fiscal system. Examples of public services with limited excludability but significant congestibility include public safety (expenditures on police and fire protection depend on the size of the population being served), public health and sanitation (sewage, water treatment, refuse collection), parks and recreation, and (unpriced) roads. Nevertheless, as already suggested, access to public services may in some cases be restricted to citizens or at least to legal immigrants or, if desired, targeted at immigrants. Policy decisions about the location of public facilities such as health clinics or schools (e.g., whether to locate such facilities in immigrant enclaves) or about whether to provide multilingual services differentially affect immigrants and natives, implicitly or explicitly.

For some public-sector activities, the fiscal impact of immigrants may be somewhat indirect. Insofar as publicly provided housing, rent subsidies, or tax preferences for the housing sector increase housing supply and lower the equilibrium price of housing, all housing consumers are made better off, regardless of immigrant or citizenship status. The same is true for subsidies that increase the supplies of medical personnel, pharmaceuticals, elder-care facilities, and the like. To the extent that these policies affect the equilibrium prices, all consumers share in the benefits and add to the fiscal burden.

The children of immigrants also affect a country's fiscal system, on both the revenue and expenditure sides, whether or not they are immigrants themselves. From an *ex ante* policy perspective, these effects are contingent on the initial arrival of the immigrant parent(s), and thus, arguably, should be included in a comprehensive analysis of the impact of immigration. To do otherwise would, in effect, amount to the assumption that immigrants will be infertile, an assumption that is certainly extreme and, for "representative" recent immigrants in western European countries, is empirically quite incorrect, since, as noted earlier, these immigrants often tend to have higher fertility rates than native western Europeans.

As these general remarks indicate, immigrants interact with a jurisdiction's fiscal system in many ways over time. A proper assessment of the fiscal impact of immigration would ideally take into account the totality of these interactions.

Immigration and Public-Pension Systems

All aspects of the fiscal impact of immigration are worthy of careful analysis. The impacts of immigrants on public-pension systems are of special interest, however, for several reasons. First, as noted earlier, public pensions are major elements of the fiscal systems of western European nations. Second, since participants in these systems pay taxes when they are young and receive benefits when they are old, public-pension systems illustrate very well the importance of considering *both* the tax and the expenditure sides of government accounts simultaneously and in an *intertemporal* con-text. Third, the benefits and costs of public pensions are comparatively eas-ily measured, at least in principle.[7]

At a basic theoretical level, the concept of "net public-pension wealth" (*NPPW*) (Feldstein, 1974) provides a convenient summary of the impact of a public-pension system on a household's lifetime wealth. *NPPW* is the pre-sent value of future public-pension benefits received by a household, net of taxes paid into the public-pension system. If $NPPW > 0$ for an individual or household, participation in the system involves a net transfer to the house-hold from the rest of society, whereas the opposite is the case if $NPPW > 0$. This variable, or its negative, also measures the present value of the impact of a household on the public-pension system.

More formally, suppose that households are life-cycle utility maximiz-ers that supply labor inelastically and have utility functions defined over lifetime consumption streams. Retirement occurs with certainty at age R, and death occurs with certainty at age D. Assume that every household supplies one unit of labor until retirement, earning w_i annually if it resides in country i. (The assumptions that labor supply and annual earnings are constant over time are made for notational simplicity.) Let c_t denote the value of consumption in period t of the life cycle and r denote a fixed mar-ket interest rate. In the absence of any government fiscal policy, the house-hold faces a lifetime budget constraint, starting at age 0, of

$$\sum_{t=0}^{D} \frac{c_t}{(1+r)^t} = \sum_{t=0}^{R} \frac{w_i}{(1+r)^t}. \tag{4.1}$$

The budget constraint for an older household is identical to equation (4.1), except that it covers a shorter horizon, beginning at some initial $t_0 > 0$.

To incorporate a public-pension system into this framework, suppose that the benefit received by a worker in country i is a lump-sum annuity of b_i, financed by a proportional payroll tax at rate τ_i. (It is straightforward to use a more realistic specification at the cost of slightly more complex notation.) Then the budget constraint facing a worker residing in country i becomes

$$\sum_{t=0}^{D} \frac{c_t}{(1+r)^t} = \sum_{t=0}^{R} \frac{(1-\tau_i)w_i}{(1+r)^t} + \sum_{t=R}^{D} \frac{b_i}{(1+r)^t}. \tag{4.2}$$

Public pensions raise lifetime wealth by providing a flow of bene-fits during retirement but reduce lifetime wealth by requiring a flow of

7. This framework is presented and discussed in more detail in Wildasin (1999). See Uebelmesser (2004) for a recent discussion of public pension systems and many additional references to the literature.

contributions during the working years. The net effect of the public-pension program on lifetime wealth for workers in country i is thus

$$NPPW_i = \sum_{t=R}^{D} \frac{b_i}{(1+r)^t} - \sum_{t=0}^{R} \frac{\tau_i w_i}{(1+r)^t}. \tag{4.3}$$

The sign and magnitude of this expression depends on market prices (wages and interest rates), individual household attributes (current age, labor market participation and earnings, ages of retirement and death), and, of course, the policy parameters: the tax rate and benefit level.

In principle, the computation of $NPPW_i$ is not a complex undertaking, but in practice, there is much room for variations in its estimation.[8] The impact of a country's public-pension system on a household net lifetime wealth depends on the household's earnings and the country's policies, as is also true when calculating the impact of migration on a country's public-pension system: how much immigrants pay in taxes or receive in benefits depends on their employment and earnings paths over the life cycle as well as on tax and expenditure policies, which are only observable retrospectively. Analysis of the historical impact of immigrants on a public-pension system, while interesting, does not provide direct information about the impact of prospective immigrants on the future of a public-pension system. The evaluation of this effect requires information that cannot be known with certainty and can only be imperfectly foreseen.

Despite its inevitable limitations, net public-pension wealth does provide a present-value measure of the fiscal interactions between a household (or individual) and a public-pension system. It takes into account both the tax contributions made by the household and the expenditures on benefits that it receives at different stages of the life cycle, discounted to the present.

8. As noted by Leimer and Lesnoy (1982) and as discussed much more fully in Leimer and Lesnoy (1980, 1981), the calculation of $NPPW_i$ is a forward-looking exercise. If a calculation of $NPPW_i$ is to be used as an explanatory variable for predicting household behavior, then what is needed is an estimate of *expected* $NPPW_i$. The savings or migration behavior of today's 20- or 30-year-olds may be affected by public pension systems in which they will participate for another half-century, and although it is reasonable to imagine that households do make forward-looking decisions, it is not at all obvious how they gauge their own life prospects (future employment and earnings, health, and mortality) or future public-sector fiscal policies over such long periods of time. The same basic issues arise in a different but related area of analysis: the effect of public pension systems on fertility. As discussed in Becker and Barro (1988, 1989) and Wildasin (1990a), future public-sector debt obligations reduce the return to child-bearing for altruistically disposed parents. Whether future public pension obligations in EU countries help to explain lower current fertility rates in this region is an intriguing hypothesis but one that presents formidable challenges for empirical research.

For western European countries, estimated net public-pension wealth is typically negative, and substantially so, for representative young workers. One way to assess this particular fiscal burden is to compare *NPPW* with lifetime wealth, that is, with the present value of lifetime earnings. This burden can easily exceed 10 percent of lifetime wealth (Wildasin, 1999). Expressed somewhat differently, participation in the public-pension systems of some western European countries would, on balance, be equivalent to imposing a payroll tax at a rate of, say, 10 percent over a household's entire lifetime.

More generally, looking beyond public-pension systems and evaluating the total fiscal system more comprehensively, one can apply the methodology of "generational accounting," an exercise that requires projections of future policy, economic, and demographic variables (see especially Auerbach, Kotlikoff, and Leibfritz, 1999). The basic finding from research on generational accounting is that current fiscal policies in advanced economies, within the context of standard demographic and economic projections, exhibit significant generational imbalances in the sense that fiscal policy, on balance, shifts resources toward those presently alive, at the expense of future generations. Existing public-sector debt obligations make up one important component of the fiscal burden that future generations face, but the generational-accounting approach makes clear that the implicit liabilities of the public sector are also quite large. Underfunded public-pension obligations—that is, the fact that net public-pension wealth is negative for current and future generations—are the outstanding example of such implicit liabilities.

Because of anticipated demographic changes, young immigrants to EU countries with attributes similar to those of existing residents are generally expected to be "net fiscal contributors." That is, the fiscal system is positively affected by the arrival of such an immigrant, taking into account the entire lifetime impact of the household's interaction with the public-pension system. From the viewpoint of the existing (native) residents of the country, this immigrant confers a fiscal benefit by adding more to the revenue side of the fiscal system than the burden imposed on the expenditure side. The immigrant produces a "net fiscal benefit" to the existing population of the country. The magnitude of the net fiscal benefit that immigrants produce varies from country to country, as is apparent from the estimates in Wildasin (1999) and Kotlikoff and Leibfritz (1999). The latter authors summarize findings on generational accounts for 17 different countries, including both developed and developing countries. For Germany and France, the present value of net fiscal contributions that would be made by a 25-year-old immigrant who is economically similar to existing residents would be in excess of $300,000 (1995 dollars). For Denmark, Sweden, the Netherlands, and Belgium, the corresponding figure lies between $200,000 and $300,000; for a few EU countries (such as Norway and Italy), this figure is less than $200,000; and in one case, that of Portugal, the figure is only about $85,000.

Differential Fiscal Impacts, by Type of Migrant and by Type of Pension System

While it may seem natural to focus on the fiscal impacts of "representative" households or immigrants, a migrant's net fiscal impact on a country, whether measured by $NPPW_i$ alone or more comprehensively, depends (1) on the demographic and economic characteristics of the migrant and (2) on the characteristics of the fiscal system—the tax and benefit structure of the public-pension system—in country i. For example, $NPPW_i$ is larger—that is, the net fiscal benefit of an immigrant is smaller—for older immigrants, since they contribute to the public-pension system for a shorter period of time before drawing benefits. Since benefits in most public-pension systems rise less than in proportion to lifetime contributions, $NPPW_i$ is smaller (more negative) for immigrants with high earnings; that is, the net fiscal benefit to country i from an immigrant is higher the higher the immigrant's earnings. Skilled workers are thus likely to be net fiscal contributors to public-pension systems. Illegal immigrants may not be able to receive benefits from the public-pension system at all (an attempt to draw benefits might lead to deportation), but the employers of such immigrants might still withhold payroll taxes (perhaps on the basis of false documentation provided by the immigrant), in which case, $NPPW_i$ is definitely negative: the worker contributes to the public-pension system but never receives benefits from it. At least from the perspective of the public-pension system, the net fiscal benefit from such an immigrant is definitely positive, even if the worker has rather low earnings. To take still one more example, since life expectancy is significantly affected by nutrition and disease in early childhood, immigrants from poor countries have lower life expectancies than those from rich countries. Holding other immigrant characteristics (including earnings) constant, $NPPW_i$ would be lower for immigrants from poor countries than for those from rich countries; the net fiscal benefit of immigrants from poor countries would be greater than that for immigrants from rich countries, other things being the same.

The same immigrant can have quite different net public-pension wealth in different countries. For instance, suppose that the public-pension system in country i is "Bismarkian," in the sense that benefits depend positively on earnings, whereas the system in country j is "Beveridgean," with benefits relatively uniform regardless of earnings. Other things being the same, $NPPW_i > NPPW_j$ for a high-earnings individual; that is, a high earner would benefit more from, or suffer less from, the system with earnings-dependent benefits. The reverse would be true for a low earner. As a further example, suppose that a country's public-pension system is changing over time and that this is anticipated by households. For instance, in view of the data described above, one might anticipate that public-pension benefits will be falling over time for many western European countries, while taxes may be rising. These changes reduce $NPPW_i$ for all households, increasing the net fiscal benefit of immigration to existing local residents.

There are, of course, many conceivable types of immigrants, and the immigration flows that actually occur result in a mix of diverse types of immigrants. The preceding remarks indicate that the net fiscal benefit (or cost) of immigration for the existing residents of a country depends not only on the total number of immigrants but also on the *composition* of the immigrant flow. For this reason, it can be misleading to speak of *the* impact of immigrants on a public-pension system. Furthermore, the *differential* fiscal impacts of *different types* of migrants mean that policies that selectively or differentially affect migration flows can have quite diverse fiscal implications.

Toward a More Complete Picture

Public-pension systems well illustrate how migration affects both the revenue and the expenditure sides of the fiscal accounts and how the fiscal impact of immigration may occur over many periods, with immigrants possibly making net fiscal contributions in some periods and imposing net fiscal burdens in other periods. The impact immigrants have on pension systems also depends on the characteristics of the immigrants and on the characteristics of the fiscal system.

These remarks are more broadly applicable to the analysis of the impact of migration on fiscal systems. The parallel with public-pension systems is particularly obvious in the case of public-sector health expenditures, the benefits of which are closely linked to age and which, like public pensions, are often financed by taxes on working populations. But these observations apply generally when considering the totality of the interactions between an immigrant and a country's fiscal system. In principle, one could ascertain the full fiscal impact of immigration by particular types of immigrants in a particular country by analyzing all of the ways in which they interact with the fiscal system over the entire period of their residence. This would, however, require knowledge not only of immigrant characteristics and how they change over time (e.g., changes in earnings, employment, and health over the life cycle) but also of the characteristics of the fiscal system and how they change over time (e.g., changes in tax rates, expenditures, and regulations affecting public-expenditure programs and tax systems).

Public-pension and health programs are by no means the only important elements of the fiscal systems of rich countries that are sensitive to migration. The revenue flows from virtually all types of taxation, whether based on consumption, income, or wealth, depend crucially on both the size and the socioeconomic composition of the population to which they are applied. For example, the revenue impacts of immigration are highly sensitive to the current and future income and wealth of immigrants. One important illustration will suffice. The top 0.2 percent of U.S. taxpayers—those at the very highest income levels (in excess of $1 million)—account for some 25.2 percent of income-tax revenues, amounting to more than $775,000 in annual taxes paid per taxpayer (U.S. Treasury, 2007).[9] Since there are only about 175,000 such taxpayers, an increase or decrease in their numbers by, say, 80,000 would have profound consequences for the U.S. fiscal system, resulting in a swing of total personal income-tax revenues of as much as 10 percent. To anticipate later discussion, it is evident from this example that "not all immigrants are created equal" from a fiscal perspective. Among other implications, it is easy to see why *gross* as well as *net* migration can be of great importance fiscal systems. An outflow of 80,000 high-income taxpayers and their replacement by an equal number of poor immigrants would drastically worsen the flow of revenues to the U.S. federal government (not to mention the subnational governments). Similar remarks apply, but with less force, to taxes that are less progressively distributed.

The effects of demographic change in relation to debt warrant explicit mention as well. Outstanding debt (explicit government debt) amounts to 50 to 100 percent of GDP for most rich countries. The obligations of debt service fall on future taxpayers, especially those with high incomes. Reductions in fertility (especially by well-educated households with high lifetime incomes), if accompanied by increases in immigration (especially of well-educated immigrants with high lifetime incomes), will shift future tax burdens away from native populations and their descendants toward immigrants and their descendants.

Because immigrants and fiscal systems are diverse and ever changing, it is difficult or impossible to arrive at definitive assessments of "the"

---

9. It may be amusing to note that many of these taxpayers are literally worth more to the fisc than their weight in gold. At current prices ($900 per ounce), an average adult male's weight equivalent (190 pounds) of gold is worth about $2.7 million. Under conservative assumptions about life expectancy and discount rate, the present value of taxes paid by very-high-income taxpayers can easily exceed this amount.

fiscal impacts of immigration. However, in addition to the generational-accounting analyses mentioned above, a growing number of recent studies shed significant light on this topic. For instance, Hansen and Lofstrom (2001, 2003) observe that while immigrants (the foreign-born) account for about 10 percent of the Swedish population, they are the recipients of about 30 percent of welfare expenditures. Moreover, "refugee" immigrants have much lower employment and much higher (and persistent) welfare participation rates than immigrants from other Nordic countries, and these differences are quite persistent over time (Hansen and Lofstrom, 2001). This means, of course, that refugee immigrants pay relatively little in taxes, in addition to imposing high costs on the public sector. For Sweden, it is clear that not all immigrants are the same, from the fiscal perspective. The composition of the immigrant flow is a matter of great importance in assessing the fiscal impact of migration. Riphahn (1998) reports generally similar findings for Germany, emphasizing that there, too, welfare expenditures on behalf of immigrants account for a very large share of total expenditures.[10] Wadensjö and Orrje (2002) present a very comprehensive assessment of the fiscal impacts of immigrants in Denmark, distinguishing again between immigrants from less developed and more developed countries and closely analyzing both tax and expenditure impacts of immigration over the life cycle. These authors also find that immigrants from poorer countries pay less in taxes and receive more in benefits than other types of immigrants.

By contrast, Collado and Iturbe-Ormaetxe (2004) find that immigrants to Spain—including recent immigrants from relatively poor countries—have employment rates as high as or higher than those of natives and earnings that are roughly 75 percent of the native level. They estimate that expansion of existing immigration flows, assuming that "marginal" immigrants are similar to existing immigrants, would have net positive fiscal impacts. Comparing results for the United States presented by Auerbach and Oreopoulos (2000) and Gustman and Steinmeier (2000), who find that immigrants have only a modest fiscal impact, Collado and Iturbe-Ormaetxe note that human capital and earnings differentials between natives and recent immigrants in the United States is substantially larger than is the case for Spain, reflecting the characteristics both of native populations and of immigrants.

---

10. In the United States, nonnatives account for about 18 percent of participants in Food Stamps, AFDC/TANF (C. R. Bollinger, personal communication), and Medicaid and (at 11 percent of the population) are thus overrepresented in the population of social-benefits recipients, though to a lesser degree than in the EU countries just mentioned. See also Bollinger and Hagstrom (2003, 2004).

Competition for Mobile Labor:
Why and in What Form?

This section explores some of the potential implications of international labor mobility for policy adjustment. The focus is mainly on the adjustment of fiscal and migration policies in rich (i.e., destination) countries, using a no-migration benchmark as a reference case. The third part of the section, however, explores the implications of global competition for skilled labor for human capital investment, both in rich and in poor (i.e., origin) countries.

Margins of Fiscal Adjustment: No Migration

As a matter of arithmetic, rich countries will have to make policy adjustments during coming decades in order to deal with intergenerational fiscal imbalances. Leaving migration aside momentarily, there are only two fundamental margins of fiscal adjustment: reductions in public expenditures or increases in revenues. Through the use of debt and other fiscal policies, these adjustments may be distributed over time and across generations in many ways. To facilitate the analysis of migration and fiscal adjustment, it is helpful, as a benchmark, to review the range of policy options in the absence of migration.

Most obviously, fiscal imbalances in key age-related expenditure programs such as public-pension and health systems can be managed by reductions in health and retirement benefits or by increases in taxes on working populations. These reforms could be achieved relatively uniformly, by scaling down all existing benefits and scaling up all existing taxes, or they could be applied more selectively, for instance, by cutting benefits or raising taxes for those with higher incomes.

Changes in other elements of the overall fiscal system may also be used to manage fiscal imbalances by reducing benefits or increasing taxes for different socioeconomic or age groups in effective terms, even if only implicitly rather than explicitly. For instance, the funding of retirement systems could be augmented with revenues from other parts of the tax system (i.e., from "general" funds) in addition to payroll taxes. By comparison with increased payroll taxes, higher levels of consumption-based taxation (such as value-added taxes, or VATs) would shift fiscal burdens toward the old, including the retired population, and would effectively reduce their retirement benefits. Taxes based on nonhuman wealth or the return to nonhuman wealth (such as comprehensive personal income taxes) would also shift burdens toward older generations relative to a payroll tax. Reductions in public expenditures other than retirement-related programs (general social assistance, unemployment, education, and infrastructure) would shift fiscal burdens toward younger age cohorts. At a basic level, the fungibility of fiscal resources implies that age-related fiscal imbalances may be managed by revenue increases or expenditure reductions throughout the fiscal system. Furthermore, these adjustments may occur rapidly, but through the use of explicit and implicit government debt, they may also be partially deferred and thus distributed across generations extending farther into the future.

The laws of fiscal arithmetic dictate that some combination of these adjustments must take place, defining a menu of policy options. How the political process will ultimately select among these options is difficult to determine. Nevertheless, different models of the political economy of policymaking over time, even if not definitive in their predictions, offer some indications of the forces at work.

First, simple voting models, in which sheer numbers can be decisive, suggest that growing numbers of elderly voters could gain increased or even complete control of the political process, maintaining or even raising public-pension benefits while being certain that the cost of ensuring these benefits is shifted to some other population group (younger workers, principally). The political power of the elderly, it would seem, can hardly weaken substantially as they grow more numerous. On the other hand, voters in any age group have diverse characteristics and preferences and do not vote uniformly. Also, different interest groups or factions can influence policymaking not only through their impact on voting but also through the expenditure of resources on lobbying and pressure-group politics.

However political interests are represented and expressed, it is important to recognize that public expenditures and taxes are not lump-sum in nature and that, in general, those who benefit from a policy are subject to diminishing marginal benefits and rising marginal costs. In simple "reduced-form" models of the political process (e.g., Becker, 1983, 1985), observed (equilibrium) policies reflect a balance or trade-off among contending groups. Distortionary taxes that give rise to an increasing "marginal cost of public funds" can help to explain the limits on majoritarian redistribution at a point in time (e.g., Meltzer and Richard, 1981) or across generations (Barro, 1979; Wildasin, 1990b).[11]

To illustrate, consider a simple overlapping-generations model with a two-period life cycle in which the utility of retirees (the old) depends only on their own consumption while the utility of the working population (the young) depends on their consumption in each period (c_1 and c_2), their

---

11. As Mulligan (2001) observes, normative analyses of the optimal structure of second-best policies (e.g., in the tradition of Mirrlees, 1971) can thus provide important insights into the equilibria of political-economy models.

leisure (*l*), the level of education provided to their children (*e*), and other public goods (*z*), as represented by a life-cycle utility function $u(c_1c_2,l,e,z)$. Suppose that the public sector provides cash transfers to the elderly as well as education for the young, and assume for the moment that the government finances incremental expenditures through pay-as-you-go changes in taxes on the earnings of young workers.

Under these assumptions, one can calculate the change in the welfare for a young household resulting from an incremental change in the level of public-pension benefits. If leisure is a normal good and if the wage and income elasticities of labor supply are not directly affected by demographic changes, one can show (see Wildasin, 1990b) that a decrease in the number of working households relative to the number of retirees reduces the net benefit (or raises the net cost) to young workers of a marginal increase in public-pension benefits. In particular, if young workers are harmed by an expansion of public-pension benefits, they are harmed *more* when they are less numerous, relative to the retired population. If their political influence (through voter turnout, lobbying, or other channels) depends on their intensity of preferences, then aging of the population reduces the equilibrium level of public-pension benefits per retiree. Similarly, a marginal increase in education spending benefits young workers (i.e., parents) less, or harms them more, when there are relatively more elderly retirees in the society. The underlying logic is the same: an increase in the number of elderly, other things being equal, requires higher public-pension expenditures, raising the shadow value of public-sector revenues and thus the cost, at the margin, of incremental public spending of any kind at all.

This discussion has assumed that incremental changes in public spending are financed through contemporaneous changes in taxes on the earnings of young workers. There are, of course, other financing possibilities, notably including deferral of taxes through incremental deficit financing. The development of a fully specified model of intergenerational political equilibrium goes beyond the scope of the present analysis, but intertemporal tax-smoothing considerations imply that distortionary earnings taxes will be utilized in all periods. Thus, an increase in the proportion of elderly in the population, which raises political pressures to limit spending financed by the current young generation, would also be expected to result in some shifting of taxes to future generations through an increase in borrowing.

In summary, population aging and associated financial stresses on the public pension and health systems are expected to lead to adjustment along virtually all margins of fiscal policy. As total pension and health expenditures on benefits for the aged increase with the aging of the population, the shadow value of public-sector resources rises. This creates incentives to raise revenue yields from all sources and to reduce expenditures of all kinds, spreading the fiscal impact of an aging population throughout the fiscal system. Higher government borrowing and reduced spending on education and infrastructure offer additional degrees of freedom for fiscal adjustment, shifting some of the fiscal costs of an aging population forward to future generations.[12]

Migration and Fiscal Competition: A Simple Model

Let us now return to the potential role of international migration in the context of a process of fiscal adjustment. As is clear from the discussion of previous sections, economic and demographic fundamentals (levels of development and age structures) imply that powerful incentives for immigration from poor to rich countries will persist for at least the next several decades. The level and composition of immigration flows experienced by individual countries will depend on local economic conditions and policies, including direct controls over migration as well as fiscal policies. Nations have incentives to structure these policies so as to ease the fiscal adjustment process.

Generational-accounting studies show that if immigrants to rich countries have characteristics broadly similar to existing residents, in terms of income or its correlates (education, health, longevity, etc.), and if they immigrate at young ages, then, as native young residents do, they provide positive net fiscal benefits to these countries. However, some immigrants might have "better" or "worse" characteristics than natives, and, as empirical analyses show, the fiscal impacts could then be quite different. Poorer, lower-skilled, sicker, and older immigrants provide smaller net fiscal benefits to native populations and may impose net fiscal burdens, whereas better-educated, wealthier, healthier, and younger immigrants bring larger positive fiscal impacts.

Rich countries therefore have incentives to attract some, but not all, types of potential immigrants and to retain some, but not all, types of native residents. To do so, they have several policy instruments at their disposal. First, they may attempt to impose direct controls on migration.

---

12. Models of intertemporal tax smoothing highlight the gradual adjustment of taxes (and, implicitly, of other expenditures) in response to fiscal shocks. The financing of World War II through borrowing is the outstanding empirical example. The above remarks similarly treat increased spending on aging populations as a "fiscal shock" that triggers policy adjustments over time. Unlike the case of World War II, the gradual and predictable nature of age-related spending implies significant scope for anticipatory adjustments in fiscal policy. At a deeper level, however, it is interesting that the baby boom itself is a demographic echo of World War II. The bulge in age-related public spending associated with the baby-boom generation can thus be viewed as a further lagged fiscal shock triggered by that war.

Restrictions on emigration are seldom imposed or enforced, so, in practice, direct migration controls usually are limited to constraints on immigration. Although these constraints appear at first glance to be rigid quantitative limits, they can be and, in fact, are quite flexible, both because the degree of enforcement of any immigration controls is a matter of policy discretion and because immigration controls can be applied in a "textured" (or discriminatory) fashion, limiting entry for some types of immigrants but not others. Second, fiscal policies affect migration incentives, and these policies can also be altered in ways that influence migration. As in the case of direct immigration controls, fiscal policies can be adjusted in many distinct respects, creating the potential to strengthen incentives that attract some types of immigrants while weakening incentives for others. Note that fiscal policies can influence emigration incentives, even though direct emigration controls may be infeasible.

The literature dealing with fiscal competition provides a framework for analyzing the choice of fiscal and regulatory policies, and their interactions, in the face of actual or potential migration.[13] A simple model, based on this literature, can be used to examine some of the key policy questions that arise in the global competition for potentially mobile workers. To begin with, consider a snapshot of an overlapping-generations model in a single period, focusing initially on a country that attracts immigrants from abroad.

Suppose that national output is a concave function $F(L)$ of the effective labor force L. Initially, there is a stock L_i^0 "native" workers of type i, where i represents worker attributes, such as skill levels, initial wealth holdings, and other characteristics that affect workers' fiscal treatment. Let the initial effective labor force be defined as $L^0 \equiv \sum_i \alpha_i L_i^0$, where α_i is the effective labor supply of a worker of type i. Workers are young and are assumed to be mobile. (More precisely, *some*, but not necessarily all, workers are assumed to be mobile.) In addition, there is a fixed population of elderly, who do not work and who are not mobile. In order to focus on the effects of policies on the native population as a whole, assume for simplicity that lump-sum redistribution between old and young native residents is possible so that their net incomes may be aggregated.

Young workers may enter the country from abroad, with M_i the number of immigrants of type i. The total effective labor force, inclusive of immigrants, is then $L = L^0 + \sum_i \alpha_i M_i$. Let τ_i be the net fiscal contribution, in present value terms, made by a worker of type i.[14] National output is

---

13 See, e.g., Wilson (1999), Wildasin (1998, 2006), and Wilson and Wildasin (2004) for overviews of this literature.

14 In terms of Auerbach-Kotlikoff generational accounting, this is the current value of lifetime taxes minus the current value of lifetime pension benefits and other cash and in-kind transfers.

paid out partly to immigrants, with $\sum_i \alpha_i M_i F'(L)$ the total gross wages paid to immigrants. Gross-wage income for the native working population is $\sum_i \alpha_i L_i^0 F'(L) = L^0 F'(L)$, and total nonwage income, assumed for simplicity to accrue solely to native residents, is $F(L) - LF'(L)$. Thus, ignoring fiscal transfers, the aggregate income of native residents is $L^0 F'(L) + F(L) - LF'(L) = F(L) - (L - L^0)F'(L) = F(L) - \sum_i \alpha_i M_i F'(L)$. Taking the fiscal system into account, the net income of native residents is

$$W = F(L) - \sum_i \alpha_i M_i F'(L) + \sum_i M_i \tau_i. \tag{4.4}$$

To connect this notation to the previous discussion, observe that immigrants may make positive or negative net transfers to native residents, depending on the values of the fiscal variables τ_i. As discussed above, it is hazardous to generalize about the empirical value of τ_i because of the diversity of immigrants and of fiscal systems. In practice, $\tau_i > 0$ for highly skilled immigrants earning sufficiently high wages in the above-ground economy since they make large positive net fiscal contributions. Conversely, τ_i may be negative for low-skilled, low-wage immigrants who receive large fiscal benefits from welfare payments or health benefits. If immigrants are prevented from enjoying welfare or health benefits because of administrative restrictions, fiscal discrimination, or illegal status, τ_i could be positive even for low-skilled immigrants. The key point is that τ_i depends on the attributes both of immigrants themselves and of the entire fiscal system, including taxes, expenditures, and, not least, the regulatory and administrative features of these systems that determine effective eligibility for benefits and effective enforcement of tax obligations. (Note that policy reforms that allow highly skilled immigrants to move into above-ground occupations that fully exploit their skills can raise their fiscal contributions.) From a policy perspective, τ_i is not empirically given but is rather to be determined. This is the perspective offered by analyses of fiscal competition.

From the viewpoint of native residents, net income W depends on the numbers of migrants of each type and on their fiscal treatment. Suppose that migrants of type i can attain lifetime net incomes of $\bar{w}_i$ in their home countries and that no rich country's policies affect $\bar{w}_i$. In the absence of any restraints on migration, net incomes for migrants in source and destination countries tend toward equality:

$$\bar{w}_i = \alpha_i F'(L) - \tau_i, \tag{4.5}$$

assuming that $M_i > 0$. If direct regulatory constraints on immigration through limitations on employment permits, visas, and so on, are feasible and are binding, then

$$\bar{w}_i < \alpha_i F'(L) - \tau_i, \tag{4.6}$$

where, in this case, the level of immigration is effectively constrained by the regulatory limit $\bar{M}_i$ so that $M_i = \bar{M}_i$.

This simple model illuminates how policies can be used to advance the interests of native residents, as described by the simple welfare indicator W. Note first that $dW/\bar{M}_i = \alpha_i F''(L) + \tau_i > 0$ if $\tau_i > 0$ and if immigration controls are binding. That is, it is advantageous to native residents to relax binding immigration constraints on migrants who make positive net fiscal contributions. Even if $\tau_i > 0$, it is still possible that relaxation of immigration constraints could benefit native residents. If τ_i is sufficiently negative, however, natives would benefit from *tighter* immigration constraints. Within this model, then, there is a rationale for the imposition of binding immigration controls on some types of potential immigrants—those who impose large fiscal burdens. The model also shows why countries have incentives to impose *selective* (or discriminatory) immigration controls, allowing free immigration for those who are net fiscal contributors.

But direct immigration controls are only one margin of policy. The model also shows which fiscal policies benefit native residents. First, note that if immigration constraints are binding, then $dW/d\tau_i = M_i > 0$. The optimal policy is to impose more taxes on immigrants, or to reduce their fiscal benefits, as long as a binding immigration quota is in place (see Sandmo and Wildasin, 1999, for more extensive discussion of this issue). An immediate corollary of this result, however, is that direct immigration controls become *irrelevant* (nonbinding) if fiscal policies are optimally adjusted, since immigration controls cannot be binding if τ_i is sufficiently high, that is, inequality (4.6) cannot hold for sufficiently large τ_i. Equivalently, binding immigration controls indicate that fiscal policy has not been optimized. These two types of policies are thus highly mutually dependent.

To characterize optimal fiscal policy still more precisely, we may now ask what value of τ_i maximizes welfare for native residents in the absence of direct immigration controls. In the absence of immigration quotas, (4.5) must hold. It follows that $dW/d\tau_i = \tau_i / F''(L)$, which is negative if $\tau_i > 0$ and positive if $\tau_i < 0$. It follows that fiscal policy is optimized only when $\tau_i = 0$ for all i; that is, net fiscal benefits and burdens should be reduced to zero for all immigrant types.

It is not difficult to incorporate emigration into this model. The same essential conclusions continue to hold. Fiscal policies that reduce the number of net fiscal contributors harm native residents, while policies that reduce the number of households imposing net fiscal burdens are beneficial to them. The optimal policy is one that shifts τ_i toward zero for potential emigrants as well as for potential immigrants.

The preceding analysis is based on a highly stylized model. Some of the conclusions based on it continue to hold, even when some assumptions are relaxed, while other elements of the model are more critical. For example, suppose that immigrants cannot migrate at zero cost but must instead incur some migration cost c. The incorporation of migration costs has an impact on the amount of migration that occurs but has no effect on the basic insights of the model. (This is easily seen by noting that introducing a migration cost c is formally equivalent to raising the value of the parameter $\bar{w}_i$ by the amount c.) It can be argued, however, that migration (a *flow*) is a kind of stock-adjustment process and that migration costs are properly modeled in an explicitly dynamic setting. In a model that allows for sluggish dynamic adjustment because of mobility costs, many of the key qualitative insights derived above continue to hold, but some must be modified quantitatively (Wildasin, 2003). In particular, the optimal fiscal burden on an imperfectly mobile resource may be not zero but positive and proportional to the speed with which the stock of the resource adjusts to changes in its net rate of return. A factor that responds very rapidly—highly liquid financial assets would be an example (see Huizinga and Nicodème, 2004)—would optimally bear a zero net fiscal burden. But it may be optimal to impose significant fiscal burdens on resources whose stocks respond only sluggishly. Some types of labor and fixed capital investments could thus face significant fiscal burdens—up to and including confiscatory burdens, if these are feasible.

To summarize, competitive pressures provide incentives for governments to adjust tax and expenditure policies in ways that are "favorable" to resources that they seek to attract and "unfavorable" to resources that they wish to repel. In the simplest cases, this would mean, for instance, cutting income taxes on the rich or reducing welfare benefits for the poor. In a pure limiting case, fiscal policies would collect revenues from all households in accordance with the cost of providing public services to them; that is, no potentially mobile households would impose net fiscal burdens or be net fiscal contributors. This, of course, does not in any way imply that taxes would approach zero, any more than competition among firms implies that prices approach zero. Rather, competition for mobile households would reduce cross-subsidies or redistribution among households by bringing taxes (and public-sector prices) into close alignment with the costs of whatever levels of public services are provided. Limiting cases are not to be taken literally, of course. The general conclusion to draw from analyses of fiscal competition is that competitive pressures are likely to constrain fiscal policies, in the direction of reduced redistribution, for resources that are relatively highly mobile. In reality, neither the international movement of people nor the adjustment of fiscal policies occurs instantaneously. The adaptation of fiscal systems to international mobility, like their response to the aging of the population, is sure to be a gradual process.

Margins of Fiscal Adjustment with Migration

Let us now consider in more detail how age-imbalanced societies may adjust their fiscal and other policies, taking into account the potential for international migration.

REFORM OF PUBLIC PENSION AND HEALTH SYSTEMS. For countries with large underfunded systems of pension and health benefits for the old, young workers with high lifetime-earnings prospects are fiscally attractive. Workers at midlife with high current earnings and good health would also be net fiscal contributors to such systems. Others, however, would make only modest contributions or could add net fiscal burdens. At a time of fiscal stress, policy reforms that shift fiscal burdens away from desired immigrants and that shift benefits toward them would encourage fiscally favorable migration flows, while policies that work in the reverse direction would discourage them.

First and most obvious, benefit reductions at the expense of the current old population, by reducing the need for taxes on working populations, would help to attract and retain young, high-skilled workers. "Private accounts" or other reforms that reduce the amounts of transfers from young to old would have a similar effect. Caps on the maximum amount of annual "contributions" to the public-pension system and health systems or closer linkages between benefits and earnings, which limit *intragenerational* redistribution within these systems, also work in the same direction. The net fiscal benefit to a country of immigrants of any type would tend to converge under such reforms, as poor immigrants are *more* attractive when the benefits they receive are reduced, whereas rich immigrants are *less* attractive when the benefits they receive are made more generous.

However, while benefit reductions would help to restore fiscal balance without imposing added burdens on young and highly skilled immigrants, competitive pressures are by no means the exclusive determinants of fiscal policies. In countries with rapidly aging native populations and immigration of young workers, rapid reductions in pension benefits that harm existing retirees or those about to retire are disproportionately burdensome to native residents. By contrast, tax increases would shift more of the burden of public-pension adjustment onto immigrants rather than natives. In EU countries, voter participation rates (and rates of political participation generally) are considerably higher for natives relative to immigrants.[15] Given that there are already substantial immigrant populations

---

15. For example, a recent survey of voting participation in European countries found that 73 percent of native residents voted in the most recent national election, whereas only 36 percent of immigrants voted (European Social Survey, 2004). In part,

in these countries, political pressures might well favor tax increases rather than benefit reductions, because the former places more of the burden of fiscal adjustment on immigrants relative to natives.

Thus, whereas competition for internationally mobile workers would create incentives to address fiscal imbalances in public-pension and health systems through benefit reductions, native residents may also be able to shift fiscal burdens to existing (and imperfectly mobile) immigrant populations through higher taxes. An important open question for students of political economy is the relative importance of the market environment—in this context, the mobility of labor—in influencing the political process in favor of a group, current and prospective immigrants, who may not have the franchise and who generally have relatively little representation in the political process. The adjustment paths followed by countries with under-funded old-age social-insurance systems will shed light on the value of the franchise and the impact of market constraints on political decision making.

MIGRATION POLICY. As noted above, immigration controls can be and sometimes are used to achieve selective migration incentives, for example, to facilitate immigration by those with high levels of education, high levels of wealth, or other desirable characteristics. Restrictions on immigration based on country of origin can provide a complementary policy instrument. The United States and Canada already have such policies in place.

In western Europe, membership in the EU limits the extent to which individual countries can impose such controls on citizens of other EU countries; freedom of movement is one of the basic rights of EU citizens. As a practical matter, the absence of internal border controls also constrains the ability of any one country to limit immigration by non-EU citizens, since such immigrants, once admitted to the EU, can move relatively freely among EU countries. Of course, free internal migration (and capital movements) can provide substantial benefits to the residents of any large region—the United States, Canada, or the EU—by facilitating the market-directed movement of workers from low- to high-productivity employment, raising output and incomes.[16] The prospect of such gains helps to

---

this reflects varying levels of eligibility to vote: 33 percent of immigrants were not eligible to vote, in contrast to only 6 percent of natives. However, even among those eligible to vote, turnout rates were much lower for immigrants (about 0.50) than for natives (about 0.75).

16. In this context, it is important to note that *gross* rates of internal migration commonly exceed *net* rates by an order of magnitude, even at large geographic scales, and have done so for decades. Although (to this author's knowledge) no estimates have yet been made of the productivity impact of *gross* migration flows within the United States or Canada, the continuous interregional movement of workers, especially highly

underpin the commitment to the principle (if not always the practice) of free internal labor mobility, deeply embedded in EU institutions (along with the principle of free internal trade) since its inception.

Limited barriers to internal migration within the EU mean that the level of enforcement of border controls by any one EU country has important spillover effects on other EU countries, presenting a potential free-rider problem. If external border controls are effectively enforced, then the EU countries can collectively limit the inflows of older, low-skilled, unhealthy, or otherwise fiscally less attractive migrants. On the other hand, countries that fail to enforce external border controls have the potential to create significant fiscal burdens on other EU countries toward which such migrants would especially be likely to move. The instances cited above concerning the high welfare participation rates of poor migrants in Sweden, Germany, and Denmark illustrate the potential difficulty that a common border may create. (Italy and Spain are often characterized as conduits to the EU for illegal immigrants from third-world countries.)

Similar issues arise in the United States vis-à-vis state governments. The fiscal implications are far different in the United States, however, since state governments account for a very modest share of the redistributive transfers undertaken by the public sector; in the EU, almost all redistributional activities are undertaken at the level of the nation rather than at the level of the EU proper. Lax enforcement of border controls by some EU countries strengthens competitive incentives to limit social benefits for the poor. In principle, these competitive pressures could be eased by coordinated commitments by EU member states to redistributive transfers, to effective border enforcement, or both. Such coordination is not easily achieved, however. "Upward reassignment" of responsibility from EU member states to the EU itself—for redistribution, border controls, or both—offers a potential alternative institutional mechanism for limiting fiscally burdensome immigration.

THE WITHERING AWAY OF THE WELFARE STATE? Large flows of migrants from poor to rich countries testify to the mobility of relatively poor and low-skilled people. Many empirical analyses, especially studies of internal migration in countries such as the United States and Canada, show that skilled and well-educated people are also highly (and even disproportionately) mobile.[17] In addition to their public-pension and health systems,

---

skilled workers, is clearly an important part of the mechanism through which human resources are matched to employment opportunities. See Wildasin (2005) for further discussion.

17. See, e.g., Kodrzycki (2001) and Bound et al. (2001) for recent examples and additional references.

which transfer resources across generations, the fiscal systems of modern rich countries also redistribute resources from rich to poor. For these countries, poor immigrants (or residents) impose large fiscal burdens, while the rich make large fiscal contributions. The world's stock of skilled workers is a valuable resource for which rich countries have incentives to compete, while low-skilled workers represent potential fiscal burdens (or more modest fiscal contributions). The extent to which tax and expenditure systems capture resources from those at the high end of the skill distribution and transfer them to those at the low end influences the attractiveness of different countries for different types of migrants.

Competition for mobile labor may create political pressures for reduced redistribution through the fiscal system. Symmetrically, reductions in the amount of fiscal redistribution may reduce political pressures for immigration controls—specifically, for limits on the immigration of poor and unskilled migrants. In earlier (pre-20th-century) eras of migration, the "welfare state" did not yet exist, and most of the gains and losses from migration accrued to or were borne by migrants themselves. The distribution of the fiscal impacts of migration is very different in an economy where public revenues and expenditures approach one-half of GDP. In such societies, important economic impacts from migration are transmitted through the fiscal system to the rest of the population, which thus has a strong incentive to limit "unfavorable" migration, if possible. If fiscal redistribution diminishes, whether because of competition for mobile resources or otherwise, the fiscal payoff to the regulation of migration diminishes, and liberalization of migration policies would become politically more attractive.[18]

CAPITAL TAX COMPETITION. Personal income taxes provide an opportunity, if desired, to tax capital as well as wage income at the household level and to do so with a progressive rate structure. This means that a household's incentive to reside in a country—household locational choices—may depend on the taxation of capital income. To attract high-income households, a country could limit the taxation of capital income by maintaining a flat rather than progressive rate structure, by relying relatively little on personal income taxes and relatively more heavily on other types of taxes (such as payroll taxes), and by providing opportunities to escape taxation by rich households through tax shelters or special tax provisions that reduce effective tax burdens on capital. Since immigrants are relatively more highly represented in younger age cohorts, a disproportionate share

---

18. Recent analysis by Hanson, Scheve, and Slaughter (2005) indicates that public opinion toward migration is less favorable in U.S. states that provide generous transfers to the poor financed by heavier taxes on the rich.

of capital income accrues to natives at present. Relatively heavy current taxation of capital income at the household level might thus be an attractive feature of a tax system if competition for mobile labor creates pressures to limit tax burdens on young mobile workers. Over time, however, immigrants can be expected to move up through the age distribution, acquiring an increasing share of capital and capital income within the country in the process. Heavier effective taxation of capital income would not deter entry by such immigrants if these taxes are expected to fall in the future. If high current taxes signal high taxes in the future, however, then the opposite would be true.[19]

Capital income can also be taxed on a source basis, for instance, through corporation income taxation. There is an extensive literature that examines source-based taxation of capital income when capital is mobile but labor is not. Suppose, however, that both workers (or at least young workers) and capital are mobile. The complementarity of labor and capital in production then implies that they tend to move together—in fixed proportions in the extreme case where capital and labor are perfect complements but at least to some degree in less extreme cases. Fiscal policies inherit this complementarity. For instance, investment subsidies that attract capital also increase the demand for labor, and taxes on workers affect not only the locational choices of labor but the flow of capital as well. In the polar case of perfect complementarity, labor and capital make up a bundled composite input, and only the fiscal treatment of the entire bundle, rather than its component parts, would be relevant for migration/capital flow incentives.

This complementarity—of inputs and of fiscal policy—is often used to justify local economic development/investment incentives on the grounds that they increase the local employment, wages, or both. In the long run, such policies increase the incentives for workers to migrate to locations with investment-promoting fiscal policies. At the international level, the recent experience of Ireland may be cited as one possible example of such a process. A favorable investment climate in Ireland is argued to have contributed to that country's rapid economic growth and an accompanying dramatic reversal of migration flows. Ireland, which for long parts of its history has been an emigration country, has recently experienced a

---

19. Analogous issues arise with respect to value-added taxation. Falling VAT rates over time are roughly equivalent to declining taxation of capital income, implying relatively high taxes on old residents and lower future taxes on those who are currently young. A policy of falling VAT rates, if anticipated, could encourage capital accumulation and immigration by young workers who expect to accumulate capital over time.

high level of immigration, which, in turn, has helped to sustain the economic expansion (see figure 4.5; Barrett, Fitzgerald, and Nolan, 2000; and Barrett, 2002).

These remarks suggest that intensified fiscal competition for *capital investment* might be one facet of a process of fiscal competition for mobile workers. Most theoretical and empirical research on fiscal competition has focused on competition for a single mobile resource and, with some noteworthy exceptions, has not yet addressed the simultaneous determination of the fiscal treatment of multiple mobile resources through multiple fiscal instruments. This is an area of ongoing research.[20]

OTHER FISCAL-POLICY MARGINS. To take one final example of a possible margin of policy adjustment, consider the relationship between monetary and fiscal policy. High fiscal deficits create pressures for (nonindependent) central banks to monetize government debt. One response to the problem of funding public pensions would be for fiscal authorities to rely on debt financing of pension benefits, which could then be accommodated by expansionary (and possibly inflationary) monetary policy. A desire to avoid such outcomes is presumably the underlying rationale for the fiscal criteria imposed on members of the EMU: fiscal discipline enhances the prospects for a credibly independent European Central Bank, or ECB. However, low fertility rates could make it increasingly difficult for EU countries to adhere to the EMU fiscal criteria because of the problem of public-pension funding.

Expansionary monetary policy at the EMU level, on the other hand, could contribute to higher output, tighter labor markets, and lower unemployment in the EU countries. This, in turn, would raise the demand for immigrants and would contribute to increased inflows of younger workers. This could constitute yet one more margin of policy adjustment by which low fertility, the aging of the European populations, and associated financial stress on public-pension systems are partly addressed through increased migration.

20. Authors such as Bucovetsky and Wilson (1991) and Keen and Marchand (1997) have discussed the implications of fiscal competition for the mix of taxes and for the composition of public expenditures, focusing on the case in which there is only a single mobile factor of production. Wilson (1995) explicitly considers the case in which both labor and capital are mobile, showing how competition for these resources affects equilibrium fiscal structures. Redoano (2004) presents an initial empirical analysis of fiscal interactions among EU countries. Wildasin (2004) investigates how the degree of factor mobility (measured by dynamic speeds of adjustment to changes in policy) can affect the structure of a fiscal regime.

Global Inequality and Human Capital Investment

The time horizon for adjustment of policy in response to population aging is long. Over such a horizon, the global stock of skilled workers can and will change. If fiscal policies in rich countries adjust in ways that raise the net incomes of highly skilled young workers, the incentive to acquire skills will rise, both within these countries and throughout the world. As noted in the original "brain drain" literature (e.g., Bhagwati and Partington, 1976) the migration of skilled workers from poor to rich countries can deplete valuable human resources from the former. To the extent that the returns to human-capital investment in poor countries accrue to other nations, the incentives to devote public-sector resources to education may diminish. On the other hand, the incentive to devote private resources to education presumably rises. For students or their families, education provides an opportunity to work in rewarding environments, whether within the home region or elsewhere. Improved opportunities elsewhere, participation in the global market for skilled labor, raise the *private* return to education. Indeed, the well-documented persistently high rates of internal migration for highly educated workers in the United States and Canada illustrate that the option to migrate is frequently exercised, which is to say that the incentive to invest in education would be diminished, in these countries, if migration options were restrained.

Global competition for skilled workers, then, should raise the private rate of return to, and thus demand for, investment in human capital. For the rich countries, reductions in the amount of fiscal redistribution, to the extent that they occur, should raise the "net" education premium, the real income differential, net of all taxes and transfers, between skilled and unskilled workers. Supply response to rising demands for human-capital investment can occur through either the private sector (purely private education) or the public sector (purely public education) or through a mix of the two (e.g., loans, tax relief, other fiscal support for education that may take place partly at private institutions, and increased reliance on tuition and fees to finance education at public institutions). Public-sector support for education is frequently justified on the grounds that young people or their families face liquidity constraints that limit their ability to invest in human capital, a constraint that is presumably more severe in poor than in rich countries. Young people from poor countries now acquire skills and education both at home and abroad; rich countries at present provide significant public support for the advanced education of students from poor countries, resulting in part in return migration of newly educated workers to the latter (a reverse brain drain) but also facilitating the retention of some portion of recent graduates. Age-related fiscal stresses in rich countries thus give rise to complex interactions with the financing of education both in rich and in poor countries. In the former, an increase in the proportion of domestically trained skilled workers can produce a fiscal dividend, but public expenditures for education are likely to be constrained by the rising marginal cost of public funds over time. In the latter, the international mobility of skilled workers limits the return to *public* investment in education even as it raises the *private* return, presumably giving rise to incentives to shift toward increased reliance on private financing where the means to do so can be found.[21]

Conclusion

Extensive research by economic historians (O'Rourke and Williamson, 1999, and numerous references therein) reminds us that "globalization" is not a new phenomenon. The experience of the 19th century demonstrates that international linkages—particularly the international movement of labor and capital but also international trade—can have profound effects on economic growth and on the distribution of income within and among countries. International migration and capital flows today, like those of earlier eras, are driven by the desire of people to relocate themselves (through migration) and their resources (through capital flows) to locations with greater economic opportunity and higher economic returns.

While globalization is not new, there are some new things under the sun. In the realm of demography, we now witness fertility rates well below replacement rates in large regions, a situation without historical precedent. Low fertility rates and rising life expectancies must, in themselves, have important impacts on labor markets and fiscal systems in rich countries. Intergenerational transfers of historically unprecedented magnitudes in these countries give rise to tight linkages between demographic and fiscal conditions. Large international fertility *differentials* imply internationally unbalanced population age structures. When coupled with large and persistent real-income differentials between high-fertility and low-fertility regions, they create powerful incentives for international migration.

For these reasons, the economic impacts of globalization, and especially the integration of markets for labor and capital, differ in important respects from previous experience. International capital flows have received a great deal of attention in the public-economics literature dealing with factor-market integration and fiscal competition. The lion's share of public-sector expenditures and revenues are closely linked to population, however, and

---

21 For further discussion of the implications of labor mobility for investment in human capital, see, e.g., Wildasin (2000), Poutvaara (2001), Andersson and Konrad (2001, 2003), and Thum and Uebelmesser (2003).

the implications of international migration are therefore of especially critical importance. Of course, the international allocation of labor and capital are far from unrelated. This linkage means that tax, expenditure, and regulatory policies must be examined with an eye to their effects on *both* capital and labor allocations and flows.

Redistribution of income requires fiscal contributions, and fiscal contributors are scarce resources in societies with extensive redistributive policies. Skilled workers play a vital role in the fiscal systems of advanced economies and may easily be "worth their weight in gold," bringing fiscal dividends of substantial size to the societies in which they reside. Competitive pressure to attract such contributors is always present but intensifies as the shadow value of fiscal resources rises. In the context of migration, this competition can take several forms. More favorable fiscal treatment of highly skilled workers is one instrument at the disposal of governments. On the tax side, more favorable treatment may include reduced progressivity of tax-rate structures or increased reliance on consumption taxation (especially through VAT or other commodity-based taxes rather than personal taxation). Highly skilled workers anticipate high lifetime earnings streams and above-average wealth accumulation, and therefore tax burdens on them can be reduced through tax deferral or avoidance devices such as favorable tax treatment of capital gains, stock options, and closely held business entities. On the expenditure side, competitive pressures favor provision of public goods and services valued especially by highly skilled workers and especially by highly skilled immigrants.

One implication of such fiscal competition is that it tends to erode the fiscal dividends that new highly skilled workers bring to a society. In the extreme, pure fiscal competition among many nations tends to unravel redistribution among the owners of mobile resources, including skilled workers, at which point the provision of public goods and services is brought into alignment with taxes. This is not, or need not be, a "race to the bottom," either in the sense that it happens rapidly (a race) or in the sense that taxes and public expenditures are driven toward zero (the bottom). On a much smaller geographical scale, protracted competition among local school districts in the United States has not produced identical levels of local education spending and taxation, even in the face of extensive state-government fiscal policies aimed at reducing dispersion of local fiscal policies, and the quality—and expense—of some public schools in the United States is far from any sort of educational bottom. Competition does, however, raise the cost of redistribution, even as it may improve efficiency.

Policy competition for skilled workers need not occur only through fiscal policy. Regulatory policies—immigration quotas are the most obvious illustration—can also have a significant effect on migration flows. This type of competition is complementary with fiscal competition. In particular, nations have incentives to ease immigration restrictions on immigrants who produce large fiscal dividends and to tighten them on immigrants who produce large fiscal burdens. Existing immigration policies in many countries already reflect this principle, in that they contain special provisions for workers who have skills in "high demand," who have the resources and intention of starting new businesses, or who in other ways are distinguished by talent, wealth, and good future prospects. Long applicant queues for such workers are evidence that a nation may reap added fiscal benefits from targeted liberalization of immigration restrictions. Lax enforcement of border controls for low-skilled workers offers an opportunity for fiscal discrimination between high- and low-skilled workers.

In this setting, it is important to understand, on the one hand, how immigration can affect the fiscal systems of these countries. At the same time, fiscal policy can affect migration incentives and flows. This discussion has examined some of the possible mechanisms of policy adjustment that EU and other rich countries may follow as they manage the fiscal stresses imposed by aging populations on their fiscal systems. Public-pension reforms are one likely consequence of these stresses. Changes in the taxation of individuals and businesses, the provision of public goods and services, and redistributive transfers are also likely to play a role in the adjustment of EU fiscal systems to new demographic structures. The competition for mobile labor, in particular, may play an important role in creating incentives for fiscal adjustment. A deep and interesting question is whether existing institutional structures for policymaking are well adapted to the management of such complex, interrelated, and potentially far-reaching policy adjustment and, if not, how demographic pressures may ultimately play a role in shaping institutional change.

References

Ablett, J. 1999. "Generational Accounting in Australia." In A. J. Auerbach, L. J. Kotlikoff, and W. Leibfritz, eds., *Generational Accounting around the World.* Chicago: University of Chicago Press, pp. 141–60.

Andersson, F., and K. Konrad. 2001. "Globalization and Human Capital Formation." IZA Discussion Paper No. 245.

———. 2003. "Human Capital Investment and Globalization in Extortionary States." *Journal of Public Economics* 87, nos. 7–8: 1539–55.

Auerbach, A. J., L. J. Kotlikoff, and W. Leibfritz, eds. 1999. *Generational Accounting around the World.* Chicago: University of Chicago Press.

Auerbach, A. J., and P. Oreopoulos. 2000. "The Fiscal Impact of US Immigration: A Generational Accounting Perspective." In J. Poterba, ed., *Tax Policy and the Economy 14.* Cambridge, MA: MIT Press.

Barrett, A. 2002. "Return Migration of Highly Skilled Irish into Ireland and Their Impact on GNP and Earnings Inequality." In OECD, *International Mobility of the Highly Skilled*. Paris: OECD, pp. 151–57.

Barrett, A., J. Fitzgerald, and B. Nolan. 2000. "Earnings Inequality, Returns to Education and Immigration into Ireland." IZA Discussion Paper No. 167.

Barro, R. J. 1979. "On the Determination of the Public Debt." *Journal of Political Economy* 87: 940–71.

Bauer, T., M. Lofstrom, and K. F. Zimmermann. 2000. "Immigration Policy, Assimilation of Immigrants, and Natives' Sentiments towards Immigrants: Evidence from 12 OECD Countries." *Swedish Economic Policy Review* 7: 11–53.

Becker, G. S. 1983. "A Theory of Competition among Pressure Groups for Political Influence." *Quarterly Journal of Economics* 98: 371–400.

———. 1985. "Public Policies, Pressure Groups, and Dead Weight Costs." *Journal of Public Economics* 28: 329–48.

Becker, G. S., and R. J. Barro. 1988. "A Reformulation of the Economic Theory of Fertility." *Quarterly Journal of Economics* 103: 1–25.

———. 1989. "Fertility Choice in a Model of Economic Growth." *Econometrica* 57: 481–501.

Bhagwati, J. N., and M. Partington. 1976. *Taxing the Brain Drain*. Amsterdam: North Holland.

Bollinger, C. R., and P. Hagstrom. 2003. "Food Stamp Program Participation of Refugees and Immigrants." University of Kentucky Center for Poverty Research Discussion Paper 2003–05.

———. 2004. "Poverty Rates of Refugees and Immigrants." University of Kentucky Center for Poverty Research Discussion Paper 2004–06.

Bound, J., J. Groen, G. Kezki, and S. Turner. 2001. "Trade in University Training: Cross-State Variation in the Production and Use of College-Educated Labor." NBER Working Paper 8555.

Bucovetsky, S., and J. D. Wilson. 1991. "Tax Competition with Two Instruments." *Regional Science and Urban Economics* 21: 333–50.

Collado, M. D., and I. Iturbe-Ormaetxe. 2004. "Quantifying the Impact of Immigration on the Spanish Welfare State." *International Tax and Public Finance* 11: 335–53.

Coulson, B. G. and D. J. Devoretz. 1993. "Human Capital Content of Canadian Immigrants: 1967–1987." *Canadian Public Policy* 29: 357–66.

Dang, T. T., P. Antolin, and H. Oxley. 2001. "Fiscal Implications of Aging: Projections of Age-Related Spending." IMF, unpublished paper.

EUPHIX. 2008. "Old-Age-Dependency Ratio Projections (1st Variant) in Iceland, Norway, Switzerland, and the EU-27, 1995–2050." www.euphix.org/object_document/05117n27112.html

European Commission. 2005. "The 2005 EPC Projections of Age-Related Expenditure: Agreed Underlying Assumptions and Projection Methodologies." *European Economy* Occasional Papers No. 19.

European Social Survey. 2004. www.europeansocialsurvey.org.

Feldstein, M. S. 1974. "Social Security, Induced Retirement, and Aggregate Capital Accumulation." *Journal of Political Economy* 82: 905–26.

Gustman, A. L., and T. L. Steinmeier. 2000. "Social Security Benefits of Immigrants and U.S. Born." In G. J. Borjas, ed., *Issues in the Economics of Immigration.* Chicago: University of Chicago Press, pp. 309–50.

Hansen, J., and M. Lofstrom. 2001. "The Dynamics of Immigrant Welfare and Labor Market Behavior." IZA Discussion Paper No. 360.

———. 2003. "Immigrant Assimilation and Welfare Participation: Do Immigrants Assimilate Into or Out of Welfare?" *Journal of Human Resources* 38: 74–98.

Hanson, G. H., K. Scheve, and M. Slaughter. 2005. "Public Finance and Individual Preferences over Globalization Strategies." NBER Working Paper 11028.

Hoefer, M., N. Rytina, and C. Campbell. 2007. "Estimates of the Unauthorized Immigrant Population Residing in the United States: January, 2006." U.S. Department of Homeland Security, Office of Immigration Statistics.

Huizinga, H., and G. Nicodème. 2004. "Are International Deposits Tax-Driven?" *Journal of Public Economics* 88: 1093–1118.

Keen, M., and M. Marchand. 1997. "Fiscal Competition and the Pattern of Public Spending." *Journal of Public Economics* 66: 33–53.

Kodrzycki, Y. K. 2001. "Migration of Recent College Graduates: Evidence from the National Longitudinal Survey of Youth." *New England Economic Review* (January–February): 3–12.

Kotlikoff, L., and W. Leibfritz. 1999. "An International Comparison of Generational Accounts." In A. J. Auerbach, L. J. Kotlikoff, and W. Leibfritz, eds., *Generational Accounting around the World.* Chicago: University of Chicago Press, pp. 73–101.

Leimer, D., and S. Lesnoy. 1980. "Social Security and Private Saving: A Reexamination of the Time Series Evidence Using Alternative Social Security Wealth Variables." Unpublished paper.

———. 1981. "Social Security, Induced Retirement, and Aggregate Capital Accumulation: A Correction and Updating by Martin Feldstein: Comment." Unpublished paper.

———. 1982. "Social Security and Private Saving: New Time-Series Evidence." *Journal of Political Economy* 90: 606–29.

Meltzer, A. H., and S. F. Richard. 1981. "A Rational Theory of the Size of Government." *Journal of Political Economy* 89: 914–27.

Mirrlees, J. A. 1971. "An Exploration in the Theory of Optimum Income Taxation." *Review of Economic Studies* 38: 175–208.

Mulligan, C. B. 2001. "Economic Limits on 'Rational' Democratic Redistribution." Unpublished paper.

OECD (Organisation for Economic Co-operation and Development). 1999. *Trends in International Migration: Continuous Reporting System on Migration.* Paris: OECD.

———. 2002. *International Mobility of the Highly Skilled.* Paris: OECD.

———. 2003. *Trends in International Migration: Continuous Reporting System on Migration, Annual Report.* Paris: OECD.

———. 2007. *International Migration Outlook: Continuous Reporting System on Migration, Annual Report.* Paris: OECD.

O'Rourke, K. H., and J. G. Williamson. 1999. "The Heckscher-Ohlin Model between 1400 and 2000: When It Explained Factor Price Convergence, When It Did Not, and Why." NBER Working Paper 7411.

Poutvaara, P. 2001. "Alternative Tax Constitutions and Risky Education in a Federation." *Regional Science and Urban Economics* 31: 355–77.

Redoano, M. 2004. "Fiscal Interactions among EU Countries." Unpublished paper presented at IIPF conference.

Riphahn, R. T. 1998. "Immigrant Participation in Social Assistance Programs: Evidence from German Guestworkers." IZA Discussion Paper No. 15.

Sandmo, A., and D. E. Wildasin. 1999. "Taxation, Migration, and Pollution." *International Tax and Public Finance* 6 (February): 39–59.

Stigler, G. J. 1957. "The Tenable Range of Functions of Local Government." In Joint Economic Committee, *Federal Expenditure Policy for Economic Growth and Stability*, reprinted in 1965 in E. S. Phelps, ed., *Private Wants and Public Needs*, rev. ed. New York: Norton, pp. 167–76.

Storesletten, K. 2000. "Sustaining Fiscal Policy through Immigration." *Journal of Political Economy* 108: 300–23.

Thum, C., and S. Uebelmesser. 2003. "Mobility and the Role of Education as a Commitment Device." *International Tax and Public Finance* 10: 549–64.

Uebelmesser, S. 2004. *Unfunded Pension Systems: Aging and Migration.* Contributions to Economic Analysis 264. Amsterdam: Elsevier.

UN (United Nations). 2000. *Replacement Migration: Is It a Solution to Declining and Aging Populations?* New York: UN, Population Division, Economic and Social Affairs.

———. 2004. *World Population to 2300.* New York: UN Population Division, Economic and Social Affairs.

U.S. Office of Immigration Statistics. 2003. "Estimates of the Unauthorized Immigrant Population Residing in the United States: 1990 to 2000." Office of Policy and Planning.

U.S. Treasury. 2007. *Statistics of Income: Individual Income Tax Returns Publication 1304, Tax Year 2005.* (Selected Income and Tax Items Classified by: Size and Accumulated Size of Adjusted Gross Income.) www.irs.gov/taxstats/.

Wadensjö, E., and H. Orrje. 2002. *Immigration and the Public Sector in Denmark.* Aarhus, Denmark: Aarhus University Press.

Wildasin, D. E. 1990a. "Non-neutrality of Debt with Endogenous Fertility." *Oxford Economic Papers* 42: 414–28.

———. 1990b. "The Political Economy of Public Expenditure with an Aging Population," published in revised form in 1991 as "The Marginal Cost of Public Funds with an Aging Population." *Journal of Population Economics* 4: 111–35; reprinted in 1992 in Dieter Bös and Sijbren Cnossen, eds., *Fiscal Implications of an Aging Population.* Berlin: Springer, pp. 23–47.

———. 1998. "Factor Mobility and Redistributive Policy: Local and International Perspectives." In P. B. Sorensen, ed., *Public Finance in a Changing World.* London: MacMillan Press, pp. 151–92.

————. 1999. "Public Pensions in the EU: Migration Incentives and Impacts." In A. Panagariya, P. R. Portney, and R. M. Schwab, eds., *Environmental and Public Economics: Essays in Honor of Wallace E. Oates*. Cheltenham, UK: Edward Elgar, pp. 253–82.

————. 2000. "Labor Market Integration, Investment in Risky Human Capital, and Fiscal Competition." *American Economic Review* 90: 73–95.

————. 2003. "Fiscal Competition in Space and Time." *Journal of Public Economics* 87: 2571–88.

————. 2004. "Competitive Fiscal Structures." Unpublished paper.

————. 2005. "Fiscal Policy, Human Capital, and Canada-US Labor Market Integration." In Richard G. Harris and Thomas Lemieux, eds., *Social and Labour Market Aspects of North American Linkages*. Calgary, Canada: University of Calgary Press, pp. 489–536.

————. 2006. "Fiscal Competition." In B. Weingast and D. Wittman, eds., *Oxford Handbook of Political Economy*. Oxford: Oxford University Press, pp. 502–20.

Wilson, J. D. 1995. "Mobile Labor, Multiple Tax Instruments, and Tax Competition." *Journal of Urban Economics* 38: 333–56.

————. 1999. "Theories of Tax Competition." *National Tax Journal* 52: 296–315.

Wilson, J. D., and D. E. Wildasin. 2004. "Capital Tax Competition: Bane or Boon?" *Journal of Public Economics* 88: 1065–91.

World Bank. 2007. "WDI Online." http://publications.worldbank.org/WDI/.

Changing Policies and
Selection Criteria

5

Skilled Immigration to America
U.S. Admission Policies in the 21st Century

SUSAN MARTIN, B. LINDSAY LOWELL,
AND MICAH BUMP

Immigration policies are the mix of international, national, and local rules and programs that aim to facilitate the admission and integration of some foreigners and prevent the entry and stay of others. In this chapter, we present an analysis of U.S. policies on legal immigration, with particular focus on the admission of highly skilled migrants for work and study. As a partial consequence of the caps and bottlenecks on permanent admissions, as well as the growing global competition for the best and the brightest international students, temporary immigrant admission programs have grown. This chapter analyzes recent developments in temporary-high–skilled-worker policy and trends in foreign-student admissions. Recent downturns in student flows, although recovering smartly, have raised concerns and pleas for reform from representatives of business and higher education.

Highly skilled migrants should be seen, especially in a globalizing world, as an integral part of the nation's labor market for knowledge workers. Yet the decision to admit foreign workers requires us to readdress the issue of who is a skilled worker, an academic debate that goes beyond either the needs of this chapter or the practicalities faced by policymakers. Simply put, most governments define highly skilled migrants most often by setting tertiary educational minimums, as well as selecting specific high-end occupations (McLaughlan and Salt, 2002). For example, the United States' well-known specialty-worker H-1B visa must meet both a minimum degree requirement of a baccalaureate and employment in a list of targeted occupations (Lowell, 2001). The educational minimum seems self-evident, while occupation is important not only because, by its nature, it excludes workers

This paper, prepared for presentation at Council on Foreign Relations and Columbia University, March 4–5, 2005, was revised in June 2007 and April 2008. We would like to thank participants at the conference, Jagdish, Bhagwati, Gordon Hanson, and an anonymous reviewer for comments on this chapter.

with little education (say, from agricultural visa programs) but also because it targets skills that are desired. The highly skilled often include science and technology occupations along with other jobs that are in high demand, such as businesspeople, managers, teachers, and health-care providers. Such highly skilled persons are essential to modern society.

Indeed, policymakers and industry leaders are once again concerned about the adequacy of the science and engineering (S&E) workforce. Most of the architecture of the current admission system was set in place by the Immigration Act of 1965 and then revisited by the 1990 act with an eye toward streamlining and expanding skill migration. Much of the impetus for the 1990 act was based on evident inadequacies in the operation of the visas for temporary work, along with a belief that the United States faced imminent shortages of skilled labor because of slowing growth in the number of college-age persons. In fact, those projections turned out to be incorrect as increasing proportions of young adults decided to pursue college education, thereby increasing supply. And there was significant growth in the number of foreign students on U.S. campuses who, in turn, supplied a burgeoning postdoctoral labor force and frequently became temporary and permanent visa holders. But the booming new economy of the 1990s appeared to demand all of the highly skilled labor available, along with large numbers of temporary foreign workers. Then the job market for scientists and engineers, the occupations for which visas are primarily issued, was depressed in the wake of the recession of 2001 and did not start to recover until about 2005.

Today, it is somewhat difficult to ascertain the strength of future demand or the availability of domestic workers without immigration (Lowell and Salzman, 2007). The S&E labor market shows signs of strength with very low rates of unemployment, as well as weakness with sluggish wage growth. On the one hand, the Bureau of Labor Statistics continues to project very strong growth, particularly for information technology, which comports with the expectations of many observers. It is anticipated that today's knowledge economy has become ever more reliant on scientists and computer engineers. Many who hold to this projection also believe that the domestic supply of U.S. workers will not be able to match demand. On the other hand, the domestic student pipeline is healthier than often asserted, while globalization is leading to increased outsourcing of jobs. So an alternative scenario holds that demand for U.S.-based jobs may not be robust and that importing immigrants could depress the job market.

Regardless, it is asserted in a number of blue-ribbon reports that U.S. economic health and dominant position in global innovation are threatened by the lack of sufficient numbers of scientists and engineers entering the workforce. The primary causes of an impending workforce shortage, it is argued, are the mediocre preparation of domestic students in the educational pipeline and an ongoing decline in their interest in pursuing S&E

careers. To addresses the assumed crisis, the consensus recommendation of business groups, public-policy makers, and educators is to expand and improve science and math education from kindergarten through college and to court foreign S&E students and workers more aggressively. It is in this context that recent congressional attempts at immigration reform have incorporated substantial changes to the admission system for highly skilled immigrants. In 2006, the Senate would have increased the number of visas for skilled immigrants roughly fivefold. In 2007, the Senate contemplated a Canadian-style point system to cultivate a greater-skill admission system. Both of these attempts failed, primarily because of conflict over resolution of illegal migration, but reform of skilled migration will almost assuredly be on the docket for the future.

This chapter addresses the base from which any future legislative changes must depart and which must be understood for any intelligent discussion of reform. We first discuss the permanent system and so-called employment-based visas. Then we discuss visas for temporary skilled workers, focusing on the specialty H-1B, which has become the visa most often singled out as requiring a boost in numbers and streamlined processing. However, there are reasons to question whether demand for H-1Bs is such that the available numbers should be ratcheted upward without regard for domestic workers. We then turn to a discussion of foreign-student visas, which upon steeply declining post-2001, drew a lot of attention and formed the basis for widespread calls for immigration reform. However, putative policy failures did not drive the decline, and it is debatable whether further streamlining of student admissions is actually necessary. In short, the U.S. system already admits a generous number of foreign students and workers. Future policy reform should put more weight on transparency in the application process, improving the timeliness with which visas are issued, and target an optimal number of immigrants.

U.S. Admission Classes: Permanent and Temporary

Much of U.S. legal-admissions policy was formulated in the 1960s, with some changes in 1990 to reflect new realities. The temporary system of migration, rather than being truly temporary, often feeds into the permanent system, which can lead to naturalization and citizenship. Historically, the temporary system was relatively small, but today, the number of skilled workers admitted annually on temporary visas outnumbers permanent visas by as much as four to one. And foreign students, rather than being a world unto themselves in pursuit of educational credentials, have become an integral part of a probationary system leading through temporary visas to ultimate permanent status.

Permanent Immigration

During the 1990s, the United States admitted about 825,000 legal immigrants each year, up from about 600,000 a year in the 1980s (not counting those legalized under the 1986 amnesty), 450,000 a year in the 1970s, and 330,000 a year in the 1960s. During the first half of the first decade of the 21st century, admissions grew to an average of 1.082 million per year, despite a short decline in the aftermath of the events of September 11, 2001.

Permanent immigrants—green-card holders—are entitled to live and work permanently in the United States and, after five years, to become naturalized U.S. citizens. The four principal bases or doors for admission are family reunification (sponsored either by green-card holders or by naturalized citizens), employment-based, diversity, and humanitarian interests. By far the largest admissions door is for relatives of U.S. residents. In 2006, the last year for which there are detailed statistics, 66 percent of the 1.266 million immigrants were granted entry because family members already resident in the United States formally petitioned the U.S. government to admit them. The second-largest category of immigrants in 2006 (20 percent) included refugees, asylees, and other humanitarian admissions. Immigrants and their family members admitted for economic or employment reasons represented 12.5 percent of admissions, and about 3.5 percent came under the diversity visa category, immigrants from countries that had not recently sent large numbers of immigrants to the United States.

Immigrants represent a significant part of the growth of the U.S. labor force each year. Most of America's legal migrants (90 percent) are chosen because of family, humanitarian, or other criteria that do not consider labor-market factors. During the past 20 years, there have been persistent calls for shifting admission numbers from family categories, under which many immigrants with less than a high school education enter, to skills-based ones that attract more highly educated immigrants. In particular, reformists propose limiting immigration to nuclear family only.[1] Proponents of extended-family migration counter that admission of extended family serves not only humanitarian purposes but economic ones as well. Extended families often work or live together, strengthening the household economy of members who would otherwise live in poverty.

The employment-based or skilled immigration category is divided into five preferences, or groupings, each with its own admission ceiling. The highest priority goes to priority workers or persons of extraordinary ability, outstanding professors and researchers, and executives and managers

---

1. For example, the immigration bill pending in the Senate at the time of this writing would eliminate more extended family categories after clearing the backlogs and shift all admissions into a point system favoring education and skills.

of multinational corporations. The second group includes professionals with advanced degrees and workers of exceptional ability. The third group is other professionals, skilled workers, and a limited number of other workers; the fourth permits entry of religious workers; and the fifth includes entrepreneurs admitted for activities that create employment. Unused numbers in higher-priority groups can be passed down to lower priorities. Although there is an overall ceiling of 140,000 employment-based visas, Congress passed legislation in 2005 that recaptured 50,000 visas that had not been used in previous years to augment the number of visas that would be available in 2005 and 2006.

Not surprisingly, the employment-based immigrants are better educated than any other class of immigrant. More than 70 percent of those listing an occupation (that is, principal applicants rather than accompanying family members) are in managerial or executive occupations and professions (more than 80 percent together). In contrast, less than 30 percent of family-sponsored immigrants are found in these highly skilled occupational categories. Diversity immigrants, for whom a high school diploma is required, are at an intermediate level, with about 52 percent finding work in these two occupational categories. Refugees for whom there are no economic screens are least likely to have had high-skilled occupations (7 percent).

Most employment-based immigrants are sponsored by employers. There are some clear advantages to such a system. Not surprisingly, rates of employment among these immigrants are very high, since they already have jobs and, generally, a supportive employer. It is also argued that employers are the best judges of the economic contributions an individual can make. A checklist, as used in a point system, may identify would-be migrants with educational or language skills, but arguably, these individuals may not have other, more difficult-to-measure capabilities, such as an ability to work in teams, that employers find valuable.

Because the U.S. system is employer-/employee-driven and a job offer is essential, 90 percent of those admitted to permanent residence in the employment-based categories are already in the United States.[2] To hire a foreign worker as a permanent resident, the employer must undertake a recruitment process that meets Department of Labor (DOL) guidelines and demonstrates that no minimally qualified U.S. worker is available. Until recently, the wait for approval was several years. There were backlogs at both stages of the approval process: first at DOL and then the Bureau of Citizenship and Immigration Services (USCIS) at the Department of

2. Other categories include large numbers of persons adjusting status in the United States, including 55 percent of immediate family of U.S. citizens.

Homeland Security (which took over responsibility from the Immigration and Naturalization Service).

During 2007, however, DOL took steps to reduce the backlog of labor-certification applications, largely by shifting to a more streamlined process that approved most applications if the information was correct on its face. USCIS has also taken steps to reduce processing delays,[3] but applications are still subject to legislative backlogs resulting from category and per-country limits. Each month, the State Department issues a bulletin describing the availability of visas based on these numerical limits. In June 2007, while visas for most countries were currently available for the EB-2 class (that is, those with advanced degrees), visas for applicants from India were current only for Indians who had applied in April 2004, more than a three-year delay. Employers and immigrants have been frustrated by the delays and tend to use temporary visa categories, because they are easier to apply for and to bridge the gap between the decision to hire the worker and the government's grant of permanent-resident status.

Temporary Workers

Temporary work categories are increasingly important as vehicles for admission of foreign workers, particularly professionals, executives, and managers. Table 5.1 shows the major temporary working visas that are defined for specific employment purposes with different regulatory requirements. Each year, hundreds of thousands of visas are issued to temporary workers and their family members (Lowell, 1999). In addition, an unknown number of foreign students are employed either in addition to their studies or immediately thereafter in practical training (see below for more on foreign students). The growth in the number of foreign professionals admitted for temporary stays reflects global economic trends. In fast-changing industries, such as information technology, having access to a global labor market of skilled professionals is highly attractive. Also, as companies contract out work or hire contingent labor to work on specific projects, the appeal of temporary visas, rather than permanent admissions, is clear. Some foreign firms, understanding that it may not be possible to undertake an entire project offshore, obtain temporary work visas to the United States so their employees can complete the job at their U.S. clients' facilities. The temporary programs also give employers and employees a

---

3. Although things have greatly improved, processing delays still exist, particularly at the CIS Texas Processing Center, which announced in June 2007 that it was reviewing applications for I-140 immigrant petitions for skilled workers and professionals that were filed on August 1, 2003.

chance to test each other before committing to permanent employment. Multinational corporations find the temporary categories useful in bringing their own foreign personnel to work or receive training in the United States. Over time, a large number of different temporary-admission visa categories have emerged, each referred to by the letter of the alphabet under which it is described in the Immigration and Nationality Act. (See table 5.1.)

As with other immigration matters, there are trade-offs in using temporary-admission categories. While they may help increase business

Table 5.1   Principal Temporary Working Visas

Visa	Worker type	Descriptive notes (visas issued 2007)
E-1,2,3	Traders and investors	Under bilateral agreements (39,300)
H-1B	Specialty workers	Most require college degree (154,000)
H-2A	Seasonal agricultural workers	Dominated by Mexico, no cap (58,800)
H-2B	Seasonal nonagricultural workers	Tourism and other industries (130,000)
I, A, G, N	Media, officials of foreign and intergovernmental organizations	May include supporting workers and family (155,000)
J-1	Exchange scholars and others	Academics, nannies, physicians; few "workers" per se (343,000)
L-1	Intracompany transfers	Managers and professionals (85,000)
O-1,2	Workers of extraordinary ability or achievement	Scientists and others, including writers (12,000)
P-1,2,3	Artists or entertainers	Includes supporting workers (35,000)
Q	Cultural exchange and training	Small program for outstanding (1,700)
R	Religious workers	Includes international bodies (10,400)
TN	Trade NAFTA	Professionals from Canada and Mexico (admission or total entries 74,000)

Source: For the TN category, only multicount data are available from the Department of Homeland Security; individual visa issuances are from the U.S. Department of State, "FY2007 NIV Workload by Category," online at www.travel.state.gov/visa/frvi/statistics/statistics_1476.html.

productivity and even generate job growth, they also render even highly skilled foreign workers more vulnerable and may, thereby, decrease wages and undermine working conditions for U.S. workers. Generally, the foreign worker is tied to the specific employer who has requested the visa. Loss of employment may also mean the threat of deportation. Moreover, because the temporary visa is so often a testing period, the foreign professional may put up with any conditions imposed by the employer, fearing loss otherwise of the chance at permanent-resident status.

SPECIALTY H-1B WORKERS. In the Immigration Act of 1990, Congress imposed restrictions on the growing use of the H visa, intended to protect the domestic worker. Originally, the visa had no numerical limitations and few labor protections. In 1990, a numerical cap of 65,000 new H-1Bs per year was imposed. A numerical cap is intended to slow down escalating demand for foreign workers and encourage internal market adjustments that are in the best long-term competitive interests of the U.S. economy (e.g., increased training, better wages and working conditions, new technologies, or innovative production strategies).

Demand for the H-1B indeed continued to grow, largely reflecting demand for the visa by the rapidly expanding information technology (IT) sector. It reflected, too, the growth in supply of foreign-born IT graduates from U.S. colleges, the changed nature and appeal of the visa, and procedural backlogs faced by those who would prefer admission via the permanent system that make the H-1B an easier alternative. In recent years, employer demand for H-1Bs has been such that the numerical cap was exceeded before the year ran out.

In response, Congress has raised the cap twice since 1998. Primarily as the result of lobbying by the IT industry, Congress passed the American Competitiveness and Work Force Improvement Act (ACWIA). That legislation, beginning in October 1998, provided an increase in available H-1B visas from 65,000 per year to 115,000 per year in 1999 and 2000 and 107,500 in 2001. ACWIA was designed to sunset in three years unless Congress voted to extend it. However, Congress did not extend the cap in the wake of September 11, 2001, and, more concretely, the recession of 2001 and the "jobless recovery" that extended through 2003. The numerical limit returned to 65,000 for fiscal year 2002, but this cap was again affected by new legislation. However, the new legislation did not extend the progressive elements of ACWIA's labor-market protections.

As a trade-off to those who opposed increased numerical limits, ACWIA included new worker protections for so-called H-1B dependent firms, those most likely to unfairly exploit the specialty worker at the expense of U.S. workers. Dependent firms are defined as those with a certain percentage (about 15 percent) of their workforce who are H-1Bs.

ACWIA also had a requirement that H-1B workers receive the same fringe benefits as U.S. workers. The act required an additional $500 fee for petitions filed, since increased to $1,000, and provided for new investigative procedures and new penalties for violations. The bulk of the fee went toward the training of displaced workers and scholarships for low-income students. Employers such as universities and federally funded research institutes were exempted from the fee.[4]

While employers welcomed the increase in the H-1B cap in ACWIA, the numbers proved insufficient given backlogs carried over from prior fiscal years and ever-growing demand. By the end of December 1998, 59,108 of the 115,000 H-1B visas available for fiscal year 1999 had been used; 19,431 of the visas were issued to migrants whose applications were held over from the previous fiscal year, and 39,677 were new cases. Indeed, available visas under the cap ran out before year's end in 1999. In fiscal year 2000, the available visas also ran out, and the Immigration and Naturalization Service stated that it would process no new applications by midyear. In response, Congress once more passed legislation, the American Competitiveness in the Twenty-first Century Act of 2000 (ACTFA), which increased the ceiling to 195,000 and exempted certain categories of employers, particularly universities and research centers, from numerical limits.

Of course, subsequently, there was a sharp downturn in the fortunes of the IT sector and large layoffs in the dot-com industries and elsewhere. While concerns with U.S. security may someday improve data-gathering capacity, there are currently no data to confirm journalistic claims that H-1Bs are either the first or the last to be fired. One can speculate that temporary workers can be less costly or burdensome to employ in a risky economy, since the employer offers no long-term commitment. Indeed, demand for H-1Bs has remained strong but not at the levels seen during the economic boom. According to the U.S. Department of Homeland Security (2003), "During FY 2003, the Congressionally-mandated cap of 195,000 beneficiaries was not reached and about 78,000 individuals, mostly initial beneficiaries, were counted against the cap. The corresponding number for FY 2002 was 79,000."

When the legislative sunset occurred, Congress did not extend the higher numbers under the cap. As of this writing, the number has reverted to 65,000. Along with ACWIA's demise, the provisions for H-1B dependent employers and training programs were also eliminated. Demand did not diminish, however. Homeland Security announced that it had received 150,000 applications in April 2007 for fiscal year 2008, beginning on October 1,

---

4. In fact, under ACTFA (see below), H-1Bs to such nonprofit institutions were, and remain, exempted from the overall cap, and their numbers have reached 20,000 and more.

2007. Unsurprisingly, H-1B interest groups see the current cap as a constraint on employer demand for H-1B workers and would like the numbers to be significantly increased.

Foreign Students

Foreign students are an increasingly important contribution to the inflow of highly skilled workers, and their numbers have also been affected by recent events. Since its passage in 1952, the Immigration and Nationality Act (INA) has controlled the admission of foreign students to the United States (Wassem, 2003). Amended multiple times, the act admits foreign students on "nonimmigrant" visas, tying their entry to a specific purpose and a temporary period of time. The vast majority of foreign students at U.S. universities enter as F-1 visa holders. Smaller numbers enter as J-1 exchange visitors admitted for specific studies. Some F-1 students later work as H-1B specialty workers in postdoctoral or other academic jobs.

To obtain their visas, applicants must demonstrate to consular officers abroad and immigration inspectors at U.S. ports of entry that they have been accepted by an approved school or exchange program. They must also not be ineligible on the INA's grounds of inadmissibility, which include concerns about security, terrorism, health, and crime. As nonimmigrants, the applicants must also overcome a presumed intent to immigrate by providing proof of strong ties to their home countries as evidence of their intentions to return.

A DECLINE IN STUDENT VISAS AFTER SEPTEMBER 11, 2001. Following a period of sustained growth, the number of foreign students coming to America declined in 2002 and did not begin to rebound strongly until 2005. That trough in the supply of enrollees raised alarms on America's campuses and beyond to stakeholders who advocate for foreign students to supply business, science, and engineering jobs after graduation. Foreign students made up about one-third (35 percent) of core science, technology, engineering, and math (STEM) enrollees in the 2000–2001 academic year, with social science enrollees adding another twelfth (for a total of 42 percent). Those proportions remain roughly the same, even though there have been enrollment losses in the computer sciences and engineering, because enrollments in physical and life science have increased.[5] Foreign students make up roughly 4 percent of STEM bachelor's graduates, 28 percent of

5. At the same time, enrollments in business and other disciplines declined (Institute of International Education, 2006a).

STEM master's graduates, and 32 percent of STEM doctoral graduates (National Science Foundation, 2006). In short, foreign students are a significant share of the U.S. STEM student body.

While concern about the decline in foreign-student numbers went beyond STEM fields, the possibility of declines in STEM is thought to be of particular concern. It is echoed in concerns that the United States is losing its dominance in research and development, or in its trade balance, its stock markets, or its energy independence. Moreover, the start of this century is not only about the economic recession highlighted by this report; it is also about a pronounced expansion of globalization. China and India, in particular, are projected to surpass the United States economically in just a few decades. The European Union has pledged itself to rebuild its educational institutions and to boost its research capacity. Many observers argue that there are putative domestic shortages of U.S. students, while at the same time, they believe that the STEM labor force will continue to grow at a breakneck speed. Thus, foreign students are thought to be critical to retaining U.S. dominance in the evolving global economy.

The decline in student-visa numbers that followed in the wake of 2001 was dramatic. There was a 20-percent drop from 2001 to 2002 in the number of F-1 student visas issued and another 8-percent drop in 2003.[6] At the same time, there was a spike in the refusal rate for F-1 visas from about 25 percent of applications just before 2002 to 34 percent in 2002 and 2003. The number of foreign graduate students applying to all fields declined 28 percent between 2003 and 2004. Subsequently, the number of foreign students enrolled in U.S. institutions leveled off in 2002 and dropped by 2.4 percent in 2003 and a further 1.3 percent in 2004.

The recent downturn in student admissions to the United States has a historical parallel from the early 1980s. We know of no marked changes in visa processing at that time. Rather, the visa decline of the mid-1980s appears to have resulted primarily from a sharp economic correction. As is the case today, it would also appear that divergent economic crises and political events, in different nations and regions, contributed to the decline.

The decline in student visas in the early 1980s was very similar to the recent decline (Lowell, Bump, and Martin, 2007). After several years of very strong growth in student admissions, a trough followed 1982 and lasted six years. There was an 11-percent drop from the high point to the low point three years into the trough, and the recovery did not start until the fifth

---

6. The best leading indicators of student numbers are "flow" data such as visa applications or issuances. A reliance on "stock" or enrollment data, which respond slowly to changes, simultaneously indicates much less shock but also less incipient rebound.

year. The most recent decline in student admissions, after 2001, is similar in that it appears that it, too, will take about six years to recover. But the most recent decline followed in the wake of more modest rates of previous growth and witnessed a much steeper decline of 18 percent by year two of the trough.

ECONOMIC REASONS FOR THE STUDENT DECLINE. Economic conditions were the most obvious reason for the early-1980s drop in visa issuances. If economic growth falters, it is more difficult to afford studies in the United States. In 1981, 10 nations were the source of half of all student admissions. Following several years of exceptional growth, GDP in these nations fell 9 percent in 1982, with GDP remaining relatively flat until a strong rebound in 1986. Likewise, in 2000, just seven nations were the source of half of all students, but they experienced a sharp drop in GDP in 2001 of 7 percent. Of course, U.S. GDP growth also stalled during both troughs and resumed in 2004 in the most recent case.

Trends across groups of nations demonstrate that economic shocks and other factors also drove the recent changes. Concurrent events particular to each nation magnified the 2001 shocks. This was compounded by the fact that compared to the earlier 1982 trough, today's students come from fewer nations than in the 1980s. Some of the potential impact was mitigated because Korea, Japan, and Mexico, three countries that accounted for one-quarter of the flow in 2001, experienced little or no 2001 shock. But eleven leading and particularly affected nations with 30 percent of the student inflow in 2001 made up 50 percent of the decline of students afterward through 2003: China, Brazil, Turkey, Saudi Arabia, Indonesia, Colombia, Venezuela, Switzerland, Kenya, Pakistan, and Argentina.[7]

COMPETITION FOR FOREIGN STUDENTS. In addition to the effects of the economic decline, the United States faces more competition from foreign countries competing for the best international students. While the United States has traditionally been the leader in attracting the largest number of the world's brightest students, the global marketplace for international students has been on an upward trend for the past three decades (OECD, 2006). The number of international students jumped from a little more than 1.0 million in 1994 to 2.7 million in 2004. Much of the competition

7. These nations were among the largest source of foreign students, for example, in the top 75 percent numbering 3,000 and more students. Each listed nation's share of the decline in student visas through 2003 exceeded its share of the total flow in 2001. None of the other 11 nations in the top three quartiles contributed disproportionately to that decline; most experienced shallow or no drop at all (Korea, Mexico, etc.).

for foreign students is concentrated in schools where instruction is carried out in English, namely the United States, the United Kingdom, Canada, Australia, and New Zealand, which have had about half of the global international-student population.

America's competitors have made policies changes in three general areas:

1. Student admissions policies.
2. Student outreach and university marketing programs.
3. Retention policies to keep desirable students in the country.

Additionally, among large nations, France and Germany increasingly provide instruction in English and have redesigned their curricula to fit in with the more universal bachelor's and master's degree formats (International Centre for Migration Policy Development, 2006).

In some cases, changes in admission policies have been coupled with new and expanded marketing strategies. For example, in 1998, France simplified its student-visa procedures, and in 2000, the French Ministry of National Education announced that it would double the number of foreign-student visas made available. Some governments have created and funded NGOs to do their educational marketing while, others have carried out the task themselves (Institute of International Education, 2007). For instance, the United Kingdom in the mid-1990s launched a £5-million global promotional campaign to educate 25 percent of students in the global market in English-speaking countries by 2005.

While it is not marketing per se, the United States provides extensive programs for potential students (Schneider, 2000). The Department of State has 450 regional educational advising coordinators who provide information and consult with U.S. embassies, as well as extensive State Department ECA cooperative arrangements with NGOs and others. In the wake of the visa downturn, the State Department conducted an assertive outreach campaign that has been credited with helping to turn around perceptions of visa difficulties and unwelcome.

However, the federal government has not actively marketed U.S. education. Some advocacy groups believe that a government-run promotional and marketing campaign is essential to maintaining U.S. domination of the marketplace. Yet some university officials do not see the need, because their foreign-student admissions are built on the prestige of their institutions and on contacts among alumni.[8] Then again, most other national

---

8. We heard these sentiments from officials of top-tier universities during interviews with stakeholders undertaken for a research project during 2007 (Lowell,

governments have responsibility for higher education, whereas the 50 states and a substantial private sector operate in the United States.

In terms of student-retention policies, a number of countries have recently modified their laws to allow for an easier transition from student to worker, especially for S&E students. This is the case for France, Germany, Australia, and Canada. For instance, Australia recently amended its point system for admitting immigrants to allot extra points to students graduating from an Australian onshore university. Canada awards points to students who stay to work in provinces with skill shortages.

Arguably, by these standards, the United States has long had in place policies that have been competitive. There have been no caps on the U.S. admission of students, and visa requirements, compared with those of other nations, have been relatively straightforward. Indeed, no one in the current debate has suggested easing educational or English requirements. And while the United States has had no de facto retention policies, in practice, it has facilitated retention. For instance, all foreign students may take advantage of one year of practical training after graduation, and many students make the transition to the H-1B, which is valid for up to six working years. Furthermore, close to three-quarters of foreign doctoral students extend their stays to work in the United States.

Besides other developed nations, competition also comes from the source countries of foreign students. Many of the major source nations, such as India and China, are expanding their college-educational systems and are educating ever greater proportions of their growing populations. Their job markets are expanding, particularly in exporting, outsourcing, and high technology. Their college graduates may be more able to avail themselves of education at home and to find employment there after graduation.

There are at least four dimensions to consider regarding this competition to date and in the future. First, the United States is not equally in competition with other English or Western nations. More than 60 percent of the U.S. foreign-student population comes from Asia, and another 12 percent is from South America. Competition for Asians is primarily with smaller Australia, increasingly the U.K. colleges, and some Asian colleges. Only Spain has substantial numbers of South American students but less than one-third the number that are in America. At least half of the foreign students in Germany and other nations come from within Europe, while France or Belgium draw half of the majority of their foreign students from Africa. The market is heavily segmented, and U.S. competition is not so

---

Bump, and Martin, 2007). It might be the case, however, that some second- and third-tier universities would benefit from increased marketing.

much with "Europe" or transitional "Asia" as it is with specific host/source nations.

Second, many developing nations have markedly expanded their tertiary-education systems.[9] India tripled the number of its institutions of higher education from 6,000 to 18,000 between 1990 and 2006; enrollments more than doubled from about 4.5 million to 10.5 million during the same period (Agarwal, 2006). During the recent attenuation of foreign enrollments in the United States between 2000 and 2004, the percentage of the college-age population enrolled in tertiary education throughout eastern Asia and the Pacific increased from 9 percent to 19 percent; that in middle-income countries from 16 percent to 27 percent (World Bank, 2006). One can readily see that educational capacity is ramping up and that the pool of students is growing.

Third, econometric research indicates that increases in educational capacity in source countries, in the number of institutions and teachers, are likely to increase the flow of students to the United States (Rosenzweig, 2006). That is primarily because student migration is strongly affected by the promise of wage opportunities, not constraints in the domestic educational capacity of the source countries. Students from today's low-wage source countries appear to seek schooling in high-wage countries as a means of augmenting their chances of obtaining a high-wage job in the United States and other nations. In fact, increasing educational capacity prepares more students to seek education abroad; the research finds that an increase in the number of colleges and in educational capacity increases the flow of foreign students to the United States.

Last, a growing population of college-age persons should also translate into significant growth in the numbers of internationally mobile students, even if their migration rates stay constant. But the potential numbers will grow very rapidly if the rate of student migration increases as the research above suggests and/or if host nations aggressively market. In nations such as China and India, the majority of the population is younger than 20. The future will unfold a baby-boom generation of unprecedented proportions. For example, the UN projects that the Indian college-age population, 18 to 23 years old, is 125 million today and will grow to 139 million by 2015.

---

9. Not mentioned at all by those who decry a loss in the market share of foreign-born students is the fact that the OECD projects that the United States will lose about 4.5 percentage points of the OECD'S *total* college-educated population by 2014 (OECD, 2006, chart A1.4). It would be as quixotic to imagine that immigration could resolve that educational loss as it is to imagine that immigration can replace the growing number of dependent persons created by population aging.

PAYING FOR EDUCATION AND DECIDING WHERE TO GO. The decision about where to study is a complex one. Cost is certainly one factor.[10] The cost of an education increased in the United States between 2001 and 2005 because the tuition charged by colleges rose very steeply (College Board, 2006). At the same time, the recession undercut the ability of foreign students to defray their costs by working, either on or off campus. Unemployment soared, particularly in those occupations in which students found most employment after graduation. The long-running "jobless recession" and that poor prognosis for employment continued to be felt through 2005. Ironically, the fact that so many foreign students banked on jobs as temporary H-1B visa holders and on jobs in information technology, which were particularly hard hit after the bubble burst, undermined the attraction of studies in the United States.

A recession's major impacts may be on off-campus jobs, but it also affects academia and foreign students.[11] The parents of most foreign undergraduates are their primary source of funding, although many may work part-time to help defray costs, while perhaps most foreign graduate students work in one capacity or another.[12] Foreign students are permitted to work on campus and, after graduation, may choose one year of optional practical training (OPT) off campus.[13] Perhaps as many as half of foreign graduates continue on in the United States through OPT, but there are no readily available statistics, and the Institute for International Education has only recently begun publishing information on OPT. However, it is reasonable to assume that the proportions of students working both on campus and on OPT are nontrivial. Most graduate students, at least in S&E fields,

10. A survey we conducted of students who chose not to come to the United States indicated that the cost of a U.S. education was a major factor in their decision (Lowell, Bump, and Martin, 2007).

11. Paradoxically, native enrollments often increase during a recession, given the opportunity cost of schooling relative to unemployment. Even if the numbers of on-campus jobs are not heavily affected, there may be increased competition for those jobs.

12. Two-thirds of *all* foreign students report their parents as their "primary" source of funding, a little less than one-quarter report their colleges, and only about 2 percent report current employment (Institute of International Education, 2006a). These data do not differentiate by undergraduate or graduate status, nor do they tell us how many students work to supplement their primary sources of funding.

13. Students who face unforeseen financial difficulties, and when no jobs are available on campus, are permitted to work off campus. After the first year, students may also work off campus, but it counts against the year of OPT. Data on students working are not readily available. For rules and limited data from the Student and Exchange Visitor Information System, see www.ice.gov/sevis/numbers/archive/2004/3rd_quarter/index.htm.

work on campus before graduation and off campus thereafter.[14] Many students make the transition to another temporary visa or even a permanent visa after graduation or OPT.

The impact of the economic cycle on student numbers can be readily seen in its connection to the recession-hit IT sector. Foreign-student enrollments in the computer sciences dropped steeply after 2001 and continued to do so through 2006 (Institute of International Education, 2006b). Engineering enrollments were affected, too, but much less than computer-science enrollments. Perhaps the engineering students hardest hit were those planning to bridge over into a computer-related job, a not unusual outcome. The greatest declines by national origin were for China and India, the origins of students most likely to plan on these fields of study.

Pending legislation would not require the U.S. government to market itself as a student destination, but it would greatly increase its attractiveness. In the first place, an increased number of skilled-migration slots would make it more possible for students to become permanent residents. Also, Congress is considering lifting requirements that student applicants intend to return home and, in fact, would make it easier for the stay. Students with graduate degrees, particularly in science and engineering, are thought to be prime candidates for potentially uncapped admissions under future employment-based visas. Like the H-1B visa, the recent downturn in numbers causes considerable consternation and lobbying.

Conclusions

The United States remains a favored destination for millions of highly skilled foreign workers and foreign students, but its continued competitiveness in attracting the best and the brightest will require substantial changes in immigration policies and administrative mechanisms. An increasing proportion of highly skilled workers enter through temporary categories with little prospect of permanent residence within a reasonable period. The numbers involved are very significant, and the pressures that drive them are likely to continue in the near future. This is not simply an IT issue. Global transformations and ongoing record low unemployment rates throughout the economy have generated calls from several other sectors in the U.S. economy for more guest workers and immigrants.

14. About 7 percent of students counted in the United States in 2006 were on OPT, which is equivalent to half of all foreign M.A. and Ph.D. graduates in that year (Institute of International Education, 2006b).

At this writing, the Senate has failed in its deliberation of legislation that would make profound changes in U.S. immigration policy, including a new temporary-worker program for lesser-skilled workers and a point system to encourage high-skilled permanent admissions. It remains to be seen whether Congress will pass comprehensive reform or continue to muddle through with ad hoc responses to episodic economic and political demands.

When employers are asked, they report that they would prefer to sponsor permanent-resident visa holders (Lowell, 1999). The permanent class is preferable in terms of domestic safeguards, because the immigrant is a free agent able to negotiate freely and leave an employer if he or she so chooses. And permanent admission is core to the American tradition of successful integration; supplementing that tradition with large populations of floating temporary visa holders runs serious risks. Admission policies for permanent-residence visas should be flexible enough to respond to changing market conditions. Statutory ceilings tend to be too inflexible to permit rapid adjustment to economic cycles and needs. Market mechanisms to regulate flows—such as fees that make the cost of hiring foreign workers equal to or greater than that for U.S. workers or auctions—would be one way to manage numbers without ceilings. Another would be to assign a commission or task force the responsibility for setting numbers and priorities each year based on assessment of supply and demand.

Congress should also rethink what is required for a successful temporary program in the future. Under current law, H-1B workers may stay six years (or more, under new provisions that allow workers to remain if their green cards are under review), hardly a length of time that even the most casual observer would think of as temporary. If temporary-worker programs are framed as transitional programs, as is the case currently for the H-1B program, there should be a sufficient number of permanent visas to permit rapid adjustment to permanent residence. Otherwise, temporary-worker programs should be truly temporary and used in cases in which short-term employment is appropriate.

In the interest of greater transparency, visas for foreign graduate students should recognize that many intend to remain in the United States to work. The high rates at which foreign students obtain H-1B visas and/or adjust to permanent residence belie current legal provisions that preclude admission of those who intend to remain. Access to postgraduate employment appears to be one of the attractions of the United States for foreign-student applicants, and they appear to be attractive employees for many U.S. companies. U.S. immigration policy should recognize this reality and acknowledge that many foreign students indeed intend to remain after graduation. In addition, student OPT should permit two years of work authorization. Foreign students are now permitted just one year of OPT, while the regulations used to permit two years. An additional year of OPT would help students defray their educational costs.

Perhaps most important, national debate is needed on the role of immigration policy in fostering the competitiveness of the United States in attracting and retaining highly skilled foreign workers and foreign students. Some questions to address: Should the federal government provide subsidies or loans to offset high tuition and living costs and, if so, at what level of education (graduate and/or undergraduate level)? Should the federal government play a greater role in marketing to international students? What should be the relative balance in temporary and permanent admissions programs?

References

Agarwal, Pawan. 2006. "Higher Education in India: The Need for Change." ICRIER Working Paper. www.icrier.org/pdf/ICRIER_WP180__Higher_Education_in_India_.pdf.

Antecol, Heather, Deborah A. Cobb Clark, and Stephen J. Trejo. 1999. "Immigration Policy and the Skills of Immigrants to the Australia, Canada, and the United States." McMaster University, Hamilton, Ontario, April.

Beck, Roy. 2001. "Roy Beck's Numbers." In Richard Lamm and Alan Simpson, eds., *Blueprint for an Ideal Legal Immigration Policy.* Washington, DC: Center for Immigration Studies.

Borjas, George. 1998. "The Economic Progress of Immigrants." National Bureau of Economic Research, Working Paper 6506. Cambridge, MA.

Carnegie Endowment, International Migration Policy Program. 1998. "The Economic Progress of Immigrants." National Bureau of Economic Research, Working Paper. Cambridge, MA.

College Board. 2006. *Annual Survey of Colleges.* New York: College Board.

DeVoretz, Don, and Samuel Laryea. 1998. *Canada's Immigration Labor Market Experience.* Vancouver: Vancouver Centre of Excellence.

DeVoretz, Don, and Yunus Ozsomer. 1999. *Immigrants and Public Finance Transfers: Vancouver, Toronto, and Montreal.* Vancouver: Vancouver Centre of Excellence.

Duleep, Harriet Orcutt, and Mark C. Regets. 1992. "The Elusive Concept of Immigrant Quality." Paper presented at the meetings of the North American Economics and Finance Association/American Economics Association.

———. 1994. "Admission Criteria and Immigrant Earnings Profiles." Paper presented at the meetings of the North American Economics and Finance Association/American Economics Association.

Ellis, Richard, and B. Lindsay Lowell. 1999. "Foreign-Origin Persons in the U.S. Information Technology Workforce." Report 3 of the IT Workforce Data Project, United Engineering Foundation. www.uefoundation.org.

———. 2003. "The Outlook in 2003 for Information Technology Workers in the USA." Report 5 of the IT Workforce Data Project for the Commission of Professionals in Science and Technology, and the United Engineering Foundation with sponsorship of the Alfred P. Sloan Foundation, Washington, DC. www.cpst.org.

Green, Alan G., and David A. Green. 1995. "Canadian Immigration Policy: The Effectiveness of the Point System and Other Instruments." *Canadian Journal of Economics* 28, no. 46:1006–41.

Greenwood, Michael, and F. A. Ziel. 1997. *The Impact of the Immigration Act of 1990 on U.S. Immigration.* Washington, DC: U.S. Commission on Immigration Reform.

Harty, Maura. 2004. "Assistant Secretary Harty's Remarks to the Houston World Affairs Council," Testimony before the Houston World Affairs Council. http://travel.state.gov/law/legal/testimony/testimony_810.html.

Hawkins, Freda. 1988. *Canada and Immigration: Public Policy and Public Concern.* Montreal: McGill Queen's University Press.

———. 1991. *Critical Years in Immigration: Canada and Australia Compared.* Montreal: McGill Queen's University Press.

Institute of International Education. 2006a. "Open Doors." *Fast Facts 2006.* http://opendoors.iienetwork.org.

———. 2006b. "Open Doors, Data Tables." http://opendoors.iienetwork.org/page/28633.

———. 2007. "Atlas of Student Mobility, Promotional Activities and Policies." http://atlas.iienetwork.org.

International Centre for Migration Policy Development. 2006. *Comparative Study on Policies toward Foreign Students: Study on Admission and Retention Policies towards Foreign Students in Industrialized Countries.* Vienna: ICMPD.

Jasso, Guillermina, et al. 1997. "The New Immigrant Survey (NIS) Pilot Study: Preliminary Results." Joint Meeting of the Public Health Conference on Records and Statistics and the Data Users Conference. Washington, DC, July.

Jasso, Guillermina, and Mark R. Rosenzweig. 1990. *The New Chosen People: Immigrants in the United States.* Chicago: Russell Sage Foundation.

Kramer, Roger G., and B. Lindsay Lowell. 1992. "Employment Based Immigration: The Rationale and Politics Behind the Immigration Act of 1990." Population Association of America. Denver, April.

Lowell, B. Lindsay. 1996. "Skilled and Family-Based Immigration: Principles and Labor Markets." In Harriet Orcutt Duleep and Phani Wunnava, eds., *Immigrants and Immigration Policy: Individual Skills, Family Ties, and Group Identities.* Greenwich, CT: JAI Press, pp. 353–71.

———. 1999. *Foreign Temporary Workers in America: Policies That Benefit the U.S. Economy.* Westport, CT: Quorom Books.

———. 2000. "H 1B Temporary Workers: Estimating the Population." Report for the Institute of Electrical and Electronic Engineers. www.ieeeusa.org/grassroots/immreform/ h1breport.pdf.

———. 2001. "The Foreign Temporary Workforce and Shortages in Information Technology." In Wayne A. Cornelius, Thomas J. Espenshade, and Idean Salehyan, eds., *The International Migration of the Highly Skilled: Demand, Supply,* and *Development Consequences in Sending and Receiving Countries.*, San Diego: University of California Press, pp. 131–62, 2001.

———. 2004. "Demand for Skilled Immigrants in Information Technology: Following the Labor Market from Bubble to Bust." *Perspectives on Work* 8, no. 1.

Lowell, B. Lindsay, Micah Bump, and Susan Martin. 2007. *Foreign Students Coming to America: The Impact of Policy, Procedures, and Economic Competition.* Washington, DC: Georgetown University Press. http://isim.georgetown.edu.

Lowell, B. Lindsay, and Hal Salzman. 2007. "Into the Eye of the Storm: Assessing the Evidence on Science and Engineering Education, Quality, and Workforce Demand." Urban Institute, Research Report. www.urban.org/publications/411562.html.

Martin, Philip, and Susan Martin. 1999. "The Politics of Globalization in Germany and the U.S.: U.S. Immigration Policy." In Carl Lankowski, ed., *Responses to Globalization in Germany and the United States: Seven Sectors Compared.* Washington, DC: American Institute for Contemporary German Studies.

Martin, Susan, Philip Martin, and B. Lindsay Lowell. 2002. "U.S. Immigration Policy: Admission of High Skilled Workers." *Georgetown Immigration Law Journal* (Spring).

McLaughlan, Gail, and John Salt. 2002. *Migration Policies towards Highly Skilled Foreign Workers.* Report to the United Kingdom Home Office, London.

Migration News. 2002. "H-1Bs, Unions, Labor," *Migration News* 9, no. 1 (January).

Moore, Steven. 2001. "A Strategic U.S. Immigration Policy for the New Economy, Blueprint." www.cis.org/articles/2001/blueprints/moore.html.

National Science Foundation. 2006. "Science and Engineering (S&E) Indicators 2006." Appendix tables. www.nsf.gov/statistics/seind06/pdf_v2.htm.

OECD (Organisation for Economic Co-operation and Development). 2006. *Education at a Glance 2006.* Paris: OECD. www.oecd.org/dataoecd/46/0/37368660.xls.

Piore, Michael. 1979. *Birds of Passage: Migrant Labor and Industrial Societies.* New York: Cambridge University Press.

Richmond, Anthony H. 1988. *Immigration and Ethnic Conflict.* New York: St. Martin's Press.

Rosenzweig, Mark R. 2006. "Global Wage Differences and International Student Flows." In S. Collins and C. Graham, eds., *Brookings Trade Forum 2006: Global Labor Markets?* Washington, DC: Brookings.

Schneider, Michael. 2000. "Others Open Doors: How Other Nations Attract International Students: Implications for U.S. Educational Exchange." Maxwell-Washington International Relations, Syracuse University, Syracuse, NY.

Smith, James B. 2003. "Assimilation across the Latino Generations." *American Economic Review* 93, no. 2 (May): 315–19.

Smith, James B., and Barry Edmonston, eds. 1997. *The New Americans: Economic, Demographic, and Fiscal Effects of Immigration.* Washington, DC: National Research Council, National Academy of Science Press.

Trempe, Robert. 1997. *Not Just Numbers: A Canadian Framework for Future Immigration.* Ottawa: Minister of Public Works and Government Services.

U.S. Commission on Immigration Reform. 1995. *Legal Immigration: Setting Priorities.* Washington, DC: USCIR. www.utexas.edu/lbj/uscir/reports.html.

————. 1997. *Becoming an American: Immigration and Immigrant Policy.* Washington, DC: USCIR. www.utexas.edu/lbj/uscir/reports.html.

U.S. Department of Commerce. 2000. Digital Economy 2000. www.esa.doc.gov/Reports/DIGITAL.pdf.

U.S. Department of Homeland Security. 2003. "Fact Sheet: H-1B Petitions Received and Approved in FY 2003." www.uscis.gov/files/article/H1-BFY2003.pdf.

U.S. Department of State. 1994. Report of the Visa Office, Bureau of Consular Affairs.

Wassem, Ruth Ellen. 2003. "Foreign Students in the United States: Policies and Legislation." Congressional Research Service, updated January 2003. http://usinfo.state.gov/usa/infousa/educ/files/foreignst.pdf.

World Bank. 2006. "Key Development Data & Statistics, Country Profiles." http://web.worldbank.org.

6

Selection Criteria and the Skill Composition of Immigrants
A Comparative Analysis of Australian and U.S. Employment Immigration

GUILLERMINA JASSO AND MARK R. ROSENZWEIG

Many developed countries of the world are contemplating expanding the inflow of skilled migrants. The most recent reforms of immigration systems in Australia and the United States, for example, shifted from promoting family reunification to enlarging the flows of "skilled" migrants—migrants selected on the basis of job skills. Information is scarce, however, on how the design of employment-based immigration selection mechanisms affects the composition of skilled immigrants or on the determinants of skilled-migration flows in general.

Two literatures assess the determinants of the skill composition of immigrants based on national statistics on immigrants or the foreign-born. The largest looks at immigration flows from the perspective of the potential migrant seeking to maximize utility and relates observed flows of the migrants to home-country conditions (e.g., Borjas, 1987). This literature, however, chiefly because of data limitations, cannot distinguish between immigrants admitted via employment criteria and those coming through other channels, including by marriage, through kinship, or without any legal basis for immigration. Given that a large portion of flows to developed

Authors are listed in alphabetical order. The New Immigrant Survey research was supported by the National Institutes of Health (NICHD and NIA) under grant HD33843, with partial support from the U.S. Citizenship and Immigration Services (DHS), the National Science Foundation, the Assistant Secretary for Planning and Evaluation (DHHS), and the Pew Charitable Trusts. We are grateful to conference participants for many useful comments on an earlier version of this chapter; and we thank the anonymous reviewers and editors for their close reading and valuable comments. We also gratefully acknowledge the intellectual and financial support of New York University and Yale University.

countries with significant immigration are via marriage, for example, this work is not very useful for assessing the consequences of enlarging the scope for skill or employment-based immigration.[1] This literature also lacks a coherent and implementable method for evaluating how sending-country conditions affect immigration flows.[2]

A second, small literature looks at the different immigration systems of developed countries and attempts to assess their effects on the composition of immigration flows. A recent example is a comparison of the Canadian and Australian immigration systems (Richardson and Lester, 2004). This study was made possible by the recent availability of survey data on immigrants for the two countries that contains information on visas— the channels by which immigrants entered. The study, however, pays little attention to the decisions by immigrants themselves and thus ignores the literature emphasizing the self-selection of immigrants and the influence of sending-country conditions. The fact that Canada and Australia have very different country neighbors, for example, is not discussed. It is unlikely that even if Canada and Australia had the same selection systems, they would experience the same inflows of immigrants. The fundamental problem is that there are essentially two observations in the study—one for Canada and one for Australia—and many differing characteristics of their selection systems, domestic labor market conditions, and neighbor characteristics. Identification of immigration system effects therefore seems unlikely if immigrant self-selection is taken into account.

In this chapter, we look at employment-based immigration flows to Australia and the United States using data from the first round of the most recent Australian survey of legal immigrants, the second cohort of the Longitudinal Survey of Immigrants to Australia (LSIA2), and the first round of the U.S. New Immigrant Survey (NIS) 2003 cohort, merged with sending-country characteristics. The survey data sets provide information on visa class, thus permitting the identification of those immigrants screened on the basis of employment skills. The hypothesis we test is that sending-country conditions and, thus, immigrant self-selection on the basis of economic gain dominate in determining the skill composition of *employment* immigrants. To carry this out, we develop an empirically tractable framework for examining the determinants of immigration flows for employment immigrants. We emphasize that key determinants of the size

1. The most recent surveys of legal immigrants to Australia and the United States indicate that 45 and 34 percent, respectively, of adult immigrants immigrated by marrying a receiving-country citizen. On marriage and migration, see also Jasso and Rosenzweig (1990a).

2. Borjas's study (1987) is empirically unsuccessful in identifying immigrant self-selection based on the model used. See also Jasso and Rosenzweig (1990b).

and skill composition of immigrant flows are how skills are priced in different countries and proximity. Thus, who a receiving country's neighbors are matters substantially more than tweaks to selection mechanisms.

Many have argued about the relative merits of an immigrant selection system based on points awarded for selected immigrant characteristics, such as in Australia and Canada, versus the U.S. system of preferences (e.g., Martin, 2004). This argument has essentially taken place without any evidence. Moreover, closer inspection of the Australian and U.S. systems for choosing employment-based immigrants suggests that there is not a fundamental difference between them. Both award visas on the basis of petitions by domestic employers for workers in particular occupations, and both are attentive in part to schooling (as will be seen below, some applicants can self-petition). The Australian system attempts through the point system to fine-tune the flow somewhat, paying a bit more attention to schooling and using a schooling floor.[3]

In the first section of the chapter, we review briefly the current selection systems for employment and skill-based immigration in Australia and the United States, showing that they contain the same essential elements but with some differences in screening. The second section describes the Australian and U.S. data on new immigrants and presents descriptive statistics on the schooling distributions of employment immigrants in the two countries based on the survey data. These show that the average schooling of Australian employment immigrants is higher than that of U.S. employment immigrants. However, the same is also true for marital immigrants in the two countries. And there is little evidence that even the English-language requirements for employment immigrants in Australia and the absence of such a requirement in the U.S. system matter in terms of the observed initial English capabilities of the immigrants. These facts suggest that factors affecting immigrant self-selection are at play. In the third section, we develop the framework of immigrant self-selection with focus on the private gains from migration for agents with differing skills based on differences in the prices of skill across countries and differing migration costs. We then show how country-specific skill prices can be identified with existing data to implement the model. The fourth section contains the econometric estimation of world skill prices based on data from the NIS Pilot survey on the home-country wages of U.S. immigrants combined with home-country information on aggregate economic characteristics that affect the home-country skill price. In the fifth section, we use the estimates to show how the skill prices of the different country

3. The U.S. Select Commission on Immigration and Refugee Policy considered the option of a point system and did not recommend it, as discussed in Jasso (1988).

neighbors of Australia and the United States differ and how the country mix of employment immigrants relative to marital immigrants differs across the two countries with respect to skill price and proximity.

Finally, we implement the model, estimating the determinants of the size and average schooling level of employment-immigration flows to the two countries. There are five principal findings:

1. Higher skill prices in sending countries decrease the number of immigrants but increase their average schooling.

2. Countries that are more distant send fewer but more highly skilled immigrants.

3. Given skill prices and proximity, countries with higher income send more immigrants, of lower skill.

4. Within a sending country, Australia attracts fewer total but higher-skill migrants than the United States. This can be attributed, however, to the fact that the skill price in Australia is lower than the U.S. skill price, so that immigration gains are greater from immigrating to the United States.

5. The estimated coefficients determining migration flows to Australia and the United States are the same for both countries.

We conclude that geography matters in the sense that who a country's neighbors are, in terms of their level and type of development, has a significant effect on the size and skill composition of employment migrants. There is no evidence that the differences in the selection mechanism used to screen employment migrants in the two countries play a significant role in affecting the characteristics of skill migration.

Employment Immigrant Selection Systems in Australia and the United States: A Brief Overview

At first glance, the United States and Australia appear to have very different systems for admitting immigrants based on employment. The United States follows the preference-category system, in which employment-based visas are allocated via five preference categories, ranging from "priority workers," the first preference, which includes three subcategories (the world-class extraordinary-ability subcategory, a subcategory for outstanding professors and researchers, and a subcategory for multinational executives) to the fifth preference, a category for investors. In all but the fourth and fifth preference categories, filing is by an employer, except for first-preference "aliens with extraordinary ability" and second-preference immigrants with a "national interest" waiver, who may petition for themselves. Australia follows a point system, in which there is a set of basic minimal requirements, and points are assigned for characteristics such as age, occupation, and Australian schooling. Every immigrant must meet a points threshold.

Moreover, the two countries appear to differ somewhat in the balance of emphasis between inputs (such as schooling) and outcomes (such as occupational and financial achievement). The U.S. system gives somewhat short shrift to inputs and places great weight on outcomes. For example, eligibility for the top subcategory of the top preference category—"aliens with extraordinary ability"—is established by providing either evidence of a major internationally recognized award or three out of 10 kinds of evidence, which include prizes, publications, sitting on panels that judge the work of others, artistic exhibitions, and high salary or commercial success in the arts, and which, significantly, do not include educational credentials (Form I-140). Similarly, the requirements for a second-preference visa based on "exceptional ability in the sciences, arts, or business," while including educational credentials as one of the six types of evidence of which three must be presented (Form I-140), nonetheless explicitly exclude educational credentials for the subset of applicants with "exceptional ability in the sciences or arts" eligible for the blanket Schedule A certification for Group II occupations: "An alien, however, need not have studied at a college or university in order to qualify for the Group II occupation" (20 CFR, part 656.5, e-CFR retrieved May 14, 2008).

In contrast, the Australian system appears to have a greater regard for inputs, stipulating age (prospective immigrants must be younger than 45), schooling (postsecondary education, such as university or trade, is required), and skills assessment (carried out by official authorities). Points are then conferred for particular levels of several characteristics: age, skill, English language, specific work experience, occupation in demand (or job offer), Australian qualifications, intended residence, and spouse skills. Age is negatively rewarded (18 to 29 years, 30 points; 30 to 34 years, 25 points; 35 to 39 years, 20 points; 40 to 44 years, 15 points). Skill points are awarded based on a combination of schooling and occupation: 60 points for an occupation with associated specific training (such as a degree or trade certificate), although in some cases, experience can substitute for training; 50 points for general professional occupations, combined with a bachelor's degree or higher, but one that need not be related to the occupation; and 40 points for a general skilled occupation (to which the requisite diploma or advanced diploma need not be related). There is no mention of achievements as in the United States—no publications, professional associations, awards, sitting on panels that judge the work of others, or financial success. Further, extra points are conferred if the intended occupation is in demand (15 points plus 5 points if the prospective immigrant also has a job offer in that occupation); occupations in demand include a mix of highly skilled and less skilled occupations, such as obstetricians, welders, hairdressers, and furniture upholsterers.

In large degree, however, the systems are similar. Australia has a list of occupations that qualify an immigrant and excludes others; this pertains to all immigrants. The U.S. system for the second- and third-preference categories requires labor certification, which is tantamount to requiring that immigrants have an occupation on an approved list. Although education is not emphasized in the U.S. system, there are categories that qualify persons based on educational qualifications, subject to having an approved occupation. Moreover, the effects of the difference in emphasis on performance and inputs depend on the real-world correlation between inputs and outcomes. If the link between inputs and outcomes is tight, then the two systems may differ in style but not in substance. There are some notable specific differences in the list of approved or desired occupations, however. In Australia, all of the major medical specialties are in demand (pathology, surgery, psychiatry, radiology, etc.). In the United States, physicians are not eligible for employment-based visas unless they were already practicing in the United States in 1978 or they sign up to practice in an underserved geographic area or a U.S. Department of Veterans Affairs facility for a total of five years out of a six-year period (in this case, they are eligible for second-preference visas). Fundamentally (setting aside physicians and perhaps age requirements), outstanding professors and researchers, outstanding athletes and artists, and a variety of skilled professionals all find their way in both systems. Even those with low levels of schooling can immigrate under each system, in the United States because schooling is not a necessary qualification for all categories, in Australia because exceptions are granted on a variety of grounds. Neither country will likely turn away an exceptional cinematographer or stunt person with a third-grade education.

The LSIA2 and the NIS

Survey Frames

The LSIA2 (Wave 1) and the NIS-2003 (Round 1) provide comparable information on a probability sample of new immigrants.[4] The characteristics of the populations represented mainly reflect in-migration and admission

---

4. For a comprehensive overview of the LSIA project, see Hugo (in press). Brief overviews of the NIS project may be found in Jasso (2008) and Jasso et al. (2003); for a comprehensive overview, see Jasso et al. (in press).

decisions, as they are little affected by emigration selectivity.[5] Both surveys also sampled from records of new immigrants and then attempted to find and interview the sampled respondents, so that the sources of initial sample attrition are comparable. The LSIA2 sampled approximately 10 percent of primary applicants (those whose characteristics determined entry eligibility) age 15 and older who became new immigrants and who entered Australia in the one-year period from September 1999 to August 2000. The adult sample portion of the NIS-2003 sampled 4.3 percent of all persons 18 and older who were admitted as permanent resident aliens, including principal applicants (comparable to Australia's "primary" applicants) and accompanying spouses in the seven-month period from May through November 2003. Both surveys oversampled primary- or principal-applicant employment immigrants, the groups that are compared in this analysis.

There are two design differences across the two surveys that should be kept in mind in comparing "new" Australian and U.S. immigrants using the two data sets. First, the LSIA2 sampled only new-arrival immigrants, those who were outside of Australia before being admitted, while the NIS sampled all immigrants who attained legal permanent residence, including those who adjusted their status and were thus already residing in the United States.[6] The NIS permits comparison of adjustees and new arrivals. A second difference in design is that new immigrants who were not residing in Australia during the survey period were not included in the LSIA2. The NIS surveyed new immigrants regardless of their residence (although modified instruments were used for the overseas respondents). In the LSIA2, 15.5 percent of survey-eligible immigrants were not interviewed, because they were residing outside Australia at the time of the survey. Finally, as in all surveys, both the LSIA2 and the NIS were unable to interview all sampled respondents. Because the eligible population, based on immigrant records in both surveys, is known, preinterview loss can be computed accurately for both surveys. For the LSIA2, the loss is 41 percent, including exclusions based on sample design; for the

5. Of course, the evaluation of a selection system should be attentive to who among the immigrants stays. This will be possible once the second wave of the NIS-2003 survey is completed. The LSIA2 already has resurveyed the initial 1999–2000 cohort. Assessments of the skill composition of populations of the foreign-born in census data cannot distinguish between immigration and emigration selectivity.

6. Many Australian new-arrival immigrants had been to Australia before immigrating but were not already living there immediately before obtaining their immigrant status. Similarly, many new-arrival U.S. immigrants had been to the United States before, and some were, in fact, already living in the United States but, for reasons rooted in U.S. immigration law and policy, applying from abroad.

NIS-2003, it is 31.4 percent.[7] Sample size for the LSIA2 is 3,124; that for the NIS-2003 adults is 8,573.

In this analysis we look at the immigrants selected on the basis of their employment or skill characteristics. These include the primary-applicant "skilled" Australian sponsored immigrants, employer-nominated immigrants, and independent immigrants. For the NIS, the comparable group consists of the principal applicants in the employment-category preferences, as discussed above. The "skilled" immigrant Australian sample size is 832; that for the NIS is 1,369. Because only 29 percent of the U.S. employment immigrants were new arrivals, we do not exclude adjustees from the U.S. sample. Adjustee status is likely to directly affect employment status, earnings, and English-language skill.[8] Accordingly, we focus our attention on the schooling of the immigrant, which is a more permanent skill characteristic.

Comparison of the Skill Distribution of Australian and U.S. Skilled Immigrants

The Australian and U.S. systems for selecting employment or skilled immigrants, as noted, are dissimilar in many ways, with the Australian system in particular appearing to screen more precisely on skill characteristics. The schooling-attainment differences across the two skill groups appear to be consistent with this: average schooling among the Australian skilled immigrants is 16.1 years; that for their U.S. counterparts is 15.5 years. Figure 6.1 provides the distribution of schooling for the two groups based on the categories used in the LSIA2 (and the only available schooling information). As can be seen, although there is a slightly higher proportion of postgraduates among the Australian skilled immigrants (38.1 percent versus 37.5 percent), the major difference between the Australian and U.S. immigrants in the skill category is in the proportion of immigrants with less than 12 years of schooling. Among Australian skilled

7. The latter rate is comparable to that of contemporary surveys carried out in developed countries.

8. Eleven percent of Australian employment immigrants were unemployed at the time of the survey. This relatively high rate of unemployment would also make an analysis of earnings problematical. New-arrival employment immigrants in the United States had an unemployment rate of less than 5 percent. This may reflect the differing labor-market conditions in the two countries, the job-offer requirement of U.S. immigration law, or the U.S. residence of new-arrival immigrants. By examining schooling, we can ignore the direct effect of domestic labor-market conditions.

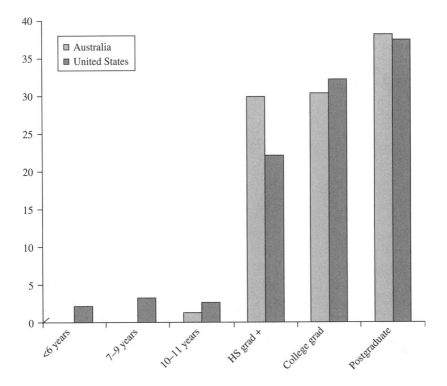

Figure 6.1 Schooling attainment of employment immigrants, by country.

immigrants, less than 1.5 percent did not complete high school, while over 8.2% of the U.S. employment immigrants did not graduate from high school.

There is no question that the availability of skill/employment visas attracts higher-skill immigrants. Figure 6.2 displays the education distribution for marital immigrants—those who obtain a visa by marrying a citizen and who are not screened on the basis of skill or employability— in the Australian and U.S. samples. As can be seen, educational attainment is considerably lower in both countries for marital compared with skilled immigrants. Average schooling for marital immigrants in Australia is 13.2 years (12.9 in the United States), with less than 10 percent (U.S. 12 percent) having postgraduate training and more than 19 percent (U.S. 26 percent) not receiving a high school diploma. It is interesting that there are more lower-schooled U.S. marital and skilled immigrants than there are among their Australian counterparts. Given that neither immigration system screens schooling in the marital category, this suggests

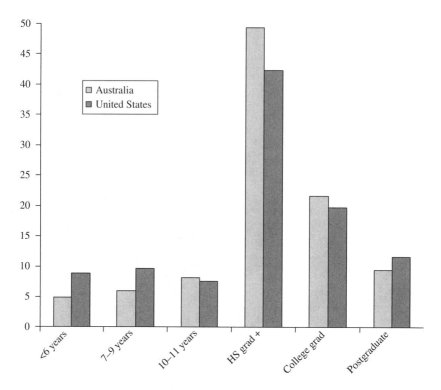

Figure 6.2 Schooling attainment of marital immigrants, by country.

that immigrant self-selection may also be playing a role in the skill-visa category.

The operation of self-selection in addition to receiving-country screening is also seen in the initial English-language ability of immigrants. As noted, the Australian immigration system screens in part based on English-language skill in the skill categories. It does not do so for marital immigrants. The U.S. system is inattentive to English skills in both categories. If screening were the only factor determining English-language ability, then we would expect to see that Australian and U.S. marital immigrants would have similar abilities in English, while Australian and U.S. skilled immigrants would have very different English-language skills. Because English ability is likely affected by duration of residence, to compare English skills across visa groups in the two countries, we restrict our attention to new arrivals, excluding the adjustees interviewed in the NIS.

Figure 6.3 displays the proportions of new-arrival immigrants who reported that they spoke English either not well or not at all, stratified

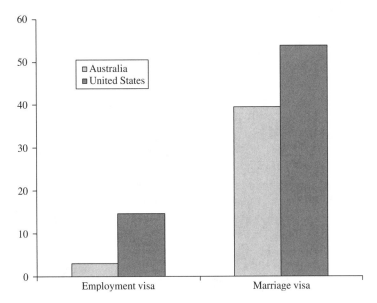

Figure 6.3 Percentage of (new arrival) immigrants speaking English not well or not at all, by visa category and country.

by visa and by country.[9] As expected based on the immigration rules, at entry among Australian immigrants, those with skill visas had greater English skills than marital immigrants, and a smaller proportion of skill immigrants in Australia had English difficulties compared with those in the United States, who were not screened on this attribute (14.7 percent versus 3.1 percent). However, marital immigrants also had more difficulty in English compared with employment immigrants among the U.S. immigrants, and the gap is even larger than in Australia between the visa groups. Moreover, the English language skill gap between the U.S. and Australian marital immigrants, with neither group being screened for English ability, is in the same direction as that between Australian and U.S. skill immigrants and is even larger in terms of percentage points (53.8 versus 39.5). Clearly, immigrant self-selection plays a role in the observed language-skill composition of immigrants. The questions are whether and how self-selection by immigrants can account for the differing skill distributions of Australian and U.S. employment immigrants and whether a distinct role for the immigrant selection systems of the two receiving countries can be identified.

9. The survey questions ascertaining language skill were identical in the two surveys, and are the same as those posed in the U.S. Census.

Skills, Skill Prices, and Immigrant Self-Selection

Immigrant Decisions, Home-Country Characteristics, and Immigrant Selectivity

In this section, we set out a simple model aimed at highlighting the important factors affecting skill differentials among immigrants due to immigrant self-selection and that can exploit available data. We assume a world economy in which there is a continuum of skills and workers have different levels of skills. Most important, rewards to skills (skill prices) differ across countries because of imperfect factor mobility. Skill may also be initially imperfectly transferable across countries.

Each worker i supplies some amount of skill units x_i. We defer the issue of the measurement of skills until the next section. The worker's wage in home country j is

$$W_{ij} = \omega_j x_i, \tag{6.1}$$

where ω_j is the skill price in country j. Thus, variation in the average wages of workers across countries is due to intercountry differences in both average skill levels and differences in the skill prices.

The initial earnings that worker i could earn in destination country u is given by

$$W_{iu} = \omega_u x_i^{\delta_{iu}}, \tag{6.2}$$

where ω_u is the destination-country skill price and δ_{iu}, $0 \leq \delta_{iu} \leq 1$, reflects the initial degree of transferability of a worker i's skills to the destination country's labor market. A worker of given skill earns a different wage in his or her origin country and initially in the destination country for two reasons: the skill price differs across the two countries, and the worker's own skill may not be fully transferable. A worker's skills may be incompletely transferable upon arrival in the destination country due to lack of job contacts, lack of familiarity with the job market or work practices, or poor English skills. With full transferability ($\delta_{iu} = 1$), the migrant can initially make use of all of his or her skill in the destination country; if the skill is initially completely nontransferable across the origin and destination countries ($\delta_{iu} = 0$), the migrant enters the destination labor market as if he or she had the lowest skill level ($x = 1$).

Given direct costs C_j and time costs $(1 + \pi_j)W_{ij}$ of migrating from j to u, the economic gain from migrating from j to u, G_{ij}, for worker i is

$$G_{ij} = x_i[\omega_u x_i^{\delta_{iu}-1} - \omega_j(1+\pi_j)] - C_j. \tag{6.3}$$

Equation (6.3) shows that for any level of direct migration costs C_j, the gains from immigrating, given a positive destination-origin skill-price differential net of migration time costs, $\omega_u > \omega_j(1 + \pi_j)$, are always higher for more highly skilled workers and for workers for whom skill transferability is high.[10]

Costs (and benefits) of migration are also psychic. Workers are assumed to (seek to) migrate from country j to country u if the utility of residing and working in u exceeds that of residing and working in j net of moving costs. The utility of residing in destination country u for a worker born in j is

$$V^u = \beta_1 \Gamma_{iu} + \beta_2(W_{iu} - W_{ij}\pi_j - C_{iu}) + \epsilon^u_i, \qquad (6.4)$$

where Γ_{iu} are amenities from living in u, such as a spouse born in u, or disamenities associated with a foreign culture and ϵ^u is a country- and worker-specific error term. The utility of the worker staying in j is

$$V^j = \beta_1 \Gamma_{ij} + \beta_2 W_{ij} + \epsilon^j_i. \qquad (6.5)$$

Taking into account the utility gain from migration accounts in part for why, for example, wages in Puerto Rico and the United States are not equalized despite the absence of legal barriers to migration and why migration may occur even if the economic gain G is negative.[11]

Given the decision rule, migrate if $V^u > V^j$, and equations (6.1) through (6.5), we can show that the skills of immigrant workers in destination countries will differ across their countries of origin given differences in home-country skill prices and moving costs. To fix ideas, assume that the marginal distributions of skills in each country are normal (or log normal), the joint stochastic or unmeasured parts of the utility functions (containing the ϵ^i) are independently and identically Gumbel-distributed, and skills and the ϵ^i are orthogonal.[12] The average skill level of immigrant workers then varies with their *home-country* skill prices according to

$$\partial E(x_i | V^u > V^j) / \partial \omega_j$$
$$= \partial E(\mu_i | -\beta_2 W_{iu} - \beta_1(\Gamma_{ij} - \Gamma_{iu}) + \epsilon^u - \epsilon^j > -\beta_2(W_{ij} - C_{ij}) / \partial \omega_j \qquad (6.6)$$
$$= \beta_2 \sigma^2(x_i) A > 0,$$

where $A = \lambda^2 + \beta_2 W_{ij}\lambda$, $\lambda = \varphi[H(P)]/\Phi[H(P)]$ (the Mills ratio) and $H(\cdot)$ is the inverse standard normal cumulative density function evaluated at the probability P that the worker chooses to migrate.

---

10. Chiswick (2000) shows that if higher skill also lowers direct migration costs, immigration will be more skill-intensive.

11. In a more elaborate analysis, the uncertainty in wages may play a role, with potential immigrants maximizing expected utility.

12. The implications of the model do not depend on these specific distributional assumptions. Such assumptions do allow for an empirically tractable analysis of multiple potential destinations, but we have simplified the framework to incorporate one potential destination, given the domination of the United States as an immigrant-receiving country.

Equation (6.6) indicates that as long as there is heterogeneity in skills among workers, immigrant workers in a destination country from sending countries with high skill prices will have higher skill levels compared with immigrant workers from low-skill-price countries of origin. The intuition is that, from equation (6.4), for given fixed monetary and psychic costs of migrating, at low skill-price differentials (when ω_j is high, for given ω_u), only the most skilled obtain a net gain from migrating, while when the differential is wide, even the least skilled experience a net gain.[13] Similarly, across destination countries, those with higher skill prices will attract, from within the same origin countries, more lower-skilled immigrants.

Immigrant skills in a destination country will also be positively associated with moving costs:

$$\partial E(x_i | V^u > V^j)/\partial C_j = (\omega_u x_i^{\delta iu-1} - \omega_j)\sigma^2(m_i)[\lambda^2 + \beta_2 C_{ij}\lambda] > 0. \quad (6.7)$$

Again, among those immigrants who incur higher costs of migrating, only those with higher skills will obtain a net positive immigration gain, all else being equal. Thus, for example, if distance and migration costs are positively associated, among immigrants from countries with the same skill prices, those from countries located farther away will tend to be more skilled and have higher earnings in the destination country. Thus, the skill composition of immigrants across destination countries will vary depending on (1) differences in the characteristics (skill prices) ω_i of the proximate sending countries and (2) differences in their own skill prices ω_u.

Determination and Measurement of Country-Specific Skill Prices

The preceding framework makes clear that to evaluate the effects of a destination country's system for selecting immigrants, it is necessary to take

---

13. Implicit in the model is a relationship between intercountry differences in skill prices and the variation in income inequality across countries. In particular, controlling for the distribution of skills, increases in the skill price of a country increase its wage inequality (and average wages). However, it is important to note that our results are not inconsistent with the claim that increased inequality for given mean income in a country can induce more lower-skilled workers to leave (Borjas, 1987). The relationship between the change in a country's income inequality and the skill selectivity of its migrants will depend on the source of the inequality change. An increase in the origin-country skill price increases incomes for all skill levels of workers but does so proportionally more for the higher-skilled. The gains from migration thus fall for all workers, leading to reduced immigration, but less so for the most skilled. However, while it is not the emphasis in our approach, it is also true that an increase in income inequality brought about, say, by reduced income support for the lower-skilled but that also holds median income constant would encourage additional migration of lower-skilled workers in our approach.

into account immigrant self-selection. And the latter will depend importantly on the distribution and levels of world skill prices. However, country-specific skill prices are not directly observed, and cannot be inferred from information on country-specific earnings inequality without concomitant information on the distribution of skills. We now discuss a method for estimating country-specific skill prices using available data, thus making it possible to assess immigrant selectivity. Two kinds of data are needed: comparable information on the wages of workers, of given skill, in every country in the world; and country-specific data on aggregate output, numbers of workers, and their average skill levels.

Assume that aggregate output Y_j in country j is produced according to Cobb-Douglas technology:

$$Y_j = AL_j^\alpha \Pi K_{nj}^\gamma, \tag{6.8}$$

where the K_{nj} are country j's stock of nonlabor resources (e.g., land, capital, minerals) and L_j is the country's aggregate stock of labor in skill, given by

$$L_j = N_j(a[x_{ij}]), \tag{6.9}$$

where N_j is the total number of workers in j and $a(\cdot)$ is a function yielding the average skill units per worker in country j.

The skill price ω_j is the marginal product of an efficiency unit of labor, given by

$$\omega_j = \alpha Y_j / N_j(a[x_{ij}]) \tag{6.10}$$

so that

$$Ln(\omega_j) = Ln\alpha + Ln(Y_j/N_j) - Ln(a[x_{ij}]). \tag{6.11}$$

Thus, the log of the skill price for any country j is just the log of labor output coefficient (in skill units) plus the log of output per worker in country j, with a coefficient of 1.0, minus the log of country j's average skill per worker. Equation (6.11) implies that among workers residing in countries with the same output per worker, those workers residing in countries where workers have higher average skill levels are paid lower skill prices, while among workers in countries with the same average worker skill levels, those in countries with higher output per worker receive higher skill prices.

Estimating (6.11) to obtain country skill prices requires data at the country level. However, although there is information on comparable measures of output per worker for all countries, the transform function $a(x_{ij})$ converting measured variables such as schooling into aggregate skill units for the economy is not known, and needs to be estimated. Moreover, the dependent variable in (6.11) is not observed.

Suppose that in addition to aggregate measures of GDP and measures of the determinants of skill, we have a random sample of workers from a random sample of countries for whom we observe their local wages, adjusted for comparability across countries based on purchasing parity, and measures of the determinants of their individual skill. In particular, suppose that a worker's level of skill depends on unobservable and observable components, μ and S (schooling), respectively, such that

$$x_i = \mu_i exp(\beta S_i). \tag{6.12}$$

Then the log of worker i's wage in country j, from (6.1), can be written as

$$Ln(W_{ij}) = Ln\alpha + Ln(Y_j/N_j) - Ln(a[x_{ij}]) + \beta_j S_{ij} + Ln\mu_{ij}. \tag{6.13}$$

Equation (6.13) indicates that the measurable log wage for worker i in country j is equal to a constant, the observable determinants of log of the country skill price from (6.12) plus the coefficient on schooling (the schooling return) times worker i's own schooling. The transform function can be estimated from (6.13), and the implication that the coefficient on the log of GDP per worker is one can be tested.

The difficulty in using (6.13) to estimate country-specific skill prices is that there do not exist comparable samples of workers from enough countries—with the same sample frame and common measures of earnings—to obtain credible estimates. Suppose, however, we have a sample of workers from different countries who immigrated to a receiving country and who report their earnings in their last jobs in their home countries. Measurement (based on common questions) of wages and worker characteristics will be comparable, with suitable conversion of currencies based on purchasing parity, and many countries will be represented. However, as noted above, immigrants are not randomly (self-)selected from the population of a country's workers. In particular, there will be selection on the unobservable component of skill μ, such that,

$$\partial E(\mu_i | V^u > V^j)/\partial \omega_j = \partial E(\mu_i | -\beta_2 W_{iu} - \beta_1(\Gamma_{ij} - \Gamma_{iu})$$
$$+ \epsilon^u - \epsilon^j > -\beta_2(W_{ij} - C_{ij})/\partial \omega_j. \tag{6.14}$$

Thus, among workers with the same schooling, those from high skill-price countries will have higher levels of unmeasured skills (positive selectivity on unobservables). The error term in (6.13) containing the unobservable component of worker earnings μ will be correlated with the determinants of the country skill price, leading to biased estimates. For example, (6.14) implies that due to immigrant selectivity, the coefficient on GDP per worker will be greater than one, biased upward. To obtain consistent estimates of (6.13) requires that this selectivity be taken into account.

One remedy is to use the standard selection-correction model (Heckman, 1979). This requires that we estimate the probability that a worker is observed in the sample, which in this case is the probability that a worker in a sending country migrates to the receiving country, compute the relevant Mills ratio λ for each immigrant, and include it among the regressors in (6.13). In our model, the probability of sample inclusion (immigration) depends on the determinants of the home-country skill price and factors affecting the costs of migration and the degree of cross-country skill transferability, from (6.4) and (6.5). The latter two sets of variables do not affect the home-country skill price, and thus the selection model is well-identified. With information on the home-country wages of a sample of immigrants, the characteristics of the economies and populations from which they came, and measures of moving costs and transferability, the skill price equation (6.13) can be estimated taking into account selection on unobservables.

Estimating Skill Prices

Data

To estimate the set of world skill prices that potentially affect the magnitude and composition of immigrant flows, we use data from the predecessor survey to the NIS-2003, the New Immigrant Survey Pilot (NIS-P), which provides the home-country earnings for a sample of new U.S. legal immigrants, combined with information on the characteristics of immigrant-sending countries. The sampling frame for the NIS-P consists of the 148,987 persons who were admitted to legal permanent residence during the months of July and August 1996. Just as for the NIS-2003, the sample of immigrants was drawn from the administrative records of the Immigration and Naturalization Service (INS), which provided information on the immigrants' age, type of visa, and country of origin, as well as the address provided by each immigrant to which his or her "green card" (the paper evidence of legal immigration status) was to be sent. The stratified random sample drawn from the records also oversampled migrants with employment visas and undersampled children; it includes 1,984 persons, of whom 1,839 were adult immigrants. Sample size for interviewed adult immigrants is 1,032. Details on the survey are given in Jasso et al. (2000).

Of the interviewed immigrants, 332 had worked in a foreign country in the 10 years before the survey and provided earnings data for their last job there. We converted the earnings in the last job abroad, provided by the immigrants in native currency units, to dollar amounts based on estimates of the country-specific purchasing power of the currencies from the Penn International Comparisons Project (ICP), described in Summers and Heston (1991). These conversion factors are explicitly designed to take into account differences in the "cost of living" across countries and to avoid the distortions associated with exchange-rate regimes in order to facilitate cross-country comparisons. The purchasing power parity (PPP) estimates thus permit comparisons of origin-country earnings across U.S. immigrants who have worked in many different countries and are comparable with their U.S. earnings, all denominated in dollars of purchasing power. Based on information on work time and pay periods, to adjust for labor-supply differences across workers, we converted all pay data to full-time earnings.

We appended to each record information on the characteristics of the immigrant's origin country using information on the last country of residence. To measure skill prices in accordance with the model, we used the real (PPP-converted) GDP per worker estimates from the Penn World Table, Mark 5.6 (Summers and Heston, 1991), supplemented with updated 1995 estimates from the ICP. We assume that in the transform function a(·), aggregate worker skills depend on schooling years and schooling quality, and thus we assembled estimates of the average schooling levels of the population age 25 and older and teacher-student ratios for primary and secondary schools from Barro and Lee (1993). Average-schooling estimates are available for a large but not complete subset of countries for which there are PPP GDP estimates. For those countries for which there are no schooling-stock estimates, we constructed a variable indicating that schooling was missing and set the schooling variable to zero.

We also appended to the micro data country-specific information related to the costs of immigration and transferability. To characterize direct migration costs, we obtained the surface distance of every potential origin country's capital to the closest major entry city in the United States. We also obtained information from the PWT 6.1 (Heston, Summers, and Aten, 2002) on GDP *per adult-equivalent*, to proxy the resources available to finance migration. As a determinant of skill transferability, we obtained information on whether English was an official language for each sending country. Finally, we appended information on the population, in 1990, of the origin countries, representing the potential pool of immigrants. The number of countries for which we have information on at least a subset of these variables is 132.[14]

---

14. The United States shares long land borders with two countries, Canada and Mexico. Canada's southern border extends 3,983 miles, and to the northwest it shares a 1,539-mile border with Alaska; Mexico's northern border spans 1,969 miles. Accordingly, for many natives of Canada and Mexico, the effective distance to the United States is zero. In the multivariate analyses reported below, it makes little difference whether the distance from Canada and Mexico to the United States is measured by zero, a small positive number, the distance from the capital to the closest major port of entry, or a dummy variable.

Estimating the Probability of Sample Selection

To account for the selectivity in the sample of immigrants, we estimate a blocked probit regression. This is equivalent to estimating a probit for immigration using individual data on samples of 132 of the world's sending-country populations. We use the population of the sending country as the population at risk of migration and the number of U.S. immigrants in the NIS-P sample as the dependent variable.[15] The number of observations is thus the population of the 132 countries, but because observations within a country are duplicates, the standard errors of coefficients are appropriately corrected.

Table 6.1 reports the blocked probit coefficients characterizing the decision to immigrate to the United States across 132 countries for two specifications, one including the school-quality measures and one without them. In both cases, the set of regressors is statistically significant, and the pseudo R^2 is respectable, given that a small micro sample of immigrants is being used. The pattern of coefficients for per-worker GDP and aggregate schooling is in conformity with the framework—in countries with higher output per worker, for given average skill, out-migration is smaller (skill prices are higher), while among countries with the same per-worker output, those with higher levels of schooling send more migrants, because the returns to skill are lower. Higher per-adult GDP, for given skill and per-worker output, leads to increased migration, suggesting the importance of resource constraints on migration, although the estimates are not precise. Most importantly for purposes of identifying selectivity in estimating the skill-price equation, distance between the country and the United States significantly deters immigration. And English-language countries, other things being equal, send more migrants to the United States.

Skill Price Estimates

Table 6.2 reports the estimates of the skill-price determinants based on the home-country wages of the sample of U.S. immigrants. The first specification omits the Mills ratio λ, while the second includes it as a regressor. The sets of country and individual-worker characteristics explain 35 percent of the total variation in home-country wages among the immigrants, and all

---

15. A more refined analysis would use the population of persons in the age group 25 to 59, corresponding to the age group of the migrants. This would require accurate information on the population age structure for all countries.

Table 6.1 Maximum Likelihood Blocked Probit Estimates: Determinants of the Probability of Being a U.S. Immigrant

Variable/specification	(1)	(2)
Log GDP per worker	−0.291	−0.187
	(1.42)	(1.02)
Log mean schooling	0.389	0.150
	(3.20)	(1.39)
Log GDP per adult-equivalent	0.060	0.230
	(0.36)	(1.21)
Distance (×10⁻⁴)	−0.259	−0.258
	(5.96)	(6.26)
English an official language	0.359	0.381
	(2.06)	(2.16)
Log teacher-pupil ratio, primary schools	—	−0.137
		(0.75)
Log teacher-pupil ratio, secondary schools	—	0.968
		(3.82)
Constant	0.580	−3.85
	(0.61)	(2.47)
Number of countries	132	132
Number of observations (country populations × 10⁻³)	4,136,943	4,136,943
Wald χ²(d.f.)	147.97 (7)	184.72 (11)
Pseudo R^2	0.16	0.18

Note: Specifications include dummy variables for missing language, distance, and teacher-pupil ratios. Z statistics in parentheses corrected for clustering of observations within countries.
Source: For immigrant information, New Immigrant Pilot Survey.

coefficients but that for the gender variable are statistically significant. The sign patterns for per-worker GDP and for schooling, moreover, conform to the model—wages are higher for workers of given education and age in countries with greater output per worker, given average country skill levels, and worker wages are lower among countries with the same output per worker but with higher average schooling levels. These results are also consistent with the migration determinant estimates of table 6.1. The point estimate in column one for per-worker GDP is greater than one, consistent with positive selectivity. And, indeed, the coefficient on λ in column two is positive. Inclusion of the Mills ratio moreover lowers the coefficient on per-worker GDP such that the hypothesis that the coefficient is one as indicated by equation (6.13) cannot be rejected.

Table 6.2   Estimates of the Determinants of the Country Log Skill Price Based on the Log Wage of U.S. Immigrants Age 25–59 in Their Home Countries

Variable/specification	OLS	OLS with selection correction
Country characteristics		
Log GDP per worker	1.41	1.35
	(5.01)	(5.21)
Log mean schooling	–1.77	–1.97
	(3.18)	(3.23)
Log teacher-pupil ratio, primary schools	–1.90	–2.17
	(3.68)	(3.80)
Log teacher-pupil ratio, secondary schools	1.44	1.36
	(2.51)	(2.56)
Immigrant skill characteristics		
Schooling	0.0683	0.0745
	(3.50)	(3.79)
Age	0.0428	0.0436
	(4.32)	(4.50)
Female	–0.169	–0.123
	(1.12)	(0.77)
λ	—	0.800
		(1.46)
Constant	–1.02	0.713
Number of countries	54	54
Number of immigrants	332	332
F (d.f., d.f.)	17.02 (10, 53)	25.33(11, 53)
R^2	0.35	0.36

Note: Specifications include dummy variables for missing country-specific schooling and teacher-pupil ratios. The *t* statistics in parentheses corrected for clustering of observations within countries.
Source: For immigrant characteristics, New Immigrant Survey Pilot.

Sending-Country Characteristics of Skilled Immigrants in Australia and the United States

The estimates (column 2) in table 6.2 can be used to estimate skill prices for all countries represented in the PWT having information on aggregate schooling. We computed average per-worker GDP over the period of 1996 to 2000 for each country and used the most recent Barro-Lee estimates of schooling levels and school inputs. To maximize the number of countries, we also used the (unreported) coefficients on the dummy variables indicating absent schooling information included in the skill-price regressions to compute skill prices for countries without this information. The resulting estimates indicate that the skill price for the United States is $70.50, while that for Australia is $64.90. Thus, everything else the same, immigrant self-selection should result in immigrants who choose to go to the United States having lower skills than those who go to Australia.

Tables 6.3 and 6.4 report the estimated skill prices for the top 10 countries sending employment immigrants to Australia, based on the LSIA2, and to the United States, based on the NIS-2003. For Australia, the top 10 countries account for 75.3 percent of all employment migration. Employment immigration is slightly more global for the United States, as the top 10 countries account for 70.6 percent of all employment immigrants. As can be seen, among the new employment immigrants in Australia, all but one of the top sending countries (Malaysia) has a lower skill price than Australia, while for the United States, all but two (Canada and Taiwan) have lower skill prices. Tables 6.3 and 6.4 show that there is considerable overlap in the countries represented by skilled migrants in the two receiving countries. However, a Kolmogorov-Smirnov test rejects the hypothesis that the skilled immigrants to Australia and the United States have the same country-of-origin distribution. For comparison, tables 6.5 and 6.6 report the top 10 country distributions of marital immigrants for the two receiving countries.[16] The distributions differ more strongly for this group of immigrants across the two receiving countries, suggesting that the marriage market may be less globally integrated than the labor market.

Differences in the selection rules employed by Australia and the United States could explain the differences in the country composition of the skilled migrants coming to the two countries. However, if geography and home-country skill prices matter in determining who chooses to migrate, the United States and Australia face different potential populations of migrants. The first column of table 6.7 reports the average distance of a person from Australia and from the United States. This is the average of the destination-/origin-country distances, weighted by population size. As can be seen, the average person in the world is closer to the United States than he or she is to Australia, by more than 1,000 miles. Indeed, there are essentially no persons residing within 1,000 miles of a major Australian city, but there are 125 million persons residing in countries bordering the

---

16. The top 10 countries represent 58.6 percent and 50.7 percent of all marital immigrants in Australia and the United States, respectively. Note that the United States is a significant sending country for Australian marital immigrants, but not vice versa.

Table 6.3   Top 10 U.S. Immigrant-Sending Countries: Employment Immigrants, 18 and Older

Country	Share in category	Distance (miles)	Estimated skill price ($)
India	0.252	7,668	12.33
Philippines	0.135	6,964	25.64
China	0.087	5,900	48.42
Mexico	0.052	0	55.12
Korea	0.050	5,609	55.73
United Kingdom	0.038	3,663	56.57
Canada	0.034	0	81.10
Taiwan	0.023	6,431	227.00
Brazil	0.019	4,458	72.60
South Africa	0.017	8,086	39.02

Source: New Immigrant Survey, 2003 cohort, round 1.

Table 6.4   Top 10 Australian Immigrant-Sending Countries: Employment Immigrants, 15 and Older

Country	Share in category	Distance (miles)	Estimated skill price ($)
United Kingdom	0.209	10,547	56.57
India	0.136	6,430	12.33
China	0.108	5,594	48.42
South Africa	0.088	6,719	39.02
Philippines	0.056	3,905	25.64
Malaysia	0.039	4,052	123.00
Pakistan	0.034	6,833	60.75
Zimbabwe	0.029	6,944	24.45
Fiji	0.028	2,146	19.52
Hong Kong	0.026	4,584	139.00

Source: Longitudinal Survey of Immigrants to Australia 2, wave 1.

United States. If distance raises the cost of migration, this would induce more lower-skill workers to seek to go to the United States than would go to Australia. However, the countries proximate to the two receiving countries also differ in skill prices. We computed the population and distance-weighted average skill price for the two countries (closer distances receive higher weights). Column 2 of table 6.7 reports the average home-country skill price faced by persons proximate to the two countries. The home-country skill price for potential migrants proximate to the United States

Table 6.5   Top 10 U.S. Immigrant-Sending Countries: Marital Immigrants, 18 and Older

Country	Share in category	Distance (miles)	Estimated skill price ($)
Mexico	0.237	0	55.12
Philippines	0.048	6,964	25.64
India	0.036	7,668	12.33
China	0.041	5,900	48.42
Colombia	0.033	1,516	35.15
Vietnam	0.027	7,301	20.65
Canada	0.024	0	81.10
Peru	0.022	2,620	23.22
United Kingdom	0.020	3,663	56.57
Japan	0.020	5,134	69.55

Source: New Immigrant Survey, 2003 cohort, round 1.

Table 6.6   Top 10 Australian Immigrant-Sending Countries: Marital Immigrants, 15 and Older

Country	Share in category	Distance (miles)	Estimated skill price ($)
China	.117	5,594	48.42
United Kingdom	.103	10,547	56.57
Philippines	.071	3,905	25.64
Lebanon	.067	8,729	93.60
Vietnam	.065	4,809	20.65
India	.043	6,430	12.33
United States	.034	7,572	70.50
Iraq	.031	8,242	
Malaysia	.029	4,052	123
Fiji	.027	2,146	19.52

Source: Longitudinal Survey of Immigrants to Australia 2, wave 1.

is higher than that for potential migrants to Australia based on geography and population size. The skill-price gain—the difference between receiving-country and sending-country skill price—is less dissimilar: $13.00 for Australian potential immigrants and $9.00 for U.S. potential immigrants. Nevertheless, the skill-price differences for potential migrants associated with the two receiving countries offset somewhat the effects of differing distances and hence migration costs.

Table 6.7   Sending Country Characteristics of Potential and Actual Immigrants, by Visa Type and Receiving Country

Receiving country	All potential immigrants		Top 10 countries of actual employment immigrants		Top 10 countries of actual marital immigrants	
	Mean distance (miles)[a]	Mean skill price ($)[b]	Mean distance (miles)[c]	Mean skill price ($)[d]	Mean distance (miles)[c]	Mean skill price ($)[d]
Australia	7,068	51.80	6,987	46.90	6,559	50.10
	(1,951)	(58.40)	(2,589)	(32.00)	(2,582)	(24.20)
United States	5,903	61.40	6,224	39.10	3,132	43.40
	(1,823)	(12.90)	(2,252)	(44.90)	(3,405)	(19.20)

[a] Population-weighted distance of all potential sending countries to the receiving country.
[b] Population- and distance-weighted country skill price across all potential receiving counties.
[c] Immigrant-weighted distance to receiving country of actual sending countries in immigrant category.
[d] Immigrant-weighted skill price of actual sending countries in immigrant category.
Source: For immigrant information, Longitudinal Survey of Immigrants to Australia 2, wave 1, and New Immigrant Survey, 2003 cohort, round 1.

Columns three and four in table 6.7 report the average distances actually traveled by and the average skill prices of the sending countries of the employment immigrants for Australia and the United States, based on the figures reported in tables 6.3 and 6.4. The average distances of the home countries represented in the flows of migrants in the two countries are more similar to the average distances of their associated potential migrants than they are to those of each other's immigrant flows. And, as expected if gains matter for migration self-selection, the average gain from migration per skill unit for persons who migrate is higher for both countries than the (potential) gain weighted by sending-country populations and distances. The last two columns of table 6.7 report the average skill prices and distances of the marital migrants in the two receiving countries. Evidently, marital migrants come from countries more proximate to the receiving countries and gain less per unit of skill on average compared with employment migrants.

Estimates of Skill Price and Migration Cost Effects on Employment Migration and Skill

Tables 6.3 to 6.7 hint at the operation of skill prices and migration costs in determining the magnitudes and skill composition of skill immigrants, but it is possible that the composition of migrants just coincidentally reflects the selection rules of the receiving countries rather than systematic choices by persons in sending countries. To explore the self-selection of immigrants more rigorously, we use the estimated country skill prices to estimate the determinants of the flow of skilled migrants separately for the two receiving countries. We test for whether the estimates conform to the immigrant selection model, in particular whether flows are smaller from sending countries with higher skill prices and at a greater distance, given resource constraints. To do this, we regress for each receiving country the ratio of employment immigrants to population in the sending country on sending-country skill price, distance to the relevant receiving country, GDP per adult, and population size. To make the coefficient estimates comparable and the coefficients interpretable in terms of actual immigrant flows, we use the sampling fractions for the two surveys to blow up the numerator for the Australian and U.S. immigrants by 10.0 and 39.7, respectively.[17]

Table 6.8 reports the estimates of the determinants of employment migration flows for both Australia and the United States. The coefficient sign patterns are the same for both receiving countries and conform to the self-selection model — the fraction of employment immigrants from a sending country is lower the higher the sending-country skill price and the less its proximity to the receiving country. The point estimates for the skill-price effects are remarkably similar for the two receiving countries, and indeed, only the effects of changes in home-country per-adult GDP appear to differ significantly. Resources appear to matter for the migration of employment immigrants to both countries—increases in income per adult, given skill prices, increase the probability of migrating—and the set of coefficients characterizing the effects of country characteristics on the flows of employment immigrants do not differ significantly across the two receiving countries.

The results in table 6.8, of course, do not imply that the systems of immigrant choice put in place in the receiving countries do not matter. The country variables explain only a small proportion of the immigrant flows. The key issue is whether the variables evidently affecting immigration self-selection explain the variation in the skills of the immigrants, net of receiving-country attributes. To examine this, we estimate the determinants of the average schooling of employment immigrants as a function of the country characteristics that influence immigration. Equation (6.11) indicates that if there is self-selection, the skill equation, conditional on immigrating, will

---

17. The LSIA2 sampled approximately 10 percent of new immigrants going to Australia in a 12-month period. The NIS-2003 sampled 4.3 percent of immigrants processed over a seven-month period.

Table 6.8   Determinants of Employment-Visa Immigration
by Receiving Country: Sample Immigrants per Country
Population (×10⁶)

Variable/country	Australia	United States
Country skill price	–20.9	–17.3
	(1.92)	(2.15)
Distance	–8.55	–1.22
	(1.38)	(1.50)
GDP per adult-equivalent	3.03	0.29
	(1.99)	(2.93)
Population	–0.0475	–.00178
	(1.43)	(0.58)
Constant	75,930	11,659
	(1.41)	(2.26)
Number of countries	132	132
R^2	0.11	0.07

Note: Absolute values of robust *t*-statistics in parentheses.
Source: For immigrant characteristics, New Immigrant Survey, 2003
cohort, round 1, and Longitudinal Survey of Immigrants to Australia
2, wave 1.

be the mirror image of the immigration equation: more skilled immigrants
will come from higher skill-price countries, net of distance effects, and
from more distant countries, given the skill price. Moreover, to the extent
that own income eases migration barriers, net of skill prices and distance,
growth in income per person in a sending country should be associated
with an increased flow of lower-skilled immigrants.

In addition to assessing whether immigrant self-selection accounts for
any variation in skill composition, we can assess whether *all* of the differences between the educational attainment of employment immigrants
in Australia and the United States, seen in figure 6.1, can be explained
by immigrant decisions. Unfortunately, because we have cross-sectional
data, we cannot identify how variation in receiving-country characteristics affects immigrant-skill composition. We can only see if net of country
characteristics effects there remains an unexplained difference in the educational attainment of Australian and U.S. skilled immigrants. However, if
there is immigrant self-selection, because the skill price in the United States
exceeds that in Australia, net of sending-country skill prices and migration
costs, immigrant educational attainment in the United States will be lower
than in Australia. If we find this, we would be unable to identify any effect
of receiving-country selection systems.

To carry out the analysis, we take the weighted (using sample weights) average of the educational attainment of the employment immigrants in the Australian and U.S. immigrant samples for each sending country and regress that on the same country variables as in the immigration equation. Given that we cannot reject similar immigration behavior for U.S. and Australian employment immigrants, seen in table 6.8, we pool both sets of immigrants, with Australian immigrants assigned the Australia-to-home-country distance and U.S. immigrants the U.S.-to-home-country distance. By pooling the samples, we expand the set of country-level observations to 148, with the Australian immigrants representing 67 countries and the U.S. immigrants representing 81 countries. Theory does not provide any guidance on functional form, so to assess robustness, we estimate linear and log-log specifications.

Table 6.9 reports the estimates of the skill selection equations for the two functional forms. The small set of country characteristics explains more than a quarter of the variation in educational attainment and more than a third of the variation in log educational attainment across employment

Table 6.9   Weighted Least Squares Estimates: Determinants of the Educational Attainment of Employment-Visa Immigrants in Australia and the United States

Variable/specification	Linear	Log-log
Country skill price	0.00406	0.02660
	(2.55)	(2.45)
Distance	0.000108	0.017200
	(2.60)	(4.51)
GDP per adult-equivalent	−0.0000213	−0.0169
	(1.65)	(1.71)
Population ($\times 10^{-3}$)	0.00116	21.20000
	(4.97)	(5.06)
Receiving country is United States	−0.454	−0.0250
	(2.31)	(1.99)
Constant	14.9	2.43
	(40.1)	(21.4)
Number of observations	148	148
R^2	0.27	0.34

Note: Absolute values of robust *t*-statistics in parentheses. Weights are the proportions of sending-country immigrants by country.
Source: For immigrant characteristics, New Immigrant Survey, 2003 cohort, round 1, and Longitudinal Survey of Immigrants to Australia 2, wave 1.

immigrants in the two countries. More important, the pattern of coefficients is consistent with immigrant self-selection, with higher skill prices abroad associated with more highly educated immigrants and greater proximity leading to less skilled migration. The results also indicate that net of country characteristics, U.S. employment immigrants have about half a year less schooling than Australian immigrants. This is consistent with the United States having a higher skill price than Australia. Thus, we cannot find any evidence of an independent effect of the differing receiving-country selection systems, although we cannot rule out such an effect.

The point estimates suggest that, for example, if the skill price in India were increased to be equal to that of China (a fourfold increase), the average educational attainment of (the fewer) Indian immigrants to Australia and the United States would be 12 percent higher. In contrast, increasing sending-country incomes fourfold, without raising the returns to skills, would lower the average skill level of (an increased number) of employment immigrants by 7 percent. Economic development in sending countries thus would affect the skill level of immigrants in developed countries, but the way in which development proceeds also appears to matter. Finally, distance matters for skill composition, but not greatly. On average, a difference in distance between receiving and sending countries of 1,000 miles (the difference between the Australian and U.S. average distances to potential migrants, table 6.7) is associated with a difference in the average educational attainment of employment immigrants of only 0.1 year (0.6 percent). Australia's geographic isolation per se evidently accounts for little of the difference between the educational attainment of employment immigrants in the United States and Australia. What matters are the skill wages of Australia's neighbors and those of the United States.

Conclusion

In this chapter, we use new survey data on employment immigrants in Australia and the United States to identify the main determinants of the size and skill composition of employment immigrants to developed countries. We emphasize the key roles of world prices of skills and country proximity. Our empirical results are consistent with the view that these factors, rather than the nuances of selection systems, dominate. There are five main findings:

1. Higher skill prices in sending countries decrease the number of immigrants but increase their average schooling.
2. Countries that are more distant send fewer but more highly skilled immigrants.

3. Given skill prices and proximity, countries with higher income send more immigrants, of lower skill.

4. Within a sending country, Australia attracts fewer total but higher-skill migrants than the United States. This can be attributed, however, to the fact that the skill price in Australia is lower than the U.S. skill price, so that immigration gains are greater from immigrating to the United States.

5. The estimated coefficients determining migration flows to Australia and the United States are the same for both countries.

We conclude that geography thus matters in the sense that who a country's neighbors are, in terms of their level and type of development, has a significant effect on the size and skill composition of employment migrants. There is no evidence that the differences in the selection mechanism used to screen employment migrants in the two countries play a significant role in affecting the characteristics of skill migration.

These results suggest that as low-income countries increase the rewards provided to skills, developed countries that seek to attract skilled immigrants will experience lower demand for visas by less skilled immigrants. And countries that newly open their borders to employment or skill-based immigration cannot necessarily use the experience of the United States or Australia to predict the composition and flows of employment immigrants to the extent that the characteristics of their neighboring countries differ substantially. Finally, not all high-skilled immigrants arrive with an employment or skill visa. Marriage is a major route to immigration, and it is not unlikely that marital migration will increase. Understanding the total world flow of skilled migrants also requires attention to the global marriage market. With new data on the visas of immigrants, new work in this domain may be possible.

References

Barro, Robert J., and Jong Wha Lee. 1993. "International Comparisons of Educational Attainment." *Journal of Monetary Economics* 32: 363–94.

Borjas, George J. 1987. "Self-Selection and the Earnings of Immigrants." *American Economic Review* 77: 531–53.

Chiswick, Barry. 1978. "The Effect of Americanization on the Earnings of Foreign-Born Men." *Journal of Political Economy* 86: 897–921.

Chiswick, Barry. 2000. "Are Immigrants Favorably Self-Selected? An Economic Analysis." In Caroline B. Brettell and James F. Hollifield, eds., *Migration Theory: Talking across Disciplines*. New York: Routledge, pp. 61–76.

Heckman, James J. 1979. "Sample Selection Bias as a Specification Error." *Econometrica* 47, no. 1: 153–62.

Heston, Alan, Robert Summers, and Bettina Aten. Penn World Table Version 6.1, Center for International Comparisons at the University of Pennsylvania (CICUP), October.

Hugo, Graeme. In press. "The Longitudinal Survey of Immigrants to Australia (LSIA)." In Beverley Morgan and Ben Nicholson, eds., *Immigration Research and Statistics Service Workshop on Longitudinal Surveys and Cross-Cultural Survey Design: Workshop Proceedings.* London: Crown, pp. 69–103.

Jasso, Guillermina. 1988. "Whom Shall We Welcome? Elite Judgments of the Criteria for the Selection of Immigrants." *American Sociological Review* 53: 919–32.

———. 2008. "New Immigrant Survey." In William A. Darity Jr., ed., *International Encyclopedia of the Social Sciences,* 2nd ed., vol. 5. Detroit: Macmillan Reference USA.

Jasso, Guillermina, Douglas S. Massey, Mark R. Rosenzweig, and James P. Smith. 2000. "The New Immigrant Survey Pilot: Overview and New Findings about Legal Immigrants at Admission." *Demography* 37: 127–38.

———. 2003. "The New Immigrant Survey in the U.S.: The Experience over Time." www.migrationinformation.org.

———. In press. "The U.S. New Immigrant Survey: Overview and Preliminary Results Based on the New-Immigrant Cohorts of 1996 and 2003." In Beverley Morgan and Ben Nicholson, eds., *Immigration Research and Statistics Service Workshop on Longitudinal Surveys and Cross-Cultural Survey Design: Workshop Proceedings.* London: Crown, 29–46.

Jasso, Guillermina, and Mark R. Rosenzweig. 1990a. *The New Chosen People: Immigrants in the United States.* New York: Russell Sage Foundation.

———. 1990b. "Self Selection and the Earnings of Immigrants: Comment." *American Economic Review* 80: 298–304.

Martin, Philip. 2004. "Migration." In Bjorn Lomborg, ed., *Global Crises, Global Solutions.* Cambridge: Cambridge University Press.

Richardson, Sue, and Laurence Lester. 2004. "A Comparison of Australian and Canadian Immigration Policies and Labour Market Outcomes." National Institute of Labour Studies, Flinders University, Adelaide, September.

Summers, Robert, and Alan Heston. 1991. "The Penn World Table (Mark 5): An Expanded Set of International Comparisons, 1950–1988." *Quarterly Journal of Economics* 106: 327–68.

7

The Role of Professional Societies in Regulating Entry of Skilled Migrants
The American Medical Association

SHERRY A. GLIED AND DEBOJYOTI SARKAR

National governments may police their borders and, through legislation and enforcement, determine how many immigrants to admit. They may also choose the balance between skilled and unskilled migration. Yet in the case of the publicly licensed professions, permission to immigrate may not constitute permission to exploit one's human capital. The authority to grant professional licenses is often devolved to the professions themselves. This authority permits the professions to influence the levels of skilled migration directly. The strongest case of such professional control over migration occurs in medicine.

Physicians trained in non-U.S. medical schools, who seek to come to the United States to practice medicine, are known as international medical graduates (IMGs).[1] IMGs today make up about 23 percent of the U.S. physician population and 24 percent of physicians in graduate residency programs.[2] About 80 percent of the IMGs entering the United States each year are foreign-born (JAMA, 1992–2004). Like all immigrants, foreign-born IMGs must meet immigration criteria (which vary from time to time) to enter the United States. In addition, in order to practice medicine, all IMGs, whether native or foreign-born, must obtain a medical license in the

This chapter draws heavily on Debojyoti Sarkar's Ph.D. dissertation (see bibliography). Jagdish Bhagwati provided the original impetus for the research. We thank Douglas Gould and Bisundev Mahato for their considerable assistance in updating the dissertation.

1. Non-U.S. medical schools are those outside the United States, Canada, and Puerto Rico. An IMG is a physician whose basic medical degree or qualification is conferred by such a non-U.S. medical school. Citizens of the United States who have completed their medical education in these non-U.S. schools are considered as IMGs, whereas foreign nationals who have graduated from medical schools in the United States, Canada, and Puerto Rico are not. The U.S.-trained physicians are called USMGs.

2. According to www.ama-assn.org/ama/pub/category/211.html.

United States. In this chapter, we examine the factors that affect the number of IMGs who enter the United States, focusing on the role of the U.S. medical profession in regulating the size of that population.

Regulating Entry into Medicine

The Council on Medical Education (COME) of the American Medical Association (AMA) in the United States regulates entry into the practice of medicine in the country. In order to practice medicine, a candidate must have completed at least four years of medical school at a recognized medical college,[3] must pass a certification examination and must complete graduate medical training in the form of a medical residency in the United States.

COME actively manages the size of the U.S. physician workforce. It does this primarily by adjusting the number of first-year positions open in U.S. medical schools. This limit on the size of the entering class restricts the ability of some American-born students to become physicians through U.S.-based medical training. These students, as well as tens of thousands of foreign students, obtain training at non-U.S. medical schools, whose size is not controlled by COME. COME, however, can indirectly regulate the number of IMGs who want to practice medicine in the United States by adjusting the stringency of the test that international applicants are required to take. Finally, as all candidates for licensure must complete a residency program, COME can regulate the size of residency programs to control the inflow. Limits on the number of residencies available are binding on USMGs as well as IMGs. However, since residency programs tend to prefer USMGs, limits on the number of residency positions have their greatest effect on IMGs.

Economists have documented the power of the U.S. medical profession to control entry and earn rents (Friedman and Kuznets, 1945; Kessel, 1958, 1970; Lindsay, 1973; Sarkar, 1995). As is the case with other professions, legislatures have ceded authority to regulate entry to the profession because medical professionals are viewed as having unique expertise to assess the quality of their peers. In the case of medicine, considerable uncertainty among policymakers and analysts regarding whether a larger supply of physicians would be socially desirable compounds this lack of knowledge about quality.

A substantial literature in health economics documents the existence of physician-induced demand in the presence of widespread health insurance. Physician-induced demand refers to a situation in which physicians subvert the usual laws of supply and demand and offset increases in supply by inducing their patients to demand additional services, shifting the demand curve upward (Reinhart, 1985). Despite a relatively inelastic demand for

---

3. See Sarkar (1995) for a complete listing.

health-care services, the presence of physician-induced demand implies that an increase in the supply of professionals will generate an increase in total expenditures on physician services. Since governments pay nearly half of all medical expenditures in the United States, the potential for such expenditure increases leads governments to be sympathetic to calls for restrictions on physician supply.

While the existence of physician-induced demand changes the welfare consequences of increasing the supply of physicians, it may not alter the profession's private interest in restricting supply to maintain the incomes of individual members. Supply expansions may lead to increased expenditures overall, but they appear to reduce the earnings of individual physicians. Moreover, many theories of physician-induced demand hypothesize that demand inducement extracts a cost from physicians, so that reducing the necessity of inducing demand to maintain income remains desirable.

While practicing physicians—and policymakers—have an interest in restricting physician supply, hospitals, which rely on medical residents to deliver care, make up a powerful countervailing force. Medical residents, completing their graduate medical education, represent about 2 percent of the U.S. hospital labor force.[4] Moreover, since 1965, hospital training of residents has been subsidized through the U.S. Medicare program. In 2002, Medicare spent more than $7.5 billion on graduate medical education (Centers for Medicare and Medicaid Services, 2005; includes both "graduate medical education" and "indirect medical education"). Hospitals have a strong interest in maintaining an adequate supply of trainees to fill their residency slots.

In sum, the professional and institutional forces governing medical education face at least three potentially conflicting goals with respect to the entry of IMGs: (1) guaranteeing the quality of medical practice in the United States, (2) maintaining the rate of return to medical training among those already practicing, and (3) providing residents to staff hospitals. The principal instrument to control the inflow of IMGs so as to realize these objectives is the stringency of the test administered to IMGs.

In this analysis, we examine how the stringency of the test administered each year adapts to changes in these three factors.

The Stringency of the Test

Formal certification of IMGs began in March 1958, when the newly formed Educational Commission for Foreign Medical Graduates (ECFMG) administered its first exam (see table 7.1 for a chronology). There were approximately

---

4. There were 5,340,000 people employed in U.S. hospitals (U.S. Department of Health and Human Services, 2003) and 98,258 residents in ACGME-accredited GME programs in 2002 (Brotherton, Rockey, and Etzel, 2003).

Table 7.1 Examinations for ECFMG Certification

Examination	Dates	Description
1. Educational Commission for Foreign Medical Graduates (ECFMG) Test	1958–1984	Format based on National Board of Medical Examiners (NBME) part I (basic sciences) and part II (clinical science) exam. A separate section includes writing a short medical case history in English. Originally called the American Qualification Exam (AMQ).
2a. Visa Qualification Examination (VQE)	1977–1984	Approximately 1,000 multiple-choice questions (half basic science, half clinical science). Half as long as NBME I and II. 1976—deemed equivalent to NBME I and II by Department of Health, Education and Welfare. Administered to IMGs outside the United States only.
2b. Federation Licensing Examination (FLEX)	1981–1985	Format similar to NBME I and II.
3a. Foreign Medical Graduate Examination in Medical Sciences (FMGEMS)	1984–1993	Replaces ECFMG and VQE. Two-day exam. Day 1, 500 multiple-choice questions (basic science). Day 2, 450 multiple-choice questions (clinical science). Topics covered and passing standards exactly the same as for the NBME test. Administered semiannually in more than 140 locations.
3b. National Board of Medical Examiners (NBME) Parts I and II	1989–1992	Part I (basic sciences) and part II (clinical sciences).
4. U.S. Medical Licensing Examination (USMLE) Parts I and II	1992–2004	Part I (basic sciences) and part II (clinical sciences).
5. ECFMG Clinical Skills Assessment (CSA)	1998–2004	Additional requirement for ECFMG certification. Includes 10 encounters with "patients" (actors).

(*continued*)

Table 7.1 *(continued)*

Examination	Dates	Description
		Two graded requirements. Integrated Clinical Encounter (ICE) focuses on data gathering. Doctor-Patient Communications (COM) focuses on interpersonal skills and English proficiency.
6. USMLE Part II Clinical Knowledge (CK) and Clinical Skills (CS)	2004–current	Clinical Knowledge is similar to USMLE part II from the past. Clinical Skills section is similar to ECFMG CSA.

Source: ECFMG Web site, Hubbard and Levit (1985), USMLE Web site, and Whelan et al. (2002).

544 medical schools outside the United States at that point; today, there are more than 1,600 (Hallock, Seeling, and Norcini, 2003). Despite a dramatic increase in domestic medical-school applications, growing prosperity following World War II, along with the baby boom, increased the demand for medical care. In 1959, a report by the Surgeon General's Consultant Group on Medical Education, known as the Bane report, predicted a shortage of physicians in the coming two decades (Blumenthal, 2004).

In 1965, amendments to the Immigration and Nationality Act (INA 65) changed the objectives of the U.S. immigration system from limiting immigrants from certain countries through a quota system to reunifying families and encouraging the growth of skilled labor. Immigration for physicians from the Eastern Hemisphere became much easier. The U.S. Department of Labor initially included physicians in the highest-priority occupation category, "schedule A," thus giving physicians automatic labor certification. In 1970, amendments to the INA allowed alien residents to apply for permanent residency without leaving the United States for two years.

In the mid-1970s, the conventional wisdom that the United States faced a shortage of physicians began to change. Moreover, many people in the medical profession and government believed that the certification test for IMGs was markedly easier than that for domestic medical graduates (Hubbard and Levit, 1985). In 1976, the second Health Professions Educational Assistance Act (HPEAA 76 or P.L. 94–484) stated that the United States had no physician shortage, rescinded the INA amendments of 1970, and required IMGs who sought visas to pass the first two parts of the National Board of Medical Examiners (NBME) test (the test administered to graduates of U.S. medical colleges) or an equivalent test and a test in English proficiency (Hubbard and Levit, 1985). Since the NBME test was not available to IMGs outside the United States, an equivalent test had to be developed. That test, the Visa Qualifying Examination (VQE), was administered for the first time in 1977. That same year, the Department of Labor removed physicians from the preferred-status category schedule A. In 1981, the Federal Licensing Examination (FLEX) was offered to IMGs as an alternative means of obtaining certification (Educational Commission for Foreign Medical Graduates, 2005). During this period, foreign physicians who were able to get visas (for other reasons) could take the ECFMG test; those who needed visas were limited to the VQE test.

In 1980, the Graduate Medical Education National Advisory Committee issued an influential report that estimated surpluses of physicians of 70,000 by 1990 and 145,000 by 2000. They estimated that 40,000 to 50,000 of the 70,000 extra physicians anticipated in 1990 would be IMGs. The report called for limitations on medical-school admissions and IMG medical training in the United States (Graduate Medical Education National Advisory Committee, 1980). In 1981, Congress stopped providing general funding for the training of new U.S. physicians (Blumenthal, 2004). In 1984, the Foreign Medical Graduate Examination in Medical Sciences (FMGEMS) replaced the existing exams (Hubbard and Levit, 1985). Beginning in 1989, IMGs were permitted to take the NBME test as an alternative to the FMGEMS.

In 1992, a three-step U.S. Medical Licensing Examination (USMLE) was introduced. This marked the first point when all prospective residents in the United States had to pass the same exam, regardless of where they had received their medical training. Also in 1992, the Council on Graduate Medical Education issued a report that warned of a surplus of physicians (Council on Graduate Medical Education, 1992). This report, like several other academic papers on the subject at that time, saw the influx of managed care in health care and believed that its dependence on primary-care physicians would cause an even greater surplus among specialized physicians and surgeons (Salsberg and Forte, 2002).

Finally, beginning in 1998, IMGs have been required to complete a Clinical Skills Assessment in addition to passing written examinations (Whelan et al., 2002). In June 2004, all medical graduates, wherever trained, had to begin taking a clinical-skills examination in the second step of the USMLE (U.S. Medical Licensing Examination, 2004).

During the same period, there have also been changes in the availability of residency positions in U.S. hospitals. In the 1983 reforms of Medicare hospital reimbursement, Congress began providing teaching hospitals with graduate medical education payments that increased in amount as a program's number of residents increased. From 1988 to 1993, the number of IMGs in residency positions increased more than 80 percent (Mullan, Politzer, and Davis, 1995).

In 1994, the Council on Graduate Medical Education recommended that first-year graduate medical education positions (residencies) be reduced to 110 percent of domestic graduates, down from 140 percent (Kindig and Libby, 1996). The Balanced Budget Act of 1997 capped the number of residents and interns at teaching hospitals at the number that worked through December 31, 1996. A phased reduction of indirect medical education (IME) payments was also initiated (Council on Graduate Medical Education, 2000). This lowered the number of residents allowed and the incentive for hospitals to accept as many new residents, since the IME payments were based on a ratio of residents to patient beds in a hospital.

Estimating the Stringency of the Test

We are interested in examining how the U.S. medical profession adjusts the stringency of the test it requires of IMGs. To do this, we need to know whether a change in the test represents an increase in the difficulty of entering the profession or an easing of entry into the profession.

A change in the stringency of the test required of IMGs affects the supply of candidates for licensure in three ways. First, as the test is costly and difficult, increases in its stringency lead fewer and better applicants to attempt it. Second, controlling for the quality of applicants taking the test, increases in stringency lead to a decline in the pass rate. Third, as test takers gain experience with a new test, preparation for the test becomes better, and pass rates, conditional on quality and test stringency, rise. Figure 7.1 describes the number of people taking the relevant IMG test each year, the pass rate on the test, and the product of these two figures, an estimate of the total number of people passing the test each year. The vertical lines show the introduction of new tests. As expected, the pass rate increases as time under a given test regime rises.

The U.S. medical profession ultimately wishes to adjust the quality and number of IMGs actually becoming licensed in the United States. That goal would argue toward using the number passing the test as the most relevant measure of stringency. However, the profession can only determine the test; other factors, including push factors, may affect the number who choose to take it. Thus, we consider two possible measures of test stringency: the pass rate on the test itself, which is arguably most in the control of the profession, and the number who pass it in a given year. We consider both variables, because the pass rate is likely to be endogenous; as the test gets harder, only more highly skilled students attempt to take it, so the pass rate may not change. The number of takers who pass the test each year, however, captures both the stringency of the test and the characteristics of students who choose to take it but also captures other push and pull elements.

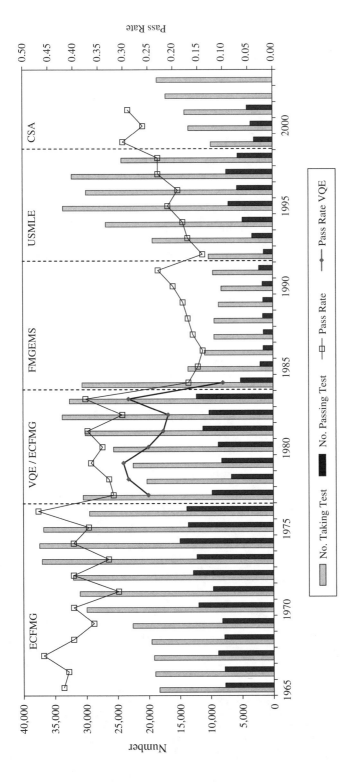

Figure 7.1 Test regimes, test takers, pass rate, and number passing.
Sources: Authors' calculation using data from ECFMG Annual Reports (various), USMLE Web site (Whelan, 2002), (Gonzalez, 1997/1998), CPS 1969–2001.

Our method requires us to know, for each test, whether it is more or less difficult than its predecessor. Since the Clinical Skills Assessment (CSA) supplements rather than replaces the USMLE test, we can safely conclude that the CSA is more stringent than its predecessor. For the other tests, we estimate the two measures of stringency controlling for the number of years since the exam was initially offered.

Information on the number of test takers and the pass rate are obtained from the USMLE Web site and from Whelan et al. (2002). To assess the effect

Table 7.2   Stringency of Exams Required for Licensure

	Pass rate		Number passing	
	VQE	No VQE	VQE	No VQE
Intercept	0.438**	0.430**	5893.856**	8401.946**
	(0.047)	(0.045)	(1338.130)	(800.233)
ECFMG/VQE	−0.032		2472.126*	
	(0.042)		(1091.170)	
FMGEMS	−0.236**	−0.225**	−4603.939**	−6497.302**
	(0.034)	(0.030)	(1091.170)	(746.908)
USMLE	−0.151**	−0.122**	−660.076**	−2726.766**
	(0.046)	(0.024)	(1211.230)	(848.285)
CSA	−0.117**	−0.10**	−2558.636**	−4830.235**
	(0.044)	(0.037)	(1453.710)	(1120.560)
Number of years since exam was introduced	0.003**	0.005**	74.468**	−104.632**
	(0.006)	(0.005)	(194.338)	(188.996)
Square of number of years since exam was introduced	0*	0*	23.523*	24.216*
	(0)	(0)	(9.917)	(10.552)
N	37	37	37	37
R^2	0.832	0.829	0.887	0.868

Note: VQE results include a dummy for 1977 VQE introduction. No VQE results exclude this variable.

Source: Authors' calculation using data from ECFMG annual reports (various), USMLE Web site, Whelan et al. (2002), Gonzalez and Zhang, (1997–1998), Wassenaar and Thran (2003), and March CPS (1969–2001). When there were two concurrent exams (ECFMG and VQE) from 1977 to 1984, we took the weighted average of the pass rates. If a new exam started in a certain year, we took the weighted average of the pass rates for the old and new exams for that year and considered the results to be part of the old exam. Standard errors in parentheses with $p < 0.05$ = *, $p < 0.01$ = **.

of the various exams on the pass rate and the number passing the test, we estimate a simple regression of exam dummies on the pass rate (number passing test), controlling for the number of years since the test was introduced and the squared number of years since introduction.

These results are reported in table 7.2 in columns 2 and 4. Using the pass-rate measure, we conclude that the 1977 ECFMG/VQE regime was not significantly different from its predecessor (the ECFMG test), the 1984 FMGEMS test was more stringent than the VQE test, but the 1992 USMLE test was less stringent than its predecessor. As noted above, we assume that the 1999 CSA test was more difficult than the USMLE test, despite the higher pass rate under this regime, because it supplemented the USMLE. In column 3, we repeat the analyses, treating the ECFMG/VQE regime as indistinguishable from the preceding regime. Again, we find that the FMGEMS test was more stringent than its predecessor, and the USMLE test was less stringent than the FMGEMS test.

Results for the number-passing measure are slightly different with respect to the ECFMG/VQE regime only. We estimate that more people, on average, passed the test under the ECFMG/VQE regime than under the pre-1977 ECFMG-only regime. In column 4, where we do not distinguish between the two regimes, we observe the same pattern as for the pass rate.

In our analyses of the factors affecting test stringency, we need a measure of changes in test stringency over time. We use the non-VQE measures because the coefficient on VQE is not significant. Using the non-VQE measure and either the pass rate or number passing, we consider three changes in the test: ECFMG/VQE to FMGEMS (harder), FMGEMS to USMLE (easier), and USMLE to CSA (harder).

Evolution of Cohort Quality, Rate of Return to Medicine, and Vacancy Rate

Cohort Quality

The COME serves the public interest by ensuring that the quality of those granted a medical license meets some standard. That standard need not be static; COME might choose to increase test stringency to raise the quality of physicians. Alternatively, if the market perceives IMGs as being of lower quality than USMGs or if market perceptions of the quality of IMGs are failing, COME might wish to increase the stringency of the exam.

The market quality of IMGs is likely to change over time as the source countries of migrants and the medical schools they attend change. In addition, IMGs tend to specialize in fields that USMGs view as less desirable, often because they cannot obtain residencies in the most desirable fields. Many IMGs work in inner cities and rural areas that USMGs tend to avoid (Kilborn, 1991; Kirk, 1991). To the extent that the returns to these less desirable specializations and locations decline over time, the market quality of IMGs will fall.

We use a method developed by George Borjas (1985) to estimate the market quality of successive cohorts of IMGs. Borjas noted that estimates of immigrant earnings measured in the cross section confounded changes in the quality of cohorts with the assimilation effect, through which earnings of immigrants increase with time in the United States. He used multiple cross sections to track the performance of specific cohorts over time, sorting out cohort quality, assimilation, and period effects. We follow his methods to examine the earnings of successive cohorts of foreign-born IMGs compared with USMGs. Our estimate provides an average measure of the quality of subsequent cohorts but does not address changes in cohort age/assimilation-earnings profiles. See Sarkar (1995) for a more complete discussion of our methodology.

DATA. We use data from the 1980, 1990, and 2000 U.S. censuses and restrict the sample to physicians working in the United States. We further restrict our sample of foreign-born physicians to those who were 25 years old or older at the time of their immigration, so as to ensure that these physicians completed their medical education abroad. We contrast the experience of cohorts who immigrated before 1950, between 1950 and 1959, between 1960 and 1964, and so on.[5] We control for the physician's experience (and the square of experience), hours worked in the preceding year, whether the physician is female, race, self-employment, sector of employment, region of the country, census year, and, for the foreign-born, years since migration (and the square of years since migration).

RESULTS. Table 7.3 describes the results of this regression. As expected, we find a strong assimilation effect. Earnings of foreign-born physicians increase, at a diminishing rate, with years in the United States. Earnings of all physicians (in CPI-adjusted terms) were 16 percent greater in 1990 than in 1980 and 24 percent greater in 2000 than in 1980.

Turning to cohort quality, we find a steady increase in the wage disadvantage of foreign-born physicians throughout this period, with the

5. The variable for the time period of immigration into the United States differs between the 1980 and 1990 census. The time period in the 1980 census is 1975 to 1980, while the corresponding time period in 1990 is 1975 to 1979 and 1980 to 1981. In order to make the groups conform, we treated the 1975-to-1979 category of the 1990 census as 1975 to 1980 and included 1980 to 1981 in the 1981-to-1984 group.

Table 7.3   The Changing Quality of Cohorts of IMGs: Pooled Census Regression

	Log of Annual Income	
	Coefficient	Standard error
Intercept	5.397**	(0.042)
Experience	0.089**	(0.001)
Experience squared	−0.002**	(0.000)
Log total hours worked	0.607**	(0.005)
Married	0.161**	(0.008)
Female	−0.339**	(0.008)
Resides in Northeast	0.013	(0.009)
Resides in South	−0.013	(0.008)
Resides in West	0.005	(0.009)
Black	−0.081**	(0.016)
Self-employed, nonincorporated	0.095**	(0.008)
Self-employed, incorporated	0.182**	(0.008)
Local government employee	−0.203**	(0.018)
State government employee	−0.183**	(0.012)
Federal government employee	−0.148**	(0.015)
Years since migration	0.018**	(0.003)
Years since migration squared	0.000**	(0.000)
Year 1990	0.162**	(0.008)
Year 2000	0.242**	(0.008)
Pre-1950 cohorts	0.039	(0.065)
1950–1959 cohort	−0.175**	(0.049)
1960–1964 cohort	−0.142**	(0.046)
1965–1969 cohort	−0.108**	(0.038)
1970–1974 cohort	−0.117**	(0.033)
1975–1980 cohort	−0.191**	(0.028)
1981–1984 cohort	−0.229**	(0.034)
1985–1990 cohort	−0.361**	(0.029)
1991–1994 cohort	−0.341**	(0.034)
1995–2000 cohort	−0.537**	(0.028)
N	76,040	
R^2	0.38	

Source: Census data from 1980, 1990, 2000. Standard errors in parentheses with $p < 0.05$ = *, $p < 0.01$ = **.

exception of the cohorts who entered in the 1960s, which have had slightly higher earnings than the 1950s entrants. This implies that the market valuation of the quality of successive cohorts of foreign-born physicians has been falling. The most likely explanation of this decline is that foreign-born physicians are much less likely to be subspecialists, and earnings of subspecialists have been increasing during this period. Regardless of the reason for the decline, however, this falling quality measure suggests one reason for COME to increase the stringency of the test required of IMGs. In our analyses, we smooth the cohort quality series using a three-year moving average. The resulting smoothed series of cohort quality is shown in figure 7.2.

Rate of Return to Medicine

The medical profession may wish to restrict the supply of IMGs in order to maintain a high rate of return to U.S. medical training. Many studies have estimated the rate of return to medical training (see Sarkar, 1995, for a summary). Following Rosen (1977), we can estimate the rate of return to medical practice as

$$R = ln(IY_2/Y_1)/s$$

where Y_2 is the earnings of physicians, Y_1 is the earnings of college graduates (without further training), and s is the length of physician training. We take s to equal 9, reflecting 4 years of medical education and 5 years of residency, including any specialty training (since we cannot separate specialist and nonspecialist physicians in our data).

Physicians typically work longer hours than nonphysicians. For this reason, Sloan and Feldman (1978) recommend adjusting the rate-of-return calculation to reflect differences in hours worked:

$$R = [ln (Y_2/Y_1) - ln (H_2/H_1)]/s$$

DATA. We use data from the annual Current Population Survey to estimate annual earnings and annual hours worked for full-time employed college graduates (those with exactly a college education). We cannot use this survey to estimate the earnings of physicians, because income data are top-coded, and many physicians earn incomes greater than the top code. In principle, various econometric techniques and empirical income distributions can be imposed to adjust for the top code (see Sarkar, 1995, for discussion). However, in the later years of our data, more than half of the physicians in the sample have incomes greater than the top-code range. This leaves us with very little information with which to estimate the top

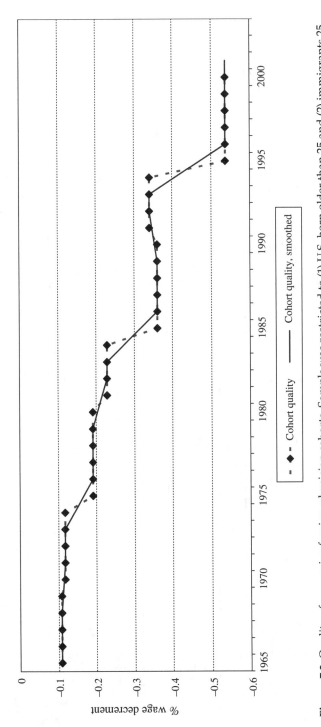

Figure 7.2 Quality of successive foreign-physician cohorts. Sample was restricted to (1) U.S.-born older than 25 and (2) immigrants 25 at the time of immigration. The dependent variable was the log of income in constant dollars (1990).
Source: Authors' calculation using Census 1980, 1990, 2000.

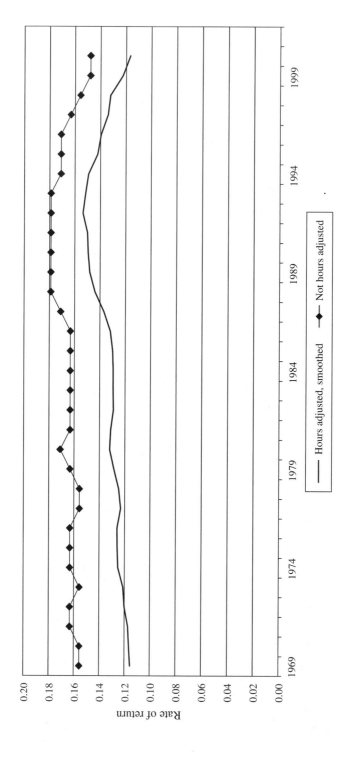

Figure 7.3 Rate of return to medical education.
Sources: Author's calculation using March CPS 1969–2001, Gonzalez (1997/1998), Wassenaar (2003), AMA data.

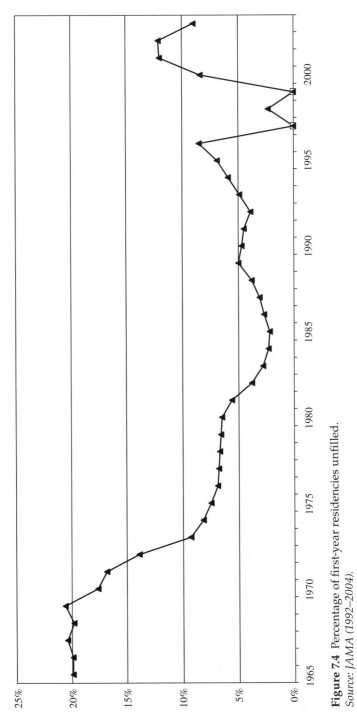

Figure 7.4 Percentage of first-year residencies unfilled.
Source: JAMA (1992–2004).

part of the distribution. Instead, we use data collected by the AMA through its Socioeconomic Monitoring Surveys (Gonzalez and Zhang, 1997–1998; Wassenaar and Thran, 2003) to capture the net earnings and hours of physicians. These figures may overstate earnings to the extent that the AMA sample selects a more-successful-than-average population of physicians.

RESULTS. Figure 7.3 presents the rate of return to medical education over time. The rate of return is consistently high, more than 12 percent, reflecting restricted entry into the profession. We compute a three-year moving average of the rate of return. The rate of return rose through the mid-1970s, flattened for a period, rose again in the early 1980s, flattened through the mid-1980s, rose very sharply in the late 1980s and early 1990s, and has fallen steadily since 1993.

Residency Vacancy Rate

We obtained data on the number of graduate medical education residencies in U.S. hospitals published periodically in the *Journal of the American Medical Association*. This source also provided information on the share of open residency positions that were filled. We compute a three-year moving average of this estimate (see figure 7.4).

Factors Affecting Test Stringency

The test governing entry of IMGs into the United States changed five times from 1958 to 1999. We hypothesized that declines in the market-perceived quality of IMGs would be expected to lead to increases in the stringency of the test, that declines in the rate of return to medicine would be expected to lead to increases in the stringency of the test, and that increases in the vacancy rate for residencies would lead to a decrease in the stringency of the test.

As the discussion above suggests, the process of revamping the test for medical licensure takes some time. We expect that these factors will affect the stringency of the test with a lag. In our analyses, we estimate results using three-year lags.[6]

---

6. Note that for those independent variables that are three-year moving averages, these lagged variables actually reflect values two to five years before the observation date. The use of lagged values also avoids the problem of reverse causality, which is unlikely to be an issue with the rate of return to medicine (since the number of new physicians is small compared with the existing pool) but could be a problem with respect to the vacancy rate.

We use the measured changes in test stringency and the time series of the three factors to estimate the effect of these factors on the decision to change the stringency of the test. We implement our analysis by conducting multinomial logit regressions (with Huber-White corrected standard errors) on the decision to hold the test constant, to make it more difficult, or to make it easier. Results are given in table 7.4.

Table 7.4   Factors Predicting Change (Easier/Harder) in the Test Required of IMGs

	Pass rate and number passing (no VQE)
Easier	
Rate of return (L3)	214.650*
	(54.471)
Residency vacancy rate (L3)	2.460
	(21.717)
Cohort quality (L3)	2.603
	(4.531)
Intercept	−33.157*
	(6.550)
Harder	
Rate of return (L3)	15.756
	(49.966)
Residency vacancy rate (L3)	9.203
	(26.502)
Cohort quality (L3)	−5.522
	(8.279)
Intercept	−7.202
	(11.136)
N	32
Pseudo R^2	0.157

Note: Multinomial logistic regression (left-out category is same test). "Pass rate" and "number passing" exclude the VQE in computation of relative test stringency. Test-stringency results from table 7.2 and from assumption that CSA test was harder than predecessor. Test stringency converted to direction of change by comparing coefficient on current test to that on preceding test. Rate of return from figure 7.3; vacancy rate from figure 7.4; cohort quality from table 7.3. All independent variables lagged three periods. Standard errors in parentheses with $p < 0.05$ = *.

We find no evidence to suggest that the residency vacancy rate influences changes in the test regime. We find that cohort quality is also not associated with changes in the test, although increases in cohort quality have a nonsignificant negative effect on the probability that the test becomes more difficult. We do, however, find that increases in the rate of return to medicine predict when the test will become easier.

We have repeated the analyses including the VQE test, and the results did not change substantively. We have also repeated the analyses including only those IMGs who took the VQE test (rather than the NBME test, which was only available to those with visas) and the pass rate on that test. Again, our result—that the rate of return to medicine predicted changes in the test regime—was robust to this modification.

In figure 7.5, we display the difference between the predicted probability that the test will become harder and the probability that it will become easier. The results suggest that the stringency of requirements placed on foreign medical graduates is likely to increase, rather than abate, in the future as the rate of return to medical education within the United States stagnates.

Conclusions

The immigration of skilled professionals depends not only on national immigration policy but also on the acquiescence of self-governing professions. Without the cooperation of professional licensing societies, people who gain skills elsewhere will have little ability to practice their professions in the United States and little incentive to migrate. This chapter suggests that the self-interest of domestic professionals is a significant determinant of physician-immigration restrictions.

The public-policy implications of these restrictions are not entirely clear. Professions regulate entry both at home and with respect to immigrants. Both types of restriction lower consumer surplus, particularly in the absence of physician-induced demand for excess care. To the extent that the United States would benefit from an increased supply of physicians, it could recruit those physicians from U.S. applicants.

One benefit to the United States of the immigration of skilled professionals is that undergraduate medical education is often heavily subsidized. In the United States, graduate medical education, at the level of residency training, is also heavily subsidized. The immigration of foreign-trained physicians saves the United States the cost of any subsidies to undergraduate medical education. The same argument suggests, however, that emigration of skilled medical professionals may reduce welfare for the sending nation, an effect compounded by the potential contributions

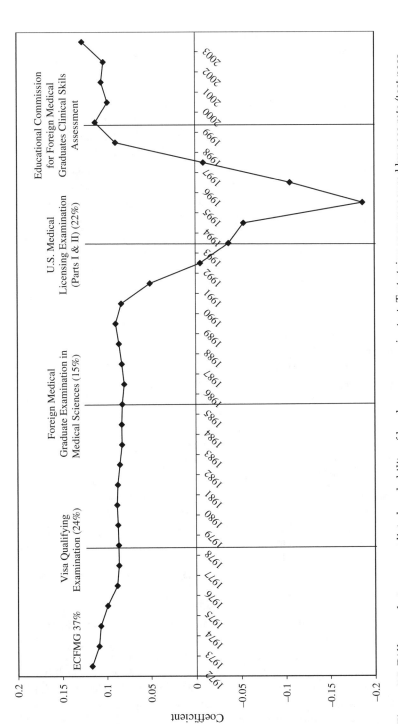

Figure 7.5 Difference between predicted probability of harder versus easier test. Test stringency measured by pass rate (test pass rates in parentheses).

Source: Coefficients from MNL regressions reported in table 7.4; test data from table 7.1; pass rates from figure 7.1. If a new exam started in a certain year, we took the weighted average of the pass rates for the old and new exams for that year and considered the results to be part of the old exam.

of these skilled professionals to the health of populations in their home countries. The brain drain of skilled medical professionals appears, for example, to be impeding the ability to address the HIV crisis in sub-Saharan Africa.

The large supply of well-trained physicians outside the United States may affect the practice of medicine and the returns to medical education here even if the migration of physicians is further discouraged. A new industry has begun to offer lower-cost medical treatment, provided by foreign medical professionals, in hospitals abroad. In some cases, these physicians provide outsourced services—such as reading diagnostic tests—in collaboration with U.S. facilities. In other cases, the foreign hospitals offer full medical services. As trade theory would predict, if lower-cost foreign physicians cannot enter the United States to treat American patients, American patients may travel abroad to obtain their services.

References

American Medical Association. 2005. "IMGs in the U.S." www.ama-assn.org/ama/pub/category/211.html.

Association of American Medical Colleges. 2005. "Medicare Direct Graduate Medical Education Payments." www.aamc.org/advocacy/library/gme/gme0001.htm.

Blumenthal, D. 2004. "New Steam from an Old Cauldron—The Physician-Supply Debate." *New England Journal of Medicine* 350, no. 17: 1780–87.

Borjas, George J, 1985. "Assimilation, Changes in Cohort Quality, and the Earnings of Immigrants." *Journal of Labor Economics* 3, no. 4: 463–89.

Brotherton, S. E., P. H. Rockey, and S. I. Etzel. 2003. "U.S. Graduate Medical Education, 2002–2003." *Journal of the American Medical Association* 290, no. 9: 1197–1202.

Centers for Medicare and Medicaid Services. 2005. "Graduate Medical Education, Indirect Medical Education Payment, Disproportionate Share Payment and Number of Hospital Beds" Data through December 31, 2004. www.cms.hhs.gov/data/download/hcris_hospital/default.asp.

Cooper, R. A., T. E. Getzen, H. J. McKee, and P. Laud. 2002. "Economic and Demographic Trends Signal an Impending Physician Shortage." *Health Affairs* 21, no. 1: 140–54.

Council on Graduate Medical Education. 1992. "Summary of Third Report: Improving Access to Health Care through Physician Workforce Reform." www.cogme.gov/rpt3.htm.

———. 2000. "Summary of Resource Paper: The Effects of the Balanced Budget Act of 1997 on Graduate Medical Education." www.cogme.gov/resource_bba.htm.

Dublin, T. D., B. S. Bloom, R. S. Knorr, and R. L. Casterline. 1985. "Where Have All the Students Gone? An Epidemiologic Study of U.S. Nationals Applying for Certification by the Educational Commission for Foreign Medical Graduates, 1969 through 1982." *Journal of the American Medical Association* 253, no. 3: 376–81.

Educational Commission for Foreign Medical Graduates. 2005. "ECFMG History." www.ecfmg.org/annuals/2002/examhist.html.

Friedman, M., and S. Kuznets. 1945. *Income from Independent Professional Practice.* New York: National Bureau of Economic Research.

Gonzalez, M. L., and P. Zhang, eds. 1997–1998. *Socioeconomic Characteristics of Medical Practice.* Chicago: American Medical Association, Center for Health Policy Research.

Graduate Medical Education National Advisory Committee. 1980. Report of the Graduate Medical Education National Advisory Committee to the Secretary, Department of Health and Human Services. Hyattsville, MD: Department of Health and Human Services.

Hallock, J. A., S. S. Seeling, and J. J. Norcini. 2003. "The International Medical Graduate Pipeline: Whether to Depend on IMGs to Remedy the U.S. Physician Shortfall Involves Global Ethical Considerations." *Health Affairs* 22, no. 4: 94–96.

Hubbard, J. P., and E. J. Levit. 1985. *The National Board of Medical Examiners, the First Seventy Years: A Continuing Commitment to Excellence.* Philadelphia: National Board of Medical Examiners, pp. 50–74, 119–29.

JAMA (Journal of the American Medical Association). 1992–2004. "Graduate Medical Education" (annual reports).

Kessel, R. A. 1958. "Discrimination in Medicine." *Journal of Law and Economics* 1: 20–53.

———. 1970. "The A.M.A. and the Supply of Physicians." *Law and Contemporary Problems* 35: 267–83.

Kilborn, P. T. 1991. "Foreign Doctors Flocking to Rescue Long-Shunned Areas of Dire Poverty." *New York Times,* November 2.

Kindig, D. A., and D. L. Libby. 1996. "Domestic Production vs. International Immigration: Options for the U.S. Physician Workforce." *Journal of the American Medical Association* 276, no. 12: 978–82.

Kirk, K. 1991. "Rural Areas Losing Appeal to Young Doctors." *Ohio Medicine* 87, no. 1 (January): 24–27.

Lindsay, C. M. 1973. "Real Returns to Medical Education." *Journal of Human Resources* 8: 331–48.

Mullan, F., R. M. Politzer, and C. H. Davis. 1995. "Medical Migration and the Physician Workforce: International Medical Graduates and American Medicine." *Journal of the American Medical Association* 273, no. 19: 1521–27.

Reinhardt, U. E. 1985. "The Theory of Physician-Induced Demand: Reflections after a Decade." *Journal of Health Economics* 4, no. 2 (June): 187–93.

Rosen, S. 1977. "Labor Quality, The Demand for Skill, and Market Selection." NBER Working Paper 0162.

Salsberg, E. S. 1998. "Development of a Framework for Revised COGME Physician Workforce Goals." Report for COGME.

Salsberg, E. S., and G. J. Forte. 2002. "Trends in the Physician Workforce, 1980–2000." *Health Affairs* 21, no. 5:165–73.

Sarkar, D. 1995. "Organized Medicine in the United States and International Medical Graduates." Ph.D. dissertation, Columbia University.

Sloan, F., and R. Feldman. 1978. "Monopolistic Elements in the Market for Physicians' Services," in W. Greenberg, ed., *Competition in the Health Care Sector: Past, Present, and Future.* Washington, DC: Federal Trade Commission.

U.S. Citizenship and Immigration Services. 2005. "Immigration and Naturalization Legislation from the Statistical Yearbook." http://uscis.gov/graphics/shared/aboutus/statistics/legishist/index.htm.

U.S. Department of Health and Human Services. 2003. Health, United States. 2003 National Center for Health Statistics. Hyattsville, MD, p. 289.

U.S. Medical Licensing Examination. www.usmle.org/scores/scores.htm.

———. 2004. "Step 2 Clinical Skills (CS) Update." www.usmle.org/step2/Step2CS/Step2Indexes/Step2CS2004update.asp.

Wassenaar, J. D., and S. L. Thran, eds. 2003. *Physician Socioeconomic Statistics.* Chicago, American Medical Association.

Whelan, Gerald P., N. E. Gary, J. Kostis, J. R. Boulet, and James A. Hallock. 2002. "The Changing Pool of International Medical Graduates Seeking Certification Training in U.S. Graduate Medical Education Programs." *Journal of the American Medical Association* 2002, no. 288: 1079–84, figure 3. http://jama.ama-assn.org/cgi/content/full/288/9/1079#TABLEJSC20153T3.

8

Individual Preferences over High-Skilled Immigration in the United States

GORDON HANSON, KENNETH SCHEVE, AND MATTHEW J. SLAUGHTER

In the United States, immigration is a source of intense political conflict. Despite widespread criticism of U.S. immigration practices, there is little consensus about how to change the management of immigrant inflows. Current immigration policy is viewed as allowing a large number of illegal aliens to enter the United States, increasing the supply of low-skilled labor in the country, and admitting individuals who place large demands on public expenditure. These outcomes, in turn, are blamed for expanding the underground economy, hurting low-income U.S. workers, and increasing fiscal deficits.

Among the more sweeping proposals for reforming U.S. immigration is the suggestion to replace the current system, in which legal admissions of permanent immigrants are based primarily on family reunification, with one in which admissions are instead based on the skill set that an individual possesses (Borjas, 1999b; Huntington, 2004). Shifting from a family-based to a skills-based admissions criterion, the reasoning goes, would allow the United States to select individuals who have high earnings potential, good prospects for succeeding in the U.S. economy, and a low likelihood of drawing on public benefits.[1]

It is unclear, however, whether there is sufficient political support to shift U.S. policy toward favoring high-skilled immigrants. The public is sharply divided over immigration. When asked about the level of U.S. immigration, nearly half of survey respondents would prefer to see the numbers admitted reduced (Scheve and Slaughter, 2001a). This opposition

For financial support, we gratefully acknowledge the National Science Foundation.
1. Presumably, the United States would also have to strengthen enforcement against illegal immigration. Otherwise, any change in legal admissions would likely be undone by a change in illegal inflows. See Hanson (2005).

is surely conditional on the nature of U.S. policies. But would changing admissions criteria reduce opposition to immigration sufficiently to make reform of U.S. immigration feasible?

Previous research offers many reasons to think the answer may be yes. Skilled immigrants have been shown to be a source of entrepreneurial activity. For example, during the 1990s information-technology boom in Silicon Valley, Chinese and Indian immigrants started new companies at an accelerating rate and accounted for 25 percent of the senior executives at all start-up firms (Saxenian, 1999). Firms started and/or populated by immigrants forge a wide range of international networks with home countries and elsewhere, which may foster economic growth by facilitating cross-border flows of ideas, capital, and goods and services (Rauch, 2001; Rauch and Trindade, 2002; Saxenian, 2002). More generally, in recent decades, skilled immigrants—many of whom were educated at American universities—have accounted for sharply increasing shares of very highly skilled segments of the U.S. labor force that are critical for supporting highly productive, highly compensated jobs. By 2000, 38 percent of all American Ph.D.s in science and engineering occupations were foreign-born, up from only 23 percent in 1990 (National Science Foundation, 2004). This evidence on the potential dynamic benefits from skilled immigrants might make natives more inclined to favor liberalization of immigration policy where they are more exposed to skilled immigration.

In this chapter, we examine individual preferences toward skilled immigration in the United States. In particular, we ask whether individuals are less opposed to immigration in states with more highly skilled immigrant populations. To implement the analysis, we combine micro data on public attitudes toward immigration with data on the size and composition of U.S. immigrant populations across regions and over time.

That opinions about immigration vary is not surprising. Immigration, like international trade, foreign investment, and other aspects of globalization, changes the distribution of income within a country. In the United States, a disproportionate number of immigrants have low skill levels, concentrating the negative labor-market effects of immigration on lower-skilled U.S. residents. In 2003, 33 percent of foreign-born adults in the United States had less than 12 years of education, compared with only 13 percent of native-born adults. By increasing the relative supply of low-skilled labor, immigration puts downward pressure on the wages of low-skilled native-born workers. Borjas (2003) finds that between 1980 and 2000, immigration had the largest effect on the low-skilled, reducing the wages of native-born high school dropouts by 9 percent.[2]

---

2. While many early studies of the labor-market consequences of immigration found that its wage impacts were small (Borjas, 1999a), recent studies find that

Consistent with these labor-market repercussions, Scheve and Slaughter (2001b) find that opposition to immigration is higher among lower-educated U.S. workers. Lower-skilled laborers' skepticism about immigration mirrors their skepticism about globalization in general.[3]

A second source of opposition to immigration relates to its consequences for public finances. Low-skilled immigrants tend to earn relatively low wages, to contribute relatively little in taxes, and to enroll in government entitlement programs with relatively high frequency. There is abundant evidence that immigrants make greater use of welfare programs than natives (Borjas and Hilton, 1996; Borjas, 1999b; Fix and Passel, 2002). This has remained true even after the 1996 reform of U.S. welfare law, which restricted immigrant access to many types of government benefits (Zimmerman and Tumlin, 1999; Fix and Passel, 2002). In U.S. states with large immigrant populations, such as California, immigration appears to increase net burdens on native taxpayers substantially (Smith and Edmonston, 1997).

The fiscal impact of immigration is reflected in public attitudes toward immigration policy. Hanson, Scheve, and Slaughter (2007) find that U.S. natives who are more exposed to immigrant fiscal pressures (i.e., individuals living in states that have large immigrant populations and that provide immigrants access to generous public benefits) are more in favor of reducing immigration. This public-finance cleavage is strongest among natives with high earnings potential (e.g., the college educated or individuals in the top income quartile), and its substantive magnitude is as large as the labor-market cleavage cited above.

In short, previous literature suggests that individual attitudes about immigration depend on an individual's skill level, the size of the immigrant population in an individual's state, and the exposure of an individual to the fiscal consequences of immigration. In this chapter, we add to this discussion the possibility that individuals also care about the skill composition of immigration.

In the first section, we develop a simple framework of voter preferences toward immigration. One channel through which the skill composition of immigration may affect individual policy preferences is through knowledge spillovers or other nonpecuniary externalities. As discussed above, high-skilled immigrants may bring new technology, new information about foreign markets, or new ways of doing business, any of which would

---

immigration depresses wages for native workers who are likely to substitute for immigrant labor (Borjas, Freeman, and Katz, 1997; Borjas, 2003).

3. See Rodrik (1997, 1998), Scheve and Slaughter (2001a, 2001b, 2001c, 2004), O'Rourke and Sinnott (2001, 2003), Mayda and Rodrik (2005), Hainmueller and Hiscox (2004), and Mayda (2006).

increase U.S. labor demand. A second channel is through its impact on the fiscal consequences of immigration. Individuals may expect higher-skilled immigrants to generate positive net fiscal transfers to native households. If either of these channels is operative, individuals may be less opposed to immigration the more skilled is the immigrant population in their region.

This reasoning depends, of course, on holding constant other individual and regional characteristics. Obviously, high-skilled immigrants are likely to compete with high-skilled natives in the labor force, which may temper the enthusiasm of high-skilled natives for high-skilled immigrant admissions. Indeed, the documented opposition of low-skilled U.S. natives to immigration appears to reflect their concerns about downward wage pressures from low-skilled immigrants. However, if high-skilled immigration creates positive fiscal benefits and/or nonpecuniary externalities, the opposition of more highly skilled natives to high-skilled immigration may be weaker than the opposition of less highly skilled native to low-skilled immigrant inflows.

Data for the analysis, described in the second section, come from several sources. We combine the 1992 and 2000 American National Election Studies (NES) surveys (Sapiro et al., 1998) with data on immigrant and native populations, labor-force participation, and use of public assistance from the U.S. Census of Population and Housing of 1990 and 2000. Additional data include information on state fiscal policies, particularly their welfare generosity in general and toward immigrants in particular. Our data allow us to exploit variation both across states and over time, such as the fact that some high-immigrant states (Massachusetts, New Jersey) have highly skilled immigrant populations while other high-immigrant states (Texas, Arizona) do not.

To preview the empirical results, reported in the third section, our main finding is that skill composition does matter but not across the board. Less highly skilled natives tend to support freer immigration more when living in states with a relatively skilled mix of immigrants. The sensitivity of less highly skilled natives' opinions to the skill composition of immigrants resonates with earlier findings of concern over the labor-market pressures of immigration. By way of conclusion, we consider the implications of our results for political prospects of proposals to reform U.S. immigration policy.

Theoretical Framework

In this section, we develop a simple framework of voter preferences to examine how cleavages regarding immigration vary across jurisdictions. While our focus is on individual economic welfare, there are surely many noneconomic determinants of attitudes toward globalization.[4] These noneconomic determinants we set aside for now, but they will be an important consideration in our empirical analysis.

Let $V(p, I_i)$ be the indirect utility enjoyed by individual i, which depends on the vector of prices for consumption goods and services p and also on after-tax income available for consumption I_i. In turn, after-tax income depends on the pretax wage income y_i, the income-tax rate t_i, and government transfers g_i, such that

$$I_i = y_i(1 - t_i) + g_i. \tag{8.1}$$

Tax rates and government transfers vary across individuals by both state of residence and level of income. Equation (8.1) assumes all income is from labor earnings and only labor earnings are taxed. Neither assumption is essential, but they simplify the presentation.

First, consider the impact on individual welfare of an increase in immigration. By differentiating the indirect utility function, we obtain the following:

$$\Delta V_i = \frac{\partial V}{\partial p} \frac{\partial p}{\partial M} \Delta M + \frac{\partial V}{\partial I_i} \frac{\partial I_i}{\partial M} \Delta M, \tag{8.2}$$

where ΔM is the change in immigration in the state in which person i resides. It is useful to reexpress this change in welfare in monetary terms. This can be done by using equation (8.1) to solve for $\partial I_i / \partial M$ in terms of the components of after-tax income and then dividing equation (8.2) by $\partial V / \partial I_i$, the marginal utility of income:

$$\frac{\Delta V_i}{\partial V / \partial I_i} = \frac{\partial V / \partial p}{\partial V / \partial I_i} \frac{\partial p}{\partial M} \Delta M + \frac{\partial y_i}{\partial M}(1 - t_i)\Delta M + \left(\frac{\partial g_i}{\partial M} - y_i \frac{\partial t_i}{\partial M}\right)\Delta M. \tag{8.3}$$

Consider the three terms on the right-hand side of equation (8.3). The first term is the monetary value of the utility change associated with immigration's impact on product prices. To the extent that immigration lowers the price at which goods are available in individual i's state (relative to labor income), this term will be positive. If the share of individual spending on nontraded services (e.g., construction, housekeeping, yard care, restaurants, lodging) is increasing in income and if these services are intensive in immigrant labor, the price impact of immigration may be largest for higher-income individuals, making them relatively more supportive of freer immigration. Looking ahead to our empirical analysis, we do not have data on individual expenditure patterns. But we do have data on other individual characteristics that may be proxy for these patterns, such

4. See, for example, Citrin et al. (1997), Scheve and Slaughter (2001a, 2001b, 2001c), Kessler (2001), O'Rourke and Sinnott (2001, 2003), Mayda and Rodrik (2005), Mayda (2006), and Hainmueller and Hiscox (2004).

as age and schooling. We will also control for any state-specific components of this price channel, because of the size of immigrant inflows or other state characteristics.

The second term on the right of (8.3) is the immigration-induced change in pretax labor income. If immigration increases the relative supply of low-skilled labor, we expect this term to be positive for high-skilled natives and negative for the low-skilled. If the only impact of skilled immigration is on the supply of labor, we would expect the opposite signs if immigrants are predominantly high-skilled. However, to the extent that high-skilled immigrants are also a source of knowledge spillovers, $\partial y_i/\partial M$ will be more positive for low-skilled individuals and less negative (or even positive) for high-skilled natives.

The third term on the right of equation (8.3) is the change in the net fiscal transfer received by individual i. This net fiscal transfer, $g_i - y_i t_i$, contains state and federal components. We assume that the federal component can be expressed as a reduced-form function of individual characteristics. The state component of the net fiscal transfer will depend on the interaction of individual characteristics and state tax and spending policies. In states with generous benefits and progressive taxation, we expect the net fiscal transfer an individual receives to be decreasing in individual income. In states with less generous benefits and less progressive taxation, we expect the correlation between fiscal transfers and income to be less negative.

How will immigration change net fiscal transfers received by natives? We assume that the arrival of immigrants is accommodated through a combination of reduced government transfers to and increased taxation of native state residents.[5] If immigrants are primarily low-skilled, then immigration is likely to reduce the net fiscal transfer received by natives, with this reduction being larger (1) in states that have larger immigrant populations and that are more generous in the public benefits they provide and (2) for high-income individuals (at least in states with progressive income taxation) (Hanson, Scheve, and Slaughter, 2007).

If immigrants are primarily high-skilled, these immigrants may make positive net fiscal transfers to U.S. native taxpayers. If increased revenues from high-skilled immigrants are not fully offset by decreased taxes or reduced borrowing, then their arrival may expand transfers received by low-income residents (especially in states that are more generous). For low-skilled natives, we thus expect $\partial g_i/\partial M \geq 0$ in the case of high-skilled immigration. In states with progressive taxation, low-income individuals pay relatively little in taxes, which makes the impact of immigration on their

---

5. Although, in principle, fiscal impact of immigration could also be accommodated through increased borrowing, all states but Vermont self-impose balanced-budget requirements of some type.

tax payments, $\partial t_i/\partial M$, small. Thus, for low-income individuals, we expect the impact of high-skilled immigration on net fiscal transfers to be weakly positive (particularly for generous states with progressive taxation).

Now consider high-income individuals. They are likely to receive little in state transfers, making $\partial g_i/\partial M$ small. But they are likely to bear a relatively large share of the state tax burden (especially in states with progressive income taxes). If the gain in tax revenues associated with high-skilled immigration is partially offset by a reduction in state tax rates, then $\partial t_i/\partial M$ will be negative (their tax rates fall). Combining terms, we expect that for high-income individuals, the impact of high-skilled immigration on net fiscal transfers will be weakly positive as well.

Finally, consider middle-income individuals. They are likely to receive less in state transfers than low-income individuals. They are also likely to pay less of their income in taxes than high-income individuals. Accordingly, we might expect immigration to affect the net fiscal transfers of middle-income individuals least of all.

In states that lack generous public benefits and progressive taxation, the impact of immigration on net fiscal transfers is likely to be relatively small for either low-income or high-income individuals. For individuals in these states, the after-tax fiscal term in (8.3) is thus likely to be dominated by the pretax price and labor-income terms.

Equation (8.3) offers a framework for how immigration cleavages may differ across individuals and fiscal jurisdictions. The pretax labor-income pressures from immigration are likely to cleave across skill groups within all jurisdictions. But there should also be after-tax fiscal pressures that vary with both skill type and the state taxing/spending regime. The perceived effects of high-skilled immigration on labor markets and public finances depend, in addition, on whether individuals expect high-skilled immigration to generate knowledge spillovers or positive net fiscal transfers to natives.

Data and Summary Statistics

The main objective of our empirical work is to provide evidence evaluating the claim that individual policy preferences about immigration are associated with the skill composition of the immigrant population. The data for our analysis come from four sources. We measure individual attitudes regarding immigration using the 1992 and 2000 American National Election Studies (NES) (Sapiro et al., 1998). Data on U.S. immigrants come from the 1990 and 2000 U.S. Census of Population and Housing and the 1994–2003 U.S. Current Population Survey. Finally, data on state fiscal policies come from the U.S. Censuses of Governments.

Immigrant Populations in U.S. States

States vary both in their exposure to immigration and in the skill composition of their immigrant populations. Figure 8.1 shows the distribution of natives and immigrants by schooling category, based on U.S. Census data. As is well documented, immigrants are concentrated at the extremes of the skill distribution. Immigrants are heavily overrepresented among those with less than a high school education, underrepresented among those with high school diplomas or some college, equally represented among those with college degrees, and slightly overrepresented among those with advanced degrees. Not surprisingly, educational attainment is strongly correlated with the economic performance of immigrants. Figure 8.2 shows that immigrants with at least a high school diploma have substantially higher earnings than the immigrant population overall. Immigrant earnings potential, as summarized by the level of schooling, may influence native perceptions of the economic consequences of immigration. Schooling affects both with whom immigrants compete in the labor market and the likelihood that immigrants draw on public benefits.

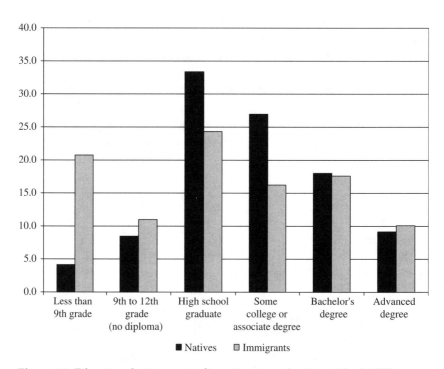

Figure 8.1 Educational attainment of immigrants and natives, March 2003.

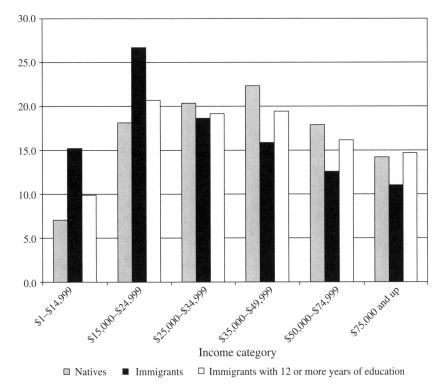

☐ Natives   ■ Immigrants   ☐ Immigrants with 12 or more years of education

Figure 8.2 Earnings distribution of immigrants and natives, 2002.

Also well known is that states vary in the size and composition of their immigrant populations. Figure 8.3, which plots the share of immigrants in the state working-age-adult population, reproduces the familiar fact that immigrants are geographically concentrated. For the United States as a whole, the immigrant-adult population share rose sharply from 1990 to 2000. In 2000, the immigrant population ratio is between 30 percent and 40 percent in two states (California, New York) and above the national average of 16.5 percent in 11 others.[6]

Immigrants with more education appear to concentrate where skilled native workers are in relatively short supply. Figures 8.4a and 8.4b plot the relative supply of high-skilled workers for state immigrant and native populations, where we measure the relative supply of skilled labor as the ratio of college graduates (individuals with 16 or more years of schooling) to high school dropouts (individuals with less than 12 years of schooling

6. These states are New Jersey, Hawaii, Florida, Nevada, Texas, Connecticut, Massachusetts, Arizona, Rhode Island, Illinois, and the District of Columbia.

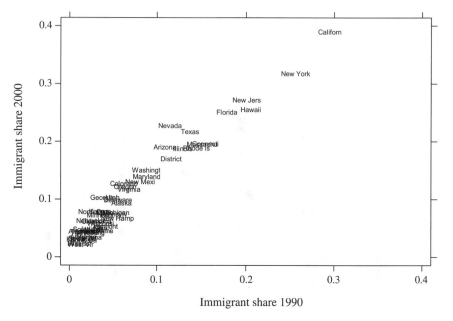

Figure 8.3 Share of immigrants in state population.

and no high school diploma). There is a negative relationship between the relative supply of immigrant and native college graduates across U.S. states. This suggests that high-skilled immigrants may be drawn to regions where the size of this labor group is relatively small among the native population. In both 1990 and 2000, U.S. states in the Southwest and on the West Coast stand out as having a relatively abundant supply of low-skilled immigrants.

Heterogeneity in state immigrant populations is also reflected in the economic performance of immigrants. Figures 8.5a and 8.5b plot the ratio of immigrant to native per-capita income against the immigrant ratio of college graduates to high school dropouts over the native ratio of college graduates to high school dropouts. There is a strong positive relationship between the relative supply of skilled immigrants and immigrant relative incomes. Immigrants have high incomes relative to natives in states in which high-skilled immigrants are relatively abundant.

Differences in schooling between immigrants and natives affect the likelihood with which the two groups use public assistance. Table 8.1 shows immigrant and native usage of different types of public assistance for the period 1994 to 2002. In 2002, immigrant-headed households were much more likely than native-headed households to participate in welfare

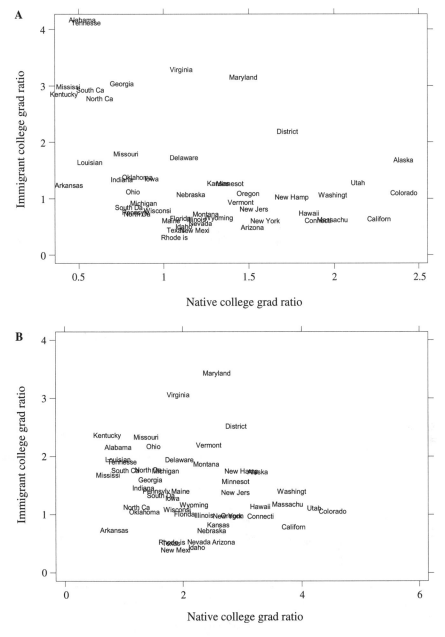

Figure 8.4 (a) Ratio of college graduates to high school dropouts, 1990. (b) Ratio of college graduates to high school dropouts, 2000.

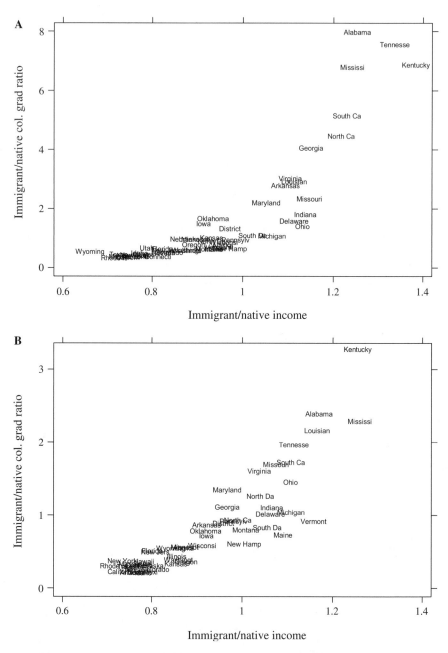

Figure 8.5 (a) Immigrant/native relative education and per capita income, 1990.
(b) Immigrant/native relative education and per capita income, 2000.

Table 8.1 Welfare Participation in More and Less Generous States

	A. Welfare Participation Rates (% of Households Receiving Some Type of Assistance)				B. Cash Program Participation Rates (% of Households Receiving Cash Assistance)			
	Natives		Immigrants		Natives		Immigrants	
	Less generous states	More generous states	Less generous states	More generous states	Less generous states	More generous states	Less generous states	More generous states
1994	16.7	13.9	22.8	25.2	7.7	7.6	8.2	14.3
1995	15.8	13.7	22.9	25.2	7.2	7.5	8.2	14.0
1996	16.2	13.9	19.3	24.0	7.0	7.6	7.4	13.1
1997	14.7	12.9	17.1	22.4	6.6	6.4	6.1	11.3
1998	13.9	12.6	16.9	21.9	5.7	6.0	5.6	10.5
1999	13.6	12.6	15.5	21.5	5.4	5.6	4.7	9.9
2000	14.0	12.9	15.4	23.7	5.1	5.1	3.4	9.1
2001	15.2	13.4	18.5	25.3	5.1	4.9	3.5	8.6
2002	16.0	13.7	20.7	25.5	4.9	4.9	3.4	8.3

(continued)

Table 8.1 *(continued)*

	C. Medicaid Participation Rates (% of Households Receiving Medicaid)				D. Food Stamp Participation Rates (% of Households Receiving Food Stamps)			
	Natives		Immigrants		Natives		Immigrants	
	Less generous states	More generous states	Less generous states	More generous states	Less generous states	More generous states	Less generous states	More generous states
1994	14.1	12.4	18.6	23.6	9.6	7.3	14.2	13.6
1995	13.5	12.4	19.5	23.6	8.6	7.1	13.1	12.6
1996	14.0	12.6	17.2	22.7	8.3	7.2	11.0	11.4
1997	12.8	11.8	15.2	20.9	7.3	6.0	9.2	10.3
1998	12.2	11.6	15.4	20.7	6.4	5.2	5.7	9.1
1999	12.2	11.7	13.8	20.7	5.8	4.6	6.2	7.7
2000	12.5	12.2	14.0	22.6	5.8	4.3	4.8	6.7
2001	13.7	12.6	17.3	24.5	6.2	4.3	5.3	6.7
2002	14.5	12.8	19.4	24.7	6.3	4.6	5.8	6.8

Source: Current Population Survey, Annual Demographic Files, various years.

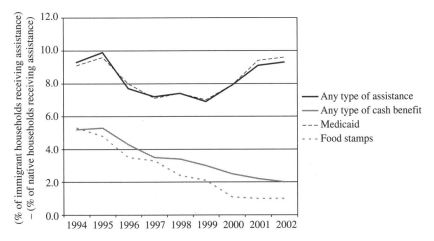

Figure 8.6 Difference in immigrant and native welfare-participation rates.

programs.[7] Among immigrant households, 24.2 percent had at least one member who used some type of social assistance, compared with 14.9 percent of native households. Immigrant households were thus 9.3 percent more likely than native households to receive public benefits (figure 8.6). Since the early 1990s, researchers have consistently found that immigrants are more likely than natives to receive social assistance (Borjas, 1999a, 2002). Given that immigrants are more likely to earn low incomes and that participation in welfare programs is means-tested, this is hardly surprising.

Figure 8.6 shows that the immigrant/native differential in overall welfare use has fluctuated over time but does not show a consistent trend. In 1994, the share of households receiving welfare was 24.6 percent for immigrants and 15.3 percent for natives, which is the same differential (9.3 percent) as in 2002. This stability is perhaps unexpected in light of important recent changes in U.S. welfare policy. In 1996, Congress undertook a major overhaul of federal welfare programs. Among other changes, the reform excluded noncitizens from access to many benefits. Congress also substituted state entitlements to federal funds with block grants, leaving states wide discretion over individual eligibility criteria. For legal

7. When considering immigrant use of public assistance, we take households (rather than individuals) as the unit of analysis. We define as an immigrant household a unit in which the household head is foreign-born. This definition thus includes in immigrant households U.S.-born children of immigrants who live with their parents. Households are the units on which government agencies assess income taxes, property taxes, and other levies. For determining individual eligibility for means-tested benefit programs, it is typically the characteristics of the household that are evaluated (Zimmermann and Tumlin, 1999).

immigrants arriving before 1996, states have the option of whether to use their federal block grants to provide this group with benefits. For legal immigrants arriving after 1996, states may not use federal block grants to provide noncitizens with benefits, but they are free to use other state funds to create substitute programs.

While the immigrant/native differential in overall welfare use hasn't changed over time, the *composition* of benefits received by immigrants and natives has changed. In 1994, immigrant households were 5.2 percent more likely than native households to receive some type of cash benefit (general assistance, AFDC, SSI) (figure 8.6). By 2002, this differential had fallen to 2.0 percent. Similarly, between 1994 and 2002, the differential between immigrant and native use of food stamps declined from 5.3 percent to 1.0 percent. Medicaid is the only major category in which the immigrant/native welfare differential didn't fall (and, in fact, increased from 9.1 percent to 9.6 percent). The share of immigrant households using all types of social assistance *except* Medicaid has declined, both in absolute terms and relative to natives. What appears to explain immigrants' continued access to Medicaid is that it is a program for which U.S.-born children are eligible, regardless of the citizenship of their parents. Many immigrant-headed households may have retained their access to Medicaid by virtue of having children who are U.S. citizens.[8]

Underlying national patterns in welfare usage, there is considerable variation across states in immigrant uptake of public assistance. Zimmermann and Tumlin (1999) categorize U.S. states according to the relative generosity of their welfare programs and immigrant access to these programs. We categorize states as providing immigrants with high access to benefits if they both provide generous welfare benefits and make these benefits relatively available to immigrants. While the level of benefits available to immigrants has changed markedly over time, the ranking of states in terms of their generosity toward immigrants has been relatively stable. Figures 8.7a and 8.7b plot the fraction of immigrant and native households receiving cash assistance in 1990 and 2000. During the 1990s, the ranking of states in terms of immigrant uptake of welfare changed relatively little, with the Northeast, the northern Midwest, and the far West having the highest fraction of immigrant households receiving cash assistance.

To summarize immigrant access to public benefits, we use Zimmermann and Tumlin's categorization.[9] Table 8.1 shows that in 2002, the immigrant/native differential in welfare use was 11.8 percent in

8. See Ku, Fremstad, and Broaddus (2003).
9. A state is considered to offer immigrants high access to benefits if the state offers generous welfare benefits and makes these benefits relatively available to immigrants.

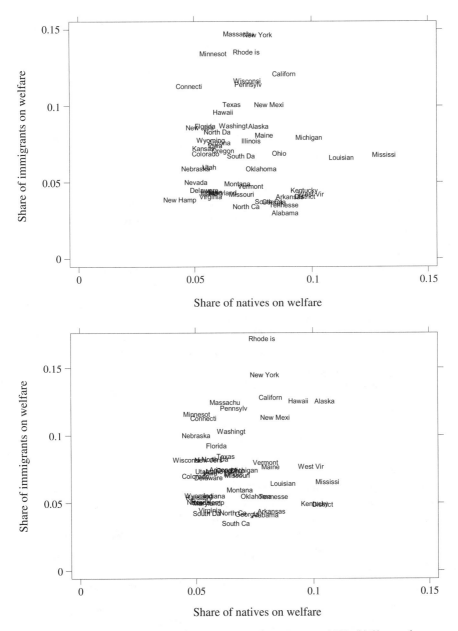

Figure 8.7 (a) Share of households receiving cash assistance, 1990. (b) Share of households receiving cash assistance, 2000.

high-immigrant-access states and 4.7 percent in low-immigrant-access states. This compares with 1994, when the differential was 11.9 percent in high-access states and 6.1 percent in low-access states, suggesting that over time, welfare use by immigrants has fallen more in low-access states. Changes in welfare use over time are more pronounced at the level of individual programs. For cash programs from 1994 to 2002, the immigrant/native differential in benefit use declined from 6.7 percent to 2.2 percent in high-access states and from 0.5 percent to –1.5 percent in low-access states; for food stamps, the decline in the immigrant/native differential was from 6.3 percent to 2.2 percent in high-access states and from 4.6 percent to –0.5 percent in low-access states. Thus, in low-access states, immigrant households actually have become less likely than native households to use public benefits associated with either cash transfers or food programs. Again, it is only for Medicaid that the immigrant/native differential in welfare uptake appears to be stable over time.

Immigrant usage of public assistance is closely related to immigrant schooling. Figures 8.8a and 8.8b plot the share of immigrant households on public assistance against the relative supply of immigrant labor that is highly skilled (the ratio of immigrant households headed by someone with 16 or more years of schooling to immigrant households headed by someone with less than 12 years of schooling).[10] There is a strong negative relationship. Before or after welfare reform, states with more highly skilled immigrant populations have lower immigrant uptake of welfare.

Public Opinion about Immigration

To evaluate differences in individual policy preferences about immigration, a key ingredient is a measure of policy opinion. The NES is an extensive survey of individual political opinions, including opinions about immigration, based on a stratified random sample of the U.S. population. These surveys also report details on respondent characteristics, including age, gender, educational attainment, location of residence, and other details on political views. To evaluate preferences toward immigration, we use the following question from the NES: "Do you think the number of immigrants

---

10. The U.S. Census of Population and Housing collects information on pretax income in the form of supplemental security income (SSI), aid for families with dependent children (AFDC, which has become temporary assistance for needy families, or TANF), and general assistance. This is a partial list of means-tested entitlement programs, as the census does not measure noncash benefits provided through programs such as food stamps, Medicaid, public housing, and so on (Borjas and Hilton, 1996).

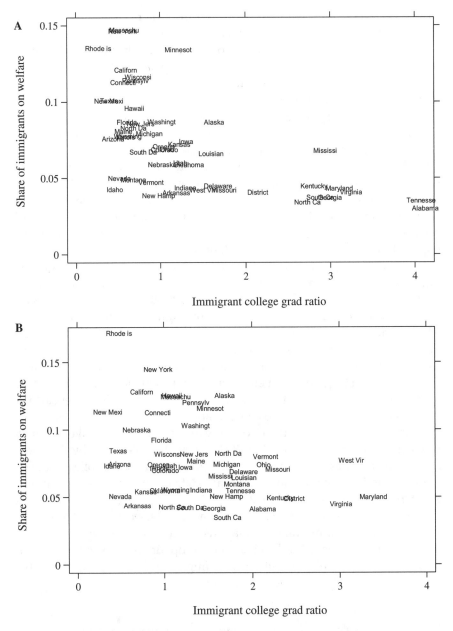

Figure 8.8 (a) Education and uptake of cash assistance among immigrants, 1990. (b) Education and uptake of cash assistance among immigrants, 2000.

from foreign countries who are permitted to come to the United States to live should be increased a little, increased a lot, decreased a little, decreased a lot, or left the same as it is now?" For the main analyses of immigration in the paper, we set the variable *immigration opinion* equal to 1 for those individuals favoring immigration to be decreased a little or a lot and 0 for those individuals favoring immigration be maintained or increased. This question requires respondents to reveal their general position on the proper direction for U.S. immigration policy. In 2000, 44.8 percent of respondents favored decreasing immigration (15.0 percent by a little, 29.8 percent by a lot), 44.5 percent favored leaving immigration unchanged, and 9.8 percent favored increasing immigration (5.8 percent by a little, 4.0 percent by a lot).

Our theoretical discussion above focused on two motivations for opposition to immigration. One is the concern that immigration put downward pressure on pretax wages for lower-skilled workers. A number of recent papers have found evidence consistent with this prediction.[11] Another motivation for opposition to immigrants is the concern that immigration imposes a fiscal burden on native taxpayers. Hanson, Scheve, and Slaughter (2007) find evidence consistent with this prediction. The focus of this chapter is on how the skill composition of the immigrant population affects the labor-market and public-finance consequences of immigration that individuals perceive. In the estimation, we examine these considerations, as well as noneconomic factors possibly correlated with an individual's stance on immigration (e.g., political beliefs, ethnicity). But before turning to these estimates, it is instructive to see if simple summary statistics reveal patterns consistent with these two considerations.

Table 8.2 shows the fraction of native-born individuals favoring new restrictions on immigration in the 1992 and 2000 NES surveys by three levels of education (less than high school, high school or some college, college graduate) and by whether an individual's state has a relatively large immigrant population.[12] In both 1992 and 2000, the lowest-educated natives (those with less than high school) are more opposed to immigration in states with larger immigrant populations. Since low-schooling natives are the group most exposed to labor-market competition from immigrants, it makes sense that their opposition to immigration is strongest where this competition is likely to be the most intense.

---

11. Scheve and Slaughter (2001a, 2001b), Kessler (2001), O'Rourke and Sinnott (2003), Mayda (2006). But also see Citrin et al. (1997) and Hainmueller and Hiscox (2004).

12. High-immigrant states are defined to be those with a ratio of immigrants to natives of at least 0.12 (the national mean in 1990). Figure 8.3 shows that this value identifies states that are spread out from the mass of states in the bottom left with low immigrant populations in both years.

Table 8.2   Support for Immigration Restrictions by Education Group and Size of State Immigrant Population

	State immigrant population	No high school	High school or some college	College graduate
1992	Low	46.0%	55.9%	40.0%
	High	56.2%	53.7%	41.0%
2000	Low	49.7%	55.3%	35.3%
	High	70.1%	49.5%	37.2%

Note: This table reports the percentage of native-born respondents stating that they would prefer immigration to be decreased (by a little or by a lot) in the NES survey for a given year. "No high school" refers to those with up to 12 years of schooling but no high school diploma, "high school or some college" refers to those with 12 to 15 years of schooling (with a high school diploma), and "college graduates" refers to those with 16 or more years of schooling. States with a high immigrant population have a ratio of immigrants to natives of at least 0.12 (the mean state immigrant/native population ratio for working-age adults in 1990). Summary statistics use NES sampling weights.

In either year, the most highly educated natives (those with a college degree) are the least opposed to immigration. However, they are somewhat more opposed to immigration in states with larger immigrant populations (where this difference is larger in 1992 than in 2000). In high-immigrant states, natives with high income potential are the group most exposed to the public-finance consequences of immigration. This is suggestive evidence that individual opposition to immigration is strongest where the fiscal burden associated with immigration is likely to be greatest. However, since table 8.2 does not control for individual characteristics, other than education, or for state characteristics, other than the size of the immigrant population, we should be cautious in interpreting these results. Below, we introduce additional controls.

To attempt to separate the labor-market versus public-finance motivations for opposition to immigration, table 8.3 adds to table 8.2 a breakdown of native public opinion according to whether an individual lives in a state in which immigrants have high access to public benefits.[13] In 1992, both low-educated natives and high-educated natives are more opposed to immigration in states in which immigrants have high access to public benefits. The same is again true for high-educated natives in 2000. These

13. In 1992, before welfare reform, high-access states are those Zimmermann and Tumlin (1999) identify as having generous public benefits. In 2000, after welfare reform, high-access states are those providing generous public benefits *and* relatively high availability of these benefits to immigrants.

Table 8.3   Support for Immigration Restrictions by Education Group and Immigrant Access to Public Benefits

	Immigrant access to public benefits	No high school	High school or some college	College graduate
1992	Low	46.2%	54.7%	37.6%
	High	56.1%	55.7%	43.7%
2000	Low	59.7%	53.6%	34.7%
	High	56.0%	50.5%	38.8%

Note: States with high immigrant access to public assistances are those with generous welfare benefits (in 1992) or with generous welfare benefits and high availability of these benefits to immigrants (in 2000) (see Zimmermann and Tumlin, 1999). See the note to table 8.2 for other details.

findings, which replicate Hanson, Scheve, and Slaughter (2007), are consistent with the theoretical framework above, in which low-income natives oppose immigration because of the perception that immigrants will crowd out their access to benefits, and high-income natives oppose immigration because of the perception that immigrants will increase their net tax burden. The differential in opposition to immigration between high-access and low-access states declines between 1992 and 2000, after welfare reform was implemented (and many noncitizens lost access to welfare benefits). Again, table 8.3 does not control for many other characteristics and so should be taken as suggestive only.

To see whether the skill composition of the immigrant population matters for attitudes about immigration policy, tables 8.4 and 8.5 reproduce tables 8.2 and 8.3, adding an additional breakdown for whether a state has a high-skilled or a low-skilled immigration population. We define a high-skilled immigration population as one in which the share of immigrants with 16 or more years of schooling in a state is above the national average in a given year.

Table 8.4 shows some evidence—especially for lower-skilled natives—that opposition to immigration is weaker where the immigrant population is more skilled. For higher-skilled natives, the reverse generally holds. In two of the three comparisons of college-graduate opinions across low-skill and high-skill immigrant states, opposition is stronger in the high-skill states. These patterns suggest that the skill composition of immigrants matters for considerations of labor-market pressures, as high-skilled immigrants presumably complement lower-skilled natives but substitute for their higher-skilled counterparts.

We see a similar pattern in table 8.5, which breaks down states according to immigrant access to public benefits and the skill composition of the

Table 8.4 Support for Immigration Restrictions by Education Group, Size of State Immigrant Population, and Composition of Immigrant Population

| | | State immigrant skills | | | | | |
| | Size of state | No high school | | High school or some college | | College graduate | |
	Immigrant population	Low	High	Low	High	Low	High
1992	Low	56.9%	42.8%	56.2%	55.8%	38.4%	40.8%
	High	56.2%	N/A	53.7%	N/A	41.0%	N/A
2000	Low	46.4%	50.8%	56.9%	54.6%	25.0%	38.5%
	High	70.6%	67.7%	48.6%	53.7%	37.8%	35.0%

Note: "High-skilled immigrant population" refers to states whose share of immigrants with a college education is above the national average. "N/A" indicates the average could not be calculated because there were too few underlying observations in that cell. See note to table 8.2 for other details.

Table 8.5 Support for Immigration Restrictions by Education Group, Immigrant Access to Public Benefits, and Composition of Immigrant Population

| | | State immigrant skills | | | | | |
| | Immigrant access to public benefits | No high school | | High school or some college | | College graduate | |
		Low	High	Low	High	Low	High
1992	Low	53.8%	42.9%	54.4%	54.9%	31.7%	42.3%
	High	59.0%	42.3%	54.8%	61.7%	45.0%	31.7%
2000	Low	66.5%	53.6%	49.8%	56.8%	34.3%	35.1%
	High	57.2%	54.4%	51.8%	47.3%	36.3%	43.4%

Note: See note to table 8.4.

immigrant population. In both years and both public-finance regimes, high school dropouts are less opposed to immigration when living in states where the state immigrant population is more educated. The opposite is true for college graduates in three of the four rows of table 8.5.

Were a primary economic consequence of immigration to increase labor-market competition for natives, we would expect low-skilled natives to be more opposed to low-skilled immigration and high-skilled natives to be more opposed to high-skilled immigration. Tables 8.4 and 8.5 offer some support for this prediction. In states where the immigrant population is more skilled, low-skilled natives are less opposed and higher-skilled natives are more opposed to liberalizing immigration. Below, we extend the analysis to a regression framework.

Before moving forward, however, it is important to discuss why we think correlations between education and opinions on immigration policy reflect labor-market issues rather than noneconomic considerations such as cultural attitudes. This issue was considered in some detail in Scheve and Slaughter (2001a, 2001b); here we highlight two important reasons for this interpretation.

One reason is that the education-opinion cleavage is robust to including a wide range of direct measures of noneconomic considerations such as racial tolerance and attitudes toward the proper role of the United States in the world. A second reason is that the education-opinion cleavage is replicated when replacing educational attainment with alternative measures of labor-market skills, such as actual earnings (e.g., average occupational wages). We prefer education over earnings because income is well known to be poorly measured, nonrandomly missing in surveys, and sensitive to transitory shocks (e.g., illness or bonuses) that do not reflect permanent earnings power.

Individual Heterogeneity and Public Opinion

To this point, we have been treating individual location decisions and state fiscal and welfare policies as exogenous or at least predetermined. It is instructive to consider how endogenizing these characteristics might affect the interpretation of the results. Suppose there is an unobserved characteristic of individuals (e.g., ancestry, family history, personal experience) that is correlated with individual policy preferences regarding immigration. All else being equal, we would expect individuals more opposed to immigration to be more likely to reside in states with smaller immigrant populations. In table 8.2, this would lead us to *understate* differences in public opinion between high-immigrant and low-immigrant states (since individuals less opposed to immigration would be more likely to live in high-immigrant states). Suppose also that states whose native population is more opposed to immigration tend to enact welfare policies that are less generous toward immigrants. In table 8.3, this would again lead us to *understate* differences in public opinion between high-immigrant and low-immigrant states (since individuals less opposed to immigration would be more likely to live in high-immigrant-access states). It appears, then, that likely patterns of correlation between unobserved individual character- istics and state immigrant populations and welfare policies would tend to dampen regional variation in public opinion, making it harder for us to find any systematic variation in attitudes toward immigration, across either individuals or regions.

We attempt to control for noneconomic factors that may affect indi- vidual attitudes toward immigration by checking the robustness of the results to the inclusion of a large set of individual characteristics as regres- sors. This is by no means a perfect solution to how unobserved charac- teristics of individuals might affect the state in which they reside, but it will give a sense of how robust the estimates are to additional covariates. We attempt to control for how heterogeneity in state native populations might have affected state welfare policies by accounting for state fixed effects in the regression. In so doing, we are assuming that changes in the state native population do not have a large effect on state welfare policies over the eight-year period that our sample covers. Given that the ranking of states in terms of their generosity toward immigrants changed relatively little during the 1990s (see figure 8.7), this assumption does not seem to be without merit. Our results are silent, however, on sources of state varia- tion in welfare policies. By controlling for state fixed effects, identification will come from the *interaction* between individual characteristics and state characteristics, as we explain below.

A final issue related to unobserved sources of variation in public opinion has to do with measurement error. Bertrand and Mullainathan (2001) argue that individual responses to subjective questions are likely to contain errors in measurement, complicating their use in econometric analysis. They are particularly suspect about using subjective responses as dependent variables, since how individuals interpret questions or the precision and sophistication with which they answer questions may be correlated with observed characteristics, such as age, education, gender, race, and so on. In the NES, one may be particularly concerned that indi- viduals at different educational levels may have different interpretations of what it means to reduce immigration by a little or a lot. There is no simple solution to this problem. We check the robustness of the results to the inclusion of individual characteristics, where we try to use character- istics that appear likely to be correlated with how individuals interpret questions (but, we hope, uncorrelated with opinions about immigration). However, this approach only partially addresses the issue. The possibil- ity of measurement error in the qualitative responses we examine sug- gests that it is important to exercise caution in interpreting the regression results.

Empirical Results

Empirical Specification

Our theoretical discussion above highlighted that immigration is likely to affect an individual's economic well-being via pretax income, posttax net fiscal transfers, and—the main argument of this chapter—perhaps by the skill mix of immigrants. Guided by this discussion, we specify a reduced-form estimating equation for individual preferences over immigration policy.

Let I^*_{ist} be a latent variable indicating opposition to immigration by a native individual i living in state s at time t. We model the determinants of I^*_{ist} as follows:

$$I^*_{ist} = \alpha_0 + \beta_j 1(Educ_{istj}) + \delta_k 1(Educ_{istk})1(Imm_{st})$$
$$+ \gamma_k 1(Educ_{istk})1(FE_{st}) + \lambda_k 1(Educ_{istk})1(ImmMix_{st}) \qquad (8.4)$$
$$+ \theta X_{ist} + \pi Z_{st} + \mu_{ist}$$

where j is an index from 1 to 3; k is an index from 1 to 4; $1(Educ_{istj})$ and $1(Educ_{istk})$ are a series of dichotomous variables indicating individual educational attainment; $1(ImmMix_{st})$ is the dichotomous variable *immigrant mix* indicating whether the immigrant mix in the state in which the respondent lives is highly skilled; $1(Imm_{st})$ is the dichotomous variable *high immigration* indicating whether the state in which the respondent lives is a high-immigration state; $1(FE_{st})$ is a dichotomous variable *fiscal exposure* indicating whether the state in which the respondent lives faces a high level of fiscal exposure to immigration; X is a vector of individual-level control variables, Z is a vector of state-level control variables; α, β, δ, γ, λ, θ, and π are parameters to be estimated; and μ_{ist} is a mean-zero random error term that reflects unobserved factors associated with individual preferences over changes in immigration policy, including the impact of immigration on unobserved determinants of wage income and fiscal transfers.

The first term in this expression, α_0, is simply a constant. The second and third terms evaluate the pretax income channel for how immigration and trade affect economic well-being. The second term is indexed by j because for $1(Educ_{istj})$ we include three indicator variables, *high school, some college,* and *college,* with *no high school* as the omitted category. The third term is indexed by k because we interact all four educational categories with the variable *high immigration* indicating whether the respondent lives in a high-immigration state.

This parameterization provides a pretax labor-market interpretation of $\beta_{1...3}$ and, when its interactions are included, $\delta_{1...4}$. In the presence of low-skilled immigration, we expect opposition to immigration to be decreasing in respondent skill levels because of its effect on earnings across skills. Thus, the coefficient for *college,* β_3, should be less than zero, and perhaps the same will hold for *some college*, β_2. If immigrants alter wages locally rather than nationally, then correlations between skills and opinion should be stronger in states with higher immigration levels. This implies that the coefficient on the interaction between *no high school* and *high immigration*, δ_1, should be greater than zero and/or that the coefficient on the interaction between *college* and *high immigration*, δ_4, should be less than zero.[14]

The fourth term in equation (8.4), $\gamma_k 1 (Educ_{istk}) 1 (FE_{st})$, evaluates if the consequences of immigration for posttax net fiscal transfers have an important effect on policy opinions. We interact all four educational variables (our proxy for different income groups) with *fiscal exposure*, a dichotomous indicator equal to one for state-years that meet two conditions: (1) they have relatively high welfare generosity, measured as above the national median welfare spending per native; and (2) they have relatively high immigration populations, defined as those states with a ratio of immigrants to natives above the national average. See Hanson, Scheve, and Slaughter (2007) for details on *fiscal exposure*.

The parameters $\gamma_{1...4}$ indicate whether respondents with *no high school*, *high school*, *some college*, and *college* in high-fiscal-exposure states are more or less likely to oppose immigration. Our theoretical discussion suggests that all respondents should be more opposed to immigration in states with high fiscal exposure to immigrants and that this should be especially true for high-income/educated individuals because of the progressivity of state tax and transfer systems. We therefore expect parameters $\gamma_{1...4}$ to be positive and increasing in magnitude.

The fifth term in equation (8.4), $\lambda_k 1 (Educ_{istk}) 1 (ImmMix_{st})$, evaluates the main argument of this chapter: that the skill mix of local immigrants has an important effect on individual economic well-being and, thus, policy opinions. To test this idea, we interact all four measures of educational attainment with *immigration mix*, a dichotomous indicator equal to one for state-years whose share of immigrants accounted for by college graduates exceeds the national average. If all natives perceive skilled immigrants to generate important dynamic and/or nonpecuniary benefits, then the parameters $\lambda_{1...4}$ should all be negative. Alternatively, if the skill mix of immigrants matters as a dimension of labor-market concerns, then we expect these parameters to be negative only for respondents with *no high school* or (perhaps) *high school*.

---

14. The interactions between schooling and whether the respondent lives in a high-immigration state may also control for the price channel through which immigration affects individual utility. If consumption patterns vary by income and education, then the effect of immigration on prices in a state will depend on the relative size of the immigrant population in the state.

The last terms in equation (8.2), θX_{ist} and πZ_{st}, estimate the effect of various individual-level and state-level control variables including *age, age squared,* dichotomous indicator variables *female* and *Hispanic, state unemployment,* a year indicator variable for 2000, and a full set of state dummy variables to account for time-invariant features of states that may influence individual attitudes toward immigration. Some of these control variables account for the price channel through which immigration affects individual utility, which depends on consumption patterns not measured in our data. These controls may also capture some noneconomic influences on policy opinions. We report results with many additional control variables that measure tolerance, isolationist sentiment, ideology, and partisanship, all of which more directly attempt to account for noneconomic determinants of policy opinions.

In equation (8.4), the latent variable I_{ist}^* is unobserved. Let I_{ist}, *immigration opinion,* be an indicator variable equal to one if an individual favors decreasing immigration (restricting trade) and zero otherwise, in which case $\Pr(I_{ist}^* > 0) = \Pr(I_{ist} = 0)$. Assuming that the idiosyncratic component of individual preferences, μ_{ist}, is normally distributed, then the following applies:

$$\Pr(I_{ist} = 1) = \Phi(\alpha_0 + \beta_j 1(Educ_{istj}) + \gamma_k 1(Educ_{istk}) 1(Imm_{st})$$
$$+ \lambda_k 1(Educ_{istk}) 1(FE_{st}) + \theta X_{ist} + \delta Z_{st}) \tag{8.5}$$

where $\Phi(\ )$ is the standard normal cdf. We will estimate various specifications of equation (8.5) as a probit and report robust standard errors clustered on states. All estimations use NES data for native-born individuals pooled across 1992 and 2000.

One concern about the specification in equation (8.5) is that U.S. natives may choose where to live in the United States based in part on a state's tax policies. In this case, unobserved individual characteristics may be correlated with state fiscal policy, and our coefficient estimates could be inconsistent. While we cannot easily remedy this type of simultaneity problem, it appears likely to work against us, biasing coefficient estimates on fiscal exposure to immigration in (8.5) toward zero. Suppose, for instance, that individuals who are particularly averse to paying taxes are more likely to locate in low-tax states. If these individuals are also those more aggravated by the fiscal consequences of immigration, then individuals with stronger antiimmigration sentiments would tend to locate in states with low fiscal exposure to immigration (and, by extension, individuals with weaker antiimmigration sentiments would tend to locate in states with greater fiscal exposure). The consequence of such self-selection would be that we would underestimate the effects of state fiscal exposure on opposition to immigration, owing to the fact that unobserved policy preferences would tend to be negatively correlated with the fiscal generosity of a state toward immigrants. Thus, our results may be sensitive to selection bias but in a manner that causes us to underestimate the effect of fiscal exposure on opposition to immigration.

Estimation Results

Our baseline specification results are reported in table 8.6. Each column of the table corresponds to a different specification of equation (8.5). The results across all four specifications replicate the finding in the literature that higher-skilled natives are less likely to support immigration restrictions. Here, opposition to immigration is weakest among college graduates. The coefficients on *college* across all four models imply that college graduates are 17 to 26 percentage points less likely to prefer fewer immigrants than are high school dropouts.

Our main result of interest is whether support for immigration is greater in states with higher skill mixes of immigrants. Model 1 examines this idea by including as a regressor *immigration mix*; here, we implicitly restrict to be equal all four parameters $\lambda_{1\ldots4}$. The coefficient estimate on *immigration mix* is significantly negative. An individual living in a state with an above-average share of college graduates in its immigrant population is 5.9 percentage points less likely to support immigration restrictions than is a comparable person living in a below-average state.

Model 2 interacts *immigration mix* with our full set of education indicators, to look for variation in the impact of immigrant skill mix on native opinions. It is clear that the restrictive model 1 masked important differences across education groups. The coefficients on the interactions between *immigration mix* and *no high school* and *high school* are negative, large in magnitude, and statistically significant. But the coefficients on the interactions between *immigration mix* and both *some college* and *college graduate* are smaller and not significantly different from zero. Only lower-skilled natives are more supportive of immigration in the presence of higher-skilled immigrants; the estimates in model 2 imply by 18.4 and 8.3 percentage points for high school dropouts and high school graduates, respectively.

This is our main finding. It is inconsistent with the hypothesis that more highly skilled immigrants elicit more support for freer immigration in all natives thanks to perceived dynamic and/or nonpecuniary benefits. Instead, it resonates with earlier findings of concern over the labor-market pressures of immigration. The opposition of lower-skilled natives to freer immigration is ameliorated when exposed to higher-skilled immigrants that likely complement rather than substitute for them in the labor market.

Table 8.6   Probit Results for Immigration-Policy Preferences, Baseline Specifications

	Model 1	Model 2	Model 3	Model 4
High school	0.039	−0.100	0.230	−0.017
	(0.082)	(0.097)	(0.198)	(0.147)
Some college	−0.143	−0.414	−0.147	−0.344
	(0.093)	(0.088)	(0.164)	(0.113)
College	−0.440	−0.629	−0.459	−0.682
	(0.094)	(0.102)	(0.228)	(0.168)
Immigration mix	−0.149			
	(0.071)			
*No high school * immigration mix*		−0.473	−0.255	−0.353
		(0.136)	(0.183)	(0.150)
*High school * immigration mix*		−0.223	−0.298	−0.230
		(0.070)	(0.089)	(0.086)
*Some college * immigration mix*		0.093	0.075	0.076
		(0.104)	(0.104)	(0.105)
*College * immigration mix*		−0.110	−0.045	−0.017
		(0.107)	(0.162)	(0.134)
*No high school * additional indicator*			0.487	0.382
			(0.184)	(0.205)
*High school * additional indicator*			0.008	0.174
			(0.189)	(0.142)
*Some college * additional indicator*			0.106	0.206
			(0.121)	(0.140)

(*continued*)

Table 8.6 *(continued)*

	Model 1	Model 2	Model 3	Model 4
*College * additional indicator*			0.231	0.440
			(0.194)	(0.163)
Observations	3,117	3,117	3,117	3,117
Log likelihood	−2,103.61	−2,095.81	−2,091.36	−1,997.26

Note: This table reports coefficient estimates for probit regressions on native individuals from the 1992 and 2000 NES surveys. The dependent variable is *immigration opinion,* equal to one for respondents who support further restricting immigration and zero otherwise. *Immigration mix* is a dichotomous indicator equal to one for state-years whose share of immigrants accounted for by college graduates exceeds the national average. *Additional indicator* is *high immigration* in model 3 and *fiscal exposure* in model 4. All specifications include the baseline control variables *age, age squared, female, Hispanic, state unemployment,* a year indicator variable for 2000, and a full set of state fixed effects. Each cell reports a coefficient estimate and a state-clustered robust standard error in parentheses. Observations are weighted using sampling weights from the NES data.

Models 3 and 4 in table 8.6 examine the robustness of this interaction between native skills and immigrant skill mix by expanding the specification of equation (8.5) to include other regressors found to matter in earlier research. Model 3 adds the interactions of individual skills with the indicator *high immigration,* for high levels of immigration. As in Hanson, Scheve, and Slaughter (2007), we find that native high school dropouts living in high-immigration states are significantly more likely to oppose freer immigration. This is consistent with immigrant inflows having local rather than national labor-market impacts. Results for *immigration mix* are attenuated for high school dropouts, with a fall in magnitude and significance for its coefficient estimate. But results for *immigration mix* interacted with *high school* are now stronger.

Finally, model 4 adds the interactions of individual skills with the indicator *fiscal exposure,* to capture states with high fiscal pressures from immigrant inflows. As in Hanson, Scheve, and Slaughter (2007), college graduates are much less supportive of freer immigration when living in states with high fiscal pressures from immigrants. For these highly skilled natives, pretax labor-market benefit of immigrant inflows may be offset by posttax fiscal costs. But, as in model 3, our results for *immigration mix* interacted with individual skills are largely unchanged. As in model 2, here in model 4, the coefficients on the interactions between *immigration mix* and *no high school* and *high school* are negative, large in magnitude, and statistically significant.

In table 8.7, we examine the robustness of our table 8.6 findings by adding to equation (8.5) additional control regressors in X_{ist}. Consistent

Table 8.7   Probit Results for Immigration-Policy Preferences, Expanded
Specifications

	Model 1	Model 2	Model 3	Model 4
High school	−0.026	−0.215	0.005	−0.150
	(0.114)	(0.145)	(0.280)	(0.203)
Some college	−0.234	−0.560	−0.410	−0.497
	(0.130)	(0.136)	(0.229)	(0.152)
College	−0.479	−0.729	−0.569	−0.763
	(0.126)	(0.133)	(0.234)	(0.181)
Immigration mix	−0.072			
	(0.124)			
*No high school * immigration mix*		−0.563	−0.419	−0.494
		(0.224)	(0.264)	(0.239)
*High school * immigration mix*		−0.155	−0.199	−0.148
		(0.128)	(0.134)	(0.130)
*Some college * immigration mix*		0.183	0.193	0.191
		(0.114)	(0.152)	(0.148)
*College * immigration mix*		−0.013	−0.006	0.075
		(0.146)	(0.193)	(0.161)
*No high school * additional indicator*			0.402	0.409
			(0.290)	(0.276)
*High school * additional indicator*			0.091	0.266
			(0.146)	(0.151)
*Some college * additional indicator*			0.180	0.261
			(0.146)	(0.165)

(*continued*)

Table 8.7   *(continued)*

	Model 1	Model 2	Model 3	Model 4
*College * additional indicator*			0.164	0.456
			(0.204)	(0.186)
Observations	2,277	2,277	2,277	2,277
Log likelihood	−1,478.91	−1,471.22	−1,469.68	−1,422.17

Note: This table reports coefficient estimates for probit regressions on native individuals from the 1992 and 2000 NES surveys. The dependent variable is *immigration opinion,* equal to one for respondents who support further restricting immigration and zero otherwise. *Immigration mix* is a dichotomous indicator equal to one for state-years whose share of immigrants accounted for by college graduates exceeds the national average. *Additional indicator* is *high immigration* in model 3 and *fiscal exposure* in model 4. All specifications include the baseline control variables *age, age squared, female, Hispanic, state unemployment,* a year indicator variable for 2000, and a full set of state fixed effects. They also include the additional control variables *government employee, ideology, isolationism, tolerance,* and *union member.* Each cell reports a coefficient estimate and a state-clustered robust standard error in parentheses. Observations are weighted using NES sampling weights.

with many earlier studies showing an important role for noneconomic considerations in shaping opinions on immigration policy, we add control regressors *government employee* (dichotomous indicator); *ideology, isolationism,* and *tolerance* (continuous, each constructed from various NES survey responses); and *union member* (dichotomous indicator). These regressors may also be correlated with Bertrand-Mullainathan measurement errors in qualitative responses about immigration.

These additional control regressors somewhat attenuate our results for our key regressor of interest, *immigrant mix.* In model 1, the coefficient estimate on *immigrant mix* is now smaller and not significantly different from zero. In models 2 through 4, the coefficient on the interaction of *immigrant mix* and *high school* remains negative but is now again smaller and not significantly different from zero. In models 2 and 4, the coefficient on the interaction between *immigration mix* and *no high school* remains negative, large in magnitude, and statistically significant. We conclude from table 8.7 that the broad pattern of table 8.6 remains but that the role for the skill mix of immigrants in shaping policy opinions is less clear.

The attenuation of the results controlling for these other factors has at least three possible interpretations. First, including measures such as *ideology, isolationism,* and *tolerance* risks introducing endogeneity into the analysis. For example, ideology may simply be a summary statistic of individuals' policy preferences including those about immigration policy. Second, the attenuation of these estimates may indicate that the effect of skilled immigration on policy opinions is through these attitudinal variables. Respondents exposed to skilled immigration may, for example, develop less isolationist and more tolerant attitudes that are correlated with less restrictionist immigration-policy positions. Finally, to extent that the attitudinal variables are exogenous and well measured, the attenuation of the estimates may indeed reflect that the effect of skill immigration on policy opinions is weaker than reported in table 8.6.

In unreported results, we examined additional factors that may shape individual opinions about immigration policy. Huntington (2004) argues that opposition to immigration may be rooted not just in the skill mix of immigrants but also in the perceived negative effects that increasing cultural, ethnic, and linguistic diversity may have on the United States. He singles out immigration from Latin America, which accounts for more than 50 percent of new immigrant inflows since 1990, as having particularly weakened American identity. To the extent that there are individuals in our data who share Huntington's views, opposition to immigration as expressed in the NES may simply be proxying for opposition to Latino immigration. To examine this idea, we included controls for the share of the state immigrant population that is from Latin America. In no specification did the inclusion of this variable affect the results reported in tables 8.6 and 8.7. Additionally, the variable was statistically insignificant in most regressions.

Conclusions

Voters today remain sharply divided over the proper direction for U.S. immigration controls. In this chapter, we have built on earlier research examining which cleavages underlie opinions on immigration policy. We have examined whether individual opinions vary with the skill mix of state immigrant inflows, above and beyond the pretax labor-market and posttax fiscal cleavages found in earlier work.

Our main finding is that skill composition does matter but not across the board. Lower-skilled natives tend to support freer immigration more when living in states with a relatively skilled mix of immigrants. The sensitivity of lower-skilled natives' opinions to the skill composition of immigrants resonates with earlier findings of concern over the labor-market pressures of immigration. It does not resonate with arguments that higher-skilled immigrants will be preferred because of perceived dynamic and/or nonpecuniary benefits.

One possible research extension of our study would be to examine the skill mix of local immigrants in finer detail. Our analysis uses state-level data. It might be that immigration opinions are especially sensitive to immigrant-skill compositions far closer to home, for example, by counties or metropolitan areas rather than entire states. For geographically large and ethnically diverse states such as California, this finer focus might strengthen our somewhat mixed results.

We close with one possible policy implication suggested by this study. As discussed in the introduction, there are many calls today for a reform of U.S. immigration policy with the broad goal of overhauling admission rules to favor more highly skilled immigrants. For various economic goals (e.g., maximizing the boost to national output), such an overhaul might make sense. Our findings in this chapter suggest that this sort of policy reform may increase support for immigration among the native constituency most opposed to liberalization: lower-skilled workers.

References

Bertrand, Marianne, and Sendhil Mullainathan. 2001. "Do People Mean What They Say? Implications for Subjective Survey Data." *American Economic Review Papers and Proceedings* 91 (May): 67–72.

Borjas, George J. 1999a. "The Economic Analysis of Immigration." In Orley C. Ashenfelter and David Card, eds., *Handbook of Labor Economics.* Amsterdam: North Holland, pp. 1697–1760.

———. 1999b. *Heaven's Door: Immigration Policy and the American Economy.* Princeton, NJ: Princeton University Press.

———. 2003. "The Labor Demand Curve Is Downward Sloping: Reexamining the Impact of Immigration on the Labor Market." *Quarterly Journal of Economics* 118, no. 4: 1335–74.

Borjas, George J., Richard B. Freeman, and Lawrence F. Katz. 1997. "How Much Do Immigration and Trade Affect Labor Market Outcomes?" *Brookings Papers on Economic Activity* 1: 1–90.

Borjas, George J., and Lynette Hilton. 1996. "Immigration and the Welfare State: Immigrant Participation in Means-Tested Entitlement Programs." *Quarterly Journal of Economics* 111, no. 2: 575–604.

Citrin, Jack, Donald Green, Christopher Muste, and Cara Wong. 1997. "Public Opinion toward Immigration Reform: The Role of Economic Motivation." *Journal of Politics* 59, no. 3: 858–81.

Fix, Michael, and Jeffrey Passel. 2002. "The Scope and Impact of Welfare Reform's Immigrant Provisions." Washington, DC: Urban Institute.

Hainmueller, Jens, and Michael J. Hiscox. 2004. "Educated Preferences: Explaining Attitudes toward Immigration in Europe." Paper prepared for presentation at the Annual Meeting of the American Political Science Association.

Hanson, Gordon. 2005. "Challenges for U.S. Immigration Policy." In C. Fred Bergsten, ed., *The United States and the World Economy: Foreign Economic Policy for the Next Decade.* Washington, DC: Institute for International Economics, pp. 343–72.

Hanson, Gordon, Kenneth Scheve, and Matthew Slaughter. 2007. "Public Finance and Individual Preferences over Globalization Strategies." *Economics and Politics* 19, no. 1 (March): 1–33.

Huntington, Samuel. 2004. "The Hispanic Challenge." *Foreign Policy* (March–April): 30–45.

Kessler, Alan. 2001. "Immigration, Economic Insecurity, and the 'Ambivalent' American Public." Working Paper No. 41. Center for Comparative Immigration Studies, UCSD.

Leighton Ku, Shawn Fremstad, and Mathew Broaddus. 2003. "Noncitizens' Use of Public Benefits Has Declined since 1996: Recent Report Paints Misleading Picture of Impact of Eligibility Restrictions on Immigrant Families." Center for Budget and Policy Priorities. www.cbpp.org/4-14-03wel.htm.

Mayda, Anna Marie. 2006. "Who Is Against Immigration? A Cross-Country Investigation of Individual Attitudes toward Immigrants." *Review of Economics and Statistics* 88: 510–30.

Mayda, Anna Marie, and Dani Rodrik. 2005. "Why Are Some People (and Countries) More Protectionist than Others?" *European Economic Review* 49: 1393–1430.

National Science Foundation. 2004. *Science and Engineering Indicators: 2004.* Washington, DC: National Science Foundation.

O'Rourke, Kevin, and Richard Sinnott. 2001. "The Determinants of Individual Trade Policy Preferences: International Survey Evidence." In S. M. Collins and D. Rodrik, eds., *Brookings Trade Forum: 2001.* Washington, DC: Brookings.

———. 2003. "Migration Flows: Political Economy of Migration and the Empirical Challenges." Working paper.

Rauch, James E. 2001. "Business and Social Networks in International Trade." *Journal of Economic Literature* 39: 1177–1203.

Rauch, James E., and Vitor Trindade. 2002. "Ethnic Chinese Networks in International Trade." *Review of Economics and Statistics* 84, no. 1: 116–30.

Rodrik, Dani. 1997. *Has Globalization Gone Too Far?* Washington, DC: Institute for International Economics.

———. 1998. "Why Do More Open Economies Have Bigger Governments?" *Journal of Political Economy* 106, no. 5: 997–1032.

Sapiro, Virginia, Steven J. Rosenstone, Warren E. Miller, and the National Election Studies. 1998. American National Election Studies, 1948–1997 [CD-ROM], ICPSR ed. Ann Arbor, MI: Interuniversity Consortium for Political and Social Research.

Saxenian, AnnaLee. 1999. *Silicon Valley's New Immigrant Entrepreneurs.* Monograph, Public Policy Institute of California.

———. 2002. *Local and Global Networks of Immigrant Professionals in Silicon Valley.* Monograph, Public Policy Institute of California.

Scheve, Kenneth F., and Matthew J. Slaughter. 2001a. *Globalization and the Perceptions of American Workers.* Washington DC: Institute for International Economics.

———. 2001b. "Labor-Market Competition and Individual Preferences over Immigration Policy." *Review of Economics and Statistics* 83, no. 1 (February): 133–45.

———. 2001c. "What Determines Individual Trade-Policy Preferences." *Journal of International Economics* 54, no. 2 (August): 267–92.

———. 2004. "Economic Insecurity and the Globalization of Production." *American Journal of Political Science* 48, no. 4 (October).

Smith, J. P., and B. Edmonston, eds. 1997. *The New Americans: Economic, Demographic, and Fiscal Effects of Immigration.* Washington, DC: National Academy Press.

Zimmermann, Wendy, and Karen Tumlin. 1999. "Patchwork Policies: State Assistance for Immigrants under Welfare Reform." Urban Institute Occasional Paper 24.

II

Effects on Source Countries

Overview

9

Skilled Immigration
The Perspective of Developing Countries

FRÉDÉRIC DOCQUIER AND HILLEL RAPOPORT

The current wave of economic globalization has opened a window of opportunity for human capital to agglomerate where it is already abundant and yet best rewarded, that is, in the most economically advanced countries. This trend has been strengthened by the gradual introduction of selective immigration policies in many OECD countries since the 1980s. What started as an effort to increase the quality of immigration in countries such as Australia or Canada has developed into an international competition for attracting the highly educated and skilled. Together with traditional self-selection effects on the supply side, this explains the overall tendency for migration rates to be much higher for the highly skilled. Globalization indicators reveal that between 1990 and 2000, the world Export/GDP ratio has been multiplied by 1.5 and the FDI/GDP ratio by three (World Trade Organization, 2004). During the same period, the total number of foreign-born individuals legally residing in the OECD member countries has also been multiplied by 1.4, with a larger increase for highly skilled migrants (by 1.64) than for low-skilled migrants (by 1.14) (Docquier and Marfouk, 2006).

What are the consequences of this human-capital flight for sending (developing) countries? In a world of perfect competition with complete markets, the free mobility of labor is pareto-improving: migrants receive higher incomes, natives in the receiving countries can share the

We thank for their comments Jose Antonio Gonzalez, Gordon Hanson, Arye Hillman, Hubert Jayet, Maurice Schiff, participants at the IZA/Urban Institute Workshop on Migration, Washington, DC, May 2004, our discussants Prachi Mishra and David Weinstein, and seminar audiences at Bar-Ilan, Ben-Gurion, Haifa, the Inter-American Development Bank, Lille, Southampton, and the World Bank. A previous version of this chapter appeared as World Bank Policy Research Working Paper 3382, August 2004. This project is part of the World Bank Migration and Development Program, which we thank for financial support.

immigration surplus, and remaining residents in the sending countries can benefit from the rise in the land/labor and capital/labor ratios. However, it is obvious that a number of "externalities" also have to be factored in. First, skilled migrants are net fiscal contributors, and their departure therefore represents a fiscal loss for those left behind (fiscal externality). Second, skilled and unskilled labor complement each other in the production process; in a context of scarcity of skilled-labor and abundant unskilled labor, as is the case in developing countries, skilled labor migration may have a substantial negative impact on unskilled workers' productivity and wages and lead to higher inequality in the home country. Third, think of an economy where human capital is the engine of growth and education decisions engender both intragenerational and intergenerational externalities (Lucas, 1988); in such a setting, brain-drain migration will negatively affect the home country's current economic performance as well as its growth prospects. And fourth, as demonstrated in various new economic geography (e.g., Hoffmann, 2003) and new growth (e.g., Klenow and Rodriguez-Clare, 2005) frameworks, skilled labor is key to attracting FDI and fostering R&D activities (technological externality).

At the same time, skilled migrants continue to affect the economy of their origin countries after they have left, be it through remittances, return migration, or participation in business and scientific networks. Putting all of these channels together and taking account of the various externalities listed above within a single model is a very complex, if not impossible, task. In this chapter, we make the simplification that the impact of highly skilled migration on source countries may ultimately be captured through its effect on the long-run level of the human capital stock there; this simplification will allow for a unified treatment of the different channels mentioned above.

How Big Is the Brain Drain?

There is clear evidence that the brain drain has increased dramatically since the 1970s. Thirty years ago, the United Nations estimated the total number of highly skilled south-north migrants for 1961–1972 at only 300,000 (UNCTAD, 1975); less than a generation later, in 1990, the US. Census revealed that there were more than 2.5 million highly educated immigrants from developing countries residing in the United States alone, excluding people younger than 25 (that is, without counting most foreign students). Country studies commissioned by the International Labor Organization also showed that nearly 40 percent of Philippines emigrants are college-educated and, more surprisingly, that Mexico in 1990 was the world's third-largest exporter of college-educated migrants (Lowell and Findlay, 2001).

Since 1990, the chief causes of the brain drain have gained in strength as a result of a combination of changes on the supply side (e.g., skill-biased technological progress, human-capital agglomeration effects) that contribute to positive self-selection among migrants and of quality-selective immigration policies on the demand side. Quality-selective immigration policies were introduced in Australia and Canada in the 1980s in the form of point systems before being gradually adopted by other OECD countries. In the United States, the Immigration Act of 1990 and the substantial relaxation of the quotas for highly skilled professionals (H-1B visas) represent a major step in that direction, while European countries such as France, Germany, Ireland, or the United Kingdom have recently adopted policies aimed at attracting a qualified workforce (OECD, 2002).

Until very recently, there were no comparative data on the magnitude of the brain drain. The first serious effort to put together harmonized international data on migration rates by education level was by William Carrington and Enrica Detragiache from the International Monetary Fund, who used U.S. 1990 Census data and other OECD statistics on international migration to construct estimates of emigration rates at three education levels (primary, secondary, and tertiary) for about 60 developing countries.[1] The Carrington-Detragiache (CD) estimates, however, suffer from four main shortcomings. First, CD assumed for each country that the skill composition of its emigration to non-U.S. OECD countries is identical to that of its emigration to the United States; for example, Nigerian immigrants in the United Kingdom are assumed to be distributed across educational categories in the same way as Nigerian immigrants in the United States. Consequently, the CD estimates are not reliable for countries for which the United States is not the main destination (transposition problem). Second, at the time Carrington and Detragiache conducted their study, the OECD immigration data (notably for the EU, Japan, Switzerland, or New Zealand) did not allow for a full decomposition of the immigrants' origin mix; more precisely, many OECD countries used to publish statistics indicating the immigrants' origin country for the top five or 10 sending countries only. For small countries not captured in these statistics, the figures reported in the CD database are therefore biased: the total number of emigrants is underestimated, and in some cases one is (mis)led to conclude that 100 percent of a given country's workers who immigrated to an OECD member country immigrated to the United States (underreporting problem); as acknowledged by Carrington and Detragiache, this may approximate the reality for Latin America but is clearly erroneous, for example, in the case of most African countries and

---

1. See Carrington and Detragiache (1998). Relying on the same assumptions, Adams (2003) provides estimates for 2000.

many Asian countries. Third, the CD data excludes south-south migration, which may be significant in some cases (e.g., migration to the Gulf States from Arab and Islamic countries or to South Africa from its neighboring countries). Finally, recall that all foreign-born individuals residing in an OECD country are defined as immigrants independent of their age at arrival; for example, Mexican-born individuals who arrived in the United States at age five or 10 and then graduated from U.S. high-education institutions later on are counted as highly skilled Mexican immigrants.

In an attempt to extend Carrington and Detragiache's work, Docquier and Marfouk (2006) collected data on the immigration structure by education levels and country of birth from most OECD countries in 1990 and 2000. They used the same methodology and definitions as Carrington and Detragiache but extended their work in a number of ways. First, census, register, and survey data reporting educational levels and countries of birth were used for all OECD countries. On this basis, Docquier and Marfouk (DM) published emigration rates by education level for 195 countries in 2000 and 174 countries in 1990. Their estimates address two of the above-mentioned problems arising from the CD database: underreporting for small countries, and transposition of the U.S. immigration education structure to the rest of the OECD countries (and, in addition, they provide data for a second year, 2000). Aggregating over countries, it appears from the DM database that the total number of adult immigrants living in the OECD area and 25 or older may be estimated at 59.0 million for 2000 and 41.8 million for 1990. Emigration rates by educational levels are then obtained by comparing the number of emigrants to the population from which they are drawn (taken from Barro and Lee, 2001), giving average emigration rates to the OECD of 1.1 percent, 1.8 percent, and 5.4 percent, respectively for low-skill, medium-skill, and high-skill workers.

Table 9.1 compares total and skilled-emigration rates in 2000 by region, income group (using the four-group classication of the World Bank), and country size (for countries with population more than 25 million, between 10 million and 25 million, between 2.5 million and 10 million, and less than 2.5 million). It shows that average migration rates are strongly decreasing with country size, which is hardly surprising, as small countries tend to be more open to trade and migration. Regarding income groups, the highest rates are observed for middle-income countries, where people have both the incentives and the means to emigrate. High-income countries (less incentive to emigrate) and low-income countries (where liquidity constraints are more binding and/or for which the transferability of human capital is problematic) exhibit the lowest rates. Finally, the analysis by region shows that the regions most affected are Africa, Central America, and, because of small-size effects, the Pacific and the Caribbean.

Table 9.1   Data by Country Group in 2000

	Rate of emigration in %		Shared of skilled workers in %	
	Total	Skilled	Among residents	Among migrants
By country size				
Large countries (pop. > 25 million)	1.3	4.1	11.3	36.4
Upper-middle (25 > pop. > 10	3.1	8.8	11.0	33.2
Lower-middle (10 > pop. > 2.5)	5.8	13.5	13.0	33.1
Small countries (pop. < 2.5)	10.3	27.5	10.5	34.7
By income group				
High-income countries	2.8	3.5	30.7	38.3
Upper-middle-income countries	4.2	7.9	13.0	25.2
Lower-middle-income countries	3.2	7.6	14.2	35.4
Low-income countries	0.5	6.1	3.5	45.1
UN least-developed countries	1.0	13.2	2.3	34.0
By region				
America	3.3	3.3	29.6	29.7
Northern America	0.5	0.9	51.3	57.9
Caribbean	15.3	42.8	9.3	38.6
Central America	11.9	16.9	11.1	16.6
South America	1.6	5.1	12.3	41.2
Europe	4.1	7.0	17.9	31.7
Eastern Europe	2.2	4.3	17.4	34.2
Northern Europe	6.8	13.7	19.9	43.2
Southern Europe	6.6	10.7	10.8	18.2
Western Europe	3.3	5.4	23.4	39.3
Africa	1.5	10.4	4.0	30.9
Eastern Africa	1.0	18.6	1.8	40.8
Middle Africa	1.0	16.1	1.6	30.9
Northern Africa	2.9	7.3	7.5	19.6
Southern Africa	1.0	6.8	8.7	62.1
Western Africa	1.0	14.8	2.4	42.0
Asia	0.8	5.5	6.3	46.8
Eastern Asia	0.5	3.9	6.3	55.5
South-central Asia	0.5	5.3	5.0	52.5
Southeastern Asia	1.6	9.8	7.9	51.4
Western Asia	3.5	6.9	11.4	22.9

(continued)

Table 9.1   (*continued*)

	Rate of emigration in %		Shared of skilled workers in %	
	Total	Skilled	Among residents	Among migrants
Oceania	4.3	6.8	27.8	45.0
Australia and New Zealand	3.7	5.4	32.7	49.2
Melanesia	4.5	44.0	2.7	45.0
Micronesia	7.2	32.3	7.1	43.6
Polynesia	48.7	75.2	7.1	22.7

Source: Docquier and Marfouk (2006).

After excluding high-income countries from our sample, the left panel of table 9.2 gives the data for developing countries only. Obviously, the size of the brain drain depends on whether it is measured in absolute or relative terms. In terms of absolute numbers (see column 1), the Philippines, India, Mexico, China, Vietnam, and Poland appear as the major sending countries. In terms of emigration rates (that is, as percentage of the native-born skilled-labor force), the rankings are, of course, very different. Columns 2 and 3 show the 30 countries for which emigration rates among the highly skilled are respectively the highest and the lowest in 2000. The brain drain appears very strong in small countries, with emigration rates as high as 80 percent in some Pacific and Carribean islands. By contrast, eastern European and South American countries exhibit relatively low brain-drain levels. It is also noteworthy that India, China, and Brazil are among the least affected countries in relative terms, despite their important contribution to the overall stock of skilled migrants at the world level.

The DM data set considers as skilled immigrants all foreign-born workers with university or postsecondary training living in an OECD country. Such a definition based on the country of birth does not account for whether education has been acquired in the home or in the host country. Depending on the objective for which the data are going to be used, such a definition could appear either too inclusive or too exclusive. For example, it would seem appropriate (or even too exclusive) if one wants to measure the extent of a country's "skilled diaspora." Conversely, it may seem too inclusive if one wants to estimate the fiscal cost of the brain drain for the source country, in which case only people with home-country higher education should be considered as skilled emigrants. Building on DM estimates, Beine, Docquier, and Rapoport (2007) used immigrants' age of entry as a proxy for where education has been acquired. They provide alternative measures of the brain drain by defining skilled immigrants as those who left their home countries after ages 12, 18, or 22 and to do so for 1990 and 2000.

Table 9.2 Skilled Emigration: Top 30 Countries in 2000

	All middle-income and low-income countries			Middle- and low-income countries with population more than 4 million		
Highest stocks 0+		Highest rates 0+ in %	Lower rates 0+ in %	Highest rates 0+ in %	Highest rates 18+ in %	Highest rates 22+ in %
Philippines	1126513	Guyana 89.0	India 4.3	Haiti 83.6	Haiti 78.3	Haiti 73.7
India	1037768	Grenada 85.1	Burma 4.0	Siena Leone 52.5	Sierra Leone 51.1	Sierra Leone 48.4
Mexico	923017	Jamaica 85.1	Paraguay 3.9	Ghana 46.8	Ghana 44.9	Mozambique 43.7
China	816916	St. Vincent and Grenadines 84.5	China 3.8	Mozambique 45.1	Mozambique 44.4	Ghana 42.3
Vietnam	506459	Haiti 83.6	Moldova 3.6	Kenya 38.4	Kenya 35.7	Kenya 33.4
Poland	449778	Trinidad and Tobago 79.3	Botswana 3.6	Laos 37.4	Uganda 32.7	Uganda 30.7
Cuba	332707	St. Kitts and Nevis 78.5	Ukraine 3.6	Uganda 35.6	Somalia 31.4	Somalia 29.9
Iran	308774	Samoa 76.4	Namibia 3.4	Angola 33.0	Angola 29.2	Angola 26.4
Jamaica	291169	Tonga 75.2	Venezuela 3.4	Somalia 32.6	Sri Lanka 26.1	Sri Lanka 24.1
Russia	290208	St. Lucia 71.1	Belarus 3.2	El Salvador 31.0	Laos 25.7	Rwanda 23.9
Taiwan	275265	Cape Verde 67.4	Burkina Faso 2.6	Sri Lanka 29.6	Rwanda 24.7	Laos 21.9
Ukraine	249155	Belize 65.5	Argentina 2.5	Nicaragua 29.6	El Salvador 23.3	Afghanistan 20.4
Colombia	233563	Dominica 64.2	Chad 2.4	Cuba 28.7	Nicaragua 22.8	Nicaragua 19.4
Pakistan	222534	Barbados 63.5	Thailand 2.4	Papua New Guinea 28.5	Afghanistan 21.5	Croatia 18.9
Romania	177076	Gambia 63.2	Libya 2.4	Vietnam 27.1	Croatia 20.7	El Salvador 18.3
Turkey	174437	Fiji 62.2	Georgia 2.3	Rwanda 25.8	Papua New Guinea 19.8	Malawi 18.0

(continued)

Table 9.2   (continued)

	All middle-income and low-income countries			Middle- and low-income countries with population more than 4 million		
Highest stocks 0+		Highest rates 0+ in %	Lower rates 0+ in %	Highest rates 0+ in %	Highest rates 18+ in %	Highest rates 22+ in %
Brazil	168367	Mauritius 56.1	Brazil 2.3	Honduras 24.4	Cuba 19.4	Papua New Guinea 17.1
South Africa	168047	Seychelles 55.8	Indonesia 2.1	Guatemala 24.2	Vietnam 19.0	Cuba 17.0
Peru	163758	Sierra Leone 52.5	Azerbaijan 2.0	Croatia 24.1	Honduras 18.9	Vietnam 15.8
Dominican Republic	155179	Suriname 47.9	Russia 1.5	Afghanistan 23.3	Guatemala 18.4	Honduras 15.2
Haiti	152715	Ghana 46.8	Kazakhstan 1.2	Dominican Republic 21.6	Malawi 18.2	Togo 15.0
Egypt	150596	Mozambique 45.1	Maldives 1.2	Togo 18.7	Togo 16.9	Zambia 14.5
Nigeria	149528	Liberia 45.0	Mongolia 1.1	Malawi 18.7	Dominican Republic 15.7	Slovakia 14.4
Serbia & Montenegro	149065	Marshall Islands 39.4	Kyrgyzstan 0.7	Cambodia 18.3	Slovakia 15.4	Guatemala 14.1
Morocco	141238	Lebanon 38.6	Uzbekistan 0.7	Senegal 17.7	Zambia 15.1	Dominican Republic 12.8
Lebanon	138237	Kenya 38.4	Bhutan 0.6	Cameroon 17.2	Cameroon 14.6	Senegal 12.5
El Salvador	127710	Micronesia 37.8	Oman 0.6	Morocco 17.0	Senegal 14.1	Serbia and Montenegro 12.3
Hungary	124463	Laos 37.4	Swaziland 0.5	Zambia 16.8	Morocco 13.4	Cameroon 12.3
Trinidad and Tobago	120329	Uganda 35.6	Tajikistan 0.4	Slovakia 16.7	Serbia and Montenegro 12.9	Morocco 12.1
Guyana	118263	Nauru 34.5	Turkmenistan 0.2	Mexico 15.3	Poland 12.2	Poland 11.2

Source: Docquier and Marfouk (2006); Beine, Docquier, and Rapoport (2007).

On the right panel of table 9.2 (columns 4 to 6), we compare the uncorrected DM rates (referred to as 0+) with the corrected rates excluding migrants who left their country before ages 18 or 22 (referred to as 18+ and 22+). For a better illustration of the phenomenon, we present data only for countries with total population higher than 4 million. Controlling for familial migration does not significantly affect the rankings, as may be seen from the table. The corrected rates are by construction lower than those calculated without age-of-entry restrictions. The correlation between corrected and uncorrected rates is very high, and the country rankings by brain-drain intensities are only mildly affected by the correction. Skilled emigration is highest (higher than 30 percent) in countries that suffered from civil war and political instability during the last decades (e.g., Haiti, Somalia, Ghana, Sierra Leone, Lebanon) and is particularly strong in Central America and sub-Saharan Africa.

Theory and Evidence

This section provides an overview of the theoretical and empirical literature on the consequences of highly skilled emigration for developing countries.[2] Roughly, three generations of economics research on the brain drain may be distinguished.

The first generation dates back to the late 1960s and includes mainly descriptive papers (see, for example, Grubel and Scott, 1966, and the collection of papers in Adams, 1968) and welfare analyses within standard trade-theoretic frameworks (Johnson, 1967; Berry and Soligo, 1969). Basically, these early contributions conclude to an essentially neutral impact of the brain drain on source countries. This is a result of the general belief that the negative externalities at work are small, if not "negligible" (Grubel and Scott, 1966, p. 270), to the fact that skilled emigrants may leave behind them part of their assets which complement remaining skilled and unskilled labor in the production process (Berry and Soligo, 1969), or simply to the role of remittances and other positive-feedback effects that act to compensate those left behind for any real loss the brain drain may cause. From a broader perspective, these studies (with the exception of Berry and Soligo) generally emphasize the benefits of free migration to the world economy as a whole and tend to disregard "nationalistic" and "outdated" claims about the alleged losses of developing countries.

The second generation of brain-drain studies is in sharp contrast with the previous one. Under the leadership of Jagdish Bhagwati, a series of

2. Commander, Kangasniemi, and Winters (2004) also survey this literature.

alternative models were developed throughout the 1970s to explore the welfare consequences of the brain drain in more reallistic institutional settings. Domestic labor-markets rigidities (Bhagwati and Hamada, 1974), informational imperfections (Hamada and Bhagwati, 1975), and fiscal and other types of externalities (Bhagwati and Hamada, 1974; Bhagwati and Rodriguez, 1975; Rodriguez, 1975; McCulloch and Yellen, 1977) were introduced to emphasize instead the negative consequences of the brain drain for those left behind. Consequently, skilled emigration was viewed as contributing to increased inequality at the international level, with rich countries becoming richer at the expense of poor countries.[3] About 20 years later, the first papers to investigate the relationship between migration and human-capital formation in an endogenous growth framework rested on similar arguments and also emphasized the negative effects of the brain drain (e.g., Miyagiwa, 1991; Haque and Kim, 1995). Together with the literature of the 1970s, these papers constitute what we may term the traditional or pessimistic view.

Finally, a third generation of brain-drain research has emerged since the mid-1990s around the idea that migration prospects can foster domestic enrollment in education in developing countries, raising the possibility for a brain drain to be beneficial to the source country (e.g., Mountford, 1997; Stark, Helmenstein, and Prskawetz, 1998; Beine, Docquier, and Rapoport, 2001). These studies look at how the country's stock of human capital is built up and how migration modifies the incentive structure faced by developing countries' residents when making their education decisions. This literature is mainly theoretical but also includes a small number of empirical studies. At the same time, the various feedback effects underlined in the early literature (remittances, return migration, and business networks) have also given rise to an important literature, also contributing to nuance the negative view still dominant in many academic and international forums.

The Model

Consider a stylized small open economy populated by two-period lived individuals. For the sake of simplicity, we assume that a composite good is produced at each period of time according to a linear production function

---

3. An additional feature of this strand of the literature is to examine different possible taxation schemes that could compensate the sending countries for the losses incurred, for example, through a "tax on brains" (later coined "Bhagwati tax") to be collected on skilled emigrants' earnings abroad and redistributed within the country of origin (Bhagwati and Dellalfar, 1973; McCulloch and Yellen, 1975; Bhagwati, 1976). See also the special issue of the *Journal of Public Economics* on "Income Taxation in the Presence of International Personal Mobility," August 1982.

$Y_t = w_t L_t$. We do not model capital accumulation and set the interest rate to zero. The labor supply L_t sums up skilled and unskilled labor. Normalizing the number of efficiency units offered by an unskilled individual to 1, a skilled individual is assumed to offer $h > 1$ such units.

The scale factor w_t measures the wage rate per efficiency unit of labor. It is endogenous and time-varying. To formalize the spill-over effects associated with human capital formation, we assume that w_t is an increasing function of the economywide average level of human capital of the workers remaining in the country H_t, itself a function of the proportion of skilled workers in that generation P_t (we write $H_t = 1 + P_t[h - 1]$, with P_t the share of skilled workers and $h > 1$ their relative productivity). Hence, the domestic wage rate per efficiency unit of labor is given by

$$w_t \equiv w(H_t)$$

with the derivative $w' > 0$.

When young, people are offered the choice between working as unskilled workers and devoting part of their time to education. There is a single education program, the cost of which is proportional to the domestic wage rate w_t. However, individuals are heterogenous in their ability to learn and may therefore be characterized by different education costs, with high-ability individuals incurring a lower cost. The cost of education for a type-c agent is denoted by cw_t, with c distributed on [0, 1] according to the cumulative distribution $F(c)$. When adult, skilled (educated) and unskilled agents work full-time, with education enhancing one's productivity and, thus, one's income, by the exogenous skill premium h. Utility is linear in consumption; there is no discounting of income and no domestic savings. In the following, we will assume for simplicity a uniform distribution of education costs and, consequently, restrict the values of h to the interval [1, 2] in order to obtain interior solutions.[4]

Without migration, the lifetime income of an uneducated agent is given by $w_t + w_{t+1}$. By contrast, the lifetime income for an educated agent is $w_t - cw_t + w_{t+1}h$. Clearly, education is worthwhile for individuals whose education cost is lower than a critical value. At the steady state ($w_{t+1} = w_t$), the condition for investing in education in an economy with no migration (henceforth denoted using the subscript n)

$$c < c_n \equiv h - 1,$$

In poor countries, however, liquidity constraints are likely to have impact on education choices. Assume, therefore, that the first-period consumption cannot be lower than a minimal threshold ϕw_t, which is assumed

---

4. Given that $c \in [0, 1]$, the restriction $h < 2$ ensures that the proportion of educated is lower than unity even when c is uniformly distributed.

to be proportional to domestic wages. Hence, an agent with education cost above $c_L \equiv 1 - \phi$ has no access to education, and the liquidity constraint may or may not be binding depending on whether $c_L \lessgtr c_n$.

Consequently, the economywide average level of human capital of the current generation of adults may be written as

$$H_n = 1 + P_n(h - 1),$$

where $P_n = Min \, [F(c_n); F(c_L)]$ measures the proportion of educated adults.

Let us now examine the impact of skilled migration on the sending economy. In our setting, the impact of migration on remaining residents is related to the way it affects the composition of the labor force. Obviously, the relationship between social welfare and skilled emigration is likely to depend on other channels. For example, skilled emigration may cause a loss of social capital (Schiff, 2002) or have redistributive effects we are abstracting from in this chapter.[5] We focus instead on the impact of the brain drain on the source country's average stock of human capital, our proxy for the country's long-run economic potential.

The Traditional View

As explained above, the literature of the 1970s developed a pessimistic view of the brain drain. Careful examination of these models reveals that their central conclusions rest on a number of critical assumptions. In particular, it is assumed that (1) migrants self-selected out of the general population, (2) there is free international mobility of skilled labor and, therefore, no uncertainty regarding future migration opportunities for the educated, and (3) there is a complete disconnection between emigrants and their countries of origin once they have left. Is such conditions, clearly, skilled emigration can only affect negatively the proportion of educated in the remaining population P.

Building on the stylized model above, consider that workers now have the possibility to emigrate toward a developed country where, because of an exogenous technological gap, one unit of human capital is paid $w^* > w_t$. The wage ratio can be written as $\omega_t = w^*/w_t = \omega(P_t)$ with $\omega' < 0$. Migration entails a cost kw^* which captures transportation, search, assimilation, and psychic costs of leaving one's home country. Individuals have to choose whether to educate (ED or NE) and whether to migrate (MI or NM). The lifetime income associated with each pair of decisions is given by

---

5. See, however, below, where we discuss such redistributive effects when education is publicly financed.

$$U(NE, NM) = w_t + w_{t+1}$$

$$U(NE, MI) = wt + w^*(1-k)$$

$$U(ED, NM) = w_t - cw_t + w_{t+1}h$$

$$U(ED, MI) = w_t - cw_t + w^*(h-k).$$

At the steady state, the condition for a positive self-selection equilibrium to emerge (i.e., skilled workers only emigrate) is

$$\omega(1-k) < 1 < \omega\left(1-\frac{k}{h}\right).$$

In this case, migration prospects have impact on the education-cost threshold required for investing in education; the condition for investing in education becomes

$$c < c_o \equiv \omega(h-k)-1,$$

which is higher than $c_n = h - 1$ providing that the self-selection condition holds.

There is strong evidence that migration prospects indeed have impact on people's decisions to invest in higher education. According to the International Office for Migration (2003), the prospects of working abroad have increased the expected return to additional years of education and have led many people to invest in more schooling, especially in occupations in high demand overseas. For example, in their survey on medical doctors working in the United Kingdom, Kangasniemi, Winters, and Commander (2007) indicate that the migration premium in the medical professions lies between 2 and 4 (in PPP values); about 30 percent of Indian M.D.s surveyed acknowledge that the prospect of emigration affected their effort put into studies; furthermore, the respondents estimate that migration prospects affect the effort of about 40 percent of current medical students in India. In the case of the software industry, Commander et al. (2004) estimate that the migration premium for Indian IT workers contemplating emigration to the United States lies between 3 and 5 (depending on the type of job) in PPP values.[6]

On the basis of survey and anecdotal evidence (and of introspection, too), one can therefore easily admit that migration prospects stimulate domestic enrollment in education. In a context of free migration and with no feedback effects, however, emigration deprives the country of its educated workforce, the proportion of educated in the remaining population

---

6. In current U.S. dollars, the migration premium is obviously much higher. Many migrants confess that they are unable to compare earnings on a PPP basis. The expected migration premium is likely to lie between the PPP and the current dollar values.

falls to zero, and the average level of human capital of remaining members falls to one. In the presence of a minimal threshold for consumption, migration can be limited by an additional liquidity constraint. Liquidity constraints here are caused by the monetary fraction of the migration costs (as psychic costs of leaving and assimilation costs are incurred only once migration has occurred). Let us denote by $k'w^* < kw^*$ this monetary component of the migration cost. Agents with education costs greater than $c_M \equiv 1 - k'\omega - \phi < c_L$ cannot both educate and migrate, so that some educated individuals remain in the home country when the threshold c_M is lower than c_n. In this case, indeed, individuals with education cost between c_M and c_n cannot afford paying for both migration and education but still have an incentive to invest in education (see case 1 in figure 9.1). When c_M is higher than c_n, however, agents who cannot afford paying migration costs have no incentive to educate, and all of the educated leave the country at the end of period 1 (see case 2 in figure 9.1).

In any event, the traditional view posits that once migration opportunities are introduced, the average level of human capital among remaining residents H_t decreases, which, in turn, depresses wages through the various externalities outlined above (Hamada, 1977; Usher, 1977; Blomqvist, 1986). Using a different perspective, Bhagwati and Hamada (1974) developed a model of wage determination in which the departure of skilled workers also reduces unskilled workers' expected earnings. The transmission mechanism involves a noncompetitive wage-setting assumed to capture the various labor markets' imperfections prevailing in developing countries. Assume that educated wages are determined by workers' unions and incorporate an element of international emulation (i.e., depend positively on wages abroad). Once skilled-workers' wages are set, unskilled workers'

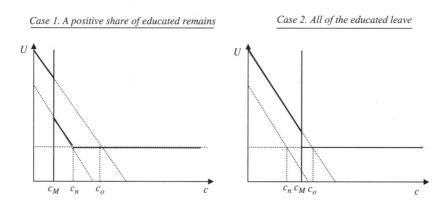

Figure 9.1 Brain drain, education choices, and liquidity constraints.

wages follow with some rule of proportionality. In this setting, skilled migration reduces skilled unemployment, meaning that wage pressures become stronger. While the net effect on skilled employment depends on the elasticity of demand for skilled-labor (determining whether the skilled labor wage bill increases), this tends to extend unemployment and reduces welfare among the uneducated.

Note that Bhagwati and Hamada (1974), as well as McCulloch and Yellen (1977), take into account the incentive effects of the brain drain on education decisions, with the increase in the expected wage for skilled workers stimulating human-capital investments; they also raise a number of questions regarding optimal public financing of education in such a context, an issue that is dealt with below.

Temporary Migration

As explained, most receiving countries have recently made admission conditions for candidate immigrants more selective. Quality-selective procedures have been put in place, and in addition, many immigration programs targeting the educated and skilled are designed for temporary immigrants. To account for this, assume that candidate immigrants are allowed to spend only a fraction γ of their working life in the destination economy. Substituting temporary for permanent visas reinforces positive self-selection among migrants: the expected return to education being lowered, fewer people invest in education, and only those at the upper-end of the ability distribution will find it beneficial to do so. Obviously, the exact impact depends on the length of the migration period. In terms of our notations, the lifetime income for educated agents is now given by[7]

$$U(ED, NM) = w_t - cw_t + w_{t+1}h$$
$$U(ED, MI) = w_t - cw_t + \gamma w^*h + (1 - \gamma)hw_{t+1} - kw^*.$$

At the steady state, emigration is optimal for skilled workers when the following condition holds:

$$\gamma h(\omega - 1) > k\omega.$$

---

7. For simplicity, we assume migration costs to be identical to the case of permanent migration. This could be justified by assuming that higher transportation costs (since people now travel both ways) strictly compensate for reduced psychological costs or that the latter are incurred during the first years following immigration. Alternatively, we could assume that in case of temporary migration, people incur a migration cost of $k' + \gamma(k - k') \equiv k''$.

If the latter condition does not hold, migration prospects have no effect on human capital formation. If it does hold, then the prospect of temporary migration stimulates human-capital investments at home.

Without liquidity constraints, the condition for investing in education then becomes

$$c < c_\gamma \equiv \gamma(\omega-1)h + h - 1 - k\omega \quad \text{if} \quad \gamma h(\omega-1) > k\omega$$
$$< c_n \equiv h - 1 \text{ if not.}$$

In the first alternative, and assuming a uniform distribution of education costs, the proportion of educated workers in the country becomes

$$P_\gamma = \frac{(1-\gamma)c_\gamma}{1-\gamma c_\gamma}.$$

In terms of incentives, the case of temporary migration is similar to the case of permanent migration, except that the incentive effect is propotional to γ. In terms of total impact, however, there is a major difference with the case of permanent visas, in that the incentive effect now partly benefits the home country. Indeed, the probability P_γ can be lower or higher than P_n. Let us denote by $\gamma^* \equiv \dfrac{k\omega}{h(\omega-1)}$ the value of γ above which skilled workers start opting for migration and, therefore, above which some migration takes place and has impact on education decisions. Formally, a possibility of "beneficial brain drain" emerges if the derivative of P_γ with respect to γ is positive at $\gamma = \gamma^*$. This derivative is given by

$$\left[\frac{\partial P_\gamma}{\partial \gamma}\right]_{\gamma(\omega-1)=k\omega} = \frac{(h-1)(h-2) + h(\omega-1) - k\omega}{[1-\gamma(h-1)]^2} \lessgtr 0.$$

If it is positive, then there is an interval of γ for which the temporary migration of skilled workers stimulates human-capital formation (i.e., raises the economywide average level of human capital).[8] However, liquidity constraints are likely to limit the size of the incentive effect. If $c_\gamma > c_L$, some agents have no access to education in spite of the fact that education is a profitable investment, and this reduces the likelihood of a beneficial brain drain. Similarly, if liquidity constraints restrict migration prospects, the incentive effect is thereby weakened. In the particular case where $c_M > c_n$, the number of individuals engaging in education is constant, and temporary migration reduces the share of educated workers.

Dos Santos and Postel-Vinay (2003) argue that a beneficial brain drain can still emerge even if the share of educated workers decreases. This is shown in a setting where growth is exogenous at destination and

---

8. Clearly, for $\gamma = 1$, the effect of the brain drain is unambiguously detrimental.

endogenous at origin, the engine of growth in the developing country being the knowledge and technology spill-overs somehow carried out by migrants returning from the more advanced economy. To the extent that returnees contribute to the diffusion of the more advanced technology they experienced abroad, emigrants' return is therefore a potential source of growth for the home country. In terms of our notations, this is as if return migrants would come back with a productivity gain $\Theta h > h$, which stimulates human-capital formation at home. The average stock of human capital then becomes

$$H = 1 + P_\gamma \left(\Theta h - 1 \right),$$

which must be compared to the case of no migration $H = 1 + P_n(h-1)$.[9]

Using a different perspective, Stark, Helmenstein, and Prskawetz (1997) elaborate on the possibility of a brain gain associated with a brain drain in a context of imperfect information with return migration. In their setting, workers' productivity is revealed at destination only after a certain period of time during which people are paid according to the average productivity of their group. Some relatively low-skilled workers will therefore find it beneficial to invest in education in order to migrate and be pooled at destination with high-skilled workers; once individuals' ability are revealed, the low-skilled workers return to their home countries, which may then benefit from their educational investments.

There is limited evidence that return migration is significant among the highly-skilled. In fact, we know that in general, return migration is characterized by negative self-selection (Borjas and Bratsberg, 1996) and is seldom among the highly skilled unless sustained growth preceded return. For example, less than a fifth of Taiwanese Ph.D.s who graduated from U.S. universities in the 1970s in the fields of science and engineering returned to Taiwan (Kwok and Leland, 1982) or Korea, a proportion that rose to about two-thirds in the course of the 1990s, after two decades of impressive growth in these countries. The figures for Chinese and Indian Ph.D.s graduating from U.S. universities in the same fields during the period 1990 to 1999 are fairly identical to what they were for Taiwan or Korea 20 years before (stay rates of 87 percent and 82 percent, respectively) (OECD, 2002). This is confirmed by a recent survey showing that in the

---

9. In a companion paper, Dos Santos and Postel-Vinay (2004) show that a change in immigration policy in the form of an increase in the share of temporary visas may benefit the sending countries. Such a change lowers the incentives to acquire education, which, in turn, lowers the premigration stock of human capital at origin, but implies a higher proportion of returnees among emigrants, which increases the country's stock of knowledge, a complement of human capital. The paper derives the theoretical conditions required for an overall positive effect to occur.

Hsinchu Science Park in Taipei, a large fraction of companies have been started by returnees from the United States (Luo and Wang, 2002). In the case of India, the evidence for the software industry is mixed. Saxenian (2001) shows that despite the quick rise of the Indian software industry, only a fraction of Indian engineers in Bangalore are returnees. On the other hand, a recent comprehensive survey of India's software industry reached more optimistic conclusions and confirmed the presence of network effects and the importance of temporary mobility. The survey, conducted among 225 Indian software firms, showed strong evidence of brain circulation, with 30 to 40 percent of the higher-level employees having relevant work experience in a developed country (Commander et al., 2004).[10]

Such specific experiences apart, return skilled migration remains relatively limited and is often more a consequence than a trigger of growth in the home country.

Uncertainty

Before 1965, the U.S. immigration policy was based on country-specific quotas. This quota system is now abolished, but various types of requirements and restrictions imposed by the United States and other countries' immigration authorities render the migration decision very uncertain. Implicit or explicit size quotas are effectively in place, and receiving an immigration visa, whether temporary or permanent, requires being in a close relationship with either relatives or employers who must then demonstrate that the migrant's skills can hardly be found among native workers. Moreover, in some countries, point systems are used to evaluate the potential contribution of immigrants to the host economy. This means that at all stages of the immigration process, there is a probability that the migration project will have to be postponed or abandoned. Individuals engaging in education investments with the prospect of migration must therefore factor in the risks involved. Paradoxically, such uncertainty, which is surely a bad thing ex-ante from the individual's perspective, creates the possibility for a brain-drain migration to generate a net human-capital gain for the home country.

Starting with Mountford (1997), a series of theoretical contributions have explored the conditions required for this possibility to materialize. This has been done in various theoretical frameworks with heterogeneous

---

10. In their survey on medical doctors working in the United Kingdom, Kangasmieni, Winters, and Commander (2004) found that "many" doctors intended to return after completing their training abroad. Note that the survey asked about intentions, not actual returns.

(Mountford, 1997; Docquier and Rapoport, 1999, Beine, Docquier, and Rapoport, 2001) and homogenous agents (Stark, Helmenstein, and Prskawetz, 1998; Vidal, 1998). As explained above, the basic idea is that in a context of uncertainty regarding future migration opportunities and of higher earnings abroad, migration prospects foster education investments (this induces an incentive or "brain" effect) which can compensate the loss from actual emigration (flight or "drain" effect), with the sign of the net effect on human-capital formation being positive or negative depending on which effect dominates.[11]

In order to incorporate these approaches within our general framework, assume that the probability of migration depends solely on the achievement of a given educational requirement, which is observable, and not on individuals' ability, which is not perfectly observable (i.e., migrants are assumed to be randomly selected among those who satisfy some kind of prerequisite with informational content regarding their ability—in our case, education).[12] The model with uncertainty is similar to an out-selection model where receiving countries accept a fraction $p > 0$ of skilled candidates and reject all unskilled applications. Assume, moreover, that the subjective probability of receiving a visa, as seen by a potential migrant, equals to the proportion of educated who effectively emigrated among the previous generation. Under these assumptions, the lifetime income for educated agents is now given by

$$U(ED, NM) = w_t - cw_t + w_{t+1}h$$
$$U(ED, MI) = w_t - cw_t + pw^*h + (1 - p)hw_{t+1} - pkw^*.$$

Uncertainty and return migration induce similar effects on the expected return to education, which is lower in both cases than in the case of a certain and permanent migration. However, several differences are

11. In a similar spirit, Katz and Rapoport (2005) develop a framework where expected wages are identical at origin and destination but are charaterized by a higher variance in the origin country. In such a context, education is imparted with an option value thanks to the possibility of migration, and the authors show that more variability raises the expected proportion of educated in the remaining population when individual abilities and domestic shocks are uniformly distributed.

12. Our simplified model assumes homogeneous skills among the educated. The size of the incentive effect would be different with heterogeneous skills (see Commander, Kangasniemi, and Winters, 2004). In reality, immigration authorities may be combining education with other selection devices such as tests of IQ or host-country language fluency. Were IQ a perfect signal of ability and the only criterion retained, migration could only be detrimental to human-capital formation at home. Still, to the extent that knowing one's skills is a discovery process or, alternatively, to the extent that IQ or other tests are imperfect signals of ability, migration prospects induce additional incentives to invest in education for some workers with intermediate ability.

worth noting. First, the incentive mechanism operates even for low values of p (remember that an incentive effect was obtained under temporary migration only for $\gamma \geq \dfrac{kw}{h(w-1)}$. Second, at $p = \gamma$, uncertainty generates more incentives to educate than temporary migration (at least at low levels of risk aversion). The reason for this is straightforward and has to do with the fact that migration costs are incurred with probability $p < 1$ under uncertainty but with probability $p = 1$ in case of temporary migration.

At the steady state, the condition for skilled migration being optimal is the same as under certainty (i.e., $1 < \omega \left[1 - \dfrac{k}{h} \right]$), but now education is worthwhile for people for whom

$$ c < c_p \equiv h - 1 + ph \left[\omega \left(1 - \frac{k}{h} \right) - 1 \right]. $$

Clearly, we have $c_p = c_n$ when $p = 0$ and $c_p = c_o$ when $p = 1$.

As in the case of temporary migration, there is a possibility of beneficial brain drain for the sending country thanks to the incentive effect. Indeed, the proportion of educated workers in the country becomes $Pp = \dfrac{(1-p)c_p}{1-pc_p}$, which can be lower or higher than P_n. A beneficial brain drain can be obtained for some ranges of p, providing that the derivative of P_p with respect to p is positive at $p = 0$. We obtain

$$ \left[\frac{\partial P_p}{\partial p} \right]_{p=0} = (h-1)(h-2) + h(\omega - 1) - kw \underset{>}{\overset{<}{-}} 0 $$

As in previous cases, liquidity constraints are likely to lower the size of the incentive effect. If $c_p > c_L$, the incentive effect will be limited to agents with education costs made up between c_n and c_L. A similar remark applies if $c_p > c_M$.

What is the empirical evidence of this "prospect" channel? To the best of our knowledge, the first study to attempt estimating the growth effects of the brain drain using cross-country comparisons is Beine, Docquier, and Rapoport (2001); in a cross section of 37 developing countries, and after controlling for remittances, they found that migration prospects have a positive and significant impact on human-capital formation at origin, especially for countries with low GDP-per-capita levels. This was a first but imperfect try, since they used gross migration rates as a proxy measure for the brain drain because of the lack of comparative data on international migration by education levels.

In a subsequent study, Beine, Docquier, and Rapoport (2008) used the DM emigration rates by education level to assess empirically the impact of the brain drain on human-capital formation in developing countries. They

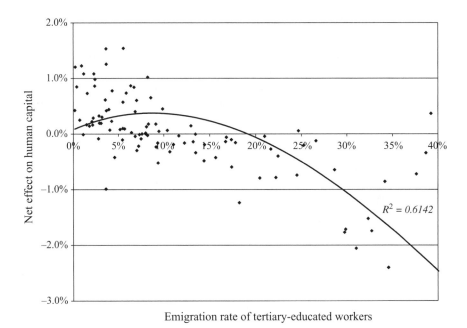

Figure 9.2 Brain drain and human capital in LDCs (with second-order polynomial trend).

find evidence of a positive impact of skilled-migration prospects on gross human-capital levels in a cross section of 127 developing countries. In contrast, Faini (2003) finds a depressing but not significant effect of tertiary emigration on domestic enrollment in higher education, a finding he attributes to the choice of would-be migrants to pursue their studies abroad. As he himself aknowledges, however, his results must be taken with caution, as they are based on enrollment data known to raise measurement problems.[13]

Beine, Docquier, and Rapoport (2008) also computed the net effect of the brain drain using counter-factual experiments: they compare the current proportion of postsecondary educated workers to their erstwhile value if skilled workers were allowed to emigrate at the same rate as unskilled workers. They find that countries combining relatively low levels of human capital and low-skilled emigration rates are likely to experience a net gain, and conversely. Figure 9.2 gives the reduced-form net effect of the brain

13. Beine et al. (2008), on the other hand, use the improved Barro and Lee data, which estimate the proportion of highly educated partly on the basis of census data, and partly on the basis of schooling data, using an inventory method aimed at limiting measurement errors.

drain on human-capital formation in developing countries. The X axis gives the DM emigration rates for the highly educated, and the Y axis gives the net impact of the brain drain on the proportion of skilled remaining in the country. The variability across countries at given migration rates is a result of the impact of other right-hand-side variables, and the curve itself is adjusted using a second-order polynomial. On the whole, there appear to be more losers than winners, and in addition, the former tend to lose relatively more than what the latter gain. Nonetheless, at an aggregate level and given that the largest developing countries are all among the winners (China, India, Indonesia, Brazil), brain-drain migration may be seen as increasing not only the total number of skilled workers worldwide but also the number of such workers living in the developing world.

Remittances

Migrants' remittances constitute another channel through which the brain drain may generate positive effects for source countries. It is well documented that workers' remittances often make a significant contribution to GNP and are a major source of income in many developing countries. Remittances impinge on households' decisions in terms of labor supply, investment, education (Hanson and Woodruff, 2003; Cox Edwards and Ureta, 2003), migration, occupational choice, and fertility, with potentially important aggregated effects. This is especially the case in poor countries where capital-market imperfections reduce the set of options available to members of low-income classes.

The literature on migrants' remittances shows that the two main motivations to remit are altruism, on the one hand, and exchange, on the other hand.[14] Altruism is primarily directed toward one's immediate family and then decreases with social distance. In contrast, no such proximity is required in the case of exchange; the exchange-based theory of remittances posits that remittances simply "buy" various types of services, such as taking care of the migrants' assets (e.g., land, cattle) or relatives (children, elderly parents) at home. Such transfers are typically observed in case of a temporary migration and signal the migrants' intention to return. A particular type of exchange takes place when remittances are de facto repayments of loans used to finance the migrants' investments in education and/or migration, with altruism and social norms and sanctions making the intergenerational contract self-enforcing. Hence, it is a priori unclear

14. See Rapoport and Docquier (2006) for a comprehensive survey of the theoretical and empirical literature on migrants' remittances.

whether educated migrants would remit more than their uneducated compatriots; the former may remit more to meet implicit commitments to reimburse the family for funding of education investments (and, in addition, they have a higher income potential), but on the other hand, they tend to emigrate with the family, on a more permanent basis, and are therefore less likely to remit (or are likely to remit less) than someone moving alone on a temporary basis.

McCormick and Wahba (2000) obtain the result that highly skilled migration may benefit those left behind in a trade-theoretic model where migration, remittances, and domestic labor-market outcomes are jointly determined and multiple equilibria arise, with the high-migration equilibrium pareto-dominating the low-migration equilibrium. In a setting closer to the one used throughout this chapter, Cinar and Docquier (2004) develop a stylized model in which skilled emigrants altruistically remit part of their earnings to relatives in the source country. They assume that each remaining resident receives an identical amount of remittances (which depends on the proportion of migrants, the intercountry wage gap, and the altruistic parameter) and characterize the transition path (i.e., the dynamics of transfers) and the long-run equilibrium of the economy.

In our basic framework with constant marginal utility of income, remittances have impact on human-capital formation only when liquidity constraints are binding. Without migration (and assuming a uniform distribution of education costs), the share of the educated is given by c_L. With migration, two opposite effects are observed. Initially, the number of educated remaining in the country falls to $c_L - c_M$. If emigrants remit part of their foreign income, liquidity constraints become less binding for recipients in the source country. The traditional negative effect can therefore, in principle, be compensated by better access to education for those left behind, with the total effect depending on the amounts transferred and on recipients' location on the cost axis.

Let us denote by T the amount of remittances received by each remaining resident at the steady state. As shown on figure 9.3, the effect of remittances is to shift c_L and c_M to the right. With a uniform distribution, and given that $(c_L + T) - (c_M + T) = c_L - c_M$, the proportion of educated and the economywide average level of human capital are given by $P_T = \dfrac{c_L - c_M}{1 - c_M - T}$ and $H_T = 1 + P_T(h - 1)$. A beneficial brain drain obtains if $H_T > H_n$, that is, if

$$T > T^* \equiv c_M \left(\frac{1}{c_L} - 1 \right).$$

In words, this means that for a beneficial brain drain to obtain through remittances, the transfer received by each remaining resident must be relatively high so that a large share of the population gains access to education. This is unlikely when migration costs are quite high (as $\partial T^*/\partial k > 0$)

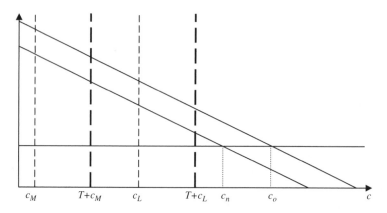

Figure 9.3 Brain drain and remittances.

and, more generally, does not seem to portray the evidence on remittance behavior in developing countries. Although remittances are generally positively correlated with donors' incomes, meaning that skilled emigrants are presumably important remitters, the results from empirical studies are mixed. Most microstudies (e.g., Lucas and Stark, 1985; Cox, Ezer, and Jimenez, 1998; Brown and Poirine, 2005) find a positive effect of education on the probability of sending remittances and on the amounts remitted after controling for income, which suggests that remittances have a loan-repayment component. However, at an aggregate level, Faini (2007) shows that migrants' remittances decrease with the proportion of skilled individuals among emigrants and concludes that "this result suggests that the negative impact of the brain drain cannot be counterbalanced by higher remittances." This does not imply that remittances by skilled migrants are negligible, especially if the proportion of temporary migrants increases; for example, Kangasniemi, Winters, and Commander (2007) show that nearly half (45 percent) of Indian medical doctors working in the United Kingdom remit income to their home country and that remitters transfer on average 16 percent of their income.

Instead of sending remittances to relatives at home, migrants may return after they have accumulated savings abroad and use such savings to promote investment projects (generally small businesses). There is much evidence that low-skill workers migrate with the aim of accumulating enough savings to access to self-employment and entrepreneurship. (See, e.g., Mesnard, 2004, and Mesnard and Ravallion, 2001, for Tunisia; Dustmann and Kirchkamp, 2002; for Turkey; Ilahi, 1999, for Pakistan; Woodruff and Zenteno, 2007; for Mexico; or McCormick and Wahba, 2001, for Egypt. The last-mentioned study also suggests that skill acquisition may be more important for relatively educated migrants than the need to overcome liquidity constraints.)

Network Effects

Our analysis has so far focused on the long-run steady state. In the short run, with unanticipated migration, emigration of educated workers is a net loss to the home country. As time goes by, however, successive cohorts adapt their education decisions, and the economywide average level of education partly (as in Figure 9.4a) or totally catches up, with a possible net gain in the long run (as in Figure 9.4b) thanks to the various channels detailed above. On the transition path, additional effects are likely to operate. In particular, there is a large economic and sociological literature emphasizing that the creation of migrants' networks facilitates exchanges of goods, factors, and ideas between the migrants' host and home countries. We now consider two types of migrant-network effects: networks that encourage trade, FDI inflows and technology diffusion and networks that encourage further migration.

An important socioeconomic literature has emerged recently to analyze the consequences of the constitution of migrants' networks on migration patterns. For example, Massey, Goldring, and Durand (1994) outline a cumulative theory of migration, noting that the first migrants usually come from the middle ranges of the socioeconomic hierarchy and are individuals who have enough resources to absorb the costs and risks of the trip but are not so affluent that working abroad is unattractive. Family and friends then draw on ties with these migrants to gain access to employment and assistance in migrating, substantially reducing the costs and risks of movement to them. This increases the attractiveness and feasibility of migration for additional members, allowing them to migrate and expand further the set of people with network connections. Migration networks can then be viewed as reducing the costs and perhaps also increasing the benefits of

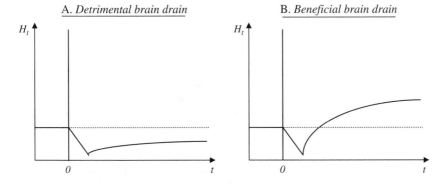

Figure 9.4 Dynamic impact of brain drain.

migration. (Bauer, Epstein, and Gang, 2007; Munshi, 2003; and McKenzie and Rapoport, 2007, find strong evidence of such network effects.) In other words, migration incentives become endogenous once networks are formed.

Building on this idea, Kanbur and Rapoport (2005) introduce networks effects at destination in a standard model of selective migration. In the spirit of Carrington, Detragiache, and Vishwanath (1996), they assume that migration costs k are decreasing with the size of the network at destination, that is, with the number of migrants already emigrated abroad. As explained above, the role of migrants' networks is to diffuse information on job availability and provide hospitality and help in job search. Hence, past migration progressively raises the expected return to education (net of migration costs) and, therefore, domestic enrollment in education.[15] For a given p or γ, this raises the optimal number of individuals engaging in education and the share of educated workers remaining in the country. In this sense, migrant networks have positive effects on human-capital formation and serve to mitigate the short-run detrimental effects of the brain drain.

Another type of network effect arises in the creation of business and trade networks; such a "diaspora externality" has long been recognized in the sociological literature and, more recently, by economists in the field of international trade. In many instances, indeed, and contrarily to what one would expect in a standard trade-theoretic framework, trade and migration appear to be complements rather than substitutes (e.g., Lopez and Schiff, 1998). Interestingly, such a complementarity has been shown to prevail mostly for trade in heterogeneous goods, where ethnic networks help in overcoming information problems linked to the very nature of the goods exchanged (Rauch and Trindade, 2002; Rauch and Casella, 2003). How the relationship of substitutability or complementarity between trade and migration is affected by the skill composition of migration, however, remains unclear. The only empirical study on this question that we are aware of is that of Lopez and Schiff (1998), who used episodes of trade liberalization to conclude to a relationship of complementarity between trade and unskilled migration, and conversely for skilled migration.[16]

15. For this incentive effect to operate, however, education must not only increase one's chances of migration but also allow access to legal, high-skill jobs. In a context where immigration is illegal and migrants can only access unskilled jobs, the prospect of migration can instead reduce education investment. See McKenzie and Rapoport (2006) on Mexico-U.S. migration and De Brauw and Giles (2006) on rural-urban migration in China.

16. A recent theoretical paper (Kar and Beladi, 2004), using a Hecksher-Ohlin framework augmented to allow for noncompetitive wage settings, comes up with predictions just opposite to the empirical findings of Lopez and Schiff.

Similarly, one may ask whether migration and FDI are substitutes (as one would expect) or complements and whether the skill composition of migration, or the sectoral composition of FDI, have impact on the relationship between the two. Again the evidence on these issues is scant. There are certainly many case studies suggesting that skilled migrants take an active part in the creation of business networks leading to FDI project deployment in their home countries. This is the case, in particular, for the software industry (Saxenian, 2001; Arora and Gambardella, 2005; Commander et al., 2004). At an aggregate level, Kugler and Rapoport (2007) investigate the migration-FDI relationship for bilateral flows between the United States and the rest of the world throughout the 1990s. They show that FDIs toward a given country are positively correlated with the initial U.S. immigration stock of that country (for both skilled and unskilled migration) but negatively correlated with the change in immigration stocks during the period studied. From this, they conclude to a relationship of contemporaneous substitutability and of dynamic complementarity between migration and FDI. Interestingly, after disaggregating the results by skill level and destination sector, they find significant relationships only for current unskilled migration and current manufacturing FDI, which appear to be substitutes, and for past skilled migration and current FDI in the service sector, which appear to be complements.

Policy Issues

Our discussion of policy issues is based on a simplified model combining liquidity constraints and uncertain migration prospects (solutions are henceforth indexed by pl). Since this kind of model relies on out-selection immigration policies, we consider that migration costs are zero ($k = k' = 0$). However, similar conclusions would be obtained through combining self-selection (which requires positive migration costs) and return migration.

Without public intervention, our model can be summarized by the following equations:

$$c_{pl} \equiv Min \ [c_O; c_M]$$
$$P_{pl} = \frac{(1-p)c_{pl}}{1 - pc_{pl}}$$

where $c_o = c_n + ph\Omega$ is the open economy critical education cost threshold, $\Omega = \omega - 1$ measures the foreign wage premium, $c_n = h - 1$ is the critical agent in the closed economy, and $c_M = 1 - \phi$ is the critical threshold of education cost when liquidity constraints are binding. The foreign wage premium Ω is endogenous and decreases with the domestic proportion of educated P_{pl}.

In this framework, we analyze the role of emigration (or immigration) policy, education policy, and (Bhagwati) tax policy on the interplay between migration and human-capital formation. These policies are evaluated in terms of their impact on the average level of human capital $H_{pl} = 1 + (h - 1)P_{pl}$ and in terms of their impact on the income of the unskilled $I_{pl} = 2w$. Basically, these two social objectives can be assimilated to efficiency and social justice. We have $\dfrac{\partial P_{pl}}{\partial c_{pl}} = \dfrac{1-p}{(1-pc_{pl})^2} > 0$; hence, for a given p, the average level of human capital increases with the critical ability. Focusing on efficiency, therefore, requires maximizing c_{pl}. Without public intervention, maximizing the proportion of educated also maximizes the welfare of uneducated agents, which means that efficient and socially just solutions coincide.

Migration Policy: The Optimal Rate of Skilled Migration

We use a diagrammatic representation in the (Ω, p) plane.

If liquidity constraints are not binding, a beneficial brain drain emerges if $P_{pl} > c_n$ or, equivalently, if

$$\Omega > \Omega_{BB}(p) \equiv \frac{(h-1)(2-h)}{h[1-p(2-h)]}.$$

This expression is an increasing and convex function of p, depicted as the BB curve in figure 9.5.

Liquidity constraints are binding if $c_{pl} > c_n$, that is, if

$$\Omega > \Omega_{LL}(p) \equiv \frac{2-h-\phi}{ph},$$

which is depicted as the LL curve in figure 9.5.

When liquidity constraints are binding, a beneficial brain drain emerges when $\dfrac{(1-p)c_M}{1-pc_M} > c_n$ or, equivalently, when $p < p_b \equiv \dfrac{2-h-\phi}{(1-\phi)(2-h)}$.

Note that p_b is the intersection between LL and BB.

The optimal rate of skilled migration depends on Ω, which is itself endogenous as it depends on human-capital accumulation and, therefore, on migration prospects. Let us define Ω_n as the foreign-wage premium prevailing at $p = 0$. If $\Omega_n > \Omega_{BB}(0) = (h - 1)(2 - h)/h$, then there is room for a beneficial brain drain over some ranges of p. Several paths of migration premium can be represented diagrammatically. In each case (i.e., for each Ω_n), the optimal migration rate corresponds to the minimal value of the (Ω, p) locus. For limited values of p, the proportion of educated increases, and the foreign-wage premium decreases with p. For a higher p, the proportion of educated decreases. The optimal migration rate lies between

0 and the BB curve (depicted as the bold curve). If liquidity constraints are binding, the incentive effect of migration vanishes, and the optimal rate of migration is constrained by the LL curve. In countries where $\Omega_n > \Omega_{BB}(0)$, a brain drain is always detrimental. The proportion of educated and the welfare of unskilled workers decrease with p. The optimal rate of migration is then zero. These results may be summarized as follows:

> As apparent from figure 9.5, the optimal migration rate is zero for relatively rich countries, that is, for countries with a low foreign-wage premium. It then increases with the foreign-wage premium Ω as long as liquidity constraints are not binding and then decreases with Ω for poor countries where liquidity constraints are binding.

In other words, there is an inverse-U- shaped relationship between optimal skilled emigration and level of development.

Education Policy

Consider now that the government collects an income tax on both educated and uneducated adults remaining in the country. The tax may be expressed in terms of educated workers' wages τwh, with τ denoting the tax rate, and is assumed to finance an education subsidy allocated to each young person

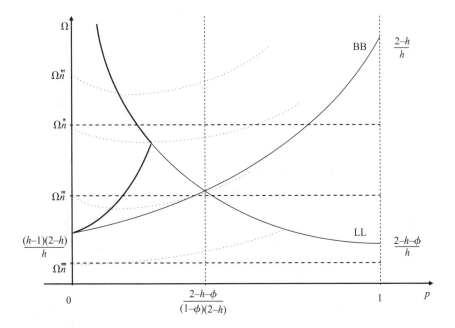

Figure 9.5 Optimal skilled-emigration rate.

opting for education; the education subsidy may itself be expressed in terms of the local wage θw. The critical education-cost threshold then becomes

$$c_O^\tau = h - 1 + \theta + ph(\Omega + r)$$
$$c_M^\tau = 1 - \phi + \theta$$
$$c_{pl}^\tau = Min \ [c_O^\tau, c_M^\tau]$$

Education policy plays a double role in the debate about the brain-drain effects. First, for a given pair (τ, θ), the condition for a beneficial brain drain to obtain is modified. Second, the brain drain requires budgetary adjustments (increasing taxes or reducing subsidies). We address these two effects separetely.

First consider that the government budget in the closed economy is balanced under the pair (τ_n, θ_n). The budget constraint implies that $\tau_n h = m\theta_n(h - 1 + \theta_n)$, where m is the number of children per adult. Assume also that liquidity constraints are not binding in the closed economy, so that $c_\tau = h - 1 + \theta_n < 1 - \phi + \theta_n$. Without fiscal adjustments (e.g., assuming that international aid allows the government to keep the policy $[\tau_n, \theta_n]$ unchanged) and assuming first that liquidity constraints are not binding (that is, $c_O^\tau \le c_M^\tau$), then a beneficial brain drain emerges if

$$\Omega > \Omega_{BB}^\tau(p) \equiv \frac{(h - 1 + \theta_n)(2 - h - \theta_n)}{h[1 - p(2 - h - \theta_n)]} - \tau_n$$

Compared with the economy without taxes and subsidies, the BB curve shifts downward: $\Omega_{BB}^\tau(p) < \Omega_{BB}(p)$. This is clearly the case for high values of p (at $p = 1$). This is also the case for small values of p, at least when the skill premium is sufficiently high (at $p = 0$, using the budget constraint, $\Omega_{BB}^\tau[0] < \Omega_{BB}[0]$ requires $\theta > \frac{[3 - 2h] - m[h - 1]}{1 + m}$, which decreases with h and m; if $m = 0$, a sufficient condition to obtain the desired condition is $h > 4/3$). On the other hand, if liquidity constraints are binding, that is, if $c_O^\tau > c_M^\tau$ (this will be the case if $\Omega > \Omega_{LL}^\tau[p] \equiv \frac{2 - h - \phi}{ph} - \tau_n$) then compared with the economy without taxes and subsidies, the LL curve will also shift downwards, but the condition for a beneficial brain drain to emerge will be

$$p < p_b^t \equiv \frac{2 - h - \phi}{(1 - \phi + \theta_n)(2 - h - \theta_n)}.$$

If the subsidy is sufficiently high $(\theta_n > \phi - h + 1)$, then p_b^τ is higher than p_b, the critical migration rate without education policy.

These results may be summarized as follows:

> If the closed-economy fiscal policy can be maintained, then education policy reinforces the likelihood of a beneficial brain

drain. As apparent from figure 9.6, the area for which a beneficial brain drain obtains in the (Ω, p) plane (see the area delimited by the solid lines) is larger than in the case without education policy (see the area delimited by the dashed lines).

Second, the brain drain generates a fiscal loss that requires fiscal adjustments such as decreasing education subsidies by $\Delta\theta$ and/or increasing taxes by $\Delta\tau$. The optimal policymix depends on the social objective of the government. Reducing education subsidies lowers the proportion of educated in both the constrained and unconstrained cases:

$$\Delta c_O^\tau = -\Delta\theta$$
$$\Delta c_M^\tau = -\Delta\theta$$

In contrast, increasing taxes stimulates education investment in the unconstrained case but has no influence on human capital accumulation in the constrained case:

$$\Delta c_O^\tau = ph\Delta\tau$$
$$\Delta c_M^\tau = 0$$

Therefore, if the government's objective is to maximize the average level of human capital (efficiency), adjusting through taxes appears to be

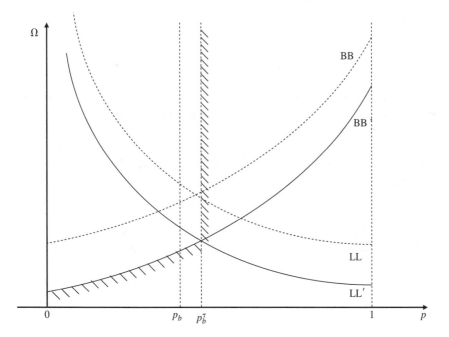

Figure 9.6 Optimal rate of migration and education policy (without budgetary adjustment).

the best option. Alternatively, if the objective is to maximize the income of unskilled workers, now defined as $I_{pl} = \omega(2 - \tau h)$, then adjusting through taxes would seem preferable in terms of efficiency but disproportionately harms the uneducated workers; if human-capital externalities are not too strong, reducing subsidies is therefore preferable for the sake of social justice.

> The fiscal adjustment to the brain drain raises a trade-off between efficiency and social justice. The optimal policy mix depends on the social-welfare function of the government.

The Case for a Bhagwati Tax

Finally, consider that the government is allowed to collect a tax (expressed in a percentage of educated workers' wages at home $\tau^* wh$) on skilled emigrants. We do not discuss here the feasibility of such a tax scheme, which obviously requires international tax cooperation between home- and host-country governments (see Desai, Kapur and McHale, 2004). Assume that the tax can be used to finance either a lump-sum transfer to the young $T^*\omega$ or an education subsidy to those opting for education (expressed in percentage of the wage rate at home $\theta^*\omega$.[17] The critical education cost then becomes

$$c_O^{\tau*} = h - 1 + ph\Omega + \theta^* - ph\tau$$
$$c_M^{\tau*} = 1 - \phi + \theta^* + T^*$$
$$c_{pl}^{\tau*} = Min\ [c_O^{\tau*}, c_M^{\tau*}].$$

In contrast to domestic taxes, a "tax on brains" (or Bhagwati tax) reduces the incentives to educate. If the proceeds from the tax are redistributed as an education subsidy, this partly compensates the negative-incentive effect just described by creating an additional incentive to educate. Both education subsidies and lump-sum transfers make liquidity constraints less binding.

The government's budget constraint becomes more complex. The number of taxpayers is now given by $Nc_{pl}^{\tau*}p$, where N denotes the number of young in the previous period. As m measures the number of children per adult, the number of young living in the origin country in the current period is equal to $N(1 - c_{pl}^{\tau*}p)m$. At the steady state, the budget constraint is given by

$$c_{pl}^{\tau*} ph\tau^* = (1 - c_{pl}^{\tau*} p)m\ [T^* + c_{pl}^{\tau*} \theta^*],$$

---

17. Allocating a lump-sum transfer to adults would simply reduce the incentive to emigrate, reinforcing the effect of the Bhagwati tax.

where the demographic growth factor (fertility minus emigration) is assumed to be positive: $(1 - c_{pl}^{\tau*} p)m > 1$.

When is a Bhagwati tax socially optimal, and how should it be redistributed?

First, let us assume that the tax revenue is used to finance an education subsidy ($T^* = 0$); this affects the critical education cost thresholds as follows:

$$c_O^{\tau*} = h - 1 + ph\Omega + \left[\frac{1 - (1 - c_{pl}^{\tau*} p)m}{(1 - c_{pl}^{\tau*} p)m} \right] ph\tau^*$$

$$c_M^{\tau*} = 1 - \phi + \frac{ph\tau^*}{(1 - c_{pl}^{\tau*} p)m}$$

Alternatively, if the tax is used to finance a lump-sum subsidy to the young ($\theta^* = 0$), then the critical thresholds become

$$c_O^{\tau*} = h - 1 + ph\Omega - ph\tau^*$$

$$c_M^{\tau*} = 1 - \phi + \frac{c_{pl}^{\tau*} ph\tau^*}{(1 - c_{pl}^{\tau*} p)m}$$

When the government aims at maximizing the stock of human capital (and, thus, the critical education cost threshold c_{pl}^{τ}), we have to distinguish between the constrained and unconstrained equilibria. Finding the critical education-cost threshold requires in most cases solving an implicit function (second-order polynomial). However, intuitive results can be obtained by comparing the effect of $ph\tau^*$ in the equations above. In the unconstrained case ($c_{pl}^{\tau*} = c_O^{\tau*}$), a Bhagwati tax always reduces the critical cost threshold $c_O^{\tau*}$. Even in the case of a detrimental brain drain, the tax reinforces the efficiency loss. The decrease is lower when the tax is redistributed as an education subsidy. On the other hand, in the constrained case ($c_O^{\tau*} = c_M^{\tau*}$), a Bhagwati tax always increases the stock of human capital and the efficiency gain is stronger when the tax is redistributed as an education subsidy.

When the governement maximizes uneducated workers' income ($I_{pl} = \omega[2 + T^*]$), two effects are obtained. First, by decreasing the average level of human capital, the Bhagwati tax reduces the local wage ω. This effect is stronger if the tax is redistributed as a lump-sum transfer to the young. However, in this case, unskilled workers share the gain from migration with emigrants. If spill-over effects are not too large, then the uneducated have a clear interest in setting a Bhagwati tax and redistributing its proceeds in a lump-sum way. These results may be summarized as follows:

> In terms of efficiency, a Bhagwati tax is detrimental in the unconstrained equilibrium and beneficial in the constrained equilibrium. In both cases, redistributing the tax revenue as an

education subsidy is more efficient than a lump-sum transfer. In terms of social justice, taxing migrants and redistributing the Bhagwati tax as a lump-sum transfer is preferable as long as spill-over effects (human-capital externalities) are not too large.

Conclusion

The main general conclusion to draw from this analysis is that for a given developing country, the optimal migration rate of its highly educated population is likely to be positive. Whether the current rate is greater or lower than this optimum is an empirical question that must be addressed country by country. A first implication, then, is that in many instances, countries that would impose restrictions on the international mobility of their educated residents, arguing, for example, that emigrants' human capital has been largely publicly financed, could, in fact, decrease the long-run level of their human-capital stock. Still, many countries experience skilled-migration rates that are clearly above optimal levels, a situation that generates static as well as dynamic losses along the lines emphasized in our stylized model. The fact that examples of excessive brain-drain rates abound reveals the difficulty for source countries to control emigration, whether skilled or unskilled. For technical, political, and moral reasons that are beyond the scope of this chapter, source countries are generally unable (with few, sad exceptions in history) to set efficient barriers to emigration; one may regret this, consider instead that emigration is an inalienable individual right, or just take this as a matter of fact that may bring about negative or positive social consequences.

Another implication of this analysis is that rich countries should not nec-essarily see themselves as free-riding on poor countries' educational efforts. The difficulty, however, is to design quality-selective immigration policies that would address the differentiated effects of the brain drain across origin countries without distorting too much the whole immigration system; this could be achieved, at least partly, by designing specific incentives to return migration to those countries most negatively affected by the brain drain and promote international cooperation aiming at more brain circulation.

References

Adams, Richard. 2003. "International Migration, Remittances and the Brain Drain: A Study of 24 Labor-Exporting Countries." World Bank Policy Research Working Paper 2972.

Adams, Walter A., ed. 1968. *The Brain Drain*. New York: Macmillan.

Arora, Ashish, and Alfonso Gambardella, eds. 2005. *From Underdogs to Tigers: The Rise and Growth of the Software Industry in Some Emerging Economies*. Oxford: Oxford University Press.

Barro, Robert J., and Jong Wha Lee. 2001. "International Data on Educational Attainment: Updates and Implications." *Oxford Economic Papers* 53, no. 3: 541–63.

Bauer, Thomas, Gil S. Epstein, and Ira N. Gang. 2007. "Herd Effects or Migration Networks? The Location Choice of Mexican Immigrants in the US." *Research in Labor Economics* 26: 199–229.

Beine, Michel, Frederic Docquier, and Hillel Rapoport. 2001. Brain Drain and Economic Growth: Theory and Evidence." *Journal of Development Economics* 64, no. 1: 275–89.

———. 2007. "Measuring International Skilled Migration: A New Database Controlling for Age of Entry." *World Bank Economic Review* 21, no. 2: 249–54.

———. 2008. Brain Drain and Human Capital Formation in Developing Countries: Winners and Losers. *Economic Journal* 118, no. 528: 631–52.

Berry, Albert R., and Ronald Soligo. 1969. "Some Welfare Aspects of International Migration." *Journal of Political Economy* 77, no. 5: 778–94.

Bhagwati, Jagdish N. 1976. *The Brain Drain and Taxation: Theory and Empirical Analysis* New York: North Holland.

Bhagwati, Jagdish N., and William Dellalfar. 1973. "The Brain Drain and Income Taxation." *World Development* 1, nos. 1–2: 94–1001.

Bhagwati, Jagdish N., and Koichi Hamada. 1974. The Brain Drain, International Integration of Markets for Professionals and Unemployment. *Journal of Development Economics* 1, no. 1: 19–42.

Bhagwati, Jagdish N., and Carlos Rodriguez. 1975. "Welfare Theoretical Analyses of the Brain Drain." *Journal of Development Economics* 2, no. 3: 195–222.

Blomqvist, Ake G. 1986. "International Migration of Educated Manpower and Social Rates of Return to Education in LDCs." *International Economic Review* 27, no. 1: 165–74.

Borjas, George J., and Bernt Bratsberg. 1996. "Who Leaves? The Outmigration of the Foreign-Born." *Review of Economics and Statistics* 78, no. 1: 165–76.

Brown, Richard P. C., and Bernard Poirine. 2005. "A Model of Migrants' Remittances with Human Capital Investment and Intrafamilial Transfers." *International Migration Review* 39, no. 2: 407–438.

Carrington, William J., and Enrica Detragiache. 1998. "How Big Is the Brain Drain?" IMF Working Paper 98.

Carrington, William J., Enrica Detragiache, and Tara Vishwanath. 1996. "Migration with Endogenous Moving Costs." *American Economic Review* 86, no. 4: 909–30.

Cinar, Dilek, and Frederic Docquier. 2004. "Brain Drain and Remittances: Implications for the Source Countries." *Brussels Economic Review* 47, no. 1: 103–18.

Commander, Simon, Rupa Chanda, Mari Kangasmieni, and Alan L. Winters. 2004. "Who Gains from Skilled Migration? Evidence from the Software Industry." Manuscript. Center for Economic Performance. London School of Economics.

Commander, Simon, Mari Kangasniemi, and Alan L. Winters. 2004. "The Brain Drain: Curse or Boon? A Survey of the Literature." In R. Badlwin and L. A. Winters, eds., *Challenges to Globalization*. Chicago: University of Chicago Press, chapter 7.

Cox, Donald, Zekeriya Ezer, and Emmanuel Jimenez. 1998. "Motives for Private Transfers over the Life Cycle: An Analytical Framework and Evidence from Peru." *Journal of Development Economics* 55, no. 1: 57–80.

Cox Edwards, Alejandra, and Manuelita Ureta. 2003. "International Migration, Remittances and Schooling: Evidence from El Salvador." *Journal of Development Economics* 72, no. 2: 429–61.

de Brauw, Alan, and John Giles. 2006. "Migrant Opportunity and the Educational Attainment of Youth in Rural China." IZA Discussion Paper 2326, September.

Desai, Mihir, Devesh Kapur, and John McHale, 2004. "Sharing the Spoils: Taxing International human Capital Flows." *International Tax and Public Finance* 11, no. 5.

Docquier, Frédéric, and Abdeslam Marfouk. 2006. "Measuring International Migration by Educational Attainment, 1990–2000." In Caglar Ozden and Maurice Schiff, eds., *International Migration, Remittances and the Brain Drain*. New York: McMillan and Palgrave, pp. 151–99.

Docquier, Frédéric, and Hillel Rapoport. (1999). "Fuite des Cerveaux et Formation de Capital Humain." *Economie Internationale* 78, no. 3: 63–71.

———. 2004. "Skilled Migration: The Perspective of Developing Countries." World Bank Policy Research Working Paper 3382, August.

Dos Santos, Manon Domingues, and Fabien Postel-Vinay. 2003. "Migration as a Source of Growth: The Perspective of a Developing Country." *Journal of Population Economics* 16, no. 1: 161–75.

———. 2004. "The Impact of Temporary Migration on Human Capital Accumulation and Economic Development." *Brussels Economic Review* 47, no. 1: 77–88.

Dustmann, Christian, and Oliver Kirchkamp. 2002. "The Optimal Migration Duration and Activity Choice after Remigration." *Journal of Development Economics* 67, no. 2: 351–72.

Faini, Riccardo. 2003. "Is the Brain Drain an Unmitigated Blessing?" UNU-WIDER Discussion Paper 2003/64, September.

———. 2007. "Remittances and the Brain Drain." *World Bank Economic Review* 21, no. 2: 177–91.

Grubel, Herbert, and Anthony Scott. 1966. "The International Flow of Human Capital." *American Economic Review* 56: 268–74.

Hamada, Koichi. 1977. Taxing the Brain Drain: A Global Point of View." In J. Bhagwati, ed., *The New International Order*. Cambridge, MA: MIT Press.

Hamada, Koichi, and Jagdish N. Bhagwati. 1975 "Domestic Distorsions, Imperfect Information and the Brain Drain." *Journal of Development Economics* 2, no. 3: 265–80.

Hanson, Gordon H., and Christopher Woodruff. 2003. "Emigration and Educational Attainment in Mexico." Mimeo. University of California at San Diego.

Haque, Nadeem U., and Aziz Jahangir. 1999. The Quality of Governance: Second-Generation Civil Reform in Africa." *Journal of African Economies* 8: 65–106.

Haque, Nadeem U., and Se-Kik Kim. 1995. " 'Human Capital Flight': Impact of Migration on Income and Growth." *IMF Staff Papers* 42, no. 3: 577–607.

Hoffmann, Anders N. 2003. "Education, Trade and Investment Liberalizations." *Journal of International Economics* 60, no. 2: 433–53.

Ilahi, Nadeem. 1999. "Return Migration and Occupational Change." *Review of Development Economics* 3, no. 2: 170–86.

International Office for Migration. 2003. *World Migration 2003: Managing Migration*. Geneva: International Organization for Migration.

Johnson, Harry. 1967. "Some Economic Aspects of the Brain Drain." *Pakistan Development Review* 7, no. 3: 379–411.

Kanbur, Ravi, and Hillel Rapoport. 2005. "Migration Selectivity and the Evolution of Spatial Inequality." *Journal of Economic Geography* 5, no. 1: 43–57.

Kangasmieni, Mari, Alan L. Winters, and Simon Commander. 2007. "Is the Medical Brain Drain Beneficial? Evidence from Overseas Doctors in the UK." *Social Science and Medicine* 65, no. 5: 915–23.

Kar, Saibal, and Hamid Beladi. 2004. "Skill Formation and International Migration: Welfare Perspective of Developing Countries." *Japan and the World Economy* 16: 35–54.

Katz, Eliakim, and Hillel Rapoport. 2005. "On Human Capital Formation with Exit Options." *Journal of Population Economics* 18, no. 2: 267–74.

Klenow, Peter J., and Andres Rodriguez-Clare. 2005. "Externalities and Growth." In P. Aghion and S. Durlauf, eds., *Handbook of Economic Growth*. Amsterdam: North Holland, pp. 817–61.

Kugler, Maurice, and Hillel Rapoport. 2007. "International Labor and Capital Flows: Complements or Substitutes?" *Economics Letters* 94, no. 2: 155–62.

Kwok, Viem, and Hayne E. Leland. 1982. "An Economic Model of the Brain Drain." *American Economic Review* 72, no. 1: 91–100.

Lopez, Ramon, and Maurice Schiff. 1998. "Migration and the Skill Composition of the Labour Force: The Impact of Trade Liberalization in LDCs." *Canadian Journal of Economics* 31, no. 2: 318–36.

Lowell, Lindsay B., and Allan M. Findlay. 2001. *Migration of Highly Skilled Persons from Developing Countries: Impact and Policy Responses*. Geneva: International Labour Office.

Lucas, Robert E. 1988. "On the Mechanics of Economic Development." *Journal of Monetary Economics* 22, no. 3: 3–42.

Lucas, Robert E. B., and Oded Stark, 1985. "Motivation to Remit: Evidence from Botswana." *Journal of Political Economy* 93: 901–18.

Luo, Yu-Ling, and Wei-Jen Wang. 2002. "High-Skill Migration and Chinese Taipei's Industrial Development." In OECD, *International Mobility of the Highly-Skilled*. Paris: OECD.

Massey, Douglas S., Luin Goldring, and Jorge Durand. 1994. "Continuities in Transnational Migration: An Analysis of Nineteen Mexican Communities." *American Journal of Sociology*, 99, no. 6: 1492–1533.

McCormick, Barry, and Jackline Wahba. 2000. "Overseas Unemployment and Remittances to a Dual Economy." *Economic Journal* 110: 509–34.

———. 2001. "Overseas Work Experience, Savings and Entrepreneurship amongst Return Migrants to LDCs." *Scottish Journal of Political Economy* 48, no. 2: 164–78.

McCullock, Rachel, and Janet T. Yellen. 1975. "Consequences of a Tax on the Brain Drain for Unemployment and Income Inequality in Less Developed Countries." *Journal of Development Economics* 2, no. 3: 249–64.

———. 1977. "Factor Mobility, Regional Development and the Distribution of Income." *Journal of Political Economy* 85, no. 1: 79–96.

McKenzie, David, and Hillel Rapoport. 2006. "Can Migration Reduce Educational Attainment? Evidence from Mexico." World Bank Policy Research Working Paper 3952, June.

———. 2007. "Network Effects and the Dynamics of Migration and Inequality: Theory and Evidence from Mexico." *Journal of Development Economics* 84, no. 1: 1–27.

Mesnard, Alice. 2004. "Temporary Migration and Capital Market Imperfections." *Oxford Economic Papers* 56: 242–62.

Mesnard, Alice, and Martin Ravallion. 2001. "Wealth Distribution and Self-Employment in a Developing Country." CEPR Discussion Paper 3026.

Miyagiwa, Kaz. 1991. "Scale Economies in Education and the Brain Drain Problem." *International Economic Review*, 32, no. 3: 743–59.

Mountford, Andrew. 1997. "Can a Brain Drain Be Good for Growth in the Source Economy?" *Journal of Development Economics* 53, no. 2: 287–303.

Munshi, Kaivan. 2003. "Networks in the Modern Economy: Mexican Migrants in the US Labor Market." *Quarterly Journal of Economics*, 118, no. 2: 549–99.

OECD (Organisation for Economic Co-operation and Development). 2002. *Trends International Migration*. Paris: OECD.

Rapoport, Hillel, and Frédéric Docquier. 2006. "The Economics of Migrants' Remittances." In S. C. Kolm and J. Mercier-Ythier, eds., *Handbook of the Economics of Giving, Reciprocity and Altruism*. Amsterdam: North Holland. Vol. 2, pp. 1135–98.

Rauch, James E., and Allessandra Casella. 2003. "Overcoming Informational Barriers to International Resource Allocation: Prices and Ties." *Economic Journal* 113, no. 484: 21–42.

Rauch, James E., and Vitor Trindade. 2002. "Ethnic Chinese Networks in International Trade." *Review of Economics and Statistics* 84, no. 1: 116–30.

Rodriguez, Carlos. 1975. "Brain Drain and Economic Growth: A Dynamic Model." *Journal of Development Economics* 2, no. 3: 223–48.

Saxenian, Anna-Lee. 2001. "Bangalore, the Silicon Valley of India?" CREDPR Working Paper 91, Stanford University.

Schiff, Maurice. 2002. "Love Thy Neighbor: Trade, Migration and Social Capital." *European Journal of Political Economy* 18, no. 1: 87–107.

Stark, Oded, Christian Helmenstein, and Alexia Prskawetz. 1997. "A Brain Gain with a Brain Drain." *Economics Letters*, 55: 227–34.

———. 1998. "Human Capital Depletion, Human Capital Formation, and Migration: A Blessing or a 'Curse'?" *Economics Letters* 60, no. 3: 363–67.

Stark, Oded, and You Qiang Wang. 2002. "Inducing Human Capital Formation: Migration as a Substitute for Subsidies." *Journal Public Economics* 86, no. 1: 29–46.

Usher, Dan. 1977. "Public Property and the Effects of Migration upon Other Residents of the Migrants' Countries of Origin and Destination." *Journal of Political Economy* 85, no. 5: 1001–20.

Vidal, Jean-Pierre. 1998. "The Effect of Emigration on Human Capital Formation." *Journal of Population Economics* 11, no. 4: 589–600.

Woodruff, Christopher, and Rene Zenteno. 2007. "Migration Networks and Micro-Enterprises in Mexico." *Journal of Development Economics* 82, no. 2: 509–28.

World Trade Organization. 2004. Trade Statistics, Historical Series 1980–2003. www.wto.org/english/res_e/statis_e/statis_e.htm.

10

Income Taxation and Skilled Migration
The Analytical Issues

JOHN DOUGLAS WILSON

The modern normative theory of income taxation is largely based on Mirrlees's pioneering 1971 article on optimal income taxation.[1] He models the design of an income tax as an exercise in policymaking under asymmetric information. The government does not know workers' productivities and so cannot tax them directly. It taxes income instead, but then workers' labor-supply decisions are distorted because they seek to lessen their tax burdens. The result is an optimal tax schedule that reflects a trade-off between efficiency and equity.

Moving to an open economy creates another avenue by which individuals might reduce or eliminate their income-tax burdens: they may move abroad. The home country may attempt to tax natives living abroad, but its ability to do so is typically quite limited. Once again, the government faces an asymmetric information problem, now involving its imperfect knowledge of opportunities available to those living abroad. A typical response to the difficulties involved in taxing foreign-source income is to tax only the domestic incomes of residents.[2] But then the opportunity to move abroad creates additional inefficiencies, tilting the efficiency-equity trade-off away from equity. The result is a less egalitarian tax system. But how much is the efficiency-equity trade-off tilted, and what factors determine the tilt? In an effort to answer these questions, this chapter reviews and synthesizes the literature on the analytics of skilled migration and income taxation.

Adding migration to an optimal income-tax model quickly introduces positive elements into the normative analysis, because the analyst must confront the issue of how the well-being of nonresidents enters the objectives

I thank Avinash Dixit and T. N. Srinivasan for helpful comments.

1. William Vickrey was cited by the Nobel Prize Committee for much earlier work on a similar model. But Mirrlees provided a method for solving the model.

2. See Pomp (1985) for an example of the problems involved in taxing the foreign incomes of emigrants.

of government decision makers. We could try to address the question using purely normative arguments. But as Mirrlees (1982) explains, welfare functions that "include all humans...are surely morally defensible, but they may be thought not to be what an adviser to a democratic state is expected to be guided by." In other words, the analyst's research will have little relevance if it requires governments to pursue objectives that are at odds with political realities. A working assumption in the research discussed in this chapter is that natives count in the measurement of national welfare, including those who move abroad (though maybe less so in some cases), whereas recent immigrants count either less or not at all. In addition, I will at times depart completely from the framework of social-welfare maximization and assume instead that tax policies are determined by a political process.

Migration also raises positive issues concerning how countries interact, including the types of strategies they pursue in their competition for skilled migrants. Some of the research reported here skirts this issue by examining the policy choices of a single country. But elsewhere, I explicitly consider the game-theoretic interactions among countries.

A number of tentative conclusions emerge from my review. First, emigration opportunities for skilled natives have the potential to eliminate completely the use of income taxation to redistribute income; this will happen in the case of an infinite migration elasticity, as described below. On the other hand, I also describe a number of models in which the progressivity of the income tax is substantial in the presence of migration opportunities; that is, average tax rates increase significantly with income. These models contain factors that limit competition for skilled migrants. In some cases, countries keep taxes high on all skilled individuals because they cannot easily identify and separately tax those individuals with poor migration opportunities. Alternatively, countries possess technological advantages, such as those arising from agglomeration economies, allowing them to tax skilled workers heavily without causing a large number to move abroad. I also discuss models in which tax policy emerges from a political process that does not fully account for subsequent migration responses.

Much of this review concerns skilled emigrants, but I also discuss immigration, including cases where its presence may lead to more income redistribution. I also point out some differences between the effects of skilled and unskilled migration.

The progressivity of a tax system is sometimes defined in terms of marginal tax rates, that is, how the tax payments on an additional dollar of income vary across individuals with different incomes. Here I argue that there is little or no connection between migration and marginal tax rates. Migration may reduce average tax rates on high-income individuals while at the same time increasing their marginal tax rates. Some of the early models of migration and income taxation assumed a linear income tax, which missed this point by restricting marginal tax rates to be the same across all levels of income. In this chapter, references to the progressivity of a tax system concern average tax rates.

The plan of this chapter is as follows. I first discuss the case where it is possible to tax the incomes of natives living abroad. Since doing so has proved difficult in practice, I next turn to the case of source-based taxation, where incomes earned abroad cannot be taxed. The benchmark model developed here lays out the case for little or no taxes on skilled residents when they are internationally mobile. Several important departures from the benchmark model are then discussed, some of which justify sizable taxes on mobile skilled residents. Whereas this analysis mainly concerns emigration, I later discuss some special issues that immigration raises for income tax policy. I also examine models with both immigration and emigration, including models where agglomeration economies have important impacts on equilibrium tax policies, and models where majority rule is used to choose taxes. Finally, I provide some concluding remarks.

Taxes on Foreign-Source Income

To better understand the second-best problems associated with taxing potential emigrants, this section describes a benchmark model in which taxing foreign-source income is possible. Information problems are first assumed away, allowing first-best policies to be employed. But the model is then extended to include such problems. For the initial model, I also assume that any public goods financed by taxes are fixed in supply, with a nonvarying cost.

Consider first a closed economy with two types of individuals, skilled and unskilled, in which the skilled earn exogenous income y_2 and the unskilled earn y_1. Assume a common utility function relating utility to consumption $u(x)$, which exhibits diminishing marginal utility. Consider the case where the government wishes to maximize the sum of the utilities of all residents. Then it is clear that the government should impose a 100-percent tax on income, using the proceeds to finance public goods and provide all workers with a uniform poll subsidy. In this manner, consumption is equalized across individuals. Otherwise, marginal utilities will differ, implying a nonoptimal income distribution.

Moving to the opposite extreme, now interpret this economy as a single "small country," where some fraction of skilled individuals emigrate and receive an exogenous income y_2^* abroad, calculated net of (exogenous) taxes paid to foreign governments. Then an emigrant's utility may be denoted $u^*(y_2^* - T_2^*)$, where T_2^* are taxes paid to the home government. The taxes collected from skilled and unskilled residents are denoted T_2

and T_1 (where a negative T_1 indicates a subsidy paid to unskilled residents). Throughout this chapter, I shall assume that the home government's welfare function gives equal weights to the utilities of native residents and emigrants.[3]

To avoid "corner solutions," in which all natives live inside or outside the country, assume that skilled and unskilled labor are both essential in the production of output. In other words, the technology is represented by a constant-returns production function, denoted $f(n_1, n_2)$, where n_1 and n_2 are the number of unskilled and skilled workers, each supplying a fixed amount of labor, and $f(0, n_2) = f(n_1, 0) = 0$. Normalizing each resident's labor supply to equal one, we may treat incomes y_1 and y_2 as the corresponding marginal products of labor, which depend on the ratio n_2/n_1. This model is henceforth referred to as the benchmark model.

The main conclusion from this model is that there should be no difference between the total tax paid by a skilled emigrant and a skilled resident. Suppose instead that the foreign tax is lower. Let us then lower the domestic tax on a skilled worker a little, while raising the tax collected from an unskilled worker to keep revenue constant at the initial population levels: $n_1 \Delta T_1 = -n_2 \Delta T_2 > 0$, where the delta symbol represents a small change.[4] As a result, more skilled workers will choose to reside in the home country, lowering their marginal product, and the skilled wage will fall until the after-tax skilled incomes have declined to their original level: $\Delta w_2 = \Delta T_2 < 0$. To satisfy the equilibrium requirement of zero economic profits, the unskilled wage will then also rise by an offsetting amount, $\Delta w_1 = \Delta T_1 > 0$, restoring the after-tax incomes of unskilled workers to their original level. But the movement of Δn_2 skilled migrants back to the home country increases tax revenue by $(T_2 - T_2^*) \Delta n_2 > 0$, creating a surplus in the government budget that can then be used to raise the utilities of unskilled workers. The original tax system could not have been optimal. By a symmetrical argument, taxes cannot be higher abroad than at home. The only possibility is for tax payments not to vary with location.

Note that this result does not mean that skilled incomes earned at home and abroad should be taxed at the same average rates. The reason is that these incomes may differ in equilibrium, as a result of locational preferences. The natural assumption to make is that skilled natives must earn a substantially higher income abroad to be willing to migrate, implying that this income is taxed less to equalize tax payments. If it were taxed the

---

3. In a dynamic model, we might expect the weight given to emigrants to diminish with their time spent abroad, increasing a government's desire to tax them more. But a government's ability to tax them more would also diminish with time spent abroad.

4. By considering a small tax change, I can use first-order approximations in the following argument.

same, then the tax system would lower home social welfare by discouraging migration. But an equal-tax-rate rule could be resurrected if the government taxed income earned abroad net of a deduction for the "cost" of going abroad. Note, too, that any taxes paid to foreign governments should also be deductible, since they are also a "cost" from the viewpoint of the home government.

Suppose now that the home country provides its residents with an exogenous supply of a public good,[5] and let the $C(n_2)$ denote its cost as a function of the number of skilled residents in the country (given the fixed number of unskilled). Then an optimal tax system will require that $T_2 - T_2^*$ equal the marginal change in $C(n_2)$ from a unit rise in n_2, which I call the "marginal congestion cost" and label MC. In other words, tax payments at home should exceed those abroad to compensate the country for the cost of providing the public good to an additional skilled resident. This marginal-cost pricing rule is needed to achieve an efficient level of migration.

I now depart from the benchmark case, while returning to the assumption of no public-good congestion. First, the case of a "large country" may be covered quickly. By the usual terms-of-trade arguments from international-trade theory, a large labor-exporting country can raise its welfare by restricting the outflow of emigrants. Doing so drives up the equilibrium wages outside the country. Such market-power arguments are of limited relevance for most labor-exporting countries, however.

More relevant is the possibility that emigrants with similar earning power within the home country nevertheless differ in their utility possibilities abroad. Reasons for such differences would include different migration costs, productivity differences abroad, or different preferences for travel abroad. If we simply expanded the previous model to allow for these heterogeneous opportunities abroad, some individuals would strictly prefer to live at home, and others would strictly prefer to emigrate. If the home government could observe these opportunities, then its optimal tax system would tailor a skilled individual's tax payments to these opportunities. As a practical matter, however, the government would face insurmountable problems in identifying each individual's opportunities for living and working abroad. If it imposed separate income-tax schedules on home income and foreign income, then it could adjust the foreign tax base to take into account the various costs of going abroad. But such adjustments could

5. In the formal model, we may assume a production process that transforms private output into the public good. Note that governments could also compete for residents through the provision of desirable public expenditures. Below, I briefly discusses a form of "expenditure competition," but most of this chapter focuses instead on the tax structures used to finance given levels of public goods and services.

not be expected to encompass all of the ways in which individuals differ in their opportunities abroad.

Recognizing these problems, Mirrlees (1982) provides a second-best analysis of optimal income taxation in an economy with heterogeneous residents and emigrants. In particular, each individual is characterized by a home productivity and a foreign productivity. In addition, he also allows emigrants to opt out of the home country's tax system. Mirrlees describes the latter possibility as "emigrating for good and severing their tax liability to the home government or indulging in other untaxable activities with greater utility." Thus, individuals are characterized by three innate attributes in this model—home productivity, foreign productivity, and productivity in nontaxed work—and each of these attributes is modeled as varying continuously across the population. The second-best problem then consists of finding two optimal income-tax schedules, one on home income and the other on foreign income. The tax system is used to redistribute income and finance an exogenous level of expenditures.

The main message arising from this analysis is that though taxes on emigrants may be lower than those on residents with the same income, the former taxes may still be substantial. Indeed, one version of the model tells us that in comparing an emigrant and a resident with the same utility, the tax collected from the emigrant is at least as high as the tax collected from the resident.

The desirability of taxing emigrants led to Jagdish Bhagwati's proposal that developing countries be allowed to exercise their income-tax jurisdictions over citizens abroad (see Bhagwati, 1976a, 1976b; Wilson, 2007). Whereas the early literature on this proposal focused more on the social costs of the brain drain, including the losses in tax revenue from migration, the case for taxing emigrant incomes as a redistributive device extends to models in which there are efficiency gains from skilled emigration (some of which are reviewed below).

One limitation of the Mirrlees model is that it ignores dynamic issues, such as the possibility that the move to nontaxable foreign work is facilitated by first doing taxable work as an emigrant. More important, experience has shown that it is extremely difficult to collect any significant amounts of tax revenue from emigrants. For this reason, few countries attempt to tax emigrants working abroad, the United States representing an important exception. Recognizing such difficulties, the following sections here will focus on the case where such taxes cannot be collected.

We have dealt so far with a single country's tax policy. But there are likely to be conflicts between "national efficiency" and "world efficiency." Such conflicts arise if the given country is large enough to exercise market power on international labor markets. But they also arise for small countries. For example, consider the emigration of some type of labor from a developing country to a developed country. Assuming no migration costs or locational preferences, world efficiency would require that this emigration continue until the marginal product of labor is equalized between the two countries. But for national efficiency, the marginal product in the developing country should equal the marginal product abroad net of taxes paid to the foreign government. In this case, the two countries could both be made better off if the developing country lowered the taxes it collected on emigrants, thereby encouraging more emigration. As observed in Wilson (1982a), however, the developing country would benefit from the efficiency gains only if it received an income transfer from the developed country. International agreements of this type are unlikely.

More generally, the inability of countries to link their government budget constraints through unfettered income transfers calls into question some of the central tenets of second-best tax theory. One of these tenets is the Diamond and Mirrlees (1971) theorem on aggregate production efficiency, which states that it is optimal for the economy to be on the frontier of its aggregate production set if all commodities are optimally taxed (including factors of production). In an international context, this theorem has been used to show that a small country should not distort its international trade, investment, and migration patterns, even if there are no lump-sum taxes. See Dixit and Norman (1980) for the case of goods trade and Gordon (1986) and Bucovetsky and Wilson (1991) for capital mobility. But the relevance of this result for the maximization of world welfare is limited, because countries possess separate budget constraints. Keen and Wildasin (2004) emphasize this limitation and provide examples of policies that may enhance world welfare, although they seem to violate the Diamond-Mirrlees theorem. One such example is the coordinated use of source-based taxes, which are shown below to be suboptimal for a single small open economy. This chapter is primarily focused on the decentralized behavior of individual countries, not on rules for coordinating decisions, but the Keen-Wildasin analysis suggests that much remains to be done on the latter topic.

Source-Based Taxation: A Benchmark Case

Recognizing the difficulties involved in taxing individuals living abroad, researchers have devoted considerable attention to source-based taxes, that is, taxes that a country imposes on only the income earned within its borders. Here I use the benchmark model from above to argue that the usefulness of source-based taxes is limited, but I later extend the model to cases in which these limitations are less severe.

In the benchmark model, skilled and unskilled workers residing in a small country provide types of labor that are imperfect substitutes (variable wage rates), but the skilled workers are able to obtain an exogenously determined utility level by emigrating. As before, the government seeks to maximize the sum of all natives' utilities, regardless of whether they emigrate. But now the home government is unable to tax the incomes of emigrants. In other words, it has access only to a "source-based tax" on income. Assume first that there are no congestion costs in public-goods provision.

The main result from this model is that no tax should be collected from skilled workers. This result is essentially a special case of my previous proof that the domestic tax T_2 must always equal the foreign tax T_2^*; simply set $T_2^* = 0$. The basic idea may be easily explained. Any attempt to collect such a tax would reduce the skilled-worker population, causing a decline in the marginal productivity of unskilled workers. The unskilled wage would fall, whereas the skilled wage would rise until skilled workers no longer wished to emigrate. Thus, any redistribution of tax burdens from skilled to unskilled workers would be offset by these wage changes. In fact, unskilled workers would be worse off, because of the revenue loss from the outflow of emigrants.

This conclusion that a small open economy will not use source-based taxation is well known in both the international tax literature and the local public economics literature, though it is often stated in the context of international capital mobility. For a restatement in a model with mobile skilled workers and immobile unskilled workers, see Proposition 4 in Wildasin (2000, p. 90). Moreover, the Diamond-Mirrlees theorem on aggregate production efficiency implies that the result extends to models in which optimal commodity taxes replace lump-sum taxes as the alternative tax instruments. Bucovetsky and Wilson (1991) show that a source-based capital tax is dominated by a tax on only labor income, although the latter tax distorts labor-leisure choices.

The local public economics literature has emphasized the corresponding result that labor mobility eliminates the ability of governments to redistribute income. Whereas the focus of this chapter is on skilled migration, similar results would be achieved in a model where it is the unskilled who are mobile. For example, see the model and subsequent discussion in Cremer and Pestieau's (2004) review of the literature on mobility and redistribution. Following common practice, they refer to the absence of income redistribution in a model with perfectly mobile unskilled workers as the "race to the bottom" result.

If we generalize the basic model by adding congestible public goods, then a role for source-based taxes is resurrected, but only as a means of compensating a country for the cost of providing mobile residents with these goods. In particular, each skilled resident should pay a tax equal to the cost of supplying another skilled person with these public goods. This cost is the "marginal congestion cost" (MC) referred to above. Nevertheless, the income tax is being used to ration public goods efficiently, rather than redistribute income.

Moving to a large open economy allows some income-redistribution activities in the presence of emigration. In this case, source-based taxes effectively shift a portion of a country's tax burden onto foreign workers; more skilled natives move abroad and compete with foreigners for skilled jobs, which depresses earnings from these jobs. As noted before, however, not many countries can be expected to satisfy this "largeness" condition in practice.

Taxing Heterogeneous Residents

This section shows that a government may find it desirable to collect substantial taxes from skilled residents if they differ in their migration opportunities, even if foreign-source income cannot be taxed. I also discuss the schedule of marginal tax rates on resident incomes. In all of the models considered here, the only choice facing individuals is whether to reside at home or abroad. Incomes available to individuals at home and abroad are treated as exogenous, leaving labor-leisure distortions to a later section.

Mirrlees (1982), discussed above, also presents an important model of source-based income taxation with heterogeneous migrants. He assumes that workers in the home country are distinguished by both "home productivities" and "foreign productivities." A type-n person has exogenous before-tax income, n, in the home country and obtains utility $u(x(n), n)$ from consumption $x(n)$, where this function is increasing in both arguments. But type-n people also possess different foreign productivities, implying that some may choose to remain at home while others emigrate. If $v(n)$ is the equilibrium level of utility for a type-n home resident, then the number of individuals who remain in the home country is described by a function $f(v(n), n)$, which is increasing in $v(n)$. This function can be used to calculate the propensity to migrate for type-n people, defined as the elasticity of their number with respect to after-tax home income x.

The government's optimal tax problem is an exercise in asymmetric information. It can observe home income and therefore infer home productivity, but it is unable to observe foreign productivities. As a result, it taxes only home income. There is again an exogenous revenue requirement (no congestion in public-goods usage.)

In contrast to what was seen above, the government has an incentive to collect positive taxes from individuals with high home productivities, because some of these individuals will not migrate—namely, those with relatively low foreign productivities. In other words, the tax system is essentially capturing some of the economic rents earned by these individuals, defined as the amount by which their incomes at home exceed the minimum incomes at which they are willing to reside in the home country. But the government is unable to observe the level of economic rent for any single individual, because of the unobservability of foreign productivities. This limits its ability to tax these rents. In the language of agency theory, the informational asymmetries enable high-skilled residents to earn "information rents."

By making assumptions about various functional forms, Mirrlees derives results suggesting that taxes can be quite high under seemingly reasonable migration elasticities, even though the only use of taxes in this model is to redistribute income. For a constant elasticity of 1/2, he finds that the share of income that is taxed away goes to 2/3 as n goes to infinity. These high tax rates no doubt reflect the assumption of fixed incomes within the home country (e.g., no labor-leisure distortions), but the example does demonstrate that reasonable levels of migration are not sufficient to produce low tax rates by themselves. Migration decisions are distorted, but the government should tolerate the resulting inefficiencies to get at the economic rents earned by some skilled residents, which can then be redistributed to unskilled residents.

Another important property of this example is that the marginal tax rate actually declines with income, obtaining a maximum of 5/6 as income approaches zero. As we shall see repeatedly, declining *marginal* tax rates are fully consistent with rising *average* tax rates. Since a marginal tax rate is the tax on another dollar, its value alone tells us nothing about an individual's tax payments per dollar on existing income. Indeed, an optimal tax system will typically involve positive marginal tax rates and negative average tax rates at low incomes, because individuals are provided with a uniform lump-sum grant, or negative tax (also called a "poll subsidy"), which is then taxed away at positive marginal rates as income rises.

In a model developed by Osmundsen (1999), even the marginal tax rate turns negative once incomes are sufficiently high, showing that skilled taxpayers can face both substantial tax burdens and a negative tax on their next dollar earned. In contrast to Mirrlees (1982), each individual divides his or her time between work at home and abroad, rather than choosing only one location to reside, and possesses a single skill parameter determining productivities at home and abroad. The income tax distorts this allocation of time. Osmundsen shows that the marginal income tax is positive for individuals with skill levels below the average skill in the home country and negative for individuals with skill levels above this average. This means that average tax rates must decline at high skill levels. With negative marginal tax rates, high-skilled individuals are encouraged to shift their work toward home, whereas low-income individuals move work abroad. Osmundsen explains this result by referring to the countervailing incentives that exist because increases in skill raise both home and foreign productivities.

There is no role for income-redistribution motives in Osmundsen's model, because utilities are linear in income, and individuals are equally weighted in the measurement of social welfare. Instead, the government raises revenue to finance public expenditures. But a related paper by Osmundsen, Schjelderup, and Hagen (2000) introduces distributional motives into the analysis by allowing welfare weights to differ across individuals, distinguished by mobility. With exogenous welfare weights, the optimal marginal tax rates on income are now positive for all workers except the least mobile. Endogenizing the welfare weights so that they are increasing in the time spent in the home country reduces the optimal marginal tax rates.

Returning to the Mirrlees model, he considers a version where the taxation of high-income individuals can be related to the properties of the joint distribution between before-tax incomes at home and abroad, denoted $g(n, m)$. Here he assumes that a type-m individual receiving after-tax income x at home moves abroad if $u_1(\gamma m) > u_1(x)$, where the function u_1 describes the relation between utility and consumption and $\gamma < 1$ reflects the disutility from going abroad to earn this income. He further assumes that $log\ m$ and $log\ n$ are distributed according to a binormal distribution with mean zero, variances σ^2_m and σ^2_n, and correlation coefficient ρ. Using these assumptions, he shows that the average and marginal taxes facing an n-person go to 100 percent as n goes to infinity if $\rho\sigma^2_m/\sigma^2_n < 1$, while they go to zero if $\rho\sigma^2_m/\sigma^2_n > 1$. Mirrlees suggests that the first case is the more relevant one. Intuitively, a low correlation between productivities, combined with a relatively high variance of home productivities, implies that there will be a sizable number of individuals with high n but low m, suggesting ample opportunities for taxing their incomes without inducing too much migration.

Comparing the results of these various papers, we see that there is agreement that average tax burdens on skilled residents can be substantial, given seemingly reasonable assumptions about migration responses, but there is considerable disagreement about marginal tax rates.

Comparing Closed and Open Economies

I now discuss how migration opportunities can greatly reduce the average taxes collected from skilled individuals while actually raising the marginal tax rates that they face. In other words, tax burdens fall, but the tax owed on another dollar may rise. This material on nonlinear tax systems draws on Wilson (1992), but first I discuss an earlier literature that restricts tax schedules to be linear.

Both of these literatures utilize the Mirrlees (1971) model of optimal income taxation to represent the trade-off between equity and efficiency in a closed economy. Workers choose how much labor to supply, denoted L, and their consumption expenditures x are financed solely by labor income: $x = wL - T(wL)$, where w is a wage rate and $T(wL)$ is the function relating tax payments to before-tax income. With a linear tax function, $x = (1 - t)wL + \alpha$, where t is a constant marginal tax rate and α is a common poll subsidy given to all workers. These workers differ in their marginal productivities, or "skill levels," which equal their wages. A high-w worker chooses to work more hours and is therefore necessarily a high-income person. Assuming that the government's expenditures are not too large, an optimal tax system (linear or nonlinear) redistributes income to low-income workers; that is, they are "tax recipients." In contrast, high-income workers are "taxpayers."

Wilson (1980) restricts that tax system to be linear and introduces migration by assuming that individuals with a given home skill differ in their foreign-utility possibilities. This specification is similar to the Mirrlees (1982) specification described above. The government's problem is to choose the tax system that maximizes the sum of utilities for a fixed group of natives, giving equal weight to residents and emigrants. The tax is used to redistribute income, not to finance public goods.

The main insight obtained from this model is that the elimination of "potential emigration" at sufficiently low or high home-skill levels leads to a rise in the optimal marginal tax rate and poll subsidy. In other words, potential emigration at these skill levels leads to less income redistribution. Potential emigrants are defined as existing at a given skill level if a small change in the marginal tax rate or poll subsidy alters the number of home-country residents with this skill. The basic idea is that the home country suffers a revenue loss from migration when a move to a more egalitarian tax system causes high-income taxpayers ($ty > \alpha$) to move abroad or low-income tax recipients ($ty < \alpha$) to migrate into the home country. But in an intermediate range of skill levels, a feasible change in the tax system toward a higher marginal tax causes either high-income workers to return home or low income workers to emigrate, and either change increases tax revenue. Thus, potential emigration in an intermediate range encourages more redistribution in the form of a higher marginal tax rate and poll subsidy. See Wilson (1982b) for further analysis. Bhagwati and Hamada (1982) also obtain conditions under which skilled migration reduces the optimal marginal tax rate, using a model that replaces labor-leisure distortions with an education decision that is distorted by the income tax.

To conclude, the results here emphasize the importance of the home-skill levels of migrants. These results depend on the use of a linear income tax, which, while restrictive, is being given increasing attention as part of flat-tax proposals in the United States.

Turning to nonlinear taxation, I follow Stiglitz (1982) and others by considering an economy with two types of workers: skilled or unskilled. As described above, each worker chooses how much labor to supply. But following the model I outlined earlier, the two types of labor now enter the home country's production function as separate arguments, implying that the skilled and unskilled wage rates vary with the ratio of skilled labor to unskilled labor. I also return to the benchmark case of an open economy facing an infinitely elastic supply of skilled workers, though the results will, of course, generalize to elasticities that are high but finite. As more skilled workers enter (exit) the country, the skilled wage falls (rises) until an equilibrium is reached, equating utility at home with the exogenous level available abroad. Social welfare in the open and closed economies is again defined to include a fixed number of home natives, regardless of whether they choose to live at home or emigrate, and taxes are used both to redistribute revenue and to finance a public good.

If wages were fixed and migration absent, then it is well known that the optimal income-tax system would include a zero marginal tax on the incomes of skilled workers. Moreover, if there were many types of workers in the economy, distinguished by skills, then this zero marginal tax would apply to the highest income earned in the economy. See Seade (1977) for a detailed discussion. The basic insight is that lowering the marginal tax at the top income to zero encourages work effort among high-income individuals, without reducing anyone's tax payments. The efficiency gains can then be distributed in a way that makes everyone better off. See figure 10.1 for an example of the budget line under the optimal tax system. The vertical axis measures consumption x, and the horizontal axis measures before-tax income $y = wL$. Indifference curves for skilled and unskilled, denoted S and U, are drawn going through their equilibrium consumption-income bundles, b for skilled and a for unskilled. As shown, redistribution from the skilled to the unskilled is constrained by an incentive-compatibility condition: holding before-tax incomes fixed, it is not possible to transfer more consumption from the skilled to the unskilled, because the skilled would then prefer the bundle meant for the unskilled.

Allowing wages to vary, as assumed here, leads to an even more striking result for a closed economy: skilled workers should face a negative marginal tax; that is, their tax payments fall as their incomes rise (see Stiglitz, 1982). By implementing a negative marginal tax, the government encourages skilled workers to increase their work effort, thereby raising the ratio of skilled labor to unskilled labor. The equilibrium skilled wage (w_2) will then

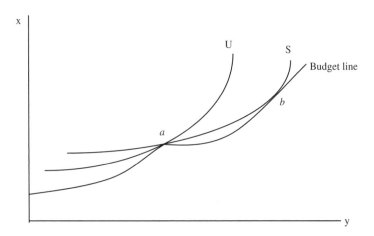

Figure 10.1 An example of the budget line under the optimal tax system.

fall, whereas the unskilled wage (w_1) will rise. These wage changes facilitate the use of income taxation to redistribute income. With no change in labor supplies, unskilled workers will earn more income, and skilled workers will earn less. In terms of figure 10.1, point a for unskilled workers shifts to the right, whereas point b shifts to the left. As a result, point a is now unattractive to skilled workers (it lies below the skilled indifference curve going through the new point b, not shown). The basic idea is that the narrower income gap reduces the attractiveness of the unskilled consumption-income bundle for skilled workers. With the incentive-compatibility constraint no longer binding, the government is now able make unskilled workers better off without making skilled workers worse off. In other words, it is optimal to subsidize skilled labor at the margin, because the resulting wage changes enable income to be redistributed in a more efficient manner.

Moving to the open economy, recall the model without labor-leisure choices, where we found that the tax payments made by each mobile skilled individual should equal the marginal congestion cost in public-goods provision, or $T_2 = MC$. In the current model, however, the optimal income tax may distort labor supplies, but the severity of the distortions can again be altered by changes in the wage structure. Whereas we previously raised w_1 and lowered w_2 by subsidizing skilled labor, now we need only lower a skilled worker's tax payment T_2. More skilled workers will choose to reside in the home country, causing w_2 to fall until skilled workers are again indifferent about emigrating, and w_1 will rise to maintain zero profits in production. If the incentive-compatibility constraint is binding, these wage changes allow income to be redistributed in a more efficient manner. We should therefore continue to reduce T_2 below MC until the cost of raising this effective subsidy just offsets the resulting efficiency gains from the improved wage structure. We have:

> For the two-type model of nonlinear income taxation, if the incentive-compatibility constraint for skilled workers is binding under the optimal tax system, then the tax paid by a high-skilled worker falls short of his or her marginal congestion cost in public-goods provision: $T_2 < MC$.
> In other words, the tax system effectively subsidizes the entry of skilled workers.

This proposition does not tell us that migration must reduce the progressivity of the tax system. If MC is sufficiently high, opening the economy could cause T_2 to rise, simply because providing public goods to skilled workers is so costly that the country wishes to encourage them to leave. This possibility seems unlikely, however. (But see below for other arguments in favor of emigration.) The proposition does tell us that migration will reduce skilled tax payments if MC is sufficiently low. With a binding incentive-compatibility constraint, the government is effectively subsidizing the entry of new skilled workers into the country (a negative $T_2 - MC$), because the resulting change in the wage structure is a more effective redistributive tool than a higher tax on these workers.

But a lower MC will reduce skilled tax payments so much that the incentive-compatibility constraint for skilled workers no longer binds. In this case, T_2 will equal the low value of MC, and both skilled and unskilled workers will face zero marginal tax rates. Reducing MC further will produce a binding incentive-compatibility constraint for unskilled workers if the government's revenue needs are sufficiently high, since high taxes then must be imposed on unskilled workers, whereas the government desires to set T_2 low to attract skilled workers. However, keeping T_2 above MC is desirable, because the resulting change in the wage structure now acts favorably on this constraint.

Putting these results together, we find that opening the economy to emigration may raise the marginal tax rate to a level above its closed-economy value (possibly to zero), while at the same time reducing or even reversing income redistribution from skilled workers to unskilled workers. Again, changes in marginal taxes have little relation to changes in average taxes.

These results should be qualified by noting that they depend on a particular pattern of factor price changes. Suppose, instead, that the two types of labor are perfect substitutes, so that relative wages are fixed. But let the country's production function exhibit decreasing returns to scale, implying the existence of profits in equilibrium (also interpreted as economic rents earned by fixed factors). If these profits are not taxed away, then there exists a role for taxing mobile workers at rates above marginal congestion costs. By using taxes to discourage workers from residing in the country, the government causes untaxed profits to decline. As a result, such taxes can be welfare improving, because they *indirectly* tax profits. In effect, the government is using the taxation of mobile residents to redistribute income indirectly from one fixed factor (recipients of profits) to another (unskilled labor).

The desirability of taxing mobile individuals in a second-best economy depends on the nature of the second-best problem. In the first model, the two types of workers are assumed to face the same tax schedule, though their marginal and average tax rates are allowed to depend on how much they choose to earn. In the second model, there are untaxed profits. A more complete analysis would model the information problems or political processes that generate these restrictions. For now, we can conclude that migration opportunities have the potential to create a highly regressive tax structure in terms of average tax rates.

Beneficial Emigration

A central property of the literature reviewed above is that the emigration of skilled individuals represents a social loss for the source country. However, other literature has sought to explain why this social loss might turn into a social gain.[6] Consider first the possibility of remittances, whereby immigrants send money back to the home country. While individuals in the home country are made better off by migration if they receive sufficient remittances, what about the remaining individuals who do not receive them? Djajic (1986) argues that this latter group may also be better off. The basic idea is that the use of remittances raises the demand for nontraded goods, thereby increasing their prices. To the extent that remaining residents are effectively net suppliers of these goods, they will then benefit from migration, even if they do not receive remittances.

Another possibility is that emigrants will return to their home countries, bringing back benefits from their stays abroad. Even without return migration, emigration may serve to establish important business networks and promote technology diffusion.

Stark and Wang (2002) develop a model in which emigration opportunities encourage source-country residents in general to invest in additional human capital, even though not all of them eventually emigrate. An important aspect of this argument is that emigration opportunities are random, so that some individuals are encouraged to invest in human capital

---

6. See Kanbur and Rapoport (2005) for a review of the "new economic approaches" to analyzing the benefits of migration.

but ultimately remain in the home country, where their investment confers benefits on the local economy.

This last mechanism suggests an avenue by which income taxation in host countries can actually be *too* progressive from the viewpoint of world welfare. By taxing skilled immigrants, a country reduces the incentives for residents in the source countries to invest in human capital. In so doing, the host tax system imposes a negative externality on the source country. The empirical relevance of this possibility deserves further study.

Wilson and Gordon (2003) provide a political-economy argument for why migration may be beneficial to both source and host countries. Their model assumes that public expenditures are controlled by self-interested government officials. In equilibrium, there is "waste" in government, represented by the excess of tax revenue over the minimum cost of providing productive public goods to residents. Government officials seek to maximize this excess revenue, because they can use it to their benefit (e.g., perks). But they nevertheless face incentives to provide public goods. In addition to raising their probabilities of remaining in office (e.g., greater voter approval), providing these public goods leads to an expansion in the tax base, which generates more revenue. A key insight here is that the tax base is likely to depend more strongly on public-goods provision in an open economy than in a closed economy. By attracting more residents into the given country, greater public-goods provision leads to higher prices of locally produced goods (housing in the Wilson-Gordon model), expanding their supplies and thereby increasing the tax base. This greater tax-base elasticity with respect to public-goods provision improves the incentives for government officials to provide public goods. We are essentially describing a form of intergovernmental competition for mobile individuals that leaves the system of countries better off than in the case of closed borders. Wilson (2005) describes a similar type of expenditure competition involving the use of public services to compete for mobile capital.

This argument can be expanded to encompass income taxation. Wilson and Gordon assume that residents choose taxes to maximize their welfare, taking into account the impact of the tax system on the behavior of government officials. If skilled individuals are mobile and are attracted to the given country by the public goods supplied there, then taxing their incomes at relatively high rates has the potential to increase the sensitivity of tax revenue to public-goods provision. As a result, a progressive tax system may be desirable, because it enhances the incentives government officials face to compete for skilled residents by providing desirable public goods and services.

Unfortunately, this last argument suggests that government officials may also possess incentives to manipulate the *pattern* of public expenditures in a way that is attractive for the mobile skilled individuals but detrimental to immobile unskilled individuals. Moreover, introducing some mobility among the unskilled would enhance such incentives, since government officials could then generate greater revenue gains by encouraging emigration among those individuals who are effectively subsidized by the tax/expenditure system. Hence, the incentives discussed here are most likely to improve the well-being of low-income residents only if they are relatively immobile and if they receive sizable benefits from the expenditure programs being used to attract high-income individuals to the country. These considerations suggest that the type of expenditure competition analyzed by Wilson and Gordon is unlikely to improve the functioning of programs with a sizable redistributive element.

Bhagwati (2004) notes that emigration opportunities are likely to benefit the source country in the case of large developing countries such as India, South Korea, the Philippines, Taiwan, and China, which have the capacity to increase their supplies of skilled professionals through education at home or abroad. But small countries with few professionals, particularly in Africa, are likely to be harmed. In both cases, however, the inability of a source country to tax natives living abroad will limit its ability to realize potential benefits. Wilson and Gordon's model raises a cautionary argument against taxes on foreign-source income that completely replace lost domestic taxes. Such taxes at this level are supported by the more traditional theory presented above, but to the extent that there do exist agency problems in government, their use would eliminate the usefulness of migration opportunities in controlling waste in government.

Returning to the case in which emigrants cannot be taxed, we could insert beneficial emigration into the previous model by adding to our "marginal congestion cost" MC a marginal benefit term MB, reflecting the lost benefits to the source country from one fewer emigrant. Then the optimal source-based tax in our benchmark model would require that each skilled resident pay a tax equal to $MC + MB$. It seems, then, that beneficial emigration could lead to higher taxes on skilled workers, producing more income redistribution than would prevail in a closed economy. Countries are essentially using high taxes to encourage their skilled citizens to leave.

This conclusion is too hasty, however, because the model fails to recognize that MB may be high only because there exist important impediments to factor mobility. Bhagwati's principle of targeting suggests that these impediments should be directly attacked. For example, if capital-market imperfections prevent potential emigrants from obtaining sufficient funding to go abroad, then the carrot of government-provided loans would seem preferable to the stick of inefficiently high domestic tax rates.

Nevertheless, the potential benefits of emigration do qualify the results above, where skilled emigration could lead to a regressive tax system. As Bhagwati (2004) suggests, these benefits are likely to vary greatly across countries.

Immigration

Some special issues arise in the case of immigration. Little changes in the benchmark model of a small country contemplating source-based taxation. If skilled immigrants are in infinitely elastic supply, they should not be taxed. Once again, trying to tax them would be self-defeating: the resulting drop in the immigrant population would lead to a reduction in unskilled wages, thereby thwarting attempts to redistribute income. But while this is the conclusion for a welfare-maximizing government, political-economy forces are particularly relevant here, because the lobbying activities of different groups of natives can be expected to take advantage of the underrepresentation of immigrants in the political process. In some cases, however, the results of such activities are consistent with the maximization of a weighted social-welfare function, with groups represented by lobbies receiving more weight. This is the message of the common-agency approach to lobbying, as developed by Grossman and Helpman (1994) and recently applied by Facchini and Willmann (2005) to the analysis of interest groups competing for protection from immigration. The latter authors emphasize that natives supplying factors complementary to those factors supplied by immigrants have a strong incentive to lobby in favor of this immigration. In our model with mobile skilled workers and immobile unskilled workers, it is the latter who benefit from skilled immigration. Thus, unskilled workers should lobby in favor of skilled immigration (perhaps through labor-union activities), whereas skilled workers lobby against it. The results in this model depend on which groups choose to lobby. Adding lobbying to our benchmark model of a small open economy will not result in restrictions on skilled immigration unless unskilled workers fail to organize and lobby. Similarly, the outcome of majority rule will depend on the voter-participation rates of factors that are complementary to skilled immigrants. See Benhabib's analysis (1996) of how the median voter chooses an immigration policy involving capital and skill requirements of immigrants.

Turning specifically to the issue of redistributive taxation, a paper by Leite-Monteiro (1997) shows that the lack of weight given to immigrants in the government objective function may actually imply that skilled immigration *raises* the taxation of skilled residents, in contrast to the literature reviewed above. He analyzes a two-country model with two types of individuals, high- and low-income. These incomes are exogenous, so there are no equity-efficiency trade-offs when the economy is closed, as in our benchmark model. Thus, income is redistributed from high-income people to low-income people until all social marginal utilities of income are equalized.

Moving to the open economy, Leite-Monteiro assumes that each country's natives can migrate to the other country but at a cost that differs among individuals with a given income. For the special case in which only high-income individuals migrate, he considers a Nash game in the taxes on high incomes.[7] When a country raises its tax rate, the number of high-income residents falls, and the resulting loss in revenue provides disincentives to redistribute income, as previously argued. However, there is a new effect. The country receiving immigrants now views their incomes as a new source of income that can be taxed to finance transfers to low-income natives. Holding the number of immigrants fixed, the addition of immigrant incomes to the tax base effectively lowers the cost of redistributing income to low-income workers, from the viewpoint of the host country. This second effect leads to excessive income redistribution relative to the case of autarky (no migration). The basic idea is that the tax that the host country collects from immigrants represents a negative externality for the immigrants' home country. The host country is essentially "exporting" some of its tax burden to the source country by taxing immigrants. This tax-exporting effect tends to raise the level of income redistribution above the level under autarky. On the other hand, the ability of potential immigrants to respond by not immigrating if taxes get too high works in the opposite direction. For a sufficiently low migration elasticity, however, income redistribution will be excessive. This will not be the case for the country of origin, where emigration has the effects described previously.

This analysis also provides one instance in which skilled and unskilled migration can have very different effects on equilibrium taxes. Consider, for example, Razin, Sadka, and Swagel's (2002) analysis of unskilled immigration. Though they assume majority rule, rather than welfare maximization, this distinction is not important for the basic argument. If low-income immigrants and natives are treated similarly by the tax system, then the immigrants' presence will raise the cost of transferring income to unskilled natives, and so the median-voter equilibrium will move toward less income redistribution. Contrary to the case of skilled immigration, this consideration reinforces our previous findings that high migration elasticities lead to less income redistribution.

These two papers raise issues about how we model the tax treatment of immigrants. Certainly, illegal immigrants would not be an important part of a country's tax system. Moreover, legal methods for differentiating

---

7. He also considers the more general case in which both types of individuals migrate, but this is not strictly a Nash game, because he assumes that each country treats the other country's taxes on high- and low-income people as both fixed, although one of the two taxes would have to change to keep the government budget balanced in the face of migration. In the current special case, the strategy variables are the taxes on the mobile individuals, allowing the taxes on immobile individuals to adjust to balance the budgets.

between the tax treatment of immigrants and natives are often available. To the extent that immigrants are separated from the tax system, countries become less constrained in their competition for desirable groups of immigrants. This competition may largely eliminate taxes on immigrants without affecting a government's ability to maintain a progressive tax system and other elements of the welfare state.

In recent years, another benefit of immigration has become increasingly important: the contributions that immigrants and their offspring make to pay-as-you-go (PAYG) public-pension systems. The distributional features of these systems bear some resemblance to a linear income tax. The idea is that pensions are financed by taxing income (a payroll tax in the United States), and the proceeds are used to finance a payment to retirees that does not rise much with lifetime income. For example, Razin and Sadka (2001) model a PAYG system in which income is taxed at a constant rate to finance a fixed retirement payment, similar to the poll subsidy above. As a result, the emigration of young skilled workers is clearly beneficial, since they are net contributors to the system.

There is an important difference, however. In a PAYG system, the current working population finances payments to the current retired population. Then the entry of additional young immigrants reduces the payments per young person needed to provide the chosen benefits to the current old. If these young immigrants then have children, the children will be available to finance retirement benefits when the current young retire. As a result, it is possible for immigrants to receive a net benefit from the social-insurance system, calculated over their lifetimes, and yet generate a positive fiscal externality for their host countries. In contrast to the linear income-tax model, the host country may therefore benefit from immigration by individuals with incomes significantly lower than the host-country average. Razin and Sadka use an overlapping-generations model to arrive at this insight.

Thus, the use of an income tax to finance a PAYG system provides additional incentives for a country to compete for immigrants through reductions in the levels of taxes imposed on them. To the extent that this immigration is concentrated among high-income immigrants, it will lead to less income redistribution, as before. The difference is that countries may no longer wish to use a less egalitarian tax system to discourage the entry of low-income immigrants, if pension concerns make population growth an important goal.

Agglomeration Economies

The models reviewed above assume constant returns to scale in production. But there is a growing literature on the efficiency benefits obtained by concentrating production activities in one country. In contrast to the previous analysis, this literature shows that more labor mobility can lead to higher taxes on the mobile workers.

Ludema and Wooton (2000) demonstrate this result in a two-country model in which the forces of agglomeration cause manufacturing activities to locate in one country, leaving the other country with only a traditional constant-returns "agricultural sector." The concentration of manufacturing takes place through the movement of manufacturing workers to the "core" country. The two countries play a Nash game in tax rates on these workers, with the objective of using the tax revenue to maximize the well-being of immobile agricultural workers. In equilibrium, the core raises its tax rate to the maximum level at which it is able to retain the manufacturing workers, given the tax rate in the "periphery" country, but this core rate is not high enough to give the periphery an incentive to offer a sufficiently low rate to induce the manufacturing workers to switch locations. The periphery is indifferent about the tax rate it imposes on manufacturing workers, because none live there in equilibrium, but the authors limit the possibilities by imposing the reasonable requirement that the tax rate is not so low (or negative) that the periphery would be worse off if the manufacturing workers actually did relocate there. This refinement produces an equilibrium with the property that lower mobility costs lead to higher tax rates. The basic idea is that if workers do not have strong preferences for location per se (distinct from preferences related to wage differences), then the core does not need to reduce its tax rate as much to induce the marginal worker to reside there. Essentially, agglomeration forces raise the real wages of mobile workers above those available elsewhere, and low mobility costs increase the rents that the core is able to extract from these workers. See Baldwin and Krugman (2004) and Kind, Knarvik, and Schjelderup (2000) for similar models but with different equilibrium concepts.

To the extent that the mobile workers here are interpreted as relatively skilled (e.g., agglomeration economies associated with the concentration of R&D activities), this model explains how more elastic supplies of migrants need not lead to a less egalitarian tax structure in the host country. Essentially, the source countries do not choose to compete, because the tax rates needed to attract migrants would be too low, given these countries' current lack of agglomeration advantages. This result would be of little comfort to those countries experiencing this "brain drain," but the assumption that the brain drain is this complete seems rather unreasonable.

Ludema and Wooton also consider the case in which agglomeration forces are weak enough to produce an equilibrium with manufacturing activities in both countries. But here increased mobility leads to lower equilibrium taxes, which is the standard result. While this line of research is certainly providing an intriguing qualification to the standard results, the models are not yet sufficiently convincing to supplant the standard results.

Voting

The focus so far has been on models where governments are both welfare maximizers and able to anticipate perfectly the future migration responses to their policies. Both assumptions are questionable. Moreover, migration responses occur over time, suggesting that they are less central to government decision making than is suggested by the static models considered here.

I will now switch from welfare-maximizing models to models in which tax policy is chosen by majority rule. There is now a large literature on migration and voting on taxes in models in which individuals differ in income. Much of this literature follows the landmark paper by Henderson, Flatters, and Mieszkowski (1974) by switching the timing of events so that government decision making takes place after individuals have chosen their equilibrium locations. Individuals choose where to reside by anticipating the future outcomes of the political processes in the different localities. Once residential decisions are made, public policies are then chosen, conditional on the existing residential populations. Having correctly anticipated these political outcomes, however, voters then have no incentive to move. If we assume that these outcomes result from majority rule, then voters will see that the chosen policies do not produce migration.[8]

A central topic in this literature is the existence or nonexistence of a "stratified equilibrium," in which individuals sort themselves across jurisdictions by income level, so that each jurisdiction contains residents with incomes lying in a different interval. Hansen and Kessler (2001a) show that a stratified equilibrium will fail to exist in models in which the incomes of a continuum of individuals are taxed to finance a public good. On the other hand, Hansen and Kessler (2001b) obtain an equilibrium by introducing a land market and assuming that jurisdictions differ sufficiently in size. The

8. An alternative interpretation of these models is that there is migration both before and after voting, but voters ignore this migration when choosing how to vote. Although the policy chosen by majority rule does not induce further migration, the outcome of voting would have differed if voters had taken migration responses into account.

small jurisdiction contains the highest-income individuals, who value most low taxes and are willing to pay high land prices to obtain them.[9]

Kessler and Hansen (2003) extend their 2001a paper by showing that the stratified equilibrium for an economy with two identical jurisdictions can be supported by interregional income transfers, whereby the rich jurisdiction transfers income to the poor jurisdiction. Moreover, they prove that the appropriately chosen transfer will raise the sum of utilities. In an international context, such interregional transfers are part of Bhagwati's (1976a, 1976b) proposal for a tax on the brain drain of skilled professionals from developing countries to developed countries, since the revenue would be returned to the developing countries. Such transfers may not only directly aid those left behind but also indirectly aid them by reducing the brain drain. Although the recent literature on beneficial migration (reviewed above) suggests a number of ways in which the brain drain is beneficial for those left behind, restrictions on emigration may still be needed to maximize these benefits. See Stark and Wang (2002) and Stark et al. (2005) for an analysis of these restrictions.

Return now to the question of how migration affects the choice of income-tax schedules, but now with majority rule replacing the welfare-maximizing governments considered above. If all jurisdictions contain populations with the same income distribution, then there is no difference between the equilibrium tax schedules and those that would be chosen by a central government, provided we are assuming that voters treat their jurisdiction's population as fixed. The more interesting case is where the equilibrium is stratified. And an equilibrium with "perfect stratification" can be obtained by assuming that there exists more jurisdictions than types of individuals (again distinguished by income). In this case, each jurisdiction contains only one income group, and so there is no income redistribution. This result agrees with the findings for welfare-maximizing governments, as reviewed above: perfect mobility eliminates the ability of jurisdictions to redistribute income. Janeba and Raff (1997) construct an equilibrium of this type, by adopting the Metzler-Richard (1981) model of voting on linear tax schedules in a closed economy to a system of many jurisdictions

9. The models discussed here assume that individuals differ only in their incomes. But equilibrium without stratification by income can be obtained by assuming that individuals also differ in tastes for a public good. For example, see Kessler and Lülfesmann (2005) and the references therein. Unlike the other models in this section, they extend their analysis to the case in which voters take into account migration responses when choosing their most-preferred tax policies. There also exists a sizable literature on the existence of an equilibrium in models with voting on taxes levied on housing. Using a model of this type, Epple and Platt (1998) also find imperfect stratification when individuals differ in both income and tastes for housing.

(which contains the labor-leisure distortions and skill differences found in the Mirrlees [1971] optimal tax model). Their message is that this equilibrium may be preferable to centralization if individuals are not too risk-averse, since majority rule will then produce too much redistribution in the centralization case.

Recent research has shown, however, that significant amounts of income redistribution can occur in a voting model that shares with our earlier benchmark model the assumptions that there are two types of individuals: mobile skilled workers and immobile unskilled workers. In particular, Hamilton and Pestieau (2005) introduce these mobility assumptions into the Mirrlees (1971) model, while retaining his use of a nonlinear income tax. With only two types of individuals, majority rule means that a country employs the minimax (Rawlsian) criterion if unskilled workers are in the majority, but it switches to the maximax criterion if skilled workers form a majority. In the latter case, the skilled workers engage in a form of "reverse income redistribution," transferring income from the unskilled to the skilled.

In contrast to the previous models, perfect labor mobility among the skilled need not eliminate income redistribution. But there exist multiple equilibria, some with income redistributed to the unskilled and others with the reverse. The possibilities depend on the ratio of skilled to unskilled workers in the world economy. Suppose that the unskilled are more numerous. Assuming that the unskilled workers do not quit working under the optimal income tax (a possibility under the assumed form of the utility function), there are two types of equilibria. In the first type, all countries have identical ratios of skilled to unskilled workers. With unskilled workers in the majority, governments maximize a Rawlsian welfare function; income taxes are used to maximize the welfare of the poorest residents, who are the unskilled. Moreover, this equilibrium is stable; increasing the ratio of skilled to unskilled in a country lowers skilled utilities in this model, not because their wages fall but rather because more taxes are collected from each skilled person as the skilled become relatively more numerous.

The second equilibrium is asymmetric. Some countries contain only unskilled workers, and others contain both but with the skilled workers in the majority. In the latter countries, income redistribution is from the unskilled to the skilled workers, implying that the skilled workers do not want to move.

Which equilibrium occurs depends on initial conditions. If the unskilled are initially in the majority everywhere, then the skilled will migrate to communities where there are fewest of them, and the process continues until equilibrium is reached with identical countries, implying Rawlsian redistribution. But if the skilled are initially in the majority in at least one country, then the skilled from countries with a majority of unskilled will possess incentives to move to countries with a majority of skilled, since this cuts their income-tax payments. An asymmetric equilibrium is then reached, with no income redistribution to the unskilled.

A useful extension of this research would involve introducing a third skill group, which might be high-skilled in developing countries but middle-skilled in developed countries. Recognizing differences in production technologies across countries would also be a valuable extension. But the simple two-type model developed by Hamilton and Pestieau nicely illustrates the basic insight that progressive taxation can survive in an economy with free migration and voting.

Conclusions

I have shown that skilled migration has the potential to reduce drastically and even reverse the use of income taxation to achieve an equitable distribution of income. But I have also discussed literature that provides important qualifications to this conclusion. Some of these qualifications are straightforward: if migration opportunities are limited for a sizable portion of the skilled population, then governments may be willing to lose the mobile fringe in order to get at the incomes of the remaining skilled residents. But more recent literature has begun to identify potential benefits that emigration may confer to the source country, and some of this literature has moved beyond the welfare-maximizing governments of earlier models, in an attempt to create a better model of the political processes that generate tax policy in an open economy. In both cases, emigration may not have as detrimental an effect on income redistribution as previously thought, at least for some countries.

To the extent that emigration does provide benefits for source countries, policies should be pursued that more fully realize their value. But a country's inability to tax emigrants can itself inhibit the use of such policies. For example, public investments in education may enhance opportunities abroad, but governments can be expected to underprovide such investments if they cannot recoup a portion of the cost by taxing the future incomes of the beneficiaries.[10] This chapter demonstrated the value of taxing foreign-source income. Bhagwati (2004, p. 215) notes that even a small tax on the incomes of Indian nationals would substantially raise Indian government revenues, a claim that receives further support from the work of Desai, Kapur, and McHale (2004).[11] An appropriately designed tax might

10. See Wildasin (2000) for a related analysis.
11. They note that if only 100,000 of the more than 1 million Indian citizens in the United States paid $5,000 each, the resulting $500 million annual revenue stream

provide governments not just with the funds for important expenditure projects but also with the incentives to make better use of their existing funds in an increasingly integrated world economy.

Bhagwati (1979) has proposed, for example, that developing countries collect a "brain-drain tax" from only those emigrants who retain their citizenship. The ability of an emigrant to avoid the tax by relinquishing citizenship in the home country provides the country's government with incentives to engage in policies that are agreeable to citizens residing abroad, including more socially productive uses of tax revenue. In other words, access to taxes on citizen-emigrant incomes may provide source governments with incentives to engage in welfare-improving competition for high-income *citizens,* rather than the competition for *residents.* Which form of competition is more important depends on a comparison of the relevant citizen and migration elasticities. Bhagwati (1979) emphasizes the economic rents immigrants earn as a result of the immigration restrictions typically imposed by developed countries. These restrictions tend to reduce the importance of competition for residents. In any case, such tax proposals suggest the need for more research not just on tax design but also on the politics of government decision making under different tax systems.

Finally, much of the research reported in this chapter concerns the design of a single country's tax system, rather than the simultaneous choice of income-tax policies by source and host countries. The voting models discussed here are one exception. More work is needed to understand the moral-hazard and adverse-selection problems that result when source and host countries attempt to tax internationally mobile workers. To the extent that countries seek to tax emigrants working abroad, there is also the issue of how the equilibria for noncooperative tax games are affected by the methods that countries employ to harmonize their tax systems, including double-taxation conventions. For example, Bond and Samuelson (1989) use a two-country model with capital mobility to show that if the source country provides tax credits for taxes paid to the host government, then the governments will choose taxes so high that all capital movements are eliminated. Such results highlight the importance of cooperative tax agreements among countries. While this chapter has emphasized the desirability of taxing foreign-source income, successfully collecting such taxes requires the aid of host countries, including the sharing of tax information.[12]

---

would still be substantial compared with India's individual income-tax base of $5.84 billion and tertiary-education budget of $2.70 billion.

12. See Keen and Ligthart (2006) for recent research on information sharing and international taxation.

References

Baldwin, Richard, and Paul Krugman. 2004. "Agglomeration, Integration and Tax Harmonization." *European Economic Review* 48: 1–23.

Benhabib, Jess. 1996. "On the Political Economy of Immigration." *European Economic Review* 40: 1737–43.

Bhagwati, Jagdish N., ed. 1976a. *Taxing the Brain Drain, Vol. 1: A Proposal.* Amsterdam: North Holland.

———, ed. 1976b. *The Brain Drain and Taxation, Vol. 2: Theory and Empirical Analysis.* Amsterdam: North Holland.

———. 1979. "International Migration of the Highly Skilled: Economics, Ethics and Taxes." *Third World Quarterly* 1: 17–30.

———. 2004. *In Defense of Globalization.* New York: Oxford University Press.

Bhagwati, Jagdish N., and Koichi Hamada. 1982. "Tax Policy in the Presence of Emigration." *Journal of Public Economics* 18: 291–317.

Bond, Eric W., and Lawrence Samuelson. 1989. "Strategic Behavior and the Rules for International Taxation of Capital." *Economic Journal* 99: 1099–1111.

Bucovetsky, Sam, and John D. Wilson. 1991. "Tax Competition with Two Tax Instruments." *Regional Science and Urban Economics* 21: 333–50.

Cremer, Helmuth, and Pierre Pestieau. 2004. "Factor Mobility and Redistribution." In V. Henderson and J. Thisse, eds., *Handbook of Regional and Urban Economics*, vol. 4. Amsterdam: North Holland.

Desai, Mihir A., Devesh Kapur, and John McHale. 2004. "Sharing the Spoils: Taxing International Human Capital Flows." *International Tax and Public Finance* 11: 663–93.

Diamond, Peter A., and James A. Mirrlees. 1971. "Optimal Taxation and Public Production I: Production Efficiency." *American Economic Review* 61: 8–27.

Dixit, Avinash, and Victor Norman. 1980. *Theory of International Trade: A Dual General Equilibrium Approach.* Cambridge: Cambridge University Press.

Djajic, S. 1986. "International Migration, Remittances and Welfare in a Dependent Economy." *Journal of Development Economics* 21: 229–34.

Epple, Dennis, and Glenn J. Platt 1998. "Equilibrium and Local Redistribution in an Urban Economy When Households Differ in Both Preferences and Incomes." *Journal of Urban Economics* 43: 23–51.

Facchini, Giovanni, and Gerald Willmann. 2005. "The Political Economy of International Factor Mobility." *Journal of International Economics* 67: 201–19.

Gordon, Roger H. 1986. "Taxation of Investment and Savings in a World Economy." *American Economic Review* 76: 1086–1102.

Grossman, Gene M., and E. Helpman. 1994."Protection for Sale." *American Economic Review* 84: 833–50.

Hamilton, Jonathan, and Pierre Pestieau. 2005. "Optimal Income Taxation and the Ability Distribution: Implications for Migration Equilibria." *International Tax and Public Finance* 12: 29–45.

Hansen, Nico A., and Anke S. Kessler. 2001a. "(Non-)Existence of Equilibria in Multicommunity Models." *Journal of Urban Economics* 50: 418–35.

———. 2001b. "The Political Geography of Tax H(e)avens and Tax Hells." *American Economic Review* 91: 1103–15.

Henderson, J. Vernon, Frank Flatters, and Peter Mieszkowski. 1974. "Public Goods, Efficiency, and Regional Fiscal Equalization." *Journal of Public Economics* 3: 99–112.

Janeba, Eckhard, and Horst Raff. 1997. "Should the Power to Redistribute Income Be (De-)Centralized? An Example." *International Tax and Public Finance* 4: 453–61.

Kanbur, Ravi, and Hillel Rapoport. 2005. "Migration Selectivity and the Evolution of Spatial Inequality." *Journal of Economic Geography* 5: 43–57.

Keen, Michael, and Jenny Ligthart. 2006. "Information Sharing and International Taxation: A Primer." *International Tax and Public Finance* 13: 81–110.

Keen, Michael, and David E. Wildasin. 2004. "Pareto-Efficient International Taxation." *American Economic Review* 94: 73–95.

Kessler, Anke S., and Nico A. Hansen. 2003. "A Positive Theory of Inter-Regional Redistribution and Constitutional Choice." Unpublished manuscript. Simon Fraser University, Burnaby, British Columbia.

Kessler, Anke S., and Christoph Lülfesmann. 2005. "Tiebout and Redistribution in a Model of Residential and Political Choice." *Journal of Public Economics* 89: 501–28.

Kind, Hans Jarle, Karen Helene Midelfart Knarvik, and Guttorm Schjelderup. 2000. "Competing for Capital in a 'Lumpy' World." *Journal of Public Economics* 78: 253–74.

Leite-Monteiro, Manuel. 1997. "Redistributive Policy with Labor Mobility across Countries." *Journal of Public Economics* 65: 229–44.

Ludema, Rodney, and Ian Wooton. 2000. "Economic Geography and Fiscal Effects of Regional Integration." *Journal of International Economics* 52: 331–37.

Metzler, Alan H., and Scott F. Richard. 1981. "A Rational Theory of the Size of Government." *Journal of Political Economy* 89: 914–27.

Mirrlees, James A. 1971. "An Exploration in the Theory of Optimal Income Taxation." *Review of Economic Studies* 38: 175–208.

———. 1982. "Migration and Optimal Income Taxes." *Journal of Public Economics* 18: 319–41.

Osmundsen, Petter. 1999. "Taxing Internationally Mobile Individuals: A Case of Countervailing Incentives." *International Tax and Public Finance* 6: 149–64.

Osmundsen, Petter, Guttorm Schjelderup, and Kare Hagen. 2000. "Personal Income Taxation under Mobility, Exogenous and Endogenous Welfare Weights, and Asymmetric Information." *Journal of Population Economics* 13: 623–37.

Pomp, Richard D. 1985. "The Experience of the Philippines in Taxing Its Nonresident Citizens." *New York University Journal of International Law and Politics* 17: 245–86.

Razin, Assaf, and Efraim Sadka. 2001. *Labor, Capital, and Finance: International Flows.* Cambridge: Cambridge University Press.

Razin, Assaf, Efraim Sadka, and Phillip Swagel. 2002. "Tax Burden and Migration: A Political Economy Theory and Evidence." *Journal of Public Economics* 85: 167–90.

Seade, J. K. 1977. "On the Shape of Optimal Tax Schedules." *Journal of Public Economics* 7: 203–35.

Stark, Oded, Alessandra Casarico, Carlo Devillanova, and Silke Uebelmesser. 2005. "The New Economics of the Brain Drain: Mapping the Gains." Unpublished manuscript. University of Bonn.

Stark, Oded, and Yong Wang. 2002. "Inducing Human Capital Formation: Migration As a Substitute for Subsidies." *Journal of Public Economics* 86: 29–46.

Stiglitz, Joseph E. 1982. "Self-Selection and Pareto Efficient Taxation." *Journal of Public Economics* 17: 213–40.

Wildasin, David E. 2000. "Labor-Market Integration, Investment in Risky Human Capital, and Fiscal Competition." *American Economic Review* 90: 73–95.

Wilson, John D. 1980. "The Effect of Potential Emigration on the Optimal Linear Income Tax." *Journal of Public Economics* 14: 339–53.

———. 1982a. "Optimal Income Taxation and Migration: A World Welfare Point of View." *Journal of Public Economics* 18: 381–97.

———. 1982b. "Optimal Linear Income Taxation in the Presence of Emigration." *Journal of Public Economics* 18: 363–79.

———. 1992. "Optimal Income Taxation and International Personal Mobility." *American Economic Review, Papers and Proceedings* 82: 191–96.

———. 2005. "Welfare-Improving Competition for Mobile Capital." *Journal of Urban Economics* 57: 1–18.

———. 2007. "Taxing the Brain Drain: A Reassessment of the Bhagwati Proposal." In Elias Dinopoulos, Pravin Krishna, Arvind Panagariya, and Kar-yiu Wong, eds., *Trade, Globalization and Poverty.* New York: Routledge.

Wilson, John D., and Roger Gordon. "Expenditure Competition." *Journal of Public Economic Theory* 5: 399–417.

African Template: The Return of the Brain Drain

11

Is the Brain Drain Good for Africa?

WILLIAM EASTERLY AND YAW NYARKO

Fear of the brain drain seems to dominate many discussions of foreign aid and national policy in developing countries. Should aid donors and government budgets subsidize formation of skills, when skilled workers might then leave for rich countries? Could poor countries possibly obtain a *positive* return from the brain drain? We argue that the answer could be yes. This is contrary to most of the received wisdom and definitely contrary to remarks and comments in the media.

These issues become more salient the poorer the source country, so Africa is the source of some of the most fearful concerns about the brain drain. The Toronto *Globe and Mail* (November 2, 2005) went so far as to write an article about the African brain drain entitled "The New Slave Trade: A Poor Country's Best Workers," in which it warned that rich countries could "suck all of the human capital out of the poor countries, leaving them forever destitute."

These fears have led to bold and imaginative proposals for solutions:

> "[C]ountries concerned about a 'brain drain' of their trained physicians to OECD markets might be able to reduce those risks by setting national training requirements slightly lower than the rich countries' standards" (World Bank and IMF, 2007).

> "Developing countries and organizations in developing countries should explore possibilities of limiting recruitment from abroad. . . . The United States and other recruiting countries should end active recruitment of health professionals from developing countries, absent agreement with those countries" (Physicians for Human Rights, 2004).

Special thanks to Jagdish Bhagwati for inviting us to the conference and for helpful suggestions, and also to Gordon Hanson, Guillermina Jasso, and Mark Rosenzweig for very helpful comments. We thank Jess Benhabib for useful comments and Silvana Melitsko and Tobias Pfutze for outstanding research assistance.

The United Kingdom has already acted on the latter suggestion, with the Department of Health issuing a list of countries (including most countries in Africa) from which recruitment of nurses is banned. The Physicians for Human Rights report includes an extensive discussion of how to prevent skilled workers in poor countries from getting around the restrictions. (Oh, no, they might check out job opportunities on the Internet!)

We argue that these fears are overblown. The brain drain has both costs and benefits for Africans. It is not at all clear that Africans are worse off because of the opportunity for skilled workers to migrate to rich countries. We engage in both theoretical and empirical exercises to evaluate the costs and benefits of the brain drain.

We build on a rich literature that gives a much more balanced picture of the possibility of "brain gain" in addition to or instead of brain drain (Mountford, 1997; Stark, Helmenstein, and Prskawetz, 1997, 1998; Beine, Docquier, and Rapoport, 2001, 2003; Stark and Wang, 2002; Docquier and Rapoport, 2004; Stark, 2004; Lucas, 2005, 2006; Faini, 2006; Clemens, 2007; Manning, 2007).

We also offer a different perspective on evaluating brain drain from what is common in aid-agency discussions. Contrary to the mercantilist presumption of development thinking that the main objective should be to maximize development of nation-states, we are concerned with the well-being (and rights) of individuals. Tanzania's development only matters because it affects the well-being of individual Tanzanians. The net benefits and costs of brain drain should be viewed from the perspective of individuals, including those who migrate. There is no reason to ignore the benefits accruing from a given policy to a Tanzanian who is no longer in Tanzania.

We are bothered by the double standard that exists in much policy discussion of the brain drain. Restrictions on mobility of Africans are discussed casually by people who would never accept limitations on their own mobility. One of the authors of this paper was born in a poor American region (West Virginia), the other in a poor African country (Ghana). There is no discussion in American policymaking circles of limiting brain drain out of West Virginia, even though there has also been a mass exodus of skills there, but the analogous situation in Ghana calls for "action plans" to limit the brain drain. Perhaps the advocates of curbing the brain drain are correct about its costs outweighing its benefits, but then they should also make the same recommendations for brain drain out of poor regions in their own countries. Individual freedom of choice regarding where to work and live is a good thing in itself, whether within or between countries, and advocates for restrictions on that freedom carry some burden of proof.

Of course, whether the brain drain has a positive or a negative effect on specific groups is an empirical issue, and we will keep an open mind about what the evidence shows and the theory suggests. To start off, we give a list of the pluses and minuses of the brain drain for Africans. This list cannot be comprehensive, but it gets us started. The implied counterfactual is that migration of skilled workers to rich countries does not take place.

Minuses (case for stopping the brain drain)
1. Skills are necessary for long-run development of the source country; therefore, skilled workers should stay at home.
2. The human capital of the migrants may have had a positive effect on the income or the growth of income of those left behind if they had stayed.
3. The human capital of the migrants may have had a positive effect on institutions or political leadership of the home society if they had stayed.
4. Family separation resulting from migration may cause both the migrants and those left behind to suffer in nonmonetary ways.

Pluses (case for letting the brain drain happen without restrictions)
1. The migrants themselves are better off, by revealed preference since migration is voluntary.
2. Family members left behind may derive indirect utility from the greater well-being of the migrants (and if the migration decision was made by the family as a whole, the family is also better off by revealed preference).
3. The migrants may send remittances back to boost the incomes of those left behind.
4. The home-country population may have stronger incentives to invest in human capital if they have the opportunity to migrate.
5. The migrants may have a positive effect on politics or institutions from abroad.
6. The threat of migration may serve as a check on the behavior of rulers at home (one specific example: it may change government's behavior in excessively taxing or paying low salaries to professionals).
7. The migrants may return home permanently or temporarily, bringing back technology.
8. The migrants may facilitate trading networks that increase source-country exports to the destination country (see Rauch on the Chinese diaspora).
9. Individual freedom is enhanced by giving individuals opportunities to migrate.

In this chapter, we will explore theoretically and empirically some of these pluses and minuses. Before doing that, we will simply put in context the scope of the African brain-drain phenomenon, describing why it seems alarming to so many people. Then we will do an exercise to place some bounds on what effect the brain drain might have had according to some simple (and, we will argue, unrealistically exaggerating the effect of the brain drain) counterfactuals. Even under these upper-bound counterfactuals, we find the quantitative significance of the brain drain to be small for Africa. Next, we will present a general theoretical framework for evaluating the brain drain's effect on the individuals concerned, and we will perform some illustrative exercises by calibrating the parameters of the model. We find plenty of reason to believe that the benefits may outweigh the costs once we take into account the gain to the migrants, the indirect utility accruing to their families, and the effect of remittances. Last, we will test empirically predictions about the effect of brain drain on skill accumulation and economic growth. We find evidence that the opportunity for brain drain does stimulate skill accumulation and that this effect seems to offset the direct loss of skills from brain drain. We find no evidence for an adverse effect of brain drain on economic growth.

The African Brain Drain in Context

The African brain drain is not so new. There were small numbers of Africans going abroad during the early 1700s for Western education. Many who went to be educated went to study religion. McWilliam (1959) tells us of a Ghanaian with the Dutch name of Jacobus Capitein, sent by the Dutch to Leyden University in the 1700s. His intellectual activities included translating the books of the apostles into the local Fante language and presenting an argument about why slavery is consistent with religious doctrines. He was ridiculed by his own people and ignored by the Europeans, and he died at 30 years of age. His generation of brain drainers were most probably very influential in translating local languages and spreading the use of the written word.

Kwegyir Aggrey is an exemplar of the brain drain. He, too, was a Ghanaian, studying at Columbia University in the 1920s, and was connected to the Phelps-Stokes fund and Caroline Phelps-Stokes, a New York philanthropist with a lifelong concern for the educational needs of the underprivileged. This connection resulted ultimately in Ghana's first coed, nondenominational school, Achimota School, which later became what is now the University of Ghana, the country's largest, oldest, and most prestigious university.

Many of the independence leaders in Africa were themselves part of a brain drain in the early 20th century. Hastings Banda, Jomo Kenyatta, and many other African independence leaders were all part of an initial brain drain, who met and strategized in the United Kingdom and the United States and then returned to fight for independence. Azikiwe, the Nigerian independence leader, studied at Lincoln University in Pennsylvania and was instrumental in bringing Kwame Nkrumah, Ghana's independence leader, to the United States, to the same institution, where the latter received a bachelor's degree in economics and sociology; he later earned a master's degree in philosophy at the University of Pennsylvania. Without that brain drain, independence may have occurred much later, if at all, in many African countries. (These independence leaders were also in contact with and in some cases contributed to the dialogue within the American civil rights movement.)

Table 11.1 describes the most recent data on the scope of the brain drain in Africa today, as compared with other regions. This table is only about the stocks of skilled emigrants (where "skilled" is defined as individuals with tertiary education) relative to other stocks and contains nothing about flows. The most straightforward statistic on the brain drain is the percentage of skilled nationals residing outside the country. We see that this statistic is worse for Africa than for most other major regions of the world, with 13 percent of African skilled workers residing outside Africa. Only Oceania and the Caribbean are much worse, and these are rather special cases—very small populations that appear not to be bound very much by immigration restrictions to nearby rich countries (Australia/New Zealand and the United States, respectively). Mexico and Central America are slightly worse than Africa, but this is also a special case because of the massive flows of all types of migrants from this region to rich countries, as shown in column 2 (the United States in this case). Africa stands out for a significant brain drain despite tiny overall emigration stocks. One way to dramatize this is to take the ratio of column 1 to column 2, which can be thought of as the ratio of probabilities of skilled emigration to overall emigration. This ratio is much higher than anywhere else in the world. A related way in which Africa stands out is that skilled migrants make up a large share of total migrants (column 3), despite the local population having a low share of skilled workers (column 4). Column 7 dramatizes this aspect by taking the ratio of column 3 to column 4, and again this ratio is far higher than anywhere else in the world.

Table 11.2 shows the same statistics as table 11.1 for all individual African countries. Cape Verde and Gambia are the countries with the highest brain drain as a percentage of skilled nationals (there is a general empirical regularity that the smallest countries have the highest brain drain).

Table 11.3 shows instead the absolute size of migration stocks by source country, as well as the shares of different regional destinations. The brain drain from Africa consists of slightly fewer than 1 million tertiary-educated people. The top two countries in absolute size are South Africa and Nigeria, not surprising given their population size. Smaller countries with

Table 11.1   Comparing Brain Drain by Region, 2000

	(1) Skilled emigrants/(skilled emigrants + skilled working-age residents)	(2) Emigrants/ (emigrants+ residents)	(3) Skilled emigrants/ all emigrants	(4) Skilled residents/ all residents	(5) Ratio of probability of emigration for skilled to overall probability of emigration (1)/(2)	(6) Ratio of probability that an emigrant will be skilled to probability that a resident will be skilled (3)/(4)
Sub-Saharan Africa	13%	1%	43%	3%	13.6	15.4
World	5%	2%	35%	11%	2.9	3.1
North America	1%	1%	58%	51%	1.1	1.1
Caribbean	43%	15%	39%	9%	2.8	4.2
Mexico/Central America	17%	12%	17%	11%	1.4	1.5
South America	5%	2%	41%	12%	3.2	3.3
Eastern Europe	4%	2%	34%	17%	1.9	2.0
Rest of Europe	9%	5%	31%	18%	1.6	1.7
Northern Africa	7%	3%	19%	9%	2.1	2.2
Eastern Asia	5%	1%	53%	6%	8.4	8.8
Western Asia	7%	4%	23%	11%	1.9	2.0
Australia/New Zealand	5%	4%	49%	33%	1.5	1.5
Oceania	49%	8%	35%	3%	6.4	11.5

Source: Docquier and Marfouk (2005).

Table 11.2 Africa Brain Drain in 2000

	(1) Skilled emigrants/ (skilled emigrants + skilled working-age residents)	(2) Emigrants/ (emigrants+ residents)	(3) Skilled emigrants/all emigrants	(4) Skilled residents/all residents
Angola	33%	3%	17%	1%
Benin	11%	0%	53%	2%
Botswana	4%	0%	34%	4%
Burkina Faso	3%	0%	30%	2%
Burundi	9%	0%	51%	2%
Cameroon	17%	1%	50%	2%
Cape Verde	67%	25%	15%	2%
Central African Republic	7%	0%	41%	2%
Chad	2%	0%	48%	2%
Comoros	21%	4%	13%	2%
Democratic Republic of the Congo	14%	1%	37%	1%
Republic of the Congo	22%	3%	40%	4%
Côte d'Ivoire	6%	1%	31%	3%
Djibouti	11%	1%	38%	2%
Equatorial Guinea	13%	4%	12%	4%
Eritrea	34%	2%	41%	2%
Ethiopia	10%	0%	49%	2%

Gabon	15%	1%	53%	3%
Gambia	63%	3%	20%	0%
Ghana	47%	2%	44%	1%
Guinea	11%	0%	26%	1%
Guinea-Bissau	24%	2%	14%	1%
Kenya	38%	2%	45%	1%
Lesotho	4%	0%	50%	1%
Liberia	45%	4%	58%	3%
Madagascar	8%	0%	43%	3%
Malawi	19%	0%	43%	1%
Mali	15%	1%	11%	1%
Mauritania	12%	1%	22%	2%
Mauritius	56%	11%	29%	3%
Mozambique	45%	1%	18%	0%
Namibia	3%	0%	51%	4%
Niger	6%	0%	49%	1%
Nigeria	11%	1%	65%	3%
Rwanda	26%	0%	48%	1%
São Tomé and Principe	22%	6%	18%	4%
Senegal	18%	3%	17%	2%

(continued)

Table 11.2 (continued)

	(1) Skilled emigrants/ (skilled emigrants + skilled working-age residents)	(2) Emigrants/ (emigrants+ residents)	(3) Skilled emigrants/all emigrants	(4) Skilled residents/all residents
Seychelles	56%	20%	37%	7%
Sierra Leone	53%	2%	50%	1%
Somalia	33%	3%	28%	2%
South Africa	8%	1%	63%	10%
Sudan	7%	0%	52%	2%
Swaziland	0%	0%	56%	4%
Tanzania	12%	1%	51%	2%
Togo	19%	1%	40%	2%
Uganda	36%	1%	46%	1%
Zambia	17%	1%	48%	2%
Zimbabwe	13%	1%	55%	5%

Source: Docquier and Marfouk (2005).

Table 11.3   African Skilled Emigrants by Source and Destination

Source	Total	Destination shares		
		America	Europe	Asia/Oceania
South Africa	168,083	37%	32%	31%
Nigeria	149,494	64%	35%	1%
Kenya	77,516	45%	49%	6%
Ghana	71,309	56%	42%	2%
Ethiopia	51,392	78%	18%	3%
Uganda	34,970	45%	52%	3%
Democratic Republic of the Congo	33,085	25%	75%	1%
Zimbabwe	32,676	28%	49%	23%
Tanzania	32,255	62%	34%	4%
Somalia	27,916	43%	53%	4%
Mauritius	23,043	22%	53%	25%
Cameroon	21,822	42%	58%	0%
Liberia	20,842	91%	8%	0%
Angola	20,449	12%	87%	1%
Sudan	18,789	60%	29%	11%
Sierra Leone	18,010	58%	41%	1%
Senegal	15,729	34%	66%	1%
Republic of the Congo	14,672	20%	79%	1%
Zambia	13,739	37%	45%	18%
Eritrea	13,144	74%	21%	5%
Côte d'Ivoire	12,088	35%	65%	0%
Madagascar	12,080	18%	81%	1%
Mozambique	10,696	15%	83%	3%
Cape Verde	8,128	53%	47%	0%
Togo	7,874	27%	73%	0%
Malawi	5,474	28%	65%	7%
Benin	4,786	25%	75%	0%
Rwanda	4,528	53%	46%	1%
Mali	3,854	22%	77%	1%
Guinea	3,668	53%	46%	1%
Gambia	3,648	32%	67%	1%
Burundi	3,557	56%	43%	1%
Mauritania	2,556	41%	59%	0%

(continued)

Table 11.3   (continued)

Source	Total	Destination shares		
		America	Europe	Asia/Oceania
Seychelles	2,426	40%	34%	25%
Gabon	2,170	11%	89%	1%
Burkina Faso	1,926	27%	73%	0%
Central African Republic	1,894	11%	88%	1%
Guinea-Bissau	1,525	1%	98%	1%
Comoros	1,349	11%	88%	0%
Chad	1,320	36%	62%	2%
Swaziland	1,053	69%	20%	11%
Niger	1,042	39%	60%	1%
Namibia	1,026	25%	40%	36%
Equatorial Guinea	1,012	1%	99%	0%
Botswana	940	23%	45%	32%
Djibouti	615	26%	70%	4%
São Tomé and Principe	571	21%	79%	1%
Lesotho	295	43%	44%	13%
Sub-Saharan Africa	961,037	47%	44%	9%

Source: Docquier and Marfouk (2005).

a history of violent upheaval also show up toward the top of the list. Kenya and Ghana are more surprising outliers as numbers 3 and 4. English-speaking countries are more likely to rank high on this list. As far as destinations, the bulk of the African brain drain is almost evenly split between Europe and the Americas, with less than 10 percent going to Asia/Oceania. However, this varies enormously by country, with Ethiopia and Liberia heavily skewed toward the Americas (presumably the United States) and Francophone countries toward Europe (presumably France).

We were able to find only two destination countries with easily accessible records on African-born immigrants (both skilled and unskilled) and their educational characteristics: the United States and the United Kingdom.

Table 11.4 shows the U.S. statistics by source country and compares Africa with other regions. Nigeria, Ethiopia, Ghana, South Africa, and Kenya again are in the top positions as source countries in this table (which shows only the top 20 source countries). However, African migrants overall are a very small share of the overall foreign-born population and truly tiny as a fraction of the total U.S. population.

Table 11.4   Statistics on Foreign-Born African Population in the United States as of 2000 Census

	Percentage of African foreign-born	% Black	% B.A. or higher	MedHH inc	% Own house
Nigeria	20.9%	93.2%	58.6	45,072	39.1
Ethiopia	10.8%	83.5%	29.5	32,215	24.5
Ghana	10.2%	93.7%	31.6	42,016	27.9
South Africa	9.9%	5.8%	55.8	69,229	55.8
Kenya	6.3%	63.6%	51.4	43,909	35.6
Liberia	6.1%	92.4%	31.1	38,341	33.2
Somalia	5.5%	71.2%	16.6	18,449	5.9
Cape Verde	4.1%	21.7%	7.2	37,443	44.4
Sierra Leone	3.2%	89.0%	31.3	42,554	31.5
Sudan	3.1%	62.2%	40.2	29,437	15.7
Eritrea	2.7%	84.6%	19.9	33,284	29.4
Cameroon	1.8%	94.9%	58.7	42,632	30.0
Uganda	1.8%	53.7%	51.5	51,758	46.6
Tanzania	1.8%	33.1%	50.2	55,185	48.2
Zimbabwe	1.7%	47.8%	50.1	50,388	44.0
Senegal	1.6%	82.2%	33.1	32,547	15.5
Côte d'Ivoire	1.1%	90.5%	34.9	33,236	16.7
Zambia	0.9%	32.9%	52.7	52,403	44.8
Gambia	0.9%	94.2%	22.5	36,522	15.2
Guinea	0.8%	85.6%	24.3	27,755	11.0
Africa	2.8%		42.8	41,196	36.2
Asia	26.4%		43.1	50,554	51.4
Europe	15.8%		29.2	42,763	63.7
Latin America	51.7%		9.6	33,519	42.5
Northern America	2.7%		33.3	46,850	68.7
Oceania	0.5%		28.6	51,425	52.4
Native-born population			24.5	42,299	68.3

Note: African-born population as percentage of native-born population: 0.3%.
Source: U.S. Census.

One phenomenon highlighted by this table is that "African immigration" to the United States has a large proportion of people who are not "black" according to U.S. Census definitions for some source countries— South Africa, Kenya, Cape Verde, Sudan, Uganda, Tanzania, Zimbabwe, and Zambia. More surprisingly for some source countries than others, there are a lot of whites, African Asians, and other nonblack groups that are part of the brain drain. We are not sure what implications this has for migration policy, if any, but it shows a different picture from the stereotypical image of black African nurses and doctors going to help white patients in the United States. As an example of how this might influence the perspective of the brain drain, those brain-drain critics who wanted the skilled migrants to stay at home to be political leaders might have to acknowledge in the counterfactual world that it would probably not have been feasible for whites or Asians to be political leaders in the source countries. Racial discrimination in the host countries is another reason to take race into consideration in evaluating brain-drain gains and losses.

Also striking in this table is how well educated the African immigrants are, with a percentage holding bachelor's degrees more than twice as high as in the native population, comparable to Asian immigrants (whose source countries have much higher tertiary enrollments) and higher than all other immigrant groups, including Europe. The same African skill bias we saw in the total emigrant stock data is very evident in the U.S. immigrant data (this may also reflect African migrants getting educated in the States). The income level of African immigrants is about the same as that of natives (the higher education of the migrants is perhaps offset by adjustment difficulties in the new environment) and obviously vastly higher than incomes in the source countries. Overall, the picture is one of migrants thriving in the destination country.

Of course, there are large differences between countries. We considered the correlation of percentage with bachelor's degrees or higher, log of household income, and home ownership on two characteristics of the immigrant population: size (in logs), and percentage black. We failed to find any effect of immigrant-population size, which conceivably might have influenced ease of adjustment to the United States, on these outcomes. Percentage black had a strong negative relationship with all three outcomes (although Cape Verde is a huge outlier), reflecting, no doubt, the higher attainment of skills in the white and Asian migrants in the source country and possibly the effects of discrimination against blacks in the United States. Despite the association of percentage with bachelor's degrees with nonblack migration, the population-weighted average percentage with bachelor's degrees is only slightly lower (40.7 percent) if we restrict the sample to source countries with blacks accounting for

Table 11.5   Source Countries for Immigrants to United Kingdom and Racial Composition

	Share of African-born population	% Black African
South Africa	19.0%	3%
Kenya	17.4%	11%
Nigeria	11.9%	87%
Ghana	7.5%	90%
Uganda	7.4%	27%
Zimbabwe	6.6%	37%
Somalia	5.8%	91%
Tanzania	4.4%	13%
Mauritius	3.6%	2%
Zambia	2.9%	24%
Sierra Leone	2.3%	87%
Malawi	1.7%	15%
Sudan	1.4%	55%
Democratic Republic of the Congo	1.1%	84%
Ethiopia	1.0%	85%
Eritrea	0.9%	90%
Angola	0.8%	64%
Gambia	0.5%	90%
Mozambique	0.4%	9%
Republic of the Congo	0.4%	81%
Cameroon	0.4%	85%
Côte d'Ivoire	0.4%	85%
Rwanda	0.3%	90%
Botswana	0.3%	54%
Burundi	0.3%	86%
Liberia	0.2%	77%
Namibia	0.2%	13%
Swaziland	0.1%	28%
Madagascar	0.1%	17%
Senegal	0.1%	63%
Togo	0.1%	88%
Guinea-Bissau	0.1%	59%

Note: African-born as percentage of total U.K. population: 2.0%.
Source: 2001 Census data.

Table 11.6   Educational Qualifications of Black African Immigrants to United Kingdom Compared with Native-Born

| | Percentage of known total | | |
	No qualifications	Vocational/ high school	College or above
All U.K.-born			
All	31%	49%	20%
Males	30%	49%	20%
Females	32%	49%	19%
Black African born outside United Kingdom			
All	16%	44%	40%
Males	12%	42%	46%
Females	19%	46%	35%

Source: 2001 Census data.

more than 80 percent of the migrants (this reflects the large population of migrants from Nigeria with very high B.A. attainment). Hence, it is still true that African immigrants have very high educational attainment if we exclude the white and Asian migrant source countries. The main source-country exceptions to the "thriving migrants" picture are Cape Verdeans (who are mostly unskilled but whose income is not so bad) and Somalians (both unskilled and low-income).

Our data on U.K. immigrants from the 2001 census confirms the importance of the same source countries as for the United States, albeit with Kenya much higher and Ethiopia much lower. Table 11.5 also confirms the significance of white and Asian migration from Africa for some important source countries such as South Africa, Kenya, Uganda, Zimbabwe, Tanzania, Zambia, and Malawi. For those who saw whites and Asians as outsiders left over from colonial times and want to see indigenous African development (not a view that we necessarily endorse), this might alter the picture of the African brain drain.

The U.K. data also confirm the skill bias in African migration (table 11.6 shows it only for black African migrants, so the picture is not altered by white or Asian migrants). More than twice as many black African migrants have a college education or above as the native-born U.K. population, and half as many are unskilled, roughly the same for both males and females.

Skill Creation in Africa

A high percentage of African government spending is on education, relative to the rest of the world. Table 11.7 shows that this is about 25 percent for Ghana and 20 percent for many African countries, such as Algeria (21.1 percent), Morocco (26.1 percent), Togo (26.4 percent), Cameroon (19.6 percent), Kenya (17 percent), Gambia (14.6 percent), Senegal (26.9 percent), and Niger (18.6 percent) (data from a 2004 Human Development Report). There is also great political pressure on the governments to increase the number of available seats in secondary schools and universities. The proportion of

Table 11.7   Public Spending on Education for Selected African Countries

	As % of total government expenditure	Tertiary education as % of government education expenditure
Algeria	21.1%	—
Angola	10.7%	3.7%
Botswana	17.0%	—
Burundi	16.7%	22.0%
Cameroon	19.6%	29.5%
Congo	14.4%	—
Ethiopia	9.4%	12.1%
Gambia	14.6%	17.8%
Ghana	24.3%	11.0%
Kenya	17.0%	21.6%
Lesotho	12.2%	—
Malawi	11.1%	20.2%
Morocco	26.1%	16.2%
Mozambique	12.0%	9.9%
Niger	18.6%	—
Senegal	26.9%	24.0%
Swaziland	19.5%	26.0%
Tanzania	11.4%	—
Togo	26.4%	29.0%
Tunisia	13.5%	18.5%
Uganda	11.5%	—
Zambia	8.7%	—

Source: Human Development Report (2004).

public expenditure on education spent on the tertiary level is more than 20 percent in countries such as Cameroon (29.5 percent), Togo (29.0 percent), Kenya (21.6 percent), Senegal (24.0 percent), and Malawi (20.2 percent).

What is the cost of producing brains—that is, of providing education to Africa's citizens? We will focus on the production of tertiary-educated citizens. The work by Hinchliffe (1987), using data for 1979 to 1984, shows unit costs of tertiary education as a multiple of per-capita GNP as averaging 8.6 for Africa, with highs of 30.0 for Tanzania, 13.0 for Upper Volta, 14.2 for Zimbabwe, and 6.0 for Ghana. The averages for Asia, Latin America, and the developed countries are 1.2, 0.9 and 0.5, respectively. By this measure, we see that education in Africa is relatively expensive. This leads, of course, to concern about the brain drain.

The Hinchliffe data are 20 years old. As indicated earlier, there has been a rapid increase in the number of students in tertiary-education institutions. This increased number as well as efficiencies in delivery would be expected to reduce the unit cost of educating students. We did our own computations, using more recent data from the UNDP Human Development Report (2004), World Development Indicators, and UNESCO (2005). Our data show smaller costs, as expected. The numbers we obtained are in the range of two and three times GNP per capita (table 11.8).[1]

Despite these high costs, African countries have rapidly increased the number of their citizens receiving education, especially tertiary education. K. Y. Amoako, in his lecture published in the Tertiary Education Series (Ghana), has studied the expansion of universities in sub-Saharan Africa. From six universities in sub-Saharan Africa in 1960, he records more than 120. Enrollments have jumped, from 1.5 million students in 1980 to 3.8 million in 1995. Francophone western Africa in the colonial era had only one university, the University of Dakar. Now there is at least one for each country. Eastern Africa had only Makerere; now there are more than a dozen. The increase from 1995 to today has been even more spectacular.

However, this expansion was starting from a very small base, and so tertiary education still reaches only a small fraction of college-age youth, as table 11.9 makes clear.

Almost all of the universities are run and paid for by the government,[2] with tuition accounting for an infinitesimally small amount of the costs. Combined with the small absolute size of the government budgets relative

1. Our computations are available upon request.
2. It has only been in recent years that governments have allowed private universities to be established in Africa. The private tuition-based universities still account for a very small percentage of the overall number of students in the tertiary-education system.

Table 11.8   Unit Costs of Higher Education
as a Multiple of Per Capita GNP

	1979–1984	2000
Botswana	7.00	1.02
Chad	—	4.21
Congo	—	1.96
Gabon	—	1.59
Ghana	5.70	1.78
Lesotho	14.20	7.50
Malawi	15.90	—
Mali	—	2.32
Niger	5.40	2.91
Rwanda	14.00	5.69
Swaziland	3.20	2.65
Tanzania	30.90	—
Togo	6.30	2.42
Upper Volta	13.20	—
Zimbabwe	12.70	—
Africa	8.60	—
Asia	1.18	—
Latin America	0.88	—
Developed countries	0.49	—

Source: Our own calculations based on Human Development
Report (2004), World Development Indicators, and UNESCO.

Table 11.9   Median Tertiary Enrollment Rates in Africa, 1991–2005

	Overall median	Female median	Male median
1991	2.06	0.70	2.74
1999	2.12	1.30	3.08
2000	2.57	1.64	3.43
2001	2.77	1.23	3.34
2002	2.91	1.88	3.67
2003	2.30	1.54	3.18
2004	2.51	1.81	3.52
2005	2.85	1.85	3.76

Source: UNESCO data.

to the needs of the population, we see why many have worried about the brain drain from Africa.

It is often these two facts—the high exodus rate of Africa's educated classes in combination with the high government subsidies of higher education—that lead to most of the outcry about the African brain drain.

Two kinds of pressures emerge. On the one hand, because of relative ease of filling up seats in the humanities, the production of graduates in these areas exceeds the ability of the economy to absorb them appropriately. On the other hand, one often hears statements in the press that there is a strong desire to have more scientists and mathematicians to help bring Africa to the technological frontier. It is interesting to note that, using Ghana as a case study, most of the seats produced in the newly formed private universities are in business and computer science. Note that the public-university bias toward humanities is similar to what often happens in the U.S. higher-education market. Graduate degrees in the humanities are often heavily advertised, with full funding given in those fields. There is a lot of soul searching in the humanities departments producing these Ph.D. degrees, since there are often no jobs in the academy.

Does the Brain Drain Explain Africa's Skill Gap?

We now begin to examine whether the brain drain is good or bad for Africa, using a variety of methods. First, we consider a counterfactual of no brain drain.

There is one aspect of Africa's brain drain that was already present in table 11.1 above, which should caution against any quick jump to brain-drain alarmism. Africa's brain drain may be unusually large relative to both total emigration and the remaining stock of skilled persons resident in Africa, but both of the latter quantities are small. Hence the size of Africa's brain drain relative to Africa's remaining residents is extremely modest (column 3 in table 11.10). Even Europe (not including eastern Europe), for example, has a bigger brain drain than Africa (see column 3 again). Suppose we posit a counterfactual in which two conditions held: (1) the brain drainers had never left home, and (2) they still would have become skilled if there had been no brain-drain opportunity. We will present evidence below against assumption 2, but let us grant it for the moment as a best-case scenario for what could happen if the brain drain were stopped.

Column 4 shows the counterfactual if both assumptions held (it is roughly equal to the sum of columns 2 and 3, except that we need to adjust the denominator to increase the number of residents by the skilled emigrants who are now assumed to have remained residents). Even if all of the African skilled emigrants had stayed at home, the share of skilled persons

Table 11.10   Does Brain Drain Explain Africa's Skill Gap? (Data from 2000)

	(1) Skilled emigrants/ (skilled emigrants + skilled working-age residents)	(2) Skilled residents/all residents	(3) Skilled emigrants/all residents	(4) Counterfactual skilled/ residents ratio if all skilled emigrants still become skilled but remain at home
Sub-Saharan Africa	13%	2.8%	0.4%	3.2%
World	5%	11.3%	0.6%	11.9%
North America	1%	51.3%	0.5%	51.5%
Caribbean	43%	9.3%	6.9%	15.2%
Mexico/Central America	17%	11.1%	2.3%	13.0%
South America	5%	12.3%	0.7%	12.9%
Eastern Europe	4%	17.4%	0.8%	18.0%
Europe (excluding eastern Europe)	9%	18.3%	1.7%	19.6%
Northern Africa	7%	8.6%	0.7%	9.2%
Eastern Asia	5%	6.0%	0.3%	6.3%
Western Asia	7%	11.4%	0.8%	12.1%
Australia/New Zealand	5%	32.7%	1.9%	33.9%
Oceania	49%	3.1%	2.9%	5.8%
15 highest counterfactual alterations in Africa				
Seychelles	56%	7.1%	9.0%	14.8%
Cape Verde	67%	2.5%	5.1%	7.2%

(continued)

Table 11.10 (continued)

	(1) Skilled emigrants/ (skilled emigrants + skilled working-age residents)	(2) Skilled residents/all residents	(3) Skilled emigrants/all residents	(4) Counterfactual skilled/ residents ratio if all skilled emigrants still become skilled but remain at home
Mauritius	56%	2.7%	3.5%	6.0%
Liberia	45%	2.6%	2.1%	4.6%
Republic of the Congo	22%	4.4%	1.3%	5.6%
Sierra Leone	53%	1.0%	1.1%	2.1%
São Tomé and Principe	22%	3.9%	1.1%	4.9%
Eritrea	34%	2.0%	1.0%	3.0%
Somalia	33%	2.0%	1.0%	3.0%
Ghana	47%	1.1%	1.0%	2.1%
South Africa	8%	10.4%	0.8%	11.1%
Zimbabwe	13%	5.3%	0.8%	6.0%
Kenya	38%	1.2%	0.7%	1.9%
Gambia	63%	0.4%	0.7%	1.1%
Equatorial Guinea	13%	3.9%	0.6%	4.5%

in the working-age population would still be very low. The share of tertiary-educated people in the population would increase only from 2.8 percent to 3.2 percent. Africa is still the region with the greatest shortage of skills, by a large margin. In fact, compared with other regions, Africa actually falls farther behind in this counterfactual world, because the Caribbean and Oceania would have benefited much more from a reversal of the brain drain than Africa. More surprisingly, Europe would have benefited more from this counterfactual of no brain drain but same skills, so the skill gap between Europe and Africa is actually higher in the counterfactual world. The only region with a smaller improvement than Africa in the counterfactual world is eastern Asia. So, if this is the right counterfactual, the skill gap between Africa and *all* other regions except eastern Asia is *smaller* with a brain drain than with no brain drain. The brain drain, even under the most unrealistic and simplistic assumption that it would be possible to have the same number of brains stay at home as are now outside the country, is not to blame for Africa's shortage of skilled professionals relative to the rest of the world.

To be sure, in some individual African nations, this counterfactual makes a significant difference. However, the number of such cases is small, and the nations so affected themselves are very small (recall that small nations have an unusually high brain drain). Table 11.10 shows the African nations with the biggest change in skill ratios in the simulation. Two nations—Seychelles and Cape Verde—would see a large change in their skill ratios in the counterfactual world. Mauritius and Liberia are the only other African nations where the change in the skill ratio is more than 2 percentage points. After that, the counterfactual change in skill ratios falls off sharply. Countries that have received a lot of attention as hot spots of brain drain, such as Ghana, South Africa, Zimbabwe, and Kenya, would see skill ratios increase by 1 percentage point or less. Even if we grant the implied counterfactual world of those who are alarmed by the brain drain, the numerical consequences for the source-country skill ratios are surprisingly small.

Overall Framework for Pluses and Minuses of the African Brain Drain for Individuals

One aspect of the brain drain that is often not mentioned is the fact that those who successfully migrate abroad often enjoy markedly improved standards of living (as demonstrated in the tables above). Parents who care about their offspring also enjoy increased utility with successful brain drain of their offspring. They may choose optimally to have taxes imposed on them to improve the school system with the sole purpose of increasing the chances that their own offspring will be able to migrate one day. These desires are no different from those of parents in rural areas or small towns in the United States who fund their school systems knowing full well that there will be next to complete brain drain of the educated from those school systems to big cities in the United States. Those parents understand fully that perhaps the only benefit of those tax payments is to see their own offspring better educated and therefore better able to drain to other regions.

It is, of course, possible that holding the given the migration outcome of their offspring fixed, they would prefer other parents' kids not to drain away. This, of course, would lead to better public and private goods for themselves—better hospitals, better government administration, shorter waits for doctors, and so on. Ex ante, however, it may be in each parent's interest to vote to allow a brain drain even if his or her own offspring has less chance of being able to drain away. We will illustrate this with some back-of-the-envelope calculations. Later, we will provide calculations that indicate that the same may be true of the society as a whole—in particular, taking into account all of the externalities, a country may decide it is in its best interests to allow and encourage a brain drain.

The message is clear: given a vote, many may decide to vote to continue the brain drain or even increase it.

Our calculations underestimate the positive aspects of the brain drain for the many reasons outlined earlier. Here we look only at utilities, remittances, and some proxy for the public goods created by educated people who stay in their home countries rather than being drained away.

Think of there being two types or ages of people in the economy, the young and the old. Suppose that there is a unit of the population that is young. Let us perform a simple static or one-period exercise. In particular, suppose that the government has resources of G which it spends on two different activities: roads and education. Let e denote the resources spent on education and H that on roads. The government therefore has the budget constraint

$$H + e = G. \tag{11.1}$$

Let $\psi = \Psi(e)$ denote the fraction of the young who will be educated when education spending is e. The function Ψ will, of course, be increasing in e, so that higher e results in a higher percentage of the young being educated. Of the educated, a fraction d will be drained off to foreign countries, with the residual fraction $1 - d$ remaining in the home country. There will therefore be three types of young: the fraction ψd who are educated and drain, the fraction $\psi(1 - d)$ who are educated and remain in their home countries, and the fraction $(1 - \psi)$ who receive no education. We now specify the utility levels of each of these three groups of young.

The educated young who do not drain, and therefore remain in their home countries, produce public goods for all in the society to consume. The precise amount y of the public goods produced depends on spending on infrastructure H, as well as the total number of educated young available, $\psi(1 - d)$, via the production function f:

$$y = f(G - e, (1 - d)\,\psi) \tag{11.2}$$

We will think of y as being the doctors and nurses, teachers and professors, engineers, and others in the country who could have migrated but did not. We will not think of this as similar to our thoughts of independence leaders, since it is unclear that merely increasing the number of educated significantly increases the chance of such once-in-a-generation leaders.

Since increasing either the infrastructure or the educated young available in the economy would be presumed to increase the output of the public good, we suppose that f is increasing in both arguments. Notice that we suppose that only the educated produce public goods. In particular, we ignore the role of the uneducated in producing public goods. There are a number of reasons for this modeling. First, we use this simplification to highlight the effect of the brain drain. Note that as the drain fraction d goes up, the production of public goods goes down. It is this important effect that we want to study. Adding the uneducated into the production function would not change our principal conclusions. Further, when looking at tertiary education, in many African countries, the educated are a very small proportion of the uneducated. Introducing the unskilled into the production function f will add few interesting insights not already captured by the first two arguments of f.

Now come the payoffs of the three different types of the young. The fraction $\psi(1 - d)$ of the young who are educated and stay within the economy receive the payoff $u^E(y)$, which depends on the quantity y of the public goods produced. Let us set $u^E(y) = cy$, where c denotes a form of "skill premium." The fraction $(1 - \psi)$ of the young who do not receive an education will be modeled as having the utility or payoff of y. The fraction ψd of the young who are educated and drain each receives an income of w^D in the countries in which they work. They also send the amount R as remittances to their families back home. The net income of the drainers is, therefore, $u^D \equiv w^D - R$. We use these very crude and simplified assumptions on the payoffs of the different types of young to enable us to focus on the brain-drain aspects of interest to us.

Now, think of a typical young person, "behind the veil," not knowing which of the three types of young they will end up being part of. The expected income u^Y of that young person is, of course, the weighted average of the three payoffs, weighted by the probability of being in each class:

$$u^Y = \psi d\,(W - R) + \psi(1 - d)\,cy + (1 - \psi)\,y. \tag{11.3}$$

Of course, one could argue that for the very rich, say, they could be sure that their offspring will be educated and may even drain. In particular, it may be better to model the three probabilities as being a function of wealth. We will argue later that we could indeed include this feature without doing much harm to our basic results.

Regarding the old, they receive an income equal to y plus whatever they receive as remittances from their offspring who successfully get an education and drain, which in expected value terms is given by

$$u^O = y + \psi dR \tag{11.4}$$

All types of the young care also about their parents' utility, U^O. This enters the utility function discounted by the factor δ^Y; in particular, the total ex ante payoff of young is

$$U^Y = u^Y + \delta^Y U^O. \tag{11.5}$$

Similarly, the old also care about the utility of their offspring; this enters their utility function additively but discounted by δ^O; in particular, the ex ante utility level of the old is

$$U^O = u^O + \delta^O U^Y. \tag{11.6}$$

The values of U^Y and U^O will be determined in an equilibrium where both equations (11.5) and (11.6) hold simultaneously. Solving those two equations simultaneously implies that if[3]

$$U^Y = \delta^Y U^O + u^Y \quad \text{and} \quad U^O = \delta^O U^Y + u^O \tag{11.7}$$

then

if

$$U^Y = \delta^Y (\delta^O U^Y + u^O) + u^Y \quad \text{so} \tag{11.8}$$

$$U^Y = \kappa [\delta^Y u^O + u^Y] \quad \text{and} \tag{11.9}$$

$$U^O = \kappa [\delta^O u^Y + u^O]. \tag{11.10}$$

where $\kappa = \dfrac{1}{1-\delta^Y \delta^O}$

---

3. The calculations follow from noting that if

$$u^Y = \delta^Y u^O + u^Y \quad \text{and} \quad u^O = \delta^O u^Y + u^O \tag{7}$$

$$U^Y = \delta^Y (\delta^O U^Y + u^O) + u^Y \quad \text{so} \tag{8}$$

$$U^Y = \kappa [\delta^Y u^O + u^Y] \quad \text{and} \tag{9}$$

$$U^O = \kappa [\delta^O u^Y + u^O]. \tag{10}$$

where $\kappa = \dfrac{1}{1-\delta^Y \delta^O}$.

and therefore

$$U^Y = \kappa \left(\delta^O u^Y + u^O \right) \qquad (11.11)$$

and

$$U^O = \kappa(\delta^O u^Y + u^O) \qquad (11.12)$$

where

$$\kappa \equiv \frac{1}{1 - \delta^Y \delta^O} \qquad (11.13)$$

Note that if either δ^Y or δ^O is 0, $\kappa = 1$.

We now have all of the ingredients to make some observations.

Too Many Educated People? The Optimal Choices of ψ and e

The function ψ maps education levels e to the fraction of the young who are educated ψ. Since ψ is by assumption strictly increasing, there is a one-to-one mapping between e and ψ, so when studying optimal choices, we can look at either variable. To study the effect of increasing ψ, we first note the following derivative:

$$\frac{\partial u^Y}{\partial \psi} = d(W - R) + (1 - d)cy - y + [\psi (1 - d) c + (1 - \psi)] \frac{\partial y}{\partial \psi} \qquad (11.14)$$

When W and d are very high relative to y, as would be expected to be the case in many poor countries, we see that $(\partial u^Y)/(\partial \psi)$ is positive. This is not surprising. An increase in the general education levels should be expected to benefit the young more than the old. Regarding the old, it is easy to see that

$$\frac{\partial U^O}{\partial \psi} = \kappa \left(\delta^O \frac{\partial u^Y}{\partial \psi} + \frac{\partial u}{\partial \psi} dR \right). \qquad (11.15)$$

If the old care about the young, and if $(\partial u^Y)/(\partial \psi)$ is large (which we just argued may be the case when W is large), then $(\partial U^O)/(\partial \psi)$ would be positive. This is the case even when $R = 0$. Hence we see that if the old are decision makers and they care for their offspring, they will set ψ as large as possible. We repeat here that this may be the same motivation behind why parents in many rural but affluent countries pay for school systems knowing full well that their offspring will leave and not directly help their communities.

If both $(\partial u^\gamma)/(\partial \psi)$ and $(\partial y)/(\partial \psi)$ are positive over their relevant domains, we obtain the conclusion that the old would prefer very high levels of education, almost to the exclusion of monies spent on roads.

To check our modeling, we ask under what conditions this would both be true and be violated. Well, if $y = f(G - e, (1 - d)\psi)$, an increase in ψ, and equivalently e, will have a negative effect via the first argument and a positive effect through the second effect. This can be seen by writing

$$\frac{\partial y}{\partial \psi} = (-f_h + [1 - d]fe)\, \frac{\partial e}{\partial \psi}. \tag{11.16}$$

In a poor country, each argument of f will most probably be small, so the usual Inada conditions will work on each argument in opposite directions. When the stock of infrastructure is very small relative to the stock of educated people, one would expect the increase in ψ to reduce y via its effect on decreasing the infrastucture level even further.

This, of course, begs another question. Despite the absurdly low levels of educated people in the country, are there too many of them relative to the size of their country? I believe that this is an issue that Yoweri Museveni has spoken about often. High education spending takes away from other infrastructure spending, which may not be optimal for the poor country with small stocks of both educated people and roads and infrastructure. One of the principle reasons for the brain drain is the lack of adequate compensation for skilled workers in their home countries relative to being abroad. The existence of a brain drain suggests that there is a larger stock of human capital than may be optimal for the economy. Perhaps there should be more spending on roads.

As an aside, we note that the above begs a bigger question. Are there too many people in Africa? In particular, are there too many people in the country relative to the "optimal" stock of people given the countries' endowments and ability to find jobs for them? Interesting work on this has been done by Lant Pritchett (2004).

Too Big a Brain Drain?

Suppose that all parameters excluding d are fixed. Does an increase in d help or hurt individuals in the economy? If either the source nation or the receiving nation can increase the rate of brain drain, everything else remaining the same, would this be for the better or for the worse?

First, note that since $y = f(G - e[1 - d]e)$, we have

$$\frac{\partial y}{\partial d} = -f_e. \tag{11.17}$$

An increase in the rate of the brain drain d has the obvious negative effect on the public-goods provision. The effect of the increase in d on the utility of the young will be made up of two parts. The first is via the effect of reduced levels of public goods on the utilities of the young who are educated but nondrained and the uneducated. The second is the increased probability of draining, which affects only the educated, since only they drain, resulting in an increase in the income from being educated and drained versus educated and not drained. These two effects are represented in the two bracketed expressions in the equations below:

$$\frac{\partial u^Y}{\partial d} = -\{f_e[\psi(1-d)c+(1-\psi)]\}+\{[\psi(W-R)]-[\psi cy]\}. \tag{11.18}$$

Clearly, if the wage of those who drain W is sufficiently large as we expect it to be, and if ψ is sufficiently large, then the first term in square brackets will dominate the other two, so that increasing d will have a net positive effect.

Regarding the effect on the old of an increase in the rate of the brain drain d, there are three effects of the model: the effect of d on the utility of the young whom they care about, the effect of d on the remittances the old will receive, and the effect of d on the public-goods provision y, which is related to the income that the old receive. These three effects are represented by the three terms on the right of the derivative equation:

$$\frac{\partial u^O}{\partial d} = \kappa\left(\delta^O\frac{\partial u^Y}{\partial d}+\psi R+\frac{\partial y}{\partial d}\right). \tag{11.19}$$

We have already argued that it is plausible to believe that the young would benefit from an increase in the brain drain—in particular, that the first term above, $(\partial u^Y)/(\partial d)$ may be positive. Similarly, the effect on remittances of an increase in d is positive and will be a benefit to the old. The one negative term is the last one, the effect of the increase in d on the public-goods provision. This will be negative, because an increase in d implies a reduction in the stock of the educated remaining within the country, which lowers the public-goods provision. If this is small relative to the other effects, then the net effect of an increase in d will be positive.

Quantifying Remittances

An interesting feature of the African brain drain is the desire by many Africans to maintain ties to their home countries. It is impressive to see the large number of Africans who send their savings in the United States to build houses slowly in their home countries for when they return. Indeed, we suspect that one can measure a migrant's savings by the height to which the building has been completed. Clearly this is a suboptimal use of the migrant's savings, since the house is not being used while the migrant is adding to it—a process that may take decades. Many cities in Mexico have now offered mortgage financing to migrants to enable them complete their houses and pay off the debts over time.

Further, for the more affluent members of the African diaspora, there are now springing up gated communities in many western African cities, which look and feel like equivalent gated communities in the United States. These cater not only to the emerging African middle classes but also to the large African diaspora living abroad.

For numerical values of the size of the remittances, there is a wide range of estimates and potentially serious problems of undercounting. Let us use Ghana as an example. Despite the high brain drain from Ghana documented earlier, official figures show only $99 million in remittances in 2005. Kenya, which has about the same-size brain drain, has more than five times that amount of remittances. It is hard to believe that Kenyan emigrants have a propensity to remit that is five times higher, although we have no direct evidence to contradict it. However, there are other reasons to think that the official data underestimate the true size of remittance receipts, a significant share of which are transmitted by travelers or through other informal channels. Correcting for these informal channels, some Bank of Ghana studies put the figure as high as $1 billion.[4]

Even with these undercounting problems, remittances in official data are still a significant part of foreign-exchange earnings in African countries, as shown in table 11.11. On average, remittances amount to 81.0 percent of foreign aid, 13.0 percent of exports, and 3.2 percent of GDP (the distribution is skewed, so medians are lower).

Regardless of the exact value of the remittances, there may be considerable scope for increasing remittance flows by reducing transaction costs associated with sending remittances.

Mexican banks and municipalities seem to be moving in this direction to capture more remittances from Mexican migrants living in the United States.

Would the Central Planner or Government Also Advocate a Brain Drain?

The computations above have taken into account the perspective of the representative old person and the representative young person. We cast this

---

4. See p. 5 of the Ghana Country Study by the Centre of Migration, Policy and Society (RO2CS008) by Adam Higazi, Oxford University.

Table 11.11   Remittances by Country in Sub-Saharan Africa

	Remittances received in million U.S. $, 2005	Remittances as ratio to foreign aid, 2004	Remittances as ratio to exports, 2004	Remittances as percent of GDP, 2005
Benin	63	17%	8%	1.5
Botswana	125	238%	2%	1.2
Burkina Faso	50	8%		1.0
Cameroon	11	1%		0.1
Cape Verde	137	81%	38%	13.9
Comoros	12	49%		3.1
Republic of the Congo	11	13%	0%	0.2
Côte d'Ivoire	160	104%	2%	1.0
Ethiopia	174	7%	8%	1.6
Gabon	6	16%	0%	0.1
Gambia	58	99%	34%	12.6
Ghana	99	6%	2%	0.9
Guinea	42	15%	5%	1.3
Guinea-Bissau	28	37%	34%	9.3
Kenya	524	58%	9%	2.8
Lesotho	327	348%	46%	22.5
Madagascar	3	0%	1%	0.1
Malawi	1	0%		0.0
Mali	155	27%	13%	2.9
Mauritania	2	1%		0.1

(continued)

Table 11.11 (*continued*)

	Remittances received in million U.S. $, 2005	Remittances as ratio to foreign aid, 2004	Remittances as ratio to exports, 2004	Remittances as percent of GDP, 2005
Mauritius	215	567%	6%	3.4
Mozambique	57	5%	3%	0.9
Namibia	16	9%	1%	0.3
Niger	60	11%	11%	1.8
Nigeria	3329	396%	6%	3.4
Rwanda	21	2%	5%	1.0
São Tomé and Principe	1	3%		1.4
Senegal	633	60%	29%	7.7
Seychelles	11	68%	1%	1.6
Sierra Leone	2	7%	11%	0.2
South Africa	658	85%	1%	0.3
Sudan	1016	159%	37%	3.7
Swaziland	81	76%	4%	3.0
Tanzania	16	1%	0%	0.1
Togo	148	292%	24%	6.7
Uganda	476	33%	36%	5.5
Sum	8728			
Average		81%	13%	3.2
Median		22%	6%	1.4

Source: World Development Indicators.

in terms of someone choosing, from an individual perspective, whether to advocate a brain drain. When we were analyzing the utilities of these representative individuals, we took into full account the effect of the brain drain on the provision of public goods. If we take the central planner as someone who cares about the utilities of representative old and young people, as described above, then it should be clear that the central-planner solution will look a whole lot like the individual optimization exercises for the young and old described above.

We now consider the perspective of a national government. On the one hand, we could think of governments as aspiring to optimize, as does the central planner. After all, this is what the governments should be doing. In that case, by caring about the utilities of the local citizenry, the governments may advocate the brain drain as outlined above.

On the other hand, one could argue that the goal of government is to optimize the output within the economy. Governments may care only about the output within the economy and not care at all about the utility of their citizens who successfully eventually migrate out of the country, and it may also not be too concerned about the utility of the parents of such emigrated people.

There are a number of ways of computing the output in the economy. The narrowest definition would be to define the objective of the governments to be that of optimizing the size of the public good y. If that is the case, then it should be fairly clear that such governments will not advocate a brain drain, since, in our model, the public goods increase with the number of educated people who remain in the economy. However, a very slightly less narrow view includes the remittances of migrants back to the home economy. If we use this definition of the objective of a government, we will conclude that the government itself may want to encourage the brain drain.

One often hears, especially in African press statements, that the government is wasting its money since it spends on students only to have them leave; those who benefit from the schooling provided by the government ought to pay back to the government the value of those benefits. In the literature on the rates of return to education, the present value of the cost of university education for the typical person is something like six times the GDP per capita of the economy. Let X denote the annual remittances of the typical person who is drained out of the economy. The net present value of this flow is about 20X at 5 percent rate of interest. Hence, so long as $X > 6/20 = 0.3$, the remittances exceed the cost of education. So long as the remittances of the typical person exceed 30 percent of GDP per capita, the remittances exceed cost. The World Bank estimated Ghana's GDP per capita at $450 in 2005, so 30 percent of this would be $135 per year.

We mentioned earlier that some put the remittances at well above the official estimates. However, let us take the official statistics, at $44 million, for Ghana and assume that these are correct (we believe they are underestimated by a factor of 10). Let N be our estimate for the number of people in the brain drain. The per-capita remittances using the official remittance figure would then be $44 million$/N$. Table 11.3 suggests that N is a little more than 71,000 Ghanaians in the West. This implies a per-capita remittance of more than $600, which is well more than 30 percent of GDP per capita.

In other words, on a straight-cash basis, remittances exceed costs of training tertiary-educated brain-drained citizens, even under exceptionally conservative assumptions.

We could go farther. Suppose that the government starts charging tuition fees. The universities are currently exceptionally overcrowded, with insufficient seats for those who would like to enter; for those who are in the system, there are large classrooms and "perchers" in dorm rooms (students staying in dorm rooms of friends unofficially). This would make the net return to government even higher, since the cost of educating students would be lower.

Then there is the new phenomenon of private universities in Africa. Although they currently do not hold large numbers of students, they are poised to become much more important in the higher education of African students. Education remains one of the most closed markets, especially in the third world. There is floating around now the idea of opening up education markets in which outsiders could compete—after all, the provision of education is a service that perhaps should be subject to the same free-trade rules as physical-commodity trades.

ROBUSTNESS SECTION. One could ask what types of considerations could make the analysis above incorrect. Some come to mind.

1. *Unequal access to the school system.* One could imagine a situation in which only the elite class has access to higher education. The elite class may therefore advocate a brain drain, while the rest of the people without access would prefer that the educated not be allowed to drain away.

In many African countries, the education system is perceived to be on the whole meritorious, at least the progression from secondary school to the universities. In that progression, there are usually nationwide examinations administered centrally and therefore with somewhat small room for abuse.

If it is the rich who have access to the school system, then the modeling assumption that is harmed will be the assumption that the probabilities of being different types of young—educated and drained, educated and nondrained and noneducated—may depend on wealth. However, even in this case, the basic structure above remains the same; what changes are the values of the probabilities. One would have to rework the numbers to see the total effect. At this time, we believe that our basic results continue to hold and in particular that there will continue to be a push toward more brain drain.

Some entry points into the school system are restricted by income; primary schooling, for example, is difficult for the very poor. On the other hand, being poor often translates to lower voting power. Our result would then say that the voting system would result in encouragement of the brain drain.

2. *Remarks on the calculations.* In our computations, we suggest that it may be optimal to set d to 1, in which case the provision of public goods could be zero, if a positive stock of the educated within the country is required for positive public-goods production. One may object to the implication of zero consumption. We do stress here that since we model utilities as linear (everything is in terms of incomes), it may be appropriate to think of y as a public good, as opposed to thinking of y as a consumption good. Furthermore, one would expect the government to impose restrictions if populations started leaving in such numbers that the remainder begins to approach zero. The Rawlings administration imposed exit visas during the height of the economic decline at the beginning of his rule of Ghana, and the communist Eastern Bloc countries have had them in place for a long period of their history.

If we do change and move to a concave utility function with utility of public goods being equal to zero, how would things change? The basic insight would remain the same. There would be pressure to increase the drainage levels. There would also be pressure to make sure that public goods remain at a minimal level. The purpose of our calculation is just to emphasis the positive aspects, which are sometimes lost in discussions of the African brain drain.

TERTIARY VERSUS PRIMARY AND SECONDARY EDUCATION. One may ask how our analysis relates to the debate on spending on tertiary as opposed to secondary and primary education. As a large proportion of the migrants are tertiary-educated, we have focused primarily on this group in our computations. There is a large literature on the returns to various types of education. That literature has often stated the higher internal rates to lower levels of education relative to tertiary (see, for example Psacharopoulos and Patrinos, 2004). We are not aware of any papers in that literature that include the possibility of emigration and the resulting remittances in their computations; this is an interesting exercise we hope that we or others are able to take up in the near future.

Measuring the Intangible Benefits of the Brain Drain

We have mentioned aspects of the early brain drain and how they assisted in the development of writing in the local languages, the establishment of formal educational institutions, and the production of the independence leaders. Given the history of many African countries—slavery, then colonialism and poverty—perhaps the optimal strategy for the national planners was to send as many people abroad to have a percentage come back with newly acquired skills, human capital, and simply knowledge about how things are done overseas. We believe that was indeed a desire of many of the postindependence leaders, who encouraged students and educated people to travel abroad to learn how foreign economies are run.

When traveling to many western African cities, it is obvious to many observers that a lot of new economic activity is being generated by people who have lived abroad for a long time and then returned to their home countries. Even more interesting are those who maintain residences both in their home countries and in the countries they drained to. Finally, there are those whose primary residence is abroad but who return to their home countries every year to assist in some way with economic development. Many have used the terminology "brain circulation" rather than "brain drain" to describe the current-day movement of educated Africans between their homes and the West.

One other argument that is often made about the brain drain is that it causes the loss of leadership of a vibrant middle class. The argument is that many of those who are drained away are the most vibrant and entrepreneurial members of their respective societies. If only they would stay in their home countries, they would be the engine of growth. Their mere presence would lead to the development of a vibrant middle class, who would insist on Western values, transparent government, and so on.

First, the exposure to outside ideas is itself an engine of growth. Having a significant portion of the population abroad means that those resident in the home countries are able to benefit via information flows, through visits, discussions, and so on, with those who have drained. Many of those who do initially drain often come back with new ideas to help develop their respective societies.

As has been stressed by the recent growth literature, ideas and knowledge form a big part of the engine of growth of nations. Independence leaders, who were initially brain-drained, realized this. Ghana had a scheme, started by Kwame Nkrumah, of what was called chartered flights. These were government subsidies to encourage Ghanaian youth in secondary schools or universities to visit the United Kingdom. Nkrumah said bluntly that he wanted his people to see how things were abroad to get an idea of where he wanted to take his country.

This circulation of brains helps in the diffusion of knowledge, which is precisely what is needed in our developing economies. Those who are part of the brain drain may be those who are the most adept at change—they, after all, are the ones who successfully migrated; perhaps they are better at implementing the change in their home country.

Some of the more exciting things going on in Ghana involve many of the drained/circulating brains. A returning Ghanaian expatriate, who had been educated at Swarthmore and then been in upper management at Microsoft, started a private high-quality university, Ashesi University. NYU has opened a study-abroad center in Ghana partially based at Ashesi. Another Ghanaian returnee from the brain drain started DataBank, one of Ghana's first investment banks. These examples are only anecdotal, but they also point to the need for more research into some of the intangible benefits of returning and circulating brain drainers.

Incentives to Form Human Capital and the Effect on Growth

Several papers (those by Oded Stark and coauthors, for example) have pointed out how, via the incentive effect on forming human capital, the possibility of a brain drain and subsequent higher wages can increase investments in human capital so much as to offset the negative effects of any brain drain.

Given the substantial apparent unemployment among graduates of universities in Ghana, it is clear that the potential to drain away is a huge incentive for many African students to work hard in school. African students have to overcome huge hurdles to get their education these days, even after they are admitted into the universities. These range from lack of textbooks, large class sizes, often distracted faculty who need to make ends meet with auxiliary activities, poorly maintained facilities, and so on. What keeps most of the students going is the prospect that they may land an opportunity abroad. If this prospect is closed too tightly, this may have an effect on the effort levels of students in the system and therefore the quality of the graduates of the school system. What is the value of a Kofi Annan in motivating Ghanaians?

The Brain Drain and the Quantity of Human Capital

The theoretical arguments that the brain drain could have a positive effect on total human-capital creation are well known. Most obviously, if the return to skills is increased by the chance at earning skilled wages abroad that are higher than those available at home, then the brain drain will create positive incentives to form human capital at home. This means that the brain drain will have offsetting effects on human capital residing in the home country: it will increase the total stock of human capital of home-country nationals, while shifting the composition of that stock toward those who reside outside the home country.[5]

In the standard infinite-horizon optimizing neoclassical growth model, with no mobility of human capital, agents invest in human capital until its marginal product is equal to the discount rate. Compared with this benchmark, an (exogenous) drain of human capital out of the country raises the marginal product of the human capital still left at home by making it scarcer. In the model, the higher marginal product of human capital would lead to more investment in human capital at home until its marginal product is once again driven down to equal the discount rate. In this simple benchmark model, the prediction is that brain drain would have zero effect on the stock of human capital left in the country—human-capital creation and brain drain cancel each other out exactly.

TESTING THE NET EFFECT ON HUMAN CAPITAL OF BRAIN DRAIN. We explore these predictions in a simple empirical framework. Let HD be skilled labor that stays at home, HF skilled labor that is abroad, and H total skilled labor ($= HD + HF$), all in stocks and all originating in the country in question. Then

$$dHD = dH - dHF \qquad (11.20)$$

where dHD means the change in skilled labor at home from 1990 to 2000. Divide through by H (initial value in 1990), so we have

$$\frac{dHD}{H} = \frac{dH}{H} - \frac{dHF}{H} \qquad (11.21)$$

Now, suppose that the formation of new skilled labor H is a positive function of the population growth rate but also of the possibility of emigration, because that raises the return to becoming skilled. So, suppose

$$\frac{dH}{H} = a + bn + c\frac{dHF}{H} \qquad (11.22)$$

where n is the growth rate of the whole population (or labor force), and c is positive if there is a positive incentive effect of brain drain on human-capital creation.

5. Beine, Docquier, and Rapoport (2001, 2003) are important previous works that also consider the positive theoretical effect of migration on human-capital creation and test these effects empirically in both human-capital accumulation and growth. We extend and update this work to develop the theoretical predictions more precisely and to cover many more countries with more up-to-date data.

To get to the equation that we will estimate, substitute (11.22) into (11.21):

$$\frac{dHD}{H} = a + bn + (c-1)\frac{dHF}{H} \qquad (11.23)$$

We will instrument for dHF/H to address reverse causality (such as omitted factors that might determine dH/H but also raise dHF/H). The interesting thing will be whether the coefficient on dHF/H is greater than -1 (because c is positive).

We measure dHF/H and dHD/H as the change in the stock of tertiary-educated nationals outside and inside the country, respectively, from 1990 to 2000, divided by the total stock of tertiary-educated population in 1990. The instruments for dHF/H are variables that we think are likely to influence brain drain to the main destination countries (United States, United Kingdom, and France): a dummy for former colony of Great Britain, a dummy for former colony of France, the log of distance from the United States, the log of distance from France, the log of distance from the United Kingdom. We also include the log of population size in 1990 as an instrument for brain drain, since small countries are usually less constrained by restrictions on immigration into the destination country. The first-stage regression is shown in table 11.12.

Table 11.12 First-Stage Regression for Brain Drain

	dHf/H
Log of distance from France	0.022
	(0.22)
Log of distance from United Kingdom	0.055
	(0.53)
Log of distance from United States	−0.107
	(2.43)*
Log of population in 1990	−0.053
	(4.17)**
Constant	1.331
	(3.80)**
Observations	157
R^2	0.26
F-statistic	11.74
P value of F-statistic	0.0000

Note: Robust t statistics in parentheses. * significant at 5%; ** significant at 1%.

The most powerful instruments seem to be the distance from the United States and the population size. The instruments do a reasonable job of explaining the variation in dHF/H with an R^2 of 0.26 and pass the weak-instruments test with an F-statistic of 11.74, so we move to the second stage.

The second-stage regression in two-stage least squares for equation (11.23) is depicted in table 11.13. The coefficient on dHF/H is actually positive, indicating that brain drain increases the stock of skilled people left at home. The instruments pass the overidentifying-restrictions test, although just barely. The coefficient on brain drain is very imprecisely estimated, so we cannot reject that it is zero. We can reject that the coefficient is -1, which is excluded by the 95 percent confidence interval for the coefficient. Since the coefficient is equal to $c - 1$, this is equivalent to c being significantly greater than zero, indicating that we do have evidence of a positive effect of the brain drain on human-capital formation. The actual estimate of c is 1.343, which is imprecisely estimated but is significantly greater than zero. So, in summary, the simple theory sketched above predicted a coefficient ($c - 1$) of zero, and the data do nothing to reject that prediction.

These results are only about the quantity of total brains. There are also good reasons to think that brain drain will have a positive effect on the

Table 11.13   Second-Stage Regression for Effect of Brain Drain on Domestic Brain Gain

	dHd/H
dHf/H	0.343
	(0.56)
Population growth	1.83
	(3.38)**
Constant	0.234
	(1.27)
Observations	157
Hansen J-statistic for overidentification (chi squared with 3 df)	7.318
P-value for J-statistic	0.0624
Coefficient of c	1.343
	(2.19)*

Note: Robust z-statistics in parentheses. * significant at 5%; ** significant at 1%.

quality of skills attained. True human capital includes both the quantity of educated people and the quality of skills they have gained. Any plausible production function for human-capital quality would have student effort as a complementary factor. So, if brain drain increases the incentive for students to work hard, then brain drain would raise the quality as well as the quantity of skills produced.

Brain Drain and Growth Regressions

A more indirect way to test the effect of brain drain is to assess its effect on economic growth. Standard growth accounting would yield one component of growth (dY/Y) explained by human-capital accumulation. Assuming neutral technical progress (A) and estimating shares from U.S. data of 0.3 for physical capital (K), 0.23 for human capital (measured as college-educated persons) at home (HD), and 0.47 for unskilled labor (L), we get the following standard growth-accounting equation:

$$\frac{dY}{Y} = \frac{dA}{A} + 0.3\frac{dK}{K} + 0.23\frac{dHD}{HD} 0.47\frac{dL}{L} \qquad (11.24)$$

Manipulating the equations above, we get an expression for dHD/HD as a function of a brain-drain variable:

$$\frac{dHD}{HD} = \frac{dH}{HD} - \frac{dHF}{HD} \qquad (11.25)$$

If we assumed that there was zero positive incentive effect on human-capital accumulation, then the predicted loss in growth caused by brain drain is then

$$\text{Loss in growth} = -0.23\frac{dHF}{HD} \qquad (11.26)$$

The predicted loss of growth based on the growth-accounting calculation is quite large in some countries (see table 11.14).

We can enter the brain-drain term (dHF/HD) on the right-hand side of equation (11.26) into a growth regression for all countries with available data and see whether it has the predicted growth effect.

The results of the growth regression may also capture more indirect ways by which brain drain could have a positive or negative effect. Brain drain could affect any of the other components of growth accounting, such as physical capital accumulation or technical change, and hence we could possibly get a coefficient that is more negative than −0.23. This approach is also more robust if there is mismeasurement of total human capital H

Table 11.14   Top 15 Countries with Largest Hypothetical
Loss in Annual Growth from Brain Drain according to
Growth Accounting

	Growth loss per annum for 1990–2000
Guyana	3.4%
Jamaica	2.8%
Haiti	2.8%
Trinidad and Tobago	2.1%
Cape Verde	1.8%
Gambia	1.5%
Bahamas	1.3%
Sierra Leone	1.3%
Mozambique	1.2%
Fiji	1.1%
Barbados	1.0%
Liberia	1.0%
Ghana	0.9%
Angola	0.8%
Suriname	0.6%

or if the skills that are draining have a different contribution to growth from those that stay at home (because of selective migration, as would be predicted by many theories). And, of course, the effect on growth is really the bottom line for whether brain drain has a negative effect on countries' economies. For all of these reasons, we supplement the exercise above with growth regressions.

When we do so, we find no negative effect of brain drain on growth. First, we do ordinary least squares. Under the ridiculously heroic assumption that all other factors that influence growth are orthogonal to brain drain, we can check the simple correlation—and we find there is none (table 11.15). We then add a variety of standard controls to the growth regression, including initial schooling. The results are fairly conventional, with "good policy" (specifically openness) and some measure of initial schooling (secondary schooling in this case) having a positive effect. Again, the brain drain shows no significant negative effect. In both regressions, we can reject the predicted coefficient on brain drain of -0.23.

We failed to find any effect of tertiary enrollment on growth. Our measure may be very noisy or otherwise flawed, but it is not so easy to establish

Table 11.15   Growth Regressions on Brain Drain and Other Controls
(Ordinary Least Squares)

	growth90_03	growth90_03	growth90_03
Brain drain	0.0002442		−0.004
	(0.22)		(−1.28)
Log income per capita, 1990		−0.009	−0.009
		(2.02)*	(2.00)*
Primary enrollment, 1990		0.0001391	0.0001354
		(1.10)	(1.08)
Secondary enrollment, 1990		0.0003832	0.0004129
		(2.96)**	(3.06)**
Tertiary enrollment, 1990		−0.0002724	−0.0003343
		(1.86)	(1.99)*
Openness variable, 1990		0.013	0.014
		(3.35)**	(3.25)**
Constant	0.011	0.05	0.053
	(2.83)**	(1.92)	(1.94)
Observations	152	87	86
R^2	0.000	0.190	0.200

Robust t-statistics in parentheses. * significant at 5%; ** significant at 1%.

the link between skills and growth. Hence, it is even less surprising that the brain drain is still insignificant in this regression.

We also explore possible reverse causality by doing two-stage least squares, using the same instruments as above. Again, the simple bivariate association fails to establish any effect of brain drain on growth, and the regression passes the tests for weak instruments and for overidentifying restrictions (table 11.16). Brain drain is still insignificant in the IV regressions with the full set of controls (with a much smaller sample). We again reject the predicted coefficient on brain drain of -0.23. Unfortunately, instrument problems bedevil this second regression, with the regression performing poorly on both weak-instruments and overidentifying-restrictions tests. However, coefficients did not shift much from the ordinary-least-squares regression, and we are not sure that IV is even required to address reverse causality problems from growth to brain drain. If poor growth caused brain drain, we would have expected the relationship to be much more negative in ordinary least squares than in IV. As it was, we found no significant negative effect in ordinary least squares in the first place.

Table 11.16   Two-Stage Least Squares Growth Regression Instrumenting
for Brain Drain

	growth90_03	growth90_03
Brain drain	0.000397	−0.005
	(0.09)	(−0.98)
Log income per capita, 1990		−0.009
		(2.08)*
Openness variable, 1990		0.015
		(3.41)**
Primary enrollment, 1990		0.000134
		−1.13
Secondary enrollment, 1990		0.000447
		(3.19)**
Tertiary enrollment, 1990		−0.00041
		(−1.95)
Constant	0.011	0.056
	(1.94)	(2.00)*
Observations	149	83
Hansen *J*-statistic (overidentification test of all instruments)	1.476	8.819
Chi-sq(3) *P* value	0.68777	0.03179
First-stage *F*-statistic	5.97	1.98
P value of first stage	0.0002	0.1068

Note: Instruments are Log of distances to United States, United Kingdom, and France; log of population in 1990. Robust *z*-statistics in parentheses. * significant at 5%; ** significant at 1%.

The bottom line, with the caveats noted above, is that we fail to find any evidence for a negative effect of brain drain either on the stock of human capital remaining in the country or on the country's growth rate.

Conclusions

We have provided some remarks on the question of the brain drain with particular reference to Africa and using Ghana as a case study of effects on individuals. Of course, much more work needs to be done in firming up many of the conjectures made.

However, we think we can make some evaluation of the brain drain based on our results. We fail to find any negative effect of brain drain on the stock of skills remaining in the source country, suggesting that skill-creation incentives offset the loss of skills one for one. We fail to find any negative effect on growth. In contrast to the zero results for the usual predicted negative effects of brain drain, we find many reasons to think that individuals are better off because of brain drain, including both the migrants and their families back in the source countries. Our back-of-the-envelope calculation for Ghana suggests that the present value of remittances more than covers the cost of educating a brain drainer. We also suggest some positive intangible effects, although these are admittedly much more speculative. On balance, therefore, theory and empirics suggest that the ability of some people in the country to go abroad and form part of the brain drain (and circulation) has had a net positive effect on individuals from the source country. In short, based on our results, we think the brain drain is good for Africa.

References

Amoako, K. Y. 2005. *Transforming Africa: An Agenda for Action.* UN Economic Commission for Africa.

Beine, Michel, Frédéric Docquier, and Hillel Rapoport. 2001. "Brain Drain and Economic Growth: Theory and Evidence." *Journal of Development Economics* 64, no. 1: 275–89.

———. 2003. "Brain Drain and LDCs' Growth: Winners and Losers." IZA Discussion Paper 819. Bonn: Forschungsinstitut zur Zukunft der Arbeit.

Clemens, Michael. 2007. "Do Visas Kill? Health Effects of African Health Professional Emigration." Center for Global Development Working Paper 114. March.

Commission for Africa. 2005. "Our Common Interest."

Docquier, Frédéric, and Abdeslam Marfouk. 2005. "International Migration by Educational Attainment (1990–2000)—Release 1.1." Update of World Bank Policy Research Working Paper 3381. Washington, DC: World Bank.

Docquier, Frédéric, and Hillel Rapoport. 2004. "Skilled Migration: The Perspective of Developing Countries." World Bank Policy Research Working Paper 3382. Washington, DC: World Bank.

Faini, R. 2006. "Remittances and Brain Drain." IZA Discussion Paper Series 214. Institute for the Study of Labor, Bonn.

Hinchliffe, K. 1987. *Higher Education in Sub-Saharan Africa.* London: Croom Helm.

Lucas, Robert E. B. 2005. *International Migration Regimes and Economic Development.* Northampton, MA: Edward Elgar.

———. 2006. "Migration and Economic Development in Africa: A Review of Evidence." *Journal of African Economies* 15, no. 2: 337–95.

Manning, C. 2007. "Brain Drain and Brain Gain: A Survey of Issues, Outcomes and Policies in the Least Developed Countries (LDCs)." Study prepared for UNCTAD as a background paper for the Least Developed Countries Report 2007. Geneva: UNCTAD.

McWilliam, H. O. A. 1959. *The Development of Education in Ghana: An Outline.* London: Longman.

Mountford, Andrew. 1997. "Can a Brain Drain Be Good for Growth in the Source Economy?" *Journal of Development Economics* 53, no. 2: 287–303.

Physicians for Human Rights. 2004. "An Action Plan to Prevent Brain Drain: Building Equitable Health Systems in Africa." Boston: Physicians for Human Rights.

Pritchett, L. 2004. "Boom Towns and Ghost Countries: Geography, Agglomeration, and Population Mobility." Center for Global Development Working Paper 36.

Psacharopoulos, G., and H. Patrinos. 2004. "Returns to Investment in Education: A Further Update." *Education Economics* 12, no. 2: 111–34.

Stark, Oded. 2004. "Rethinking the Brain Drain." *World Development* 32, no. 1: 15–22.

Stark, Oded, Christian Helmenstein, and Alexia Prskawetz. 1997. "A Brain Gain with a Brain Drain." *Economics Letters* 55, no. 2: 227–34.

———. 1998. "Human Capital Depletion, Human Capital Formation, and Migration: A Blessing or a Curse?" *Economics Letters* 60, no. 3: 363–67.

Stark, Oded, and Yong Wang. 2002. "Inducing Human Capital Formation: Migration as a Substitute for Subsidies." *Journal of Public Economics* 86, no. 1: 29–46.

UN Conference on Trade and Development. 2007. "The Least Developed Countries Report: Knowledge, Technological Learning, and Innovation for Development.

UN Millennium Project. 2005. "Investing in Development: A Practical Plan to Achieve the Millennium Development Goals." Main report.

World Bank. 2006. "Global Economic Prospects 2006: Economic Implications of Remittances and Migration." Washington, DC: World Bank.

World Bank and IMF. 2005. "Global Monitoring Report."

———. 2007. "Global Monitoring Report."

Indian Template: Taxation

12

Taxation and Skilled Indian Migration to the United States
Revisiting the Bhagwati Tax

JOHN McHALE

Between 1990 and 2000, the number of Indian-born residents of the United States rose from 450,000 to just more than 1 million. This diaspora is rich in human capital. Of the population ages 25 to 64, 40 percent had attained bachelor's degrees and a further 40 percent had graduate degrees. Their total income is estimated to have surpassed $40 billion in 2000 (equivalent to roughly 10 percent of Indian GDP in that year), and they paid an estimated $8 billion in U.S. income taxes and a further $2.5 billion in Social Security taxes. Although inferring India's fiscal loss resulting from the absence of this population from the domestic tax base is not straightforward, it is estimated to be between 0.2 percent and 0.6 percent of Indian GDP (Desai, Kapur, and McHale, 2004). Of course, the U.S.-resident Indian diaspora is an outlier in terms of its concentration of human capital. However, many other countries with far lower concentrations have far larger *shares* of their total tertiary-educated populations living abroad. While it is estimated that 4.2 percent of the total tertiary-educated Indian-born stock were living in Organisation for Economic Co-operation and Development (OECD) countries in 2000, this number was 14.2 percent for Mexico, 14.8 percent for the Philippines, and an astounding 82.5 percent for Jamaica (Docquier and Marfouk, 2004).

Following a series of analytical and policy papers by Jagdish Bhagwati and others in the 1970s, the idea of imposing some form of

This chapter draws heavily on previous joint work with Mihir Desai and Devesh Kapur. Of course, they are in no way responsible for any errors in analysis or opinions set forth here. Arvind Panagariya and Mihir Desai, my discussants at the conference, provided valuable advice for improving the chapter. I also received many useful suggestions from the conference participants. I owe a particular debt to the editors, Jagdish Bhagwati and Gordon Hanson, for their unstinting support and advice.

emigration-related tax on such human-capital-rich diasporas was widely debated.[1] But the proposal ran into a sea of objections—practical and principled—and the understandable vested interests of the would-be tax bases. The tax seems to have fallen from the policy agenda during the 1980s and 1990s. Even the Filipino government, which had long tried to tax its sizable diaspora, finally gave up in the late 1990s.

There are a number of reasons to take a fresh look at the Bhagwati tax.[2] First, as a result of the work of Docquier and Marfouk and others, we now have much better measures from census and survey data of the number of emigrants residing in rich countries (by at least crude skill aggregations). These data show skilled-emigration rates that are extremely high for a number of poor countries, especially for smaller countries located close to large, rich economies.[3] Skilled-emigration rates are highest for the Caribbean region (41 percent) and also high for much of Africa (27 percent for western Africa and 18 percent for eastern Africa). Moreover, the data show that skilled-emigration rates rose for a number of vulnerable regions during the 1990s—particularly in Africa—in part reflecting an increased bias toward skill-focused immigrant selection in rich countries. There is also reason to expect that rich-country immigration policies will become even more skill-focused in the coming decades, as governments grapple with the fiscal consequences of aging populations, fill gaps in their own educational output, and seek advantage in technologically advanced global industries (see Kapur and McHale, 2005a). The resulting absence of human capital will put enormous strains on poor-country tax bases.

Second, there is a renewed appreciation that poor countries face large investment gaps that trap them in poverty and that a significant part of the needed investment must come through the public sector (UN Millennium Project, 2005). Fiscal resources are needed to fund badly needed investments in education, health care, environmental protection, and infrastructure.

---

1. See, in particular, the volumes edited by Bhagwati (1976), Bhagwati and Partington (1976), and Bhagwati and Wilson (1989).
2. In reviewing the earlier literature, it has been both reassuring and occasionally discouraging to see any supposedly novel ideas being anticipated and extensively analyzed. I thus make no claim to novelty. My main objective in this chapter is to see if the balance of arguments has shifted with changes in global economics and politics and also to utilize new data on emigrant stocks for better quantifying of the possibilities for the tax. But, as noted by Bhagwati (1989, p. xix), the issue belongs to the "interface of economics with law, sociology, politics, and moral philosophy," so that my particular mixing of elements will have some inevitable idiosyncrasies.
3. Emigration rates are defined here as the number of emigrants of a given skill level as a share of the total number of workers at that skill level (i.e., emigrants and nonemigrants). Thus, this emigration rate measures relative stocks rather than the outflow rate per unit of time.

Although increased aid and debt relief are important parts of the solution, there is increasing interest in "innovative" mechanisms for making fiscal transfers to poor countries to help make up inevitable shortfalls (see, for example, the papers collected in Atkinson, 2005). This could be a sign that innovative, emigration-related fiscal instruments would get a more sympathetic hearing now than they did three decades ago.

Third, advances in international transportation and communication mean that a country's diaspora is now more connected to the country of origin than before. Many emigrants are now truly "transnationals," with enduring connections to both their new and former homes. These connections are strengthened by the increasing trend toward allowing dual nationality and expanding rights possessed by dual nationals.[4] An important component of Bhagwati's original case for emigrant taxation was the anomaly of what he called "representation without taxation" (Bhagwati, 1979). This is where emigrants receive the privileges of citizenship—right of travel, right of return, right to own property, right to vote, among others—without balancing tax obligations. Technological and political developments have almost certainly raised the willingness to pay for citizenship privileges, making emigrant taxation both more practical to implement and easier to defend on principle.[5]

The idea of connections also provides a useful way to think about the many effects of skilled emigration on poor countries—both good and bad. Borrowing a lens from sociologists, we can view individuals as being embedded in a web of intra- and international connections. Take the example of a would-be emigrant doctor. Before emigration, the doctor is connected to others in many ways: through product and factor markets (as a provider of health-care services), through family relationships (as a provider of income), through formal and informal "communities of practice"

---

4. Although I do think importance of transnationalism has increased, I certainly do not claim that it is a new phenomenon. Bhagwati was already pointing to it in the late 1970s: "We are, in a sense, back to the nomadic culture. We are born in one country, get educated there and elsewhere, work over a lifetime in several countries and may retire perhaps in a country different from the one we were born in. However, the most characteristic tendency of the modern, high skilled migrants in this complex world is that they typically tend to retain their nationality and their ethnic ties. The world has collapsed into a manageable geographical unit, with cheap transportation, conferences and foundation financed short term visits for virtually all those who fall in the highly skilled categories. Few change nationalities any longer, even when they change residence permanently. The professional and especially the academic world is truly international and the pressures of assimilation that led to the 'melting pot,' and the need to affirm loyalty to one's host nation by changing nationality, are no longer operative in anything like the same degree" (Bhagwati, 1979 [1983], p. 63).

5. A possible positive side effect of citizenship-based taxation is that governments have an incentive to provide better treatment to their nonresident citizens.

(as a member of an information-sharing social network of physicians), and through citizenship (as a voter and taxpayer). Some of these connections would strain but not break if the doctor emigrates. For example, the doctor may send remittances to remaining family members or continue to share information with former colleagues. The citizenship connection may or may not be broken, depending in part on the rules relating to dual citizenship in the two countries. Even where citizenship is retained, however, the taxpayer connection is almost always broken, since the vast majority of countries—the United States being the outstanding exception—do not attempt to tax the foreign-earned income of their nonresident citizens. The important questions for this chapter are (1) whether the fiscal connection *should* be broken, and (2) what instruments might be used for emigration-related fiscal transfers.

Answering these questions would have less urgency if we could be sure that skilled emigration did not hurt poor countries. For some sectors, of some countries, at some times, emigration has probably helped more than hurt.[6] The importance of the Silicon Valley Indian diaspora to the development of the Indian IT sector, the role of returning Irish in sustaining the "Celtic tiger" boom of the 1990s, and the Philippines' long-standing policy of encouraging emigration to generate remittances are possible examples of emigration yielding a net benefit to the domestic economy. But skilled emigration can also be devastating; witness the contribution of physician and nurse emigration to the health-system crises in a number of African countries. Even the Philippines, with its history of "exporting" health professionals, is now experiencing severe domestic shortages.

But the argument for emigrant taxation does not necessarily depend on poor countries actually being hurt by emigration. Bhagwati's original case for the tax put more emphasis on providing a more fair sharing of the overall gains from emigration, and—most important—the enduring obligations of citizenship. While I certainly agree with the broader justification, I do think that harm to poor countries appreciably strengthens the case, and it also justifies looking beyond the option of emigrant taxation to see what other instruments rich countries could use to compensate poor countries for emigration-related losses.

Absent Human Capital:
The U.S.-Resident Indian Diaspora

Table 12.1 provides estimates of skilled-emigration rates for 13 developing-country and emerging-market regions. The regions are listed in

6. See Kapur and McHale (2005b).

Table 12.1   Tertiary-Educated Emigration Rates to OECD Countries, by Region, Population 25 and Older

| | Tertiary-educated emigration rates | | | |
	1990	2000	Difference	2000/1990
Caribbean	41.4	40.9	−0.5	0.99
Western Africa	20.7	26.7	6.0	1.29
Eastern Africa	15.5	18.4	2.9	1.19
Central America	12.9	16.1	3.2	1.25
Central Africa	9.8	13.3	3.5	1.36
Southeastern Asia	10.3	9.8	−0.5	0.95
Northern Africa	6.8	6.2	−0.6	0.91
Western Asia	6.9	5.8	−1.1	0.84
South America	4.7	5.7	1.0	1.21
Southern Africa	6.9	5.3	−1.6	0.77
South-central Asia	4.0	5.1	1.1	1.28
Eastern Europe	2.3	4.5	2.2	1.96
Eastern Asia	4.1	4.3	0.2	1.05

Note: The emigration rate equals the number of emigrants divided by the domestically resident population plus the number of emigrants.
Source: Docquier and Marfouk (2004).

descending order of the emigration rate in 2000. The emigration rate used here is actually a *relative stock* concept: focusing on the population 25 and older, it gives the number of tertiary-educated emigrants as a percentage of the domestic tertiary-educated population *plus* the number of tertiary-educated emigrants.[7] Thus, it measures the percentage of a country's total tertiary-educated population that is absent from the country at a particular point in time. The table also shows the percentage-point change in the emigration rate between 1990 and 2000 and the ratio of the 2000 rate to the 1990 rate. The highest rate in both years is for the Caribbean region. Almost 41 percent of those 25 and older born in a Caribbean country with a tertiary education are living in an OECD country in 2000. While the emigration rate for the Caribbean region was stable through the 1990s, this rate rose quite dramatically for the two African regions that are next on the list. The rate rose from 20.7 percent to 26.7 percent for western Africa (a 29-percent increase) and from 15.5 percent to 18.9 percent for eastern Africa

7. See Docquier and Marfouk (2004) for details on the data and methods.

(a 19-percent increase). The rate was also high and rising for the Central America and central Africa regions. Of course, each of these regional rates hides a great deal of within-region diversity. For the Caribbean region, for example, the rate in 2000 ranged from a high of 82.5 percent in Jamaica to a low of 21.7 percent in the Dominican Republic.

My later illustrative examples of the revenue-raising potential of different fiscal instruments focus solely on the Indian emigrant stock living in the United States. Table 12.2 provides estimates of U.S.-specific emigration rates using the same methodology as table 12.1.[8] The table shows that the U.S-resident Indian-born population age 25 and older rose from about 304,000 in 1990 to almost 837,000 in 2000 (a 175-percent increase). A substantial number of these came on H-1B visas, the availability of which was greatly expanded in the latter part of the 1990s. Notwithstanding the increase in numbers, the U.S.-specific tertiary emigration rate remained relatively low in 2000, at 2.7 percent. As mentioned above, this compares with 14.2 percent for Mexico, 10.5 percent for the Philippines, and 78.6 percent for Jamaica. The Indian diaspora in the United States does stand out in terms of its human-capital intensity. Based on the 2000 U.S. Census, 80 percent of the Indian-born age 25 and older had tertiary degrees. This compares with 14 percent of Mexicans, 73 percent of Filipinos, and 45 percent of Jamaicans.

Table 12.3 provides more detail on the human-capital intensity of this absent Indian population. The table provides detailed educational attainment data for U.S.-born, Indian-born, and other foreign-born populations ages 18 to 64. A glance at relative graduate-level attainment makes the point dramatically. Roughly 40 percent of the Indian-born resident in the United States circa 2000 had graduate degrees, which compares with 9 percent for both the U.S.-born and other foreign-born populations. Table 12.4 shows how this educational attainment translates into income for those ages 18 to 64. The table shows the percentage of each of the three populations with an income falling into ranges that are based on given percentages of the U.S.-born median income for the relevant year. For example, we see that in 2000, 14 percent of the Indian-born population earned incomes more than 400 percent of the U.S.-born median income ($92,504), compared with 5 percent of the U.S.-born and 3 percent of the other foreign-born populations. Clearly, though relatively small in number, this Indian diaspora represents a potentially large absent tax base.

Although it is the size of this absent tax base that is of primary interest from the point of view of emigrant taxation, it is also useful to measure the fiscal loss to India from the absence of these individuals. Of course,

---

8. These estimates are based on the work of Carrington and Detragiache (1998) and Adams (2003).

Table 12.2 Emigration Rates to the United States, by Education Level, Population 25 and Older

Country of birth	U.S. resident population (≥25)				Emigration rate, 1990				Emigration rate, 2000			
	1990	2000	Change	% Chg.	Total	Primary	Secondary	Tertiary	Total	Primary	Secondary	Tertiary
Mexico	2,743,638	6,374,825	3,631,187	132	7.1	1.7	20.9	10.3	11.7	9.7	14.7	14.2
Philippines	728,454	1,163,555	435,101	60	2.2	0.1	4.4	6.6	3.5	0.6	2.2	10.5
India	304,030	836,780	532,750	175	0.1	0.1	0.1	1.1	0.2	0.1	0.2	2.7
China	404,579	846,780	442,201	109	0.1	0.1	0.1	1.4	0.1	0.1	0.2	2.2
El Salvador	263,625	619,185	355,560	135	10.2	1.6	66.6	26.1	19.5	11.0	53.4	28.3
Dominican Republic	187,871	527,520	339,649	181	5.9	0.6	29.7	14.2	11.4	5.0	29.8	19.9
Jamaica	159,913	449,795	289,882	181	11.8	0.4	23.4	67.5	25.0	4.5	29.0	78.6
Colombia	162,739	402,935	240,196	148	1.1	0.1	3.7	5.6	2.1	0.4	3.8	9.0
Guatemala	127,346	341,590	214,244	168	3.3	0.4	29.1	13.5	7.1	3.7	23.0	20.5
Peru	86,323	220,815	134,492	156	0.9	0.1	2.3	3.0	1.8	0.3	2.4	4.0
Pakistan	52,717	165,425	112,708	214	0.1	0.1	0.2	2.4	0.3	0.1	0.5	6.0
Brazil	53,904	154,250	100,346	186	0.1	0.1	0.7	0.6	0.2	0.1	0.5	1.1
Egypt	53,261	96,660	43,399	81	0.3	0.1	0.4	2.5	0.3	0.1	0.2	2.2
Bangladesh	12,385	69,180	56,795	459	0.1	0.1	0.1	0.6	0.1	0.1	0.3	2.2
Turkey	43,605	64,780	21,175	49	0.2	0.1	0.7	1.5	0.2	0.1	0.4	1.3
Indonesia	32,172	53,170	20,998	65	0.1	0.1	0.1	1.4	0.1	0.1	0.1	0.7
Sri Lanka	8,715	21,820	13,105	150	0.1	0.1	0.1	3.8	0.2	0.1	0.1	5.3
Sudan	2,496	12,730	10,234	410	0.1	0.1	0.1	1.8	0.1	0.1	0.3	3.3
Tunisia	2,816	5,555	2,739	97	0.1	0.1	0.3	1.6	0.1	0.1	0.2	1.3

Note: For each education category, the emigration rate equals the number of emigrants divided by the domestically resident population plus the number of emigrants.
Source: Carrington and Detragiache (1998) for 1990 and Adams (2003) for 2000. Both sources combine U.S Census data with Barro-Lee human-capital stock data.

Table 12.3   Educational Attainment for Native-, Indian, and Other Foreign-Born, Ages 25–64, 1990, 1994–2001

	Population shares					Graduate breakdown		
	<High school	High school graduate	Some college	Bachelor's degree	Graduate level	Master's	Professional	Ph.D.
Native-born								
1990	17	32	28	15	8	5	2	1
1994	13	36	27	16	8	6	1	1
1995	12	35	28	17	8	6	2	1
1996	12	35	28	18	8	6	1	1
1997	11	35	28	18	8	6	1	1
1998	11	35	28	18	8	6	1	1
1999	10	34	28	19	9	6	1	1
2000	10	34	29	19	9	7	1	1
2001	9	33	29	19	9	7	1	1
Indian-born								
1990	12	11	14	27	36	21	9	6
1994	8	9	15	35	32	17	11	4
1995	8	10	12	26	44	24	13	7
1996	8	13	12	30	38	27	7	4
1997	7	16	10	34	33	23	6	4
1998	6	14	15	35	31	22	5	3
1999	6	10	10	36	38	25	7	6

(continued)

369

Table 12.3 (continued)

	Population shares					Graduate breakdown		
	<High school	High school graduate	Some college	Bachelor's degree	Graduate level	Master's	Professional	Ph.D.
2000	6	8	9	35	41	27	6	8
2001	3	9	10	40	38	28	6	4
Other foreign-born								
1990	38	20	20	13	9	5	2	1
1994	34	25	17	16	8	5	2	2
1995	35	25	17	15	8	5	2	2
1996	35	23	18	15	8	5	2	2
1997	34	24	18	16	9	5	2	2
1998	33	25	16	17	9	6	2	2
1999	33	25	17	16	9	6	2	2
2000	32	26	17	16	9	5	2	2
2001	32	25	17	17	9	5	2	2

Note: The five columns under "population shares" display the percentage of native-born, Indian-born, or other foreign-born ages 25 to 64 living in the United States who have attained various levels of education for years 1990 and 1994–2001. For those who have attained "graduate level," a further breakdown by degree ty pe is provided in the three columns under "Graduate Breakdown."

Source: Desai, Kapur, and McHale (2004), based on data from IPUMS for 1990 and March CPS for 1994–2001.

370

Table 12.4   Income Distribution for Native-Born, Indian-Born, and Other
Foreign-Born, Ages 18–64, 1990, 1994–2001

		Population shares (as % of native-born median)				
	Median	0–50%	50–100%	100–200%	200–400%	>400%
Native-born						
1990	$20,293	33	17	27	18	4
1994	$19,836	31	19	28	18	4
1995	$20,100	30	20	28	18	5
1996	$20,626	30	20	29	17	4
1997	$21,418	30	20	29	17	4
1998	$21,580	30	20	29	16	4
1999	$22,826	30	20	30	16	4
2000	$23,126	30	20	29	16	5
2001	$23,925	29	21	30	16	4
Indian-born						
1990	$20,670	35	14	21	20	10
1994	$21,943	32	14	24	21	9
1995	$24,980	28	14	26	22	11
1996	$25,145	31	16	25	19	10
1997	$24,301	29	18	24	21	8
1998	$27,915	29	15	23	24	9
1999	$31,715	30	11	24	26	9
2000	$29,986	35	9	18	24	14
2001	$28,121	34	11	18	25	12
Other foreign-born						
1990	$14,483	39	21	23	13	4
1994	$13,053	42	23	21	11	3
1995	$13,803	41	24	21	11	4
1996	$13,562	42	24	22	10	3
1997	$13,729	41	24	22	10	3
1998	$14,443	40	25	21	10	4
1999	$14,816	41	26	21	9	3
2000	$15,510	40	26	21	11	3
2001	$16,084	37	26	23	10	3

Note: The second column shows the median incomes for native-born, Indian-born, or other
foreign-born ages 18 to 64 living in the United States for years 1990 and 1994–2001 in 2001 U.S.
dollars. The five columns under "population shares" display the percentage of native-born, Indian-
born, or other foreign-born ages 18 to 63 living in the United States for years 1990 and 1994–2001
that lie between various fractions and multiples of the median native-born income for that year.

Source: Desai, Kapur, and McHale (2004), based on data from IPUMS for 1990 and March CPS for
1994–2001.

the challenge is to calculate what they would earn if they were instead living and working in India and, based on those counterfactual earnings, what taxes would be paid. Mihir Desai, Devesh Kapur, and I (2008) have attempted this calculation. The most difficult part of this estimate is to produce a counterfactual earnings distribution. We use two methods, each of which has drawbacks. One method is to take the observed income distribution for this population and translate it into Indian incomes using an appropriate conversion factor. An upper bound is provided by the assumption that incomes are equalized between the two countries in purchasing-power parity terms, implying Indian incomes that are about one-fifth of U.S. incomes in dollar terms. This probably overstates the counterfactual Indian incomes for segments subject to visa constraints. It is straightforward to scale down the estimated distribution if we think that equalized purchasing power adjusted to real earnings assumption is unrealistic.[9]

Our second method is more computationally involved. We first econometrically estimate human-capital-based earnings and participation regressions using data from the 50th round (1993–1994) of the National Sample Survey. We then run the observed human-capital characteristics of the U.S.-resident Indian population through this model to obtain a counterfactual earnings distribution. We find that this method leads to substantially lower earnings estimates. Because of the selectivity of the emigrant stock, these econometrically based estimates may be biased downward.

To estimate lost tax revenues in India from emigration, we use the PPP-based method to estimate the counterfactual earnings of Indian emigrants in India. With the counterfactual earnings distribution in hand, the next step is to estimate the absence-related net fiscal loss. On the tax side, we calculate income-tax losses by running the counterfactual income through Indian income-tax schedules for the appropriate year, and we calculate indirect tax losses using estimates of indirect tax payments per unit of gross national income. On the expenditure side, we calculate expenditure savings by first identifying expenditure categories for which they are likely to be expenditure savings (essentially everything except interest payments and national defense) and then making an estimate of how much is saved for each individual. This latter step is unavoidably imprecise, and we use two fairly extreme assumptions to provide upper and lower bounds. First, we assume that government expenditure on an individual is proportional to his or her income. This means that the better-off individuals are better able to extract services from the government. To calculate the expenditure saving, we simply take expenditure per unit of income and multiply it by the counterfactual income estimate of the emigrant. Second, we assume that

9. See Desai, Kapur, and McHale (2004) for a further discussion of the limitations of this method.

everyone receives an equal share of expenditure, so that the expenditure saving is just equal to expenditure per person. Not surprisingly, use of this method leads to negligible expenditure-savings estimates given the small size of the emigrant stock relative to the large total Indian population.

What, then, is the absence-related net fiscal impact? Using our PPP-based method for estimating the counterfactual earnings distribution, we find that net fiscal loss is equal to 0.58 percent of Indian GDP using the per-capita method for calculating the expenditure savings and 0.24 percent when we use the income-based method.[10] Again, there are reasons to be concerned that this approach overestimates the emigration-induced tax loss. As a partial off-set to this fiscal loss, we estimate that the increased tax take resulting from remittances is on the order of about 0.1 percent of GDP. To the extent that the case for emigrant taxation depends on the loss to the poor-losing country, these numbers show that this one component of the overall loss is quite sizable, even for a case in which the emigrant stock is less than one-tenth of one percent of domestic population. But, as I argued above, the case for emigrant taxation can depend on more than just burden on those remaining behind.

Principles

Some candidate principles might guide the choice of emigration-related fiscal instruments. Four general principles are considered: the instrument should not impede freedom of international movement; it should be consistent with an efficient global allocation of skills; it should be fair to receiving countries, sending countries, and the emigrants themselves; and it should not impose an undue administrative burden or violate fundamental national and international laws.

Freedom of Movement

All restrictions on the freedom of movement between countries are prima facie unwelcome restrictions on liberty. Of course, there are more or less defensible reasons for such restrictions—keeping out threats to national security, protecting domestic jobs and wages, restricting the entry of those who are likely to be fiscal burdens, preventing the transmission of disease, sustaining domestic culture, and so on. These rationales have led to severe restrictions on international migration, and many are even denied the option of international travel.

10. The net fiscal loss is negligible when we use the model-based method to estimate the counterfactual distribution under either expenditure-saving assumption.

How much should we worry that emigrant taxes would further impede freedom of movement? One concern is that taxes aimed at high-earning emigrants would hit the group of poor-country citizens that have the best access to rich-country labor markets. In thinking about the defensibility of taxes, however, we must start from the quantity-restricted regime that we currently find. As I discuss further below, these quantity restrictions tend to produce large rents—payments in excess of what is required to induce them to migrate—for those lucky enough to obtain a visa.[11] Taking a modest portion of this rent in taxes is unlikely to affect the decision to emigrate. Even where some individuals choose to forgo the emigration option, a place may be opened up for someone else when the country is operating a quota system. Moreover, if some of tax revenue goes to the receiving country, or if the tax leads to a better-selected immigrant pool, there may actually be an incentive to relax the quantity restriction. Perhaps most fundamentally, although few of us like paying taxes of any kind, taxes at reasonable rates are generally considered compatible with a free society. It is not obvious that modest emigrant taxes should be singled out as unacceptable on liberty grounds.

Efficient Allocation

Fiscal instruments should be chosen to allow for the most economically efficient allocation of individuals across countries. There are, of course, different definitions of efficiency. To be concrete, I assume that efficiency requires the maximization of total global income adjusted for purchasing-power parity.[12] I assume initially that there are no market failures and no fiscal system. If international migration is driven only by real income comparisons, then a completely free international migration regime will maximize global income. A tax on emigrant incomes would then distort international migration decisions and lower global income.[13] Of course,

11. Jasso, Rosenzweig, and Smith (2002) find evidence of very large income gains for a sample of permanent immigrants to the United States. For those individuals for which they have pre- and postimmigration income data, they find an increase of almost $21,000 (from $17,080 to $37,989).

12. The purchasing-power parity adjustment takes into account how the opportunity cost of an individual's expenditure on nontraded goods varies by location.

13. This assumes that that tax policy will change migration flows. Although I know of no empirical study that examines how tax changes per se affect migration flows, there is ample evidence that migration is affected by income differences between sending and receiving regions (see, for example, Hatton and Williamson, 2005).

once we allow for preexisting distorting taxes—such as national income taxes—it may not be the case that zero emigrant taxes leads to the most efficient allocation. Suppose, for example, that tax rates are higher in the poorer sending country than they are in the richer receiving country, leading to excessive emigration. An appropriately chosen emigrant tax would then be efficiency-enhancing.

Market failures can also motivate emigrant taxation. To take a plausible example, suppose there are positive knowledge spillovers from skilled workers and that these spillovers tend to be localized and of greater value to poorer countries with weak existing knowledge bases. Completely free migration would again lead to excessive emigration from a global-efficiency perspective. Again, emigrant taxes do not necessarily misallocate global labor.

This discussion has again ignored the pervasive quantitative restrictions that already exist on international migration and the consequent rents that result. Bhagwati (1983, p. 54) notes that his initial motivation for exploring emigrant taxation was the potential for nondistorting taxation that these rents provide: "If these highly skilled migrants earn rents by successfully getting past the immigration restrictions, why not tax these rents and utilize the resulting tax revenues for developmental spending in the origin or in poor countries *en bloc?* Taxation of rents is just about the oldest and most respectable idea in the economic theory of taxation; and here would be an added source of revenues of poor countries' development programs." The taxation of such rents will not distort global labor allocation, and, to the extent that it replaces other, more distorting taxes, it will actually be efficiency-enhancing. The point of these arguments is not that emigration taxation necessarily increases the efficiency of global labor allocation, which seems a stretch, but that the efficiency case is more complex than it might appear.

Before leaving the discussion of efficiency, it is important to mention the important work initiated by the Bhagwati tax proposal on the optimal structure of the domestic tax system.[14] (See chapter 10 for a detailed review of this work.) Typically, the papers assume that the goal is to maximize social welfare (allowing for the possibility of inequality aversion) rather than pure efficiency. One question addressed is how international labor mobility affects the optimal domestic tax structure when emigrant taxation is not possible. Another is the optimal tax structure when emigrant taxation is feasible. The results are sometimes surprising and quite sensitive to model assumptions. For example, although it seems intuitive that the possibility of emigration without the possibility of emigrant taxation would make the optimal tax structure less progressive, the presence of

---

14. See the papers collected in Bhagwati and Wilson (1989).

"income effects"—whereby emigration lowers domestic tax receipts for any tax structure—can actually lead to higher marginal tax rates on domestic income. The implications of mobility for the optimal tax structure also turn out to be quite sensitive to where in the domestic income distribution emigrants are drawn from.

Fairness

Freedom and efficiency concerns provide possible rationales for avoiding emigrant taxation. But I think the greatest concern is over the fairness of such taxation. The fairness complaint has two main components: (1) it is unfair to tax emigrants at higher rates than others in the destination labor market (horizontal inequity); and (2) it is unfair to tax those who have left the country and are no longer benefiting from public goods and services. The earlier Bhagwati tax literature debated three positive fairness-based defenses.

(1) *Fair share of the spoils.* The idea here is that skilled migration leads to substantial overall gains. As noted above, the restricted nature of the international migration regime means that the gains to the emigrants themselves can be very large. With the recent concerns that rich countries are expressing about their "competitiveness in the international market for talent," it is reasonable to suppose that rich countries also obtain substantial gains from the highly skilled emigrants they target. The "brain circulation" literature has drawn attention to the various ways in which the poor countries themselves gain from their most talented individuals joining the diaspora: remittances, investments, business facilitation, knowledge-sharing networks, and skill-enhanced returns. The argument for providing more of the overall gains to the source countries does not necessarily depend on them losing out, however, but on giving them a fairer share of the overall gains.

(2) *Compensation.* The focus on brain circulation has certainly opened up debate about the effect of skilled emigration on development. But it strains credulity to think that a poor country with already limited human capital losing its best and brightest—its engineers, doctors, entrepreneurs, institutional reformers—would typically be better off when these people are somewhere else. The compensation rationale is based on using fiscal instruments to ensure that poor countries are not net losers from the lost human capital; that is, the emigration should provide an *actual* Pareto improvement and not just a potential one.

(3) *Enduring obligations.* In his advocacy for emigrant taxation, Bhagwati made use of the foregoing two fairness-based arguments. But the greatest weight was ultimately put on a third: obligations that an emigrant owes

to his or her country of origin. One source of obligation stems from the privileges of ongoing citizenship, such as the rights to vote, travel, own property, and so on. He pointed to the anomaly of "representation without taxation"—or privileges without obligations:

> [P]rofessional migrants retain their national status and associated rights, including often the right to vote, but carry no corresponding tax obligation, even of a minimal nature. The situation is one of "representation without taxation." The anomaly is particularly compounded because typically these highly skilled migrants are among the more prosperous and successful even prior to their migration, and their ability to work abroad renders them the more taxable, and almost totally untaxed, citizens of their countries. When one considers that in Albert Hirchman's apt conceptualization, these migrants have chosen to "exit" but have retained "voice" and "loyalty," it appears legitimate to regard their escaping the tax system as altogether incongruous. (Bhagwati, 1979 [1983, pp. 63–64])

Besides ongoing privileges of citizenship, past benefits received could also be a source of ongoing obligation. Most obviously, the emigrant is likely to have received publicly funded education. This education can be viewed as part of an implicit intergenerational contract. It might be considered unfair for an individual to renege on this implicit obligation by emigrating without fiscal obligation.

Before leaving the topic of fairness, I want to return to horizontal equity. On the face of it, it does seem unfair that an immigrant faces a higher rate of taxation than a native-born worker earning the same income. I think this is the main reason many people recoil from the idea of emigrant taxation. It should be noted, however, that in the case of international migration, the principle of horizontal equity pulls in different directions. While it seems unfair that an immigrant faces a higher total rate of taxation than a similarly situated native-born worker, it also seems unfair that an emigrant earning a given total income faces a lower rate of taxation than a worker back in the source country would pay on that income.[15] This is an example of the more general problem noted by Sen (1992), whereby equality in one space (the space of incomes of identically situated workers in a given receiving country) implies inequality in another space (the space of incomes of workers of a given nationality earning identical pretax incomes in different countries).

---

15. This is likely to happen since the worker in the poor home country is likely to reach the highest tax rates at a much lower income level.

Administrative/Legal Feasibility

Worries about liberty, efficiency, and fairness mean little if the proposals at issue are so administratively costly as to make them infeasible or are in clear violation of national or international law. A large part of the debate surrounding the original Bhagwati proposal related to the question of feasibility, and I think it is fair to say that the proposal evolved to meet the objections (Partington, 1976). For example, concerns about the unconstitutionality of differential taxation of immigrants in the United States led to a focus on taxes that would be imposed on emigrant incomes by the sending country rather than the receiving country (Oldman and Pomp, 1976). However, the long tradition in the United States of taxing a citizen's global income made it clear that such citizenship-based taxation is feasible under international law.

I think it is also fair to say that even the modified proposal failed to gain traction largely because of administrative difficulties that remained (see Pomp, 1989, for a review of the difficulties that the Filipino government had in administrating its emigrant tax). But it is possible that what was infeasible then is feasible now.

What has changed? First, advances in information and communication technology should now make it easier to keep track of emigrant incomes and tax obligations. Second, increased government cooperation in the form of tax treaties has improved the infrastructure of sharing income- and tax-related information. Third, the increased numbers of high-earning emigrants allow governments to take advantage of economies of scale in tax administration. Fourth, and I think most important, the value or retaining home-country citizenship has changed, as major sending countries such as India and the Philippines extend more privileges to their diasporas, and these privileges become more valuable in a era of cheap international travel and growing international business contacts. Put simply, skilled elites have more reason to value their "transnationalism." The net result of these changes is likely to be improvement in the administrative capability to charge for citizenship privileges and also an increase in the willingness to pay for such privileges.

I find that emigrant taxation does face serious principled objections. But starting from a point where international mobility is already highly constrained, these objections hardly seem unanswerable. Although various principled objections were made in the earlier debate, administrative infeasibility—and vested interests—is probably what really doomed the proposal. The administrative environment—if not the vested interests—has changed sufficiently to warrant giving these proposals another look.

Selected Fiscal Instruments

Exit Taxes

Exit taxes have a bad name. Though less objectionable than outright restrictions on exit, they tend to be seen as unwarranted obstacles to freedom of movement. Large exit taxes can amount to de facto exit prohibitions for those with low incomes and limited access to credit. Their association with the despised Soviet exit tax on talented émigrés (many of whom were Jewish) has not helped their reputation.

Can a case be made for exit taxes? Although I will argue that there are better options for transferring resources to skill-losing countries, I do not think that exit taxes can be dismissed out of hand. The most convincing rationale is one based on intergenerational debt. Young people receive publicly funded services such as education and face an implicit obligation to help finance spending for the next generation during their working lives. Leaving after completing one's education could be viewed as reneging on this implicit debt, and exit taxes used to make the debt explicit. Another way of looking at the intergenerational transfer system is that education is considered "free" conditional on later tax payments (means permitting). If the individual decides to leave, it is not obviously unfair to make this implicit debt explicit and repayable. I hasten to add that this debt should not be so onerous as effectively to prohibit exit and should be at least partially repayable in installments after emigration. One advantage of an exit tax that is independent of income is that it is relatively easy to administer. From an enforcement point of view, this debt could be treated the same way as any other debt in terms of sanctions for nonpayment, though emigrants may have few assets that could be seized and may care little about credit standing in their former homes. To provide an incentive for repayment, citizenship privileges could be made conditional on being in good standing on the debt.

How much revenue might such a tax raise? To get a sense of the revenue potential, I use the Indian-born population resident in the United States as an illustrative tax base. One problem in making an estimate is that although we have relatively good information on the educational attainment of Indians in the United States, we do not know whether this education was acquired at home or abroad. From survey evidence, we do know that it is not unusual for the highest degrees to be earned in the United States. For example, Saxenian (2002) finds that 63 percent of her sample of Indian Silicon Valley respondents earned their highest degrees in the United States, though this number is less than found in her samples of Chinese (83 percent) and Taiwanese respondents (91 percent).

For illustrative purposes, suppose we look at Indians present at the time of the 2000 census. Limiting the sample to those who are 25 or older and also to those who entered since 1990, this gives us a population of 465,729. Assuming that we impose an average tax of $15,000, this yields just more than $7 billion, or $0.7 billion a year (roughly 0.15 percent of GDP in 2000) if we assume a constant flow during the 10 years.

Sending-Country Imposed Taxes

Although it is an administrative virtue, a troubling aspect of the exit tax is that it is independent of income and thus raises concerns of vertical equity. Even if the exit tax is related to education level, we may think it unfair that the tax is insensitive to the emigrant's success in the new labor market. More generally, past education might be viewed as too narrow a basis for the emigrant's obligation, with the most important source of obligation being continuing citizen privileges rather than past educational services. A sending-country-imposed income tax on overseas citizens—or simply a Bhagwati tax—is an obvious alternative.

The legal basis for such citizenship-based (as opposed to residence-based) taxation is well established. The United States has always taxed the global income of its citizens, and the Philippines, Mexico, and Eritrea have used such taxation at various times (see Desai, Kapur, and McHale, 2004). As discussed above, the challenges faced by poor countries in administering the tax are probably the most important reason the original Bhagwati proposal was not widely adopted. Pomp (1989) provides a sobering account of the early experience of the Filipino government in trying to impose the tax in various ways, with the government finally abandoning these attempts in 1997.

Are there reasons to believe that the tax would be any more feasible now than when Bhagwati first proposed it? For the reasons outlined above, I think the answer is yes. The most important of these reasons is that privileges of citizenship are worth more in a more interconnected world where emigrants—and especially highly skilled emigrants—live a transnational life. Neither do I think the cost of administering such taxes is necessarily disqualifying. Following the original proposal, the tax could be set as a surcharge on foreign taxes paid. The only service required of receiving countries would be to provide verification that this was indeed the amount of tax paid, which would be done at the request of the emigrant.

How much might a Bhagwati tax raise? Based on estimates from the March 2000 CPS, Indian-born residents of the United States paid $2.5 billion in Social Security taxes and $8.0 billion in income taxes. (On a per-capita basis, this amounts to $2,440 in Social Security taxes and $7,904 in income taxes.) Limiting the surcharge to income taxes only, a surcharge of 10 percent would raise $0.8 billion per year. If we further limit the tax base to the Indian-born who are not U.S. citizens, the surcharge would raise $0.4 billion, though it is not obvious that the tax would need to be so limited given that dual citizenship is now allowed.

Emigration-Related Development Aid

The first two proposals describe instruments that expand the fiscal reach of sending countries to at least a subset of their absent populations. I now turn to two proposals that involve fiscal transfers from receiving countries to sending countries based on observed emigration outcomes. I assume that the motivation is that the rich receiving countries wish to share the spoils of emigration with poor sending countries or a desire to compensate the poor countries for the losses they experience. Imposing such losses on human-capital-scarce developing countries might be thought to put an extra burden on particular poor countries, for which general aid policies do not compensate. Pursuing such emigration-specific compensation might also be seen as better than the alternative of restricting the overseas recruitment activities of their private or even public sectors (e.g., health- and education-sector recruitment).

A virtue of this type of policy is its relative administrative simplicity, since it could rely on aggregate immigration stock or flow data rather than individual income data. The chief drawbacks are that it places no burden on the likely largest beneficiaries from emigration—the emigrants themselves—and it requires cooperation and goodwill from receiving countries. Even where the receiving countries are sensitive to damage done by scarce human-capital recruitment, they may be reluctant to provide these extra transfers to human-capital-losing countries, especially when there are other countries that are so poor that they do not have much human capital to lose.

How much might such a policy transfer to poor countries? As an illustration, I take the example of Indian emigration to the United States once again. Suppose that the transfer is based on the average annual increase in the stock of tertiary-educated Indians residing in the United States based on a comparison of the 1990 and 2000 censuses. Limiting attention to the population 25 and older, we find that the stock of Indian-born rose from 304,030 in 1990 to 836,780 in 2000, an increase of 532,750. If we further assume that 80 percent of the stock has a tertiary education (which is the exact share for 2000), then there is net increase of 426,200 in the stock of U.S.-resident, tertiary-educated Indians, or 42,620 a year. A one-time transfer of $1,000 for each one-person increase in the stock would then yield

Table 12.5 Some Options for Emigration-Related Fiscal Instruments

	Free movement	Efficient allocation	Fairness	Administrative/legal feasibility
Exit charges	Potential to be a significant obstacle for credit-constrained individuals	Limited impact on emigration decisions given large intramarginal emigration rents	Defensible as fair: (1) sharing of emigration rents with home country, (2) compensation for home-country losses, or (3) return for *past* citizen privileges (e.g., public education)	Moderate obstacles; may be hard to enforce; likely to be looked upon with disfavor by the international community (in part because of comparisons to the infamous Soviet exit tax)
Sending-country-imposed income taxes	Some disincentive for emigration (depends on level of tax)	Limited impact on emigration decisions given large intramarginal emigration rents	Defensible as fair: (1) sharing of emigration rents with home country, (2) compensation for home-country losses, or (3) return for *continuing* citizen privileges	Moderate to substantial obstacles (probably minimized when applied as a surcharge on foreign taxes); likely to require cooperation of receiving-country governments; unlikely to face legal impediments

(continued)

Table 12.5 (continued)

	Free movement	Efficient allocation	Fairness	Administrative/legal feasibility
Emigration-related development aid	Minimal obstacles; may make rich countries less willing to accept poor-country immigrants	Minimal impact	Defensible as a fair sharing of migration spoils or fair compensation for the losses borne by losing countries	Limited obstacles; requires accurate measures of foreign-born/native populations (together with income/skill characteristics) by country of origin
Receiving-country tax sharing (e.g., sharing Social Security taxes of eventual returnees)	Minimal obstacles; may make rich countries less willing to accept poor-country immigrants	Minimal impact; might encourage efficient return migration	Defensible as a fair sharing of migration spoils or fair compensation for the losses borne by losing countries	Places a relatively small additional burden on Social Security administrations as they keep track of contributors' country of origin; need to verify that people actually do leave

the relatively small sum of $0.04 billion per year. Alternatively, an ongoing transfer of $1,000 based on the tertiary-educated stock in 2000 of 669,424 (836,780 × 0.8) would lead to a transfer of roughly $0.7 billion per year. The transfer could be adjusted based on the income level of the losing country—with poorer countries receiving larger transfers—and also utilize finer detail on the education attainment of the human-capital stock.

Receiving-Country Tax Sharing

The development aid proposal has the attractive feature that it does not require that receiving countries keep track of immigrant incomes and tax payments. On the other hand, rich countries might be unwilling to share the spoils with poor countries without concrete evidence that spoils exist. Tax receipts on emigrant incomes provide one such concrete sign. Given the long-term fiscal gaps that most rich countries face, it might seem fanciful to think scarce fiscal revenues will be shared. Indeed, it probably is fanciful that *income*-tax receipts would be shared, since these taxes fund expenditures that typically benefit immigrants just as much as natives. A possible exception is the Social Security tax paid by immigrants who do not stay long enough to obtain benefit entitlements. (This is 10 years for retirement-income benefits in the United States, for example.) As noted above, Indian-born residents of the United States paid almost $2.5 billion in Social Security taxes in 2000. If we assume an emigrant return rate of 30 percent before the 10-year minimum contribution period, we could imagine (just about) that $0.75 billion is returned to the Indian government to provide for Social Security of these returnees.

Conclusions

As a rule, I try to avoid advocating major new forms of taxation. I am an emigrant myself, so good sense would dictate more discretion in advocating emigrant taxation in particular. But the almost complete absence of citizenship-based taxation by poor countries together with the rising phenomenon of transnational citizenship is puzzling—and I think anachronistic.

The illustrative examples outlined above were designed so that each instrument considered yielded roughly three-quarters of a billion dollars to the Indian government in 2000, or roughly 0.15 percent of that year's GDP. I think these examples show that instruments can be designed that raise substantial revenue without putting undue burden on the diaspora or the rich-country government. Of course, the India-U.S. dyad is an outlier in terms of its concentration of human capital. On the other hand, the skilled-emigration rate from India is actually relatively low, limiting the revenue potential for the Indian government. Although their emigrant populations have lower concentrations of human capital, countries in the Caribbean, Central America, and Africa in particular have potentially much larger untapped revenue sources when measured as a share of their economies because of the sheer size of their skilled diasporas. Given the concern about the low net resource transfer to these poor regions, it may be time to put the Bhagwati tax (and related instruments) back on the agenda.

References

Adams, Richard. 2003. "International Migration, Remittances and the Brain Drain: A Study of 24 Labor-Exporting Countries." World Bank Policy Research Working Paper 2972.

Atkinson, Anthony. 2005. *New Sources of Development Finance*. Oxford: Oxford University Press.

Bhagwati, Jagdish, ed. 1976a. *Taxing the Brain Drain, Vol. 1: A Proposal*. Amsterdam: North Holland.

——, ed. 1976b. *Taxing the Brain Drain, Vol. 2: Theory and Empirical Analysis*. Amsterdam: North Holland.

——. 1979. "International Migration of the Highly Skilled: Economics, Ethics and Taxes." *Third World Quarterly* 1, no. 13: 17–30; reprinted in 1983 in Robert Feenstra, ed., *Essays in Economic Theory, Vol. 2: International Factor Mobility*. Cambridge, MA: MIT Press.

——. 1983. "The Economic Analysis of International Migration." In Robert Feenstra, ed., *Essays in Economic Theory, Vol. 2: International Factor Mobility*. Cambridge, MA: MIT Press, chapter 4.

——. 1989. "Preface." In Jagdish Bhagwati and John Wilson, eds., *Income Taxation and International Mobility*. Cambridge, MA: MIT Press.

Bhagwati, Jagdish, and John Wilson, eds. 1989. *Income Taxation and International Mobility*. Cambridge, MA: MIT Press.

Carrington, William, and Enrica Detragiache. 1998. "How Big Is the Brain Drain?" IMF Working Paper 98/102.

Desai, Mihir, Devesh Kapur, and John McHale. 2004. "Sharing the Spoils: Taxing International Human Capital Flows." *International Taxation and Public Finance* 11: 663–39.

——. 2008. "The Fiscal Impact of High Skilled Emigration: Flows of Indians to the U.S." *Journal of Development Economics*.

Docquier, Frédéric, and Abdeslam Marfouk. 2004. "Measuring the International Mobility of Skilled Workers (1990–2000), Release 1.0." World Bank Working Paper 3381.

Hatton, Timothy, and Jeffrey Williamson. 2005. *Global Migration and the World Economy: Two Centuries of Policy and Performance.* Cambridge, MA: MIT Press.

Jasso, Guillermina, Mark Rosenzweig, and James Smith. 2002. "The Earnings of U.S. Immigrants: World Skill Prices, Skill Transferability and Selectivity, New Immigrant Survey Project." http://nis.princeton.edu/publications.htm.

Kapur, Devesh, and John McHale. 2005a. *Give Us Your Best and Brightest: The Global Hunt for Talent and Its Impact on the Developing World.* Washington DC: Brookings.

————. 2005b. "Sojourns and Software: Internationally Mobile Human Capital and High Tech Industry Development in India, Ireland and Israel." In Ashish Arora and Alfonso Gambardella, eds., *Underdogs to Tigers: The Rise and Growth of the Software Industry in Some Emerging Economies.* Oxford: Oxford University Press.

Oldman, Oliver, and Richard Pomp. 1976. "The Brain Drain: A Tax Analysis of the Bhagwati Proposal." in Jagdish Bhagwati, ed., *Taxing the Brain Drain, Vol. 1: A Proposal.* Amsterdam: North Holland.

Partington, Martin. 1976. "Taxing the Brain Drain: A Report on the Bellagio Conference." In Jagdish Bhagwati, ed., *Taxing the Brain Drain, Vol. 1: A Proposal.* Amsterdam: North Holland.

Pomp, Richard. 1989. "The Experience of the Philippines in Taxing Its Nonresident Citizens." In Jagdish Bhagwati and John Wilson, eds., *Income Taxation and International Mobility.* Cambridge, MA: MIT Press.

Saxenian, AnnaLee. 2002. *Local and Global Networks of Immigrant Professionals in Silicon Valley.* San Francisco: Public Policy Institute of California.

Sen, Amartya. 1992. *Inequality Reexamined.* Cambridge, MA: Harvard University Press.

UN Millennium Project. 2005. *Investing in Development: A Practical Plan to Achieve the Millennium Development Goals.* London: Earthscan.

Index

UNIVERSITY OF WOLVERHAMPTON
LEARNING & INFORMATION SERVICES